STATISTICAL CONCEPTS: A SECOND COURSE

THIRD EDITION

Richard G. Lomax
The Ohio State University

LEA

LAWRENCE ERLBAUM ASSOCIATES, PUBLISHERS

2007   Mahwah, New Jersey   London

Credits

Tables found in the Appendix have been reprinted from the following sources: Tables 1, 2, 3, 4, 5, 6 from Pearson, E. S. & Hartley, H. O. (1966), *Biometrika Tables for Statisticians*, respectively Tables 1, 12, 8, 18, 14, 47, by permission of Oxford University Press; Table 7 from Dunnett, C. W. (1955), A multiple comparison procedure for comparing several treatments with a control, *Journal of the American Statistical Association*, *50*, 1096–1121, by permission of the American Statistical Association, and from Dunnett, C. W. (1964), New tables for multiple comparisons with a control, *Biometrics*, *20*, 482–491, by permission of the Biometric Society; Table 8 from Games, P. A. (1977), An improved *t* table for simultaneous control of *g* contrasts, *Journal of the American Statistical Association*, *72*, 531–534, by permission of the American Statistical Association; Table 9 from Harter, H. L. (1960), Tables of range and studentized range, *Annals of Mathematical Statistics*, *31*, 1122–1147, by permission of the Institute of Mathematical Statistics; Table 10 from Bryant, J. L. & Paulson, A. S. (1976), An extension of Tukey's method of multiple comparisons to experimental designs with random concomitant variables, *Biometrika*, *63*, 631–638, by permission of Oxford University Press.

Senior Acquisitions Editor: Debra Riegert
Senior Editorial Assistant: Rebecca Larsen
Cover Design: Tomai Maridou
Full-Service Compositor: MidAtlantic Books & Journals, Inc.

This book was typeset in 10/13 pt. Times Roman, Italic, Bold, and Bold Italic with Optima.

Lawrence Erlbaum Associates, Inc., Publishers
10 Industrial Avenue
Mahwah, New Jersey 07430
www.erlbaum.com

CIP information for this volume can be obtained by contacting the Library of Congress.

ISBN 978-0-8058-5850-1—0-8058-5850-4 (paper)
ISBN 978-1-4106-1643-2—1-4106-1643-6 (e book)

Books published by Lawrence Erlbaum Associates are printed on
acid-free paper, and their bindings are chosen for strength and durability.

Printed in the United States of America

10 9 8 7 6 5 4 3 2 1

*This book is dedicated to
my family and to all of
my former students.*

CONTENTS

PREFACE

APPROACH

I know, I know! I've heard it a million times before. When you hear someone at a party mention the word **statistics** or **statistician**, you probably say "I hate statistics" and turn the other cheek. In the more than 25 years I have been in the field of statistics, I can only recall four or five times when someone did not have that reaction. Enough is enough. With the help of this text, the "I hate statistics" slogan will become a distant figment of your imagination.

As the title suggests, this text is designed for a course in statistics for students in education and the behavioral sciences. We begin with the most basic introduction to statistics in the first chapter and proceed through intermediate statistics. Unlike many other statistics textbooks, this book includes topics that are comprehensive enough for either a single course or a two-course sequence (e.g., nonparametric procedures, modern alternative procedures, advanced analysis of variance and regression models). The text is designed for you to become a better-prepared researcher and a more intelligent consumer of research. I do not assume that you have extensive or recent training in mathematics. Many of you have only had algebra, some more than 20 years ago. I also do not assume that you have ever had a statistics course. Rest assured, you will do fine.

I believe that a text should serve as an effective instructional tool. You should find this text to be more than a reference book; you might actually use it to learn statistics (what an oxymoron, that a statistics book can actually teach something). This text is not a theoretical statistics book, nor is it a cookbook on computing statistics, or a statistical software manual. Recipes have to be memorized, consequently you tend not to understand how or why you obtain the desired product. As well, knowing how to run a statistics package without understanding the concepts or the output is not particularly useful. Thus concepts drive the field of statistics.

GOALS AND CONTENT COVERAGE

My goals for this text are lofty, but the effort and its effects will be worthwhile. First, the text provides a comprehensive coverage of topics that could be included in an undergraduate or graduate one- or two-course sequence in statistics. The text is flexible enough so that instructors can select those topics that they desire to cover as they deem relevant in their particular discipline. In other words, chapters and sections of chapters from this text can be included in a statistics course as the instructor sees fit. Most of the popular as well as many of the lesser-known procedures and models are described in the text. A particular feature is a thorough and up-to-date discussion of assumptions, the effects of their violation, and how to deal with their violation.

The first five chapters of the text cover basic descriptive statistics, including ways of representing data graphically, statistical measures which describe a set of data, the normal distribution and other types of standard scores, and an introduction to probability and sampling. The remainder of the text covers different inferential statistics. In chapters 6 through 10 we deal with different inferential tests involving means (e.g., t tests), proportions, variances, and correlations. In chapters 11 through 16, all of the basic analysis of variance (ANOVA) models are considered. Finally, in chapters 17 and 18 we examine various regression models.

Second, the text communicates a conceptual, intuitive understanding of statistics, which requires only a rudimentary knowledge of basic algebra, and emphasizes the important concepts in statistics. The most effective way to learn statistics is through the conceptual approach. Statistical concepts tend to be easy to learn because (a) concepts can be simply stated, (b) concepts can be made relevant thorough the use of real-life examples, (c) the same concepts are shared by many procedures, and (d) concepts can be related to one another.

This text will help you to reach these goals. The following indicators will provide some feedback as to how you are doing. First, there will be a noticeable change in your attitude towards statistics. Thus one outcome is for you to feel that "statistics isn't half bad," or "this stuff is OK." Second, you will feel comfortable using statistics in your own work. Finally, you will begin to "see the light." You will know when you have reached this highest stage of statistics development when suddenly, in the middle of the night, you wake up from a dream and say "now I get it." In other words, you will begin to think statistics rather than think of ways to get out of doing statistics.

PEDAGOGICAL TOOLS

The text contains several important pedagogical features to allow you to attain these goals. First, each chapter begins with an outline (so you can anticipate what will be covered), and a list of key concepts (which you will need to really understand what you are doing). Second, realistic examples from education and the behavioral sciences are used to illustrate the concepts and procedures covered in each chapter. Each of these examples includes an examination of the various procedures and necessary assumptions, running SPSS and developing an APA style write-up, as well as tables, figures, and SPSS output to assist you. Third, the text is based on the conceptual approach. That is, material is covered so that you obtain a good understanding of statistical concepts. If you know the concepts, then you know statistics. Finally, each chapter ends with two sets of problems, computational and conceptual. Pay particular attention to the conceptual problems as they provide the best assessment of your understanding of the concepts in the chapter. I strongly suggest using the example data sets and the computational problems for additional practice through available statistics software. This will serve to reinforce the concepts covered. Answers to the odd-numbered problems are given at the end of the book.

NEW TO THE THIRD EDITION

A number of changes have been made in the second edition based on the suggestions of reviewers, instructors, and students. These improvements have been made in order to better achieve the goals of the text. The changes include the following: (a) sections have been added to most chapters on SPSS, which includes input, output, and APA style write-ups using the example dataset; (b) a CD has been inserted into the text with every dataset used in the text (i.e., both chapter examples and end of chapter problems) in SPSS format; (c) more information on confidence intervals, effect size measures, and power has been added; (d) the sequence of the regression and ANOVA chapters has been altered to provide a better conceptual flow to the text and so that the ANOVA and regression chapters are as independent as possible; (e) additional regression models have been added; (f) computations have been minimized so that more space is available for the discussion of concepts and statistical software; (g) additional end of chapter problems have been added, including more realistic examples as well as interpretive problems; (h) content throughout the book has been updated since the previous edition and numerous additional references have been provided; and (i) an Instructor's Resource CD containing all of the solutions to the end of chapter problems, statistical humor, and other instructional materials is free to adoptees.

ACKNOWLEDGMENTS

There are many individuals whose assistance enabled the completion of this book. First, I would like to thank the following individuals whom I studied statistics and research design with at the University of Pittsburgh: Jamie Algina, Lloyd Bond, Jim Carlson, Bill Cooley, Harry Hsu, Lou Pingel, Charles Stegman, and Neil Timm. Next, numerous colleagues have played an important role in my personal and professional life as a statistician. Rather than include an admittedly incomplete listing, I just say "thank you" to all of you. You know who you are.

Thanks also to all of the wonderful people at Lawrence Erlbaum Associates, in particular, to Ray O'Connell for inspiring this project back in 1986 when I began writing the second course text, and to Debra Riegert for supporting the development of subsequent texts and editions. I am most appreciative of the insightful suggestions provided by the reviewers of this text, Tim Konold (University of Virginia), L. Suzanne Dancer (University of Texas at Austin), Douglas Maynart (SUNY, New Paltz) and Patrick Markey (Villanova University). A special thank you to all of the terrific students that I have had the pleasure of teaching at the University of Pittsburgh, the University of Illinois—Chicago, Louisiana State University, Boston College, Northern Illinois University, the University of Alabama, and The Ohio State University. For all of your efforts, and the many lights that you have seen and shared with me, this book is for you. I am most grateful to my family, in particular, to Lea and Kristen. It is because of your love and understanding that I was able to cope with such a major project. Thank you one and all.

—RGL

1

ONE-FACTOR ANALYSIS OF VARIANCE—FIXED-EFFECTS MODEL

Chapter Outline

Key Concepts

1.   Between- and within-groups variability
2.   Sources of variation
3.   Partitioning the sums of squares
4.   The ANOVA model

Your first course in statistical concepts exposed you to descriptive statistics and an introduction to inferential statistics. We pick up the trail of statistics where the first course left off. In this chapter we consider the most basic ANOVA model, known as the one-factor analysis of variance model. Recall the independent t test from where the means from two independent samples were compared. What if you wish to compare more than two means? The answer is to use the **analysis of variance**. At this point you may be wondering why the procedure is called the analysis of variance rather than the analysis of means, because the intent is to study possible mean differences. One way of comparing a set of means is to think in terms of the variability among those means. If the sample means are all the same, then the variability of those means would be zero. If the sample means are not all the same, then the variability of those means would be somewhat greater than zero. In general, the greater the mean differences, the greater is the variability of the means. Thus mean differences are studied by looking at the variability of the means; hence, the term analysis of variance is appropriate rather than analysis of means (further discussed in this chapter).

We use X to denote our single **independent variable**, which we typically refer to as a **factor**, and Y to denote our **dependent** (or **criterion**) **variable**. Thus the one-factor ANOVA is a bivariate or two variable procedure. Our interest here is in determining whether mean differences exist on the dependent variable. Stated another way, the researcher is interested in the influence of the independent variable on the dependent variable. For example, a researcher may want to determine the influence that method of instruction has on statistics achievement. The independent variable or factor would be method of instruction and the dependent variable would be statistics achievement. Three different methods of instruction that might be compared are large lecture hall instruction, small-group instruction, and computer-assisted instruction. Students would be randomly assigned to one of the three methods of instruction and at the end of the semester evaluated as to their level of achievement in statistics. These results would be of interest to a statistics instructor in determining the most effective method of instruction. Thus, the instructor may opt for the method of instruction that yields the highest mean achievement.

There are a number of new concepts introduced in this chapter. These concepts include the following: independent and dependent variables; between- and within-groups variability; fixed-

and random-effects; the linear model; partitioning of the sums of squares; degrees of freedom, mean square terms, and F ratios; the ANOVA summary table; balanced and unbalanced models; and alternative ANOVA procedures. Our objectives are that by the end of this chapter, you will be able to (a) understand the characteristics and concepts underlying the one-factor ANOVA, (b) generate and interpret the results of a one-factor ANOVA, and (c) understand and evaluate the assumptions of the one-factor ANOVA.

1.1   CHARACTERISTICS OF THE ONE-FACTOR ANOVA MODEL

This section describes the distinguishing characteristics of the one-factor ANOVA model. Suppose you are interested in comparing the means of two independent samples. Here the independent t test would be the method of choice (or perhaps Welch's t' or the Mann-Whitney-Wilcoxon test). What if your interest is in comparing the means of more than two independent samples? One possibility is to conduct multiple independent t tests on each pair of means. For example, if you wished to determine whether the means from five independent samples are the same, you could do all possible pairwise t tests. In this case the following null hypotheses could be evaluated: $\mu_1 = \mu_2, \mu_1 = \mu_3, \mu_1 = \mu_4, \mu_1 = \mu_5, \mu_2 = \mu_3, \mu_2 = \mu_4, \mu_2 = \mu_5, \mu_3 = \mu_4,$ $\mu_3 = \mu_5,$ and $\mu_4 = \mu_5.$ Thus we would have to carry out 10 different independent t tests. The number of possible pairwise t tests that could be done for J means is equal to $\frac{1}{2} [J (J - 1)].$

Is there a problem in conducting so many t tests? Yes, the problem has to do with the probability of making a Type I error (i.e., α), where the researcher incorrectly rejects a true null hypothesis. Although the α level for each t test can be controlled at a specified nominal level, say .05, what happens to the overall α level for the entire set of tests? The overall α level for the entire set of tests (i.e., α_{total}), often called the **experiment-wise Type I error rate**, is larger than the α level for each of the individual t tests.

In our example we are interested in comparing the means for 10 pairs of groups. A t test is conducted for each of the 10 pairs of groups at $\alpha = .05$. Although each test controls the α level at .05, the overall α level will be larger because the risk of a Type I error accumulates across the tests. For each test we are taking a risk; the more tests we do, the more risks we are taking. This can be explained by considering the risk you take each day you drive your car to school or work. The risk of an accident is small for any one day; however, over the period of a year the risk of an accident is much larger.

For C independent (or orthogonal) tests the experiment-wise error is as follows.

$$\alpha_{total} = 1 - (1 - \alpha)^C$$

Assume for the moment that our 10 tests are independent (although they are not). If we go ahead with our 10 t tests at $\alpha = .05$, then the experiment-wise error rate is

$$\alpha_{total} = 1 - (1 - .05)^{10} = 1 - .60 = .40$$

Although we are seemingly controlling our α level at the .05 level, the probability of making a Type I error across all 10 tests is .40. In other words, in the long run, 4 times out of 10 we will make a Type I error. Thus we do not want to do all possible t tests. Before we move on, the experiment-wise error rate for C dependent tests (which would be the case when doing all possible pairwise t tests, as in our example) is more difficult to determine, so let us just say that

$$\alpha \le \alpha_{total} \le C\alpha$$

Are there other options available to us where we can maintain better control over our experiment-wise error rate? The optimal solution, in terms of maintaining control over our overall α level as well as maximizing power, is to conduct one overall test, often called an **omnibus test**. Recall that power has to do with the probability of correctly rejecting a false null hypothesis. The omnibus test could assess the equality of all of the means simultaneously and is the one used in the analysis of variance. The one-factor analysis of variance, then, represents an extension of the independent t test for two or more independent sample means, where the experiment-wise error rate is controlled.

In addition, the one-factor ANOVA has only one independent variable or factor with two or more levels. The independent variable is a discrete or grouping variable, where each subject responds to only one level. The levels represent the different samples or groups or treatments whose means are to be compared. In our example, method of instruction is the independent variable with three levels: large lecture hall, small-group, and computer-assisted. There are two ways of conceptually thinking about the selection of levels. In the fixed-effects model, all levels that the researcher is interested in are included in the design and analysis for the study. As a result, generalizations can only be made about those particular levels of the independent variable that are actually selected. For instance, if a researcher is only interested in three methods of instruction—large lecture hall, small-group and computer-assisted—then only those levels are incorporated into the study. Generalizations about other methods of instruction cannot be made because no other methods were considered for selection. Other examples of fixed-effects independent variables might be SES, gender, specific types of drug treatment, age group, weight, or marital status.

In the random-effects model, the researcher randomly samples some levels of the independent variable from the population of levels. As a result, generalizations can be made about all of the levels in the population, even those not actually sampled. For instance, a researcher interested in teacher effectiveness may have randomly sampled history teachers (i.e., the independent variable) from the population of history teachers in a particular school district. Generalizations can then be made about other history teachers in that school district not actually sampled. The random selection of levels is much the same as the random selection of individuals or objects in the random sampling process. This is the nature of inferential statistics, where inferences are made about a population (of individuals, objects, or levels) from a sample. Other examples of random-effects independent variables might be randomly selected classrooms, types of medication, animals, or time (e.g., hours, days). The remainder of this chapter is concerned with the fixed-effects model. Chapter 5 discusses the random-effects model in more detail.

In the fixed-effects model, once the levels of the independent variable are selected, subjects (i.e., persons or objects) are randomly assigned to the levels of the independent variable. In certain situations, the researcher does not have control over which level a subject is assigned to. The groups already may be in place when the researcher arrives on the scene. For instance, students may be assigned to their classes at the beginning of the year by the school administration. Researchers typically have little input regarding class assignments. In another situation, it may be theoretically impossible to assign subjects to groups. For example, as much as we might like, researchers cannot randomly assign individuals to an age level. Thus, a distinction needs to be made about whether or not the researcher can control the assignment of subjects to groups. Although the analysis will not be altered, the interpretation of the results will be. When researchers have control over group assignments, the extent to which they can generalize their findings is greater than for those researchers who do not have such control. For further information on the differences between true experimental designs (i.e., with random assignment) and quasi-experimental designs (i.e., without random assignment), see Campbell and Stanley (1966) and Cook and Campbell (1979).

Moreover, in the model being considered here, each subject is exposed to only one level of the independent variable. Chapter 5 deals with models where a subject is exposed to multiple levels of an independent variable; these are known as **repeated-measures models**. For example, a researcher may be interested in observing a group of young children repeatedly over a period of several years. Thus, each child might be observed every 6 months from birth to age 5 years. This would require a repeated-measures design because the observations of a particular child over time are obviously not independent observations.

One final characteristic is the measurement scale of the independent and dependent variables. In the analysis of variance, it is assumed that the scale of measurement on the dependent variable is at the interval or ratio level. If the dependent variable is measured at the ordinal level, then the nonparametric equivalent, the Kruskal-Wallis test, should be considered (discussed later in this chapter). If the dependent variable shares properties of both the ordinal and interval levels (e.g., grade point average), then both the ANOVA and Kruskal-Wallis procedures should be considered to cross-reference any potential effects of the measurement scale. As previously mentioned, the independent variable is a grouping or discrete variable, so it can be measured on any scale.

In summary, the characteristics of the one-factor analysis of variance fixed-effects model are as follows: (a) control of the experiment-wise error rate through an omnibus test; (b) one independent variable with two or more levels; (c) the levels of the independent variable are fixed by the researcher; (d) subjects are randomly assigned to these levels; (e) subjects are exposed to only one level of the independent variable; and (f) the dependent variable is measured at least at the interval level, although the Kruskal-Wallis one-factor ANOVA can be considered for an ordinal level dependent variable. In the context of experimental design, the one-factor analysis of variance is often referred to as the **completely randomized design**.

1.2 THE LAYOUT OF THE DATA

Before we get into the theory and analysis of the data, let us examine one tabular form of the data, known as the layout of the data. We designate each observation as Y_{ij}, where the j subscript tells us what group or level the observation belongs to and the i subscript tells us the observation or identification number within that group. For instance, Y_{34} would mean this is the third observation in the fourth group or level of the independent variable. The first subscript ranges over $i = 1, ..., n$ and the second subscript ranges over $j = 1, ..., J$. Thus there are J levels of the independent variable and n subjects in each group, for a total of $Jn = N$ total observations. For now, presume there are n subjects in each group in order to simplify matters; this is referred to as the **equal *n*'s** or **balanced case**. Later on in this chapter, we consider the **unequal *n*'s** or **unbalanced case**.

The layout of the data is shown in Table 1.1. Here we see that each column represents the observations for a particular group or level of the independent variable. At the bottom of each column are the sample group means ($\overline{Y}_{.j}$), with the overall sample mean ($\overline{Y}_{..}$) to the far right. In conclusion, the layout of the data is one form in which the researcher can think about the data.

1.3   ANOVA THEORY

This section examines the underlying theory and logic of the analysis of variance, the sums of squares, and the ANOVA summary table. As noted previously, in the analysis of variance mean differences are tested by looking at the variability of the means. This section shows precisely how this is done.

1.3.1   General Theory and Logic

We begin with the hypotheses to be tested in the analysis of variance. In the two-group situation of the independent *t* test, the null and alternative hypotheses for a two-tailed test are as follows:

$$H_0: \mu_1 = \mu_2$$
$$H_1: \mu_1 \neq \mu_2$$

In the multiple-group situation, we have already seen the problem that occurs when multiple independent *t* tests are conducted for each pair of population means (i.e., increased likelihood of a Type I error). We concluded that the solution was to use an omnibus test where the equality

TABLE 1.1
Layout for the One-Factor ANOVA Model

	Level of the Independent Variable					
	1	*2*	*3*	...	*J*	
	Y_{11}	Y_{12}	Y_{13}	...	Y_{1J}	
	Y_{21}	Y_{22}	Y_{23}	...	Y_{2J}	
	Y_{31}	Y_{32}	Y_{33}	...	Y_{3J}	
	.	.	.	...	.	
	.	.	.	...	.	
	.	.	.	...	.	
	Y_{n1}	Y_{n2}	Y_{n3}	...	Y_{nJ}	
mean:	$\overline{Y}_{.1}$	$\overline{Y}_{.2}$	$\overline{Y}_{.3}$	...	$\overline{Y}_{.J}$	$\overline{Y}_{..}$

of all of the means could be assessed simultaneously. The hypotheses for the omnibus analysis of variance test are as follows:

$$H_0: \mu_1 = \mu_2 = \mu_3 = ... = \mu_J$$
$$H_1: \text{not all the } \mu_j \text{ are equal}$$

Here H_1 is purposely written in a general form to cover the multitude of possible mean differences that could arise. These range from only two of the means being different to all of the means being different from one another. Thus, because of the way H_1 has been written, only a nondirectional alternative is appropriate. If H_0 were to be rejected, then the researcher might want to consider a multiple comparison procedure so as to determine which means or combination of means are significantly different (see chap. 2).

As was mentioned in the introduction to this chapter, the analysis of mean differences is actually carried out by looking at variability of the means. At first this seems strange. If one wants to test for mean differences, then do a test of means. If one wants to test for variance differences, then do a test of variances. These statements should make sense because logic pervades the field of statistics. And they do for the two-group situation. For the multiple-group situation, we already know things get a bit more complicated.

Say a researcher is interested in the influence of amount of daily study time on statistics achievement. Three groups were formed based on the amount of daily study time in statistics, ½ hour, 1 hour, and 2 hours. Is there a differential influence of amount of time studied on subsequent mean statistics achievement (e.g., statistics final exam)? We would expect that the more one studied statistics, the higher the statistics mean achievement would be. One possible outcome in the population is where the amount of study time does not influence statistics achievement; here the population means will be equal. That is, the null hypothesis of equal group means is true. Thus the three groups will actually be three samples from the same population of students, with mean μ. The means are equal; thus there is no variability among the three group means. A second possible outcome in the population is where the amount of study time does influence statistics achievement; here the population means will not be equal. That is, the null hypothesis is false. Thus the three groups will not be three samples from the same population of students, but rather, each group will represent a sample from a distinct population of students receiving that particular amount of study time, with mean μ_j. The means are not equal, so there is variability among the three group means. In summary, the statistical question becomes whether the difference between the sample means is due to the usual sampling variability expected from a single population, or the result of a true difference between the sample means from different populations.

We conceptually define **within-groups variability** as the variability of the observations within a group combined across groups, and **between-groups variability** as the variability between the group means. In Fig. 1.1, the horizontal axis represents low and high variability within the groups. The vertical axis represents low and high variability between the groups. In the upper left-hand plot, there is low variability both within and between the groups. That is, performance is very consistent, both within each group as well as across groups. Here within- and between-group variability are both low, and it is quite unlikely that one would reject H_0. In the upper right-hand plot, there is high variability within the groups and low variability between the groups. That is, performance is very consistent across groups, but quite variable within each group. Here within-

Variability Within-Groups

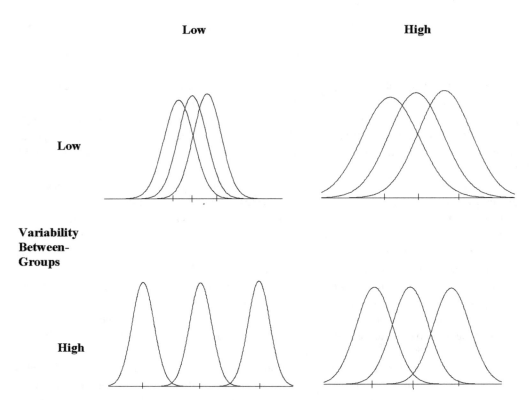

FIG. 1.1   Conceptual look at between- and within-groups variability.

group variability exceeds between-group variability, and again it is quite unlikely that one would reject H_0. In the lower left-hand plot, there is low variability within the groups and high variability between groups. That is, performance is very consistent within each group, but quite variable across groups. Here between-group variability exceeds within-group variability, and it is quite likely that one would reject H_0. In the lower right-hand plot, there is high variability both within and between the groups. That is, performance is quite variable within each group, as well as across the groups. Here within- and between-group variability are both high, and depending on the relative amounts of between- and within-group variability, one may or may not reject H_0. In summary, the optimal situation when seeking to reject H_0 is the one represented by high variability between the groups and low variability within the groups.

1.3.2   Partitioning the Sums of Squares

The partitioning of the sums of squares is a new concept in this chapter, which is also an important concept in regression analysis (from chaps. 7 & 8). In part this is because both are forms of the general linear model (GLM) (to be further discussed). Let us begin with the total sum of squares in Y, denoted as SS_{total}. The term SS_{total} represents the amount of total variation in Y.

The next step is to partition the total variation into variation between the groups, denoted by SS_{betw}, and variation within the groups, denoted by SS_{with}. In the one-factor analysis of variance we therefore partition SS_{total} as follows:

$$SS_{total} = SS_{betw} + SS_{with}$$

or

$$\sum_{i=1}^{n}\sum_{j=1}^{J}\left(Y_{ij} - \overline{Y}_{..}\right)^2 = \sum_{i=1}^{n}\sum_{j=1}^{J}\left(\overline{Y}_{.j} - \overline{Y}_{..}\right)^2 + \sum_{i=1}^{n}\sum_{j=1}^{J}\left(Y_{ij} - \overline{Y}_{.j}\right)^2$$

where SS_{total} is the total sum of squares due to variation among all of the observations without regard to group membership, SS_{betw} is the between-groups sum of squares due to the variation between the group means, and SS_{with} is the within-groups sum of squares due to the variation within the groups combined across groups. We refer to this particular formulation of the partitioned sums of squares as the **definitional** (or **conceptual**) **formula**, because each term literally defines a form of variation.

Due to computational complexity and computational error, the definitional formula is rarely used with real data. Instead **computational formula** for the partitioned sums of squares are used for hand computations. However, since nearly all data analysis at this level utilize computer software, we defer to the software to actually perform an analysis of variance (SPSS details are provided toward the end of this chapter). A complete example of the analysis of variance is also considered later in this chapter.

1.3.3 The ANOVA Summary Table

An important result of the analysis is the **ANOVA summary table**. The purpose of the summary table is to literally summarize the analysis of variance. A general form of the summary table is shown in Table 1.2. The first column lists the sources of variation in the model. As we already know, in the one-factor model the total variation is partitioned into between-groups variation and within-groups variation. The second column notes the sums of squares terms computed for each source (i.e., SS_{betw}, SS_{with}, and SS_{total}).

The third column gives the degrees of freedom for each source. Recall that, in general, degrees of freedom has to do with the number of observations that are free to vary. For example, if a sample mean and all of the sample observations except for one are known, then the final observation is not free to vary. That is, the final observation is predetermined to be a particular

TABLE 1.2
Analysis of Variance Summary Table

Source	SS	df	MS	F
Between groups	SS_{betw}	$J - 1$	MS_{betw}	MS_{betw}/MS_{with}
Within groups	SS_{with}	$N - J$	MS_{with}	
Total	SS_{total}	$N - 1$		

value. For instance, say the mean is 10 and there are three observations, 7, 11, and an unknown observation. First, the sum of the three observations must be 30 for the mean to be 10. Second, the sum of the known observations is 18. Therefore the unknown observation must be 12. Otherwise the sample mean would not be exactly equal to 10.

For the between-groups source, the definitional formula is concerned with the deviation of each group mean from the overall mean. There are J group means, so the df_{betw} must be $J - 1$. Why? If there are J group means and we know the overall mean, then only $J - 1$ of the group means are free to vary. In other words, if we know the overall mean and all but one of the group means, then the final unknown group mean is predetermined. For the within-groups source, the definitional formula is concerned with the deviation of each observation from its respective group mean. There are n observations in each group; consequently, there are $n - 1$ degrees of freedom in each group and J groups. Why are there $n - 1$ degrees of freedom in each group? If there are n observations in each group, then only $n - 1$ of the observations are free to vary. In other words, if we know the group mean and all but one of the observations for that group, then the final unknown observation for that group is predetermined. There are J groups, so the df_{with} is $J(n - 1)$ or $N - J$. For the total source, the definitional formula is concerned with the deviation of each observation from the overall mean. There are N total observations; therefore the df_{total} must be $N - 1$. Why? If there are N total observations and we know the overall mean, then only $N - 1$ of the observations are free to vary. In other words, if we know the overall mean and all but one of the N observations, then the final unknown observation is predetermined.

Why is the number of degrees of freedom important in the analysis of variance? Suppose two researchers have conducted similar studies, except Researcher A uses 20 observations per group and Researcher B uses 10 observations per group. Each researcher obtains a SS_{with} of 15. Would it be fair to say that the result for the two studies is the same? Such a comparison would be unfair because SS_{with} is influenced by the number of observations per group. A fair comparison would be to weight the SS_{with} terms by their respective number of degrees of freedom. Similarly, it would not be fair to compare the SS_{betw} terms from two similar studies based on different numbers of groups. A fair comparision would be to weight the SS_{betw} terms by their respective number of degrees of freedom. The method of weighting a sum of squares term by the number of degrees of freedom on which it is based yields what is called a **mean squares** term. Thus $MS_{betw} = SS_{betw}/df_{betw}$ and $MS_{with} = SS_{with}/df_{with}$, as shown in the fourth column of Table 1.2. They are referred to as mean squares because they represent a summed quantity that is weighted by the number of observations used in the sum itself, like the mean. The mean squares terms are also variance estimates because they represent the sum of the squared deviations from a mean divided by their degrees of freedom, like the sample variance s^2.

The last column in the ANOVA summary table, the F value, is the summary test statistic of the summary table. The F value is computed by taking the ratio of the two mean squares or variance terms. Thus for the one-factor ANOVA fixed-effects model, the F value is computed as $F = MS_{betw}/MS_{with}$. When developed by Sir Ronald A. Fisher in the 1920s, this test statistic was originally known as the variance ratio because it represents the ratio of two variance estimates. Later the variance ratio was renamed the F ratio by George W. Snedecor (who worked out the table of F values, discussed momentarily) in honor of Fisher (F for Fisher).

The F ratio tells us whether there is more variation between groups than there is within groups, which is required if we are to reject H_0. Thus if there is more variation between groups than there is within groups, then MS_{betw} will be larger than MS_{with}. As a result of this, the F ratio of MS_{betw}/MS_{with} will be greater than 1. If, on the other hand, the amount of variation between groups is about the same as there is within groups, then MS_{betw} and MS_{with} will be about the same, and the F ratio will be approximately 1. Thus we want to find large F values in order to reject the null hypothesis. The F test statistic is then compared with the F critical value so as to make a decision about the null hypothesis. The critical value is found in the F table of Appendix Table 4 as $_{\alpha}F_{(J-1,N-J)}$. Thus the degrees of freedom are $df_{betw} = J - 1$ for the numerator of the F ratio and $df_{with} = N - J$ for the denominator of the F ratio. The significance test is a one-tailed test so as to be consistent with the alternative hypothesis. The null hypothesis is rejected if the F test statistic exceeds the F critical value.

If the F test statistic exceeds the F critical value, and there are more than two groups, then it is not clear where the differences among the means lie. In this case, some multiple comparison procedure should be used to determine where the mean differences are in the groups; this is the topic of chapter 2. When there are only two groups, it is obvious where the mean difference lies, between groups 1 and 2. For the two-group situation, it is also interesting to note that the F and t test statistics follow the rule of $F = t^2$, for a nondirectional alternative hypothesis in the independent t test. This result occurs when the numerator degrees of freedom for the F ratio is 1. In an actual ANOVA summary table (shown in the next section), except for the source of variation column, it is the values for each of the other entries that are listed in the table. For example, instead of seeing SS_{betw}, we would see the computed value of SS_{betw}.

1.4 THE ANOVA MODEL

In this section we introduce the analysis of variance linear model, the estimation of parameters of the model, effect size measures, confidence intervals, power, and finish up with an example.

1.4.1 The Model

The one-factor ANOVA fixed-effects model can be written in terms of population parameters as

$$Y_{ij} = \mu + \alpha_j + \varepsilon_{ij}$$

where Y is the observed score on the dependent (or criterion) variable for individual i in group j, μ is the overall or grand population mean (i.e., regardless of group designation), α_j is the group effect for group j, and ε_{ij} is the random residual error for individual i in group j. The residual error can be due to individual differences, measurement error, and/or other factors not under investigation (i.e., other than X). The population group effect and residual error are computed as

$$\alpha_j = \mu_{.j} - \mu$$

and

$$\varepsilon_{ij} = Y_{ij} - \mu_{.j}$$

respectively, and $\mu_{.j}$ is the population mean for group j, where the initial dot subscript indicates we have averaged across all i individuals in group j. That is, the group effect is equal to the difference between the population mean of group j and the overall population mean, whereas the residual error is equal to the difference between an individual's observed score and the population mean of group j. The group effect can also be thought of as the average effect of being a member of a particular group. A positive group effect implies a group mean greater than the overall mean, whereas a negative group effect implies a group mean less than the overall mean. Note that in a fixed-effects one-factor model, the population group effects sum to zero. The residual error in the analysis of variance represents that portion of Y not accounted for by X.

1.4.2   Estimation of the Parameters of the Model

Next we need to estimate the parameters of the model μ, α_j, and ε_{ij}. The sample estimates are represented as $\overline{Y}_{..}$, a_j, and e_{ij}, respectively, where the latter two are computed as

$$a_j = \overline{Y}_{.j} - \overline{Y}_{..}$$

and

$$e_{ij} = Y_{ij} - \overline{Y}_{.j}$$

respectively. Note that $\overline{Y}_{..}$ represents the overall sample mean, where the double dot subscript indicates we have averaged across both the i and j subscripts, and $\overline{Y}_{.j}$ represents the sample mean for group j, where the initial dot subscript indicates we have averaged across all i individuals in group j.

1.4.3   Effect Size Measures, Confidence Intervals, and Power

There are various effect size measures to indicate the strength of association between X and Y, that is, the relative strength of the group effect. Let us briefly examine η^2, ω^2, and Cohen's (1988) f. First η^2 (eta) is known as the correlation ratio (generalization of R^2) and represents the proportion of variation in Y explained by the group mean differences in X. We find η^2 to be

$$\eta^2 = \frac{SS_{\text{betw}}}{SS_{\text{total}}}$$

It is well known that η^2 is a positively biased statistic (i.e., overestimates the association). The bias is most evident for n's less than 30. Another effect size measure is ω^2 (omega), which is less biased than η^2. We determine ω^2 as

$$\omega^2 = \frac{SS_{\text{betw}} - (J-1)\, MS_{\text{with}}}{SS_{\text{total}} + MS_{\text{with}}}$$

A final effect size measure is f developed by Cohen (1988). We find f as

$$f = \sqrt{\frac{\eta^2}{1 - \eta^2}}$$

These are the most common measures of effect size used for ANOVA models, both in statistics software and in print. Cohen's (1988) subjective standards can be used as follows to interpret these effect sizes: small effect, $f = .1$, η^2 or $\omega^2 = .01$; medium effect, $f = .25$, η^2 or $\omega^2 = .06$; large effect, $f = .40$, η^2 or $\omega^2 = .14$. Note that these are subjective standards developed for particular areas of inquiry; your discipline may use other standards. For further discussion, see Keppel (1982), O'Grady (1982), Wilcox (1987), Cohen (1988), Keppel and Wickens (2004), and Murphy and Myors (2004; which includes software).

Confidence interval procedures are often useful in providing an interval estimate of a population parameter (i.e., mean or mean difference); these allow us to determine the accuracy of the sample estimate. One can form confidence intervals around any sample group mean from an ANOVA (provided in software such as SPSS), although confidence intervals for means have more utility for multiple comparison procedures, as discussed in chapter 2. Confidence interval procedures have also been developed for several effect size measures (Fidler & Thompson, 2001; Smithson, 2001).

As for power (the probability of correctly rejecting a false null hypothesis), one can consider either planned power (*a priori*) or observed power (*post hoc*), as discussed in previous chapters. In the ANOVA context, we know that power is primarily a function of α, sample size, and effect size. For planned power, one inputs each of these components either into a statistical table or power chart (nicely arrayed in texts such as Cohen, 1988, or Murphy & Myors, 2004), or into statistical software (such as Power and Precision, Ex-Sample, Gpower, or the software contained in Murphy & Myors, 2004). Planned power is most often used by researchers to determine adequate sample sizes in ANOVA models, which is highly recommended. Many disciplines recommend a minimum power value, such as .80. Thus these methods are a useful way to determine the sample size that would generate a desired level of power. Observed power is determined by some statistics software, such as SPSS, and indicates what the power actually was in a completed study.

1.4.4 An Example

Consider now an example problem used throughout this chapter. Our dependent variable is the number of times a student attends statistics lab during one semester (or quarter), whereas the independent variable is the attractiveness of the lab instructor (assuming each instructor is of the same gender and is equally competent). The researcher is interested in whether the attractiveness of the instructor influences student attendance at the statistics lab. The attractiveness groups are defined as follows: Group 1, unattractive; Group 2, slightly attractive; Group 3, moderately attractive; and Group 4, very attractive. Students were randomly assigned to a group at the beginning of the semester, and attendance was taken by the instructor. There were eight students in each group for a total of 32. Students could attend a maximum of 30 lab sessions. In Table 1.3 we see the raw data and sample statistics (means and variances) for each group and overall (far right).

The results are summarized in the ANOVA summary table as shown in Table 1.4. The test statistic is compared to the critical value $_{.05}F_{3,28} = 2.95$ obtained from Appendix Table 4, using the .05 level of significance. The test statistic exceeds the critical value, so we reject H_0 and conclude that level of attractiveness is related to mean differences in statistics lab attendance. The exact probability value (*p* value) given by SPSS is .001.

TABLE 1.3

Data and Summary Statistics for the Statistics Lab Example

Number of Statistics Labs Attended by Group

	Group 1	Group 2	Group 3	Group 4	
	15	20	10	30	
	10	13	24	22	
	12	9	29	26	
	8	22	12	20	
	21	24	27	29	
	7	25	21	28	
	13	18	25	25	
	3	12	14	15	
mean:	11.1250	17.8750	20.2500	24.3750	18.4063
variance:	30.1250	35.2679	53.0714	25.9821	56.4425

TABLE 1.4

Analysis of Variance Summary Table—Statistics Lab Example

Source	SS	df	MS	F
Between groups	738.5938	3	246.1979	6.8177*
Within groups	1,011.1250	28	36.1116	
Total	1,749.7188	31		

*${}_{.05}F_{3,28} = 2.95$

Next we examine the group effects and residual errors. The group effects are estimated as

$$a_1 = \overline{Y}_{.1} - \overline{Y}_{..} = 11.125 - 18.4063 = -7.2813$$

$$a_2 = \overline{Y}_{.2} - \overline{Y}_{..} = 17.875 - 18.4063 = -0.5313$$

$$a_3 = \overline{Y}_{.3} - \overline{Y}_{..} = 20.250 - 18.4063 = +1.8437$$

$$a_4 = \overline{Y}_{.4} - \overline{Y}_{..} = 24.375 - 18.4063 = +5.9687$$

Thus group 4 has the largest positive group effect, while group 1 has the largest negative group effect. In chapter 2 we use the same data to determine which group means, or combination of group means, are statistically different. The residual errors for each individual by group are shown in Table 1.5 and discussed later in this chapter.

TABLE 1.5
Residuals for the Statistics Lab Example by Group

Group 1	Group 2	Group 3	Group 4
3.875	2.125	−10.250	5.625
−1.125	−4.875	3.750	−2.375
0.875	−8.875	8.750	1.625
−3.125	4.125	−8.250	−4.375
9.875	6.125	6.750	4.625
−4.125	7.125	0.750	3.625
1.875	0.125	4.750	0.625
−8.125	−5.875	−6.250	−9.375

Finally we determine the effect size measures. First the correlation ratio η^2 is

$$\eta^2 = \frac{SS_{betw}}{SS_{total}} = \frac{738.5938}{1,749.7188} = .4221$$

Next ω^2 is found to be

$$\omega^2 = \frac{SS_{betw} - (J-1)\, MS_{with}}{SS_{total} + MS_{with}} = \frac{738.5938 - (3)\, 36.1116}{1,749.7188 + 36.1116} = .3529$$

Lastly f is equal to

$$f = \sqrt{\frac{\eta^2}{1 - \eta^2}} = \sqrt{\frac{.4221}{1 - .4221}} = .8546$$

Based on these effect size measures, we conclude that there is a large effect size for the influence of instructor attractiveness on lab attendance. In addition, if we rank the instructor group means from unattractive (lowest mean) to very attractive (highest mean), we see that the more attractive the instructor, the more inclined the student is to attend lab. We examine multiple comparison procedures with this example data in chapter 2.

1.5 ASSUMPTIONS AND VIOLATION OF ASSUMPTIONS

There are three standard assumptions that are made in analysis of variance models, which we are already familiar with from the independent t test. We see these assumpions often in the remainder of this text. The assumptions are concerned with independence, homogeneity of variance, and normality. We also mention some techniques that are appropriate to use in evaluating each assumption.

1.5.1 Independence

The first assumption is that each sample is an independent random sample from their respective population. In other words, each sample is randomly drawn for a population and observations are independent of one another (both within samples and across samples). The use of independent random samples is crucial in the analysis of variance. The F ratio is very sensitive to violation of the independence assumption in terms of increased likelihood of a Type I and/or Type II error (e.g., Glass, et al., 1972). This effect can sometimes even be worse with larger samples (Keppel & Wickens, 2004). A violation of the independence assumption may affect the standard errors of the sample means and thus influence any inferences made about those means. One purpose of random assignment of individuals to groups is to achieve independence. If each individual is only observed once and individuals are randomly assigned to groups, then the independence assumption is usually met. If individuals work together during the experiment (e.g., discussion group, group work), then independence may be compromised. Thus a carefully planned, controlled, and conducted research design is the key to satisfying this assumption.

The simplest procedure for assessing independence is to examine residual plots by group. If the independence assumption is satisfied, then the residuals should fall into a random display of points for each group. If the assumption is violated, then the residuals will fall into some type of cyclical pattern. The Durbin-Watson statistic (1950, 1951, 1971) can be used to test for autocorrelation. Violations of the independence assumption generally occur in three situations: when observations are collected over time; when observations are made within blocks; or when observation involves replication. For severe violations of the independence assumption, there is no simple "fix" (e.g., Scariana and Davenport, 1987). For the example data, a plot of the residuals by group is shown in Figure 1.2, and there does appear to be a random display of points for each group.

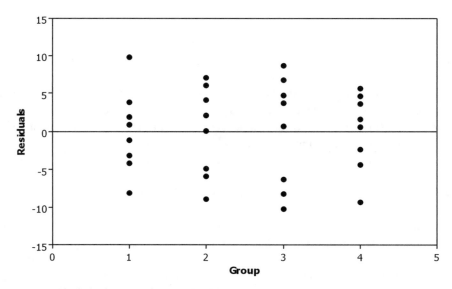

FIG. 1.2   Residual plot by group for statistics lab example.

1.5.2   Homogeneity of Variance

The second assumption is that the variances of each population are equal. This is known as the assumption of **homogeneity of variance** or **homoscedasticity**. A violation of the homogeneity assumption can lead to bias in the SS_{with} term, as well as an increase in the Type I error rate and possibly an increase in the Type II error rate. There are two sets of research that have investigated violations of this assumption, classic work and more modern work.

The classic work largely resulted from Box (1954a) and Glass, et al. (1972). Their results indicated that the effect of the violation was small with equal or nearly equal n's across the groups. There is a more serious problem if the larger n's are associated with the smaller variances (actual α > nominal α, which is a liberal result), or if the larger n's are associated with the larger variances (actual α < nominal α, which is a conservative result) [note that Bradley's (1978) criterion is used in this text, where the actual α should not exceed 1.1 to 1.5 times the nominal α]. Thus the suggestion was that heterogeneity was only a concern when there were unequal n's. The classic work only examined minor violations of the assumption (the ratio of largest variance to smallest variance being relatively small), and unfortunately has been largely adapted in textbooks and by users.

The modern work has been conducted by researchers such as Brown and Forsythe (1974), and Wilcox (1986, 1987, 1988, 1989), and nicely summarized by Coombs, et al. (1996). In short, this work indicates that the effect of heterogeneity is more severe than previously thought (poor power; α can be greatly affected), even with equal n's (although having equal n's does reduce the magnitude of the problem). Thus F is not even robust to heterogeneity with equal n's.

Suggestions for dealing with such a violation include (a) using alternative procedures such as the Welch, Brown-Forsythe, and James procedures (e.g., Myers & Well, 1995; Coombs, et al., 1996; Glass & Hopkins, 1996; Wilcox, 1996; Wilcox, 2003; Keppel & Wickens, 2004), (b) reducing α (e.g., Weinberg & Abramowitz, 2002; Keppel & Wickens, 2004), or (c) transforming Y (such as $\sqrt{Y}$, $1/Y$, or log Y) (e.g., Weinberg & Abramowitz, 2002; Keppel & Wickens, 2004). The alternative procedures will be more fully described later in this chapter.

In a plot of residuals versus each value of X, the consistency of the variance of the conditional residual distributions may be examined. Another method for detecting violation of the homogeneity assumption is the use of formal statistical tests. The traditional homogeneity tests (e.g., Levene's test) are commonly available in statistical software, but are not robust to nonnormality. Unfortunately the more robust homogeneity tests are not readily available. For the example data, the residual plot of Fig. 1.2 shows similar variances across the groups, and Levene's test suggests the variances are not different ($p = .451$).

1.5.3   Normality

The third assumption is that each of the populations follows the normal distribution. The F test is relatively robust to moderate violations of this assumption (i.e., in terms of Type I and II error rates). Specifically, effects of the violation will be minimal except for small n's, for unequal n's, and/or for extreme nonnormality. Violation of the normality assumption may be a result of outliers. The simplest outlier detection procedure is to look for observations that are more than two or three standard errors from their respective group mean. Formal procedures for the detection of outliers are now available in many statistical packages.

The following graphical techniques can be used to detect violations of the normality assumption: (a) the frequency distributions of the scores or the residuals for each group (through stem-and-leaf plots, box plots, or histograms), (b) the normal probability or quantile plot, or (c) a plot of group means versus group variances (which should be independent of one another). There are also several statistical procedures available for the detection of nonnormality (e.g., the Shapiro-Wilk test, 1965). Transformations can also be used to normalize the data. For instance, a nonlinear relationship between X and Y may result in violations of the normality and/or homoscedasticity assumptions.

In the example data, the residuals shown in Figure 1.2 appear to be somewhat normal in shape, especially considering the groups have fairly small n's. In addition, for the residuals overall, skewness $= -.2389$ and kurtosis $= -1.0191$, indicating a small departure from normality. Thus it appears that all of our assumptions have been satisfied for the example data.

A summary of the assumptions and the effects of their violation for the one-factor analysis of variance design is presented in Table 1.6. Note that in some texts the assumptions are written in terms of the residuals rather than the raw scores, but this makes no difference for our purposes.

1.6   THE UNEQUAL n's OR UNBALANCED DESIGN

Up to this point in the chapter, we have only considered the equal n's or balanced case where the number of observations is equal for each group. This was done only to make things simple. However, we need not assume that the n's must be equal (as some textbooks incorrectly do). This section briefly describes the **unequal n's** or **unbalanced case**. For our purposes, the major statistical software handle the analysis of this case for the one-factor model without any special attention. Thus, interpretation of the analysis, the assumptions, and so forth are the same as with the equal n's case. As described in chapter 3, things become a bit more complicated for the unequal n's or unbalanced case with multiple independent variables (or factors).

1.7   ALTERNATIVE ANOVA PROCEDURES

There are several alternatives to the parametric one-factor fixed-effects ANOVA. These include the Kruskal-Wallis (1952) one-factor ANOVA, the Welch (1951) test, the Brown-Forsythe

TABLE 1.6
Assumptions and Effects of Violations: One-Factor Design

Assumption	Effect of Assumption Violation
Independence	Increased likelihood of a Type I and/or Type II error in the F statistic; influences standard errors of means and thus inferences about those means
Homogeneity of variance	Bias in SS_{with}; increased likelihood of a Type I and/or Type II error; less effect with equal or nearly equal n's; effect decreases as n increases
Normality	Minimal effect with moderate violation; effect less severe with large n's, with equal or nearly equal n's, and/or with homogeneously shaped distributions

(1974) procedure, and the James (1951) procedures. You may recognize the Welch and Brown–Forsythe procedures as similar alternatives to the independent t test.

The Kruskal-Wallis test makes no normality assumption about the population distributions, although it assumes similar distribution shapes, yet still assumes equal population variances across the groups (although heterogeneity has some effect, it is less than with the parametric ANOVA). When the normality assumption is met, or nearly so (i.e., with mild nonnormality), the parametric ANOVA is slightly more powerful than the Kruskal-Wallis test (i.e., less likelihood of a Type II error). Otherwise the Kruskal-Wallis test is more powerful.

The Kruskal-Wallis procedure works as follows. First, the observations on the dependent measure are ranked, regardless of group assignment (the ranking is done by the computer). That is, the observations are ranked from first through last, disregarding group membership. The procedure essentially tests whether the average of the ranks are different across the groups such that they are unlikely to represent random samples from the same population. Thus, according to the null hypothesis, the mean rank is the same for each group, whereas for the alternative hypothesis the mean rank is not the same across groups. The test statistic is H and is compared to the critical value $_\alpha\chi^2_{J-1}$. The null hypothesis is rejected if the test statistic H exceeds the χ^2 critical value.

There are two situations to consider with this test. First, the χ^2 critical value is really only appropriate when there are at least three groups and at least five observations per group (i.e., the χ^2 is not an exact sampling distribution of H). When you are only comparing two groups use the Mann-Whitney-Wilcoxon test. The second situation is when there are tied ranks, which affect the sampling distribution of H. Typically a midranks procedure is used, which results in an overly conservative Kruskal-Wallis test. A correction for ties is commonly used. Unless the number of ties is relatively large, the effect of the correction is minimal.

Using the statistics lab data as an example, we perform the Kruskal-Wallis analysis of variance. The test statistic $H = 13.0610$ is compared with the critical value $_{.05}\chi^2_3 = 7.81$, from Appendix Table 3, and the result is that H_0 is rejected ($p = .005$). Thus the Kruskal-Wallis result agrees with the result of the parametric analysis of variance. This should not be surprising because the normality assumption apparently was met. Thus, one would probably not have done the Kruskal-Wallis test for the example data. We merely provide it for purposes of explanation and comparision.

In summary, the Kruskal-Wallis test can be used as an alternative to the parametric one-factor analysis of variance under nonnormality and/or when data are ordinal. Under normality and with interval/ratio data, the parametric ANOVA is more powerful than the Kruskal-Wallis test, and thus is the preferred method of the two.

Next we briefly consider the following procedures for the heteroscedasticity condition: the Welch (1951) test; the Brown-Forsythe (1974) procedure; and the James (1951) first- and second-order procedures (more fully described by Myers & Well, 1995; Coombs, et al., 1996; Wilcox, 1996; and Wilcox, 2003). These procedures do not require homogeneity. Current research suggests that (a) under homogeneity the F test is slightly more powerful than any of these procedures, and (b) under heterogeneity each of these alternative procedures is more powerful than the F, although the choice among them depends on several conditions, making a recommendation somewhat complicated (e.g., Clinch & Keselman, 1982; Tomarken & Serlin, 1986; Coombs, et al., 1996). The Kruskal-Wallis test is widely available in the major statistical software, and the Welch and Brown-Forsythe procedures are available in the SPSS one-way ANOVA module. Wilcox (1996, 2003) also provides assistance for these alternative procedures.

1.8   SPSS

Finally we consider the use of SPSS for the statistics lab example, including an APA style para-graph of the findings. Note that SPSS needs the data to be in a specific form for any of the analyses below to proceeed, which is different from the layout of the data in Table 1.1. For a one-factor ANOVA, the dataset must consist of two variables or columns. One column or variable is for the level of the independent variable, and the second is for the dependent variable. Each row then represents one individual, indicating the level or group that individual is a member of (1, 2, 3, or 4 in our example), and their score on the dependent variable. Thus we wind up with two long columns of group values and scores.

To conduct a parametric ANOVA through the GLM module, go to the "Analyze" pulldown, into "General Linear Model," and then into the "Univariate" procedure. Click the dependent variable (e.g., labs attended) into the "Dependent Variable" box, and click the fixed-effects fac-tor variable into the "Fixed Factor(s)" box. Click on the "Options" button to obtain such infor-mation as "Descriptive Statistics," "Estimates of effect size," "Observed power," and "Homo-geneity tests" (i.e., Levene's test) (those are the options that I typically utilize). Click on "Continue" to return to the original dialog box. To obtain a profile plot of means, click on the "Plots" button, move the factor variable name into the "Horizontal axis" box, click on "Add" to generate the plot, and finally click on "Continue" to return to the original dialog box. Then click on "OK" to run the analyses. Selected results are shown in the top three panels of Table 1.7 (ANOVA summary table, information about overall or grand mean, and information about group means, respectively) and the profile plot is shown in Fig. 1.3.

Results from some of the recommended alternative procedures can be obtained from two other SPSS modules. The Kruskal-Wallis procedure is one of the nonparametric tests in SPSS. Beginning with the "Analyze" pulldown, go into "Nonparametric Statistics," then into "K Inde-pendent Samples." Click the dependent variable into the "Test Variable List" box and the fac-tor variable into the "Grouping Variable" box. You also have to click on "Define Range" to indicate the values of the grouping variable you wish to use (1 to 4 in the example). In the lower left portion of the screen check "Kruskal-Wallis H" to generate that test, then click on "OK" to find the results as depicted in the fourth panel of Table 1.7.

The Welch and Brown-Forsythe procedures can be found within the One-Way ANOVA pro-gram. From the "Analyze" pulldown, go into "Compare Means," then into "One-Way ANOVA." First click the appropriate variables into the "Dependent List" and "Factor" boxes. Click on the "Options" button to find the Welch and Brown-Forsythe procedures, as well as descriptive statistics, Levene's homogeneity of variance test, and a profile plot of means. Then click on "Continue" to return to the original dialog box and click on "OK" to run those procedures. Selected results are given in the bottom panel of Table 1.7. For further details on the use of SPSS for these procedures, be sure to examine books such as Page, Braver, and MacKinnon (2003), or Morgan, Leech, and Barrett (2005).

Finally we come to an example paragraph of the results for the statistics lab example. From Table 1.7 we see that the ANOVA is statistically significant ($F = 6.818$, $df = 3,28$, $p = .001$), effect size is rather large ($\eta^2 = .422$), and observed power is quite strong (.956). The means were 11.125 for the unattractive level, 17.875 for the slightly attractive level, 20.250 for the moderately attractive level, and 24.375 for the very attractive level. The profile plot (Fig. 1.3) depicts that with increasing instructor attractiveness there was a corresponding increase in mean

TABLE 1.7
Selected SPSS Results for the Statistics Lab Example

Tests of Between-Subjects Effects

Dependent Variable: dv

Source	Type III Sum of Squares	df	Mean Square	F	Sig	Partial Eta Squared	Observed Power[a]
group	738.594	3	246.198	6.818	.001	.422	.956
Error	1011.125	28	36.112				
Corrected Total	1749.719	31					

a. Computed using alpha = .05

1. Grand Mean

Dependent Variable: dv

Mean	Std. Error	95% Confidence Interval	
		Lower Bound	Upper Bound
18.406	1.062	16.230	20.582

2. Group

Dependent Variable: dv

group	Mean	Std. Error	95% Confidence Interval	
			Lower Bound	Upper Bound
1.00000	11.125	2.125	6.773	15.477
2.00000	17.875	2.125	13.523	22.227
3.00000	20.250	2.125	15.898	24.602
4.00000	24.375	2.125	20.023	28.727

Test Statistics[a,b]

	dv
Chi-Square	13.061
df	3
Asymp. Sig.	.005

a. Kruskal Wallis Test
b. Grouping Variable: group

Robust Tests of Equality of Means

dv

	Statistic[a]	df1	df2	Sig.
Welch	7.862	3	15.454	.002
Brown-Forsythe	6.818	3	25.882	.002

a. Asymptotically F distributed.

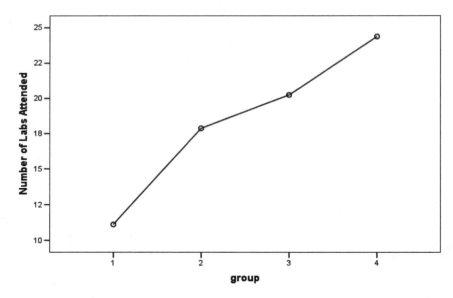

FIG. 1.3   Profile plot for statistics lab example.

lab attendance. In examining the residual plot, skewness and kurtosis statistics, and Levene's homogeneity of variance test ($p = .451$), we determined the assumptions were satisfied. For completeness, we also conducted several alternative procedures. The Kruskal-Wallis test ($p = .005$), the Welch procedure ($p = .002$), and the Brown-Forsythe procedure ($p = .002$) also indicated a significant effect, providing further support for the assumptions being satisfied.

1.9   SUMMARY

In this chapter, methods involving the comparision of multiple group means for a single independent variable were considered. The chapter began with a look at the characteristics of the analysis of variance including: (a) control of the experiment-wise error rate through an omnibus test; (b) one independent variable with two or more fixed levels; (c) individuals are randomly assigned to groups and then exposed to only one level of the independent variable; and (d) the dependent variable is at least measured at the interval level. Next, a discussion of the theory underlying ANOVA was conducted. Here we examined the concepts of between- and within-groups variability, sources of variation, and partitioning the sums of squares. The ANOVA model was examined. Some discussion was also devoted to the ANOVA assumptions, their assessment, and how to deal with assumption violations. Finally, alternative ANOVA procedures were described. At this point you should have met the following objectives: (a) be able to understand the characteristics and concepts underlying the one-factor ANOVA, (b) be able to compute and interpret the results of a one-factor ANOVA, and (c) be able to understand and evaluate the assumptions of the one-factor ANOVA. Chapter 2 considers a number of multiple comparison procedures for further examination of sets of means. Chapter 3 returns to the analysis of variance and discusses models for which there are more than one independent variable.

PROBLEMS

Conceptual Problems

1. Data for three independent random samples each of size four are analyzed by a one-factor analysis of variance fixed-effects model. If the values of the sample means are all equal, what is the value of MS_{betw}?
    a.   0
    b.   1
    c.   2
    d.   3

2. For a one-factor analysis of variance fixed-effects model, which of the following is always true?
    a. $df_{betw} + df_{with} = df_{tot}$
    b. $SS_{betw} + SS_{with} = SS_{tot}$
    c. $MS_{betw} + MS_{with} = MS_{tot}$
    d.   all of the above
    e.   both a and b

3. Suppose that $n_1 = 19$, $n_2 = 21$, and $n_3 = 23$. For a one-factor ANOVA, the df_{with} would be
    a.   2
    b.   3
    c.   60
    d.   63

4. In a one-factor ANOVA, H_0 asserts that
    a.   all of the population means are equal.
    b.   the between-groups variance estimate and the within-groups variance estimate are both estimates of the same population variance.
    c.   the within-groups sum of squares is equal to the between-groups sum of squares.
    d.   both a and b

5. For a one-factor ANOVA comparing three groups with $n = 10$ in each group, the F ratio would have degrees of freedom equal to
    a.   2, 27
    b.   2, 29
    c.   3, 27
    d.   3, 29

6.   Which of the following is not necessary in ANOVA?

    a.   Observations are from random and independent samples.

    b.   The dependent variable is measured on at least the interval scale.

    c.   Populations have equal variances.

    d.   Equal sample sizes are necessary.

7.   If you find an F ratio of 1.0 in a one-factor ANOVA, it means that

    a.   between-group variation exceeds within-group variation.

    b.   within-group variation exceeds between-group variation.

    c.   between-group variation is equal to within-group variation.

    d.   between-group variation exceeds total variation.

8.   Suppose students in grades 7, 8, 9, 10, 11, and 12 were compared on absenteeism. If ANOVA were used rather than multiple t tests, the probability of a Type I error would be less. True or False?

9.   Mean square is another name for variance or variance estimate. True or False?

10.   In ANOVA each independent variable is known as a level. True or False?

11.   A negative F ratio is impossible. True or False?

12.   Suppose that for a one-factor ANOVA with $J = 4$ and $n = 10$ the four sample means are all equal to 15. I assert that the value of MS_{with} is necessarily equal to zero. Am I correct?

13.   With $J = 3$ groups, I assert that if you reject H_0 in the one-factor ANOVA you will necessarily conclude that all three group means are different. Am I correct?

14.   The homoscedasticity assumption is that the population scores from which each of the samples are drawn are normally distributed. True or False?

15.   When analyzing mean differences among more than two samples, doing independent t tests on all possible pairs of means

    a.   decreases the probability of a Type I error.

    b.   does not change the probability of a Type I error.

    c.   increases the probability of a Type I error.

    d.   Cannot be determined from the information provided.

16.   Suppose for a one-factor fixed-effects ANOVA with $J = 5$ and $n = 15$, the five sample means are all equal to 50. I assert that the F test statistic cannot be significant. Am I correct?

17.   The independence assumption in ANOVA is that the observations in the samples do not depend on one another. True or False?

18. For $J = 2$ and $\alpha = .05$, if the result of the independent t test is significant, then the result of the one-factor fixed-effects ANOVA is uncertain. True or false?

19. A statistician conducted a one-factor fixed-effects ANOVA and found the F ratio to be less than 0. I assert that this means the between-groups variability is less than the within-groups variability. Am I correct?

Computational Problems

1. Complete the following summary table for a one-factor analysis of variance, where there are four groups receiving different headache medications, each with 16 observations, and $\alpha = .05$.

Source	SS	df	MS	F	Critical Value and Decision
Between	9.75	—	—	—	—
Within	—	—	—		
Total	18.75	—			

2. A social psychologist wants to determine if type of music has any effect on the number of beers consumed by people in a tavern. Four taverns are selected that have different musical formats. Five people are randomly sampled in each tavern and their beer consumption monitored for three hours. Complete the following one-factor ANOVA summary table using $\alpha = .05$.

Source	SS	df	MS	F	Critical Value and Decision
Between	—	—	7.52	5.01	—
Within	—	—	—		
Total	—	—			

3. A psychologist would like to know whether the season (fall, winter, spring, summer) has any consistent effect on people's sexual activity. In the middle of each season a psychologist selects a random sample of $n = 25$ students. Each individual is given a sexual activity questionnaire. A one-factor ANOVA was used to analyze these data. Complete the following ANOVA summary table ($\alpha = .05$).

Source	SS	df	MS	F	Critical Value and Decision
Between	—	—	—	5.00	—
Within	960	—	—		
Total	—	—			

4. The following five independent random samples are obtained from five normally distributed populations with equal variances. The dependent variable is number of bank transactions in one month and the groups are five different banks.

Group 1	Group 2	Group 3	Group 4	Group 5
16	16	2	5	7
5	10	9	8	12
11	7	11	1	14
23	12	13	5	16
18	7	10	8	11
12	4	13	11	9
12	23	9	9	19
19	13	9	9	24

Use SPSS to conduct a one-factor analysis of variance to determine if the group means are equal using $\alpha = .05$. Plot the group means and interpret the results.

Interpretive Problem

Using the statistics survey dataset from the CD, use SPSS to conduct a one-factor fixed-effects ANOVA, where political view is the grouping variable ($J = 5$) and the dependent variable is a variable of interest to you (the following variables look interesting: books; TV; exercise; drinks; GPA; GREQ; CDs; hair appointment). Then write an APA type paragraph describing the results.

2

MULTIPLE COMPARISON PROCEDURES

Chapter Outline

1. Concepts of multiple comparison procedures
   Contrasts
   Planned versus post hoc comparisons
   The Type I error rate
   Orthogonal contrasts
2. Selected multiple comparison procedures
   Planned analysis of trend
   Planned orthogonal contrasts
   Planned contrasts with reference group: Dunnett method
   Other planned contrasts: Dunn (or Bonferroni) and Dunn-Sidak methods
   Complex post hoc contrasts: Scheffe' and Kaiser-Bowden methods
   Simple post hoc contrasts: Tukey HSD, Tukey-Kramer, Fisher LSD, and
       Hayter tests
   Simple post hoc contrasts for unequal variances: Games-Howell, Dunnett T3
       and C tests
   Follow-up tests to Kruskal-Wallis

Key Concepts

1.   Contrast
2.   Simple and complex contrasts
3.   Planned and post hoc comparisons
4.   Contrast- and family-based Type I error rates
5.   Orthogonal contrasts

In this chapter our concern is with multiple comparison procedures that involve comparisons among the group means. Recall from chapter 1 the one-factor analysis of variance where the means from two or more samples were compared. What do we do if the omnibus F test leads us to reject H_0? First, consider the situation where there are only two samples (e.g., assessing the effectiveness of two types of medication), and H_0 has already been rejected in the omnibus test. Why was H_0 rejected? The answer should be obvious. Those two sample means must be significantly different, as there is no other way that the omnibus H_0 could have been rejected (e.g., one type of medication is more effective than the other).

Second, consider the situation where there are more than two samples (e.g., three types of medication), and H_0 has already been rejected in the omnibus test. Why was H_0 rejected? The answer is not so obvious. This situation is one where a **multiple comparison procedure** (MCP) would be quite informative. Thus for situations where there are at least three groups and the analysis of variance (ANOVA) H_0 has been rejected, some sort of MCP is necessary to determine which means or combination of means are different. Third, consider the situation where the researcher is not even interested in the ANOVA omnibus test, but is only interested in comparisons involving particular means (e.g., certain medications are more effective than a placebo). This is a situation where a MCP is useful for evaluating those specific comparisons.

If the ANOVA omnibus H_0 has been rejected, why not do all possible independent t tests? First return to a similar question from Chapter 1. There we asked about doing all possible pairwise independent t tests rather than an ANOVA. The answer there was to do an omnibus F test. The reason was related to the probability of making a Type I error (i.e., α), where the researcher incorrectly rejects a true null hypothesis. Although the α level for each t test can be controlled at a specified nominal level, say .05, what would happen to the overall α level for the set of tests? The overall α level for the set of tests, often called the family-wise Type I error rate, would be larger than the α level for each of the individual t tests. The optimal solution, in terms of maintaining control over our overall α level as well as maximizing power, is to conduct one overall omnibus test. The omnibus test assesses the equality of all of the means simultaneously.

The same concept can be applied to the multiple comparison situation. Rather than doing all possible pairwise independent t tests, where the family-wise error could be quite large, one should use a procedure that controls the family-wise error in some way. This can be done with multiple comparison procedures. As pointed out later in the chapter, there are two main methods for taking the Type I error rate into account.

This chapter is concerned with several important new concepts, such as a contrast, planned versus post hoc comparisons, the Type I error rate, and orthogonal contrasts. The remainder of the chapter consists of selected multiple comparison procedures, including when and how to apply them. The terms **comparison** and **contrast** are used here synonymously. Also, MCPs are only applicable for comparing levels of an independent variable that are fixed, in other words, for fixed-effects independent variables, and not for random-effects independent variables. Our objectives are that by the end of this chapter, you will be able to (a) understand the concepts underlying the MCPs, (b) select the appropriate MCP for a given research situation, and (c) determine and interpret the results of MCPs.

2.1 CONCEPTS OF MULTIPLE COMPARISON PROCEDURES

This section describes the most important characteristics of the multiple comparison procedures. We begin by defining a contrast, and then move into planned versus post hoc contrasts, the Type I error rates, and orthogonal contrasts.

2.1.1 Contrasts

A **contrast** is a weighted combination of the means. For example, one might wish to contrast the following means: (a) Group 1 with Group 2, or (b) the combination of Groups 1 and 2 with Group 3. Statistically a contrast is defined as

$$\psi_i = c_1 \mu_{.1} + c_2 \mu_{.2} + \cdots + c_J \mu_{.J}$$

where the c_j are known as contrast coefficients (or weights), which are positive and negative values and define a particular contrast ψ_i, and the $\mu_{.j}$ are population group means. In other words, a contrast is simply a particular combination of the group means, depending on which means the researcher is interested in comparing. It should also be noted that to form a fair or legitimate contrast, $\Sigma_j c_j = 0$ for the equal n's or balanced case, and $\Sigma_j (n_j c_j) = 0$ for the unequal n's or unbalanced case.

For example, suppose you want to compare the means of Groups 1 and 3 for $J = 4$, and call this contrast 1. The contrast would be written as

$$\psi_1 = c_1 \mu_{.1} + c_2 \mu_{.2} + c_3 \mu_{.3} + c_4 \mu_{.4}$$
$$= (+1)\mu_{.1} + (0)\mu_{.2} + (-1)\mu_{.3} + (0)\mu_{.4}$$
$$= \mu_{.1} - \mu_{.3}$$

What hypotheses are we testing when we evaluate a contrast? The null and alternate hypotheses of any specific contrast can be written simply as

$$H_0: \psi_i = 0$$

and

$$H_1 : \psi_i \neq 0$$

respectively. Thus we are testing whether a particular combination of means, as defined by the contrast coefficients, are different. How does this relate back to the omnibus F test? The null and alternate hypotheses for the omnibus F test can be written in terms of contrasts as

$$H_0 : \text{all } \psi_i = 0$$

and

$$H_1 : \text{at least one } \psi_i \neq 0$$

respectively. Here the omnibus test is determining whether any contrast that could be formulated for the set of J means is significant.

Contrasts can be divided into simple or pairwise contrasts, and complex or nonpairwise contrasts. A simple or pairwise contrast is a comparison involving only two means. Let us take as an example the situation where there are $J = 3$ groups. There are three possible distinct pairwise contrasts that could be formed: (a) $\mu_{.1} - \mu_{.2} = 0$, (b) $\mu_{.1} - \mu_{.3} = 0$, and (c) $\mu_{.2} - \mu_{.3} = 0$. It should be obvious that a pairwise contrast involving Groups 1 and 2 is the same contrast whether it is written as $\mu_{.1} - \mu_{.2} = 0$, or as $\mu_{.2} - \mu_{.1} = 0$. In terms of contrast coefficients, these three contrasts could be written in the form of a table as

	c_1	c_2	c_3
$\psi_1 : \mu_{.1} - \mu_{.2} = 0$	$+1$	-1	0
$\psi_2 : \mu_{.1} - \mu_{.3} = 0$	$+1$	0	-1
$\psi_3 : \mu_{.2} - \mu_{.3} = 0$	0	$+1$	-1

where each contrast is read across the table to determine its contrast coefficients. For example, the first contrast ψ_1 does not involve Group 3 because that contrast coefficient is zero, but does involve Groups 1 and 2 because those contrast coefficients are not zero. The coefficients are $+1$ for Group 1 and -1 for Group 2; consequently we are interested in examining the difference between Groups 1 and 2. Written in long form so that we can see where the contrast coefficients come from, the three contrasts are as follows:

$$\psi_1 = (+1)\mu_{.1} + (-1)\mu_{.2} + (0)\mu_{.3} = \mu_{.1} - \mu_{.2}$$
$$\psi_2 = (+1)\mu_{.1} + (0)\mu_{.2} + (-1)\mu_{.3} = \mu_{.1} - \mu_{.3}$$
$$\psi_3 = (0)\mu_{.1} + (+1)\mu_{.2} + (-1)\mu_{.3} = \mu_{.2} - \mu_{.3}$$

An easy way to remember the number of possible unique pairwise contrasts that could be written is $\frac{1}{2}[J(J - 1)]$. Thus for $J = 3$ the number of possible unique pairwise contrasts is 3, whereas for $J = 4$ the number of such contrasts is 6.

A complex contrast is a comparison involving more than two means. Continuing with the example of $J = 3$ groups, we might be interested in testing the contrast $\mu_{.1} - \frac{1}{2}(\mu_{.2} + \mu_{.3})$. This contrast is a comparison of the mean for Group 1 with the average of the means for Groups 2 and 3. In terms of contrast coefficients, this contrast would be written as

$$
\begin{array}{cccc}
 & c_1 & c_2 & c_3 \\
\psi_4: \mu_{.1} - \frac{1}{2}\mu_{.2} - \frac{1}{2}\mu_{.3} = 0 & 1 & -\frac{1}{2} & -\frac{1}{2}
\end{array}
$$

Written in long form so that we can see where the contrast coefficients come from, this complex contrast is as follows:

$$
\psi_4: = (+1)\mu_{.1} + (-\tfrac{1}{2})\mu_{.2} + (-\tfrac{1}{2})\mu_{.3} = \mu_{.1} - \tfrac{1}{2}\mu_{.2} - \tfrac{1}{2}\mu_{.3}
$$

The number of unique complex contrasts is greater than $\frac{1}{2}[J(J - 1)]$ when J is at least 4; in other words, the number of such contrasts that could be formed is quite large when there are more than three groups. Note that the total number of unique pairwise and complex contrasts is $[1 + \frac{1}{2}(3^J - 1) - 2^J]$ (Keppel, 1982). Thus for $J = 4$, one could form 25 total contrasts.

Many of the multiple comparison procedures are based on the same test statistic, which we introduce here as the "standard t." The standard t ratio for a contrast is given as

$$
t = \frac{\psi'}{s_{\psi'}}
$$

where $s_{\psi'}$ represents the standard error of the contrast as

$$
s_{\psi'} = \sqrt{MS_{error} \sum_{j=1}^{J} \left(\frac{c_j^2}{n_j} \right)}
$$

where the prime (i.e., $'$) indicates that the contrast is based on sample data, and n_j refers to the number of observations in group j.

2.1.2   Planned Versus Post hoc Comparisons

This section examines specific types of contrasts or comparisons. One way of classifying contrasts is whether the contrasts are formulated prior to the research or following a significant omnibus F test. **Planned contrasts** (also known as specific or a priori contrasts) involve particular comparisons that the researcher is interested in examining prior to data collection. These planned contrasts are generally based on theory, previous research, and/or hypotheses. Here the researcher is interested in certain specific contrasts a priori, where the number of such contrasts is usually small. Planned contrasts are done without regard to the result of the omnibus F test. In other words, the researcher is interested in certain specific contrasts, but not in the omnibus F test that examines all possible contrasts. In this situation the researcher could care less about the multitude of possible contrasts and need not even examine the F test; but rather the concern is only with a few contrasts of substantive interest. In addition, the researcher may not be as concerned with the family-wise error rate for planned comparisons because only a few of them will actually be carried out. Fewer planned comparisons are usually conducted (due to their specificity) than post hoc comparisons (due to their generality), so planned contrasts generally yield narrower confidence intervals, are more powerful, and have a higher likelihood of a Type I error than post hoc comparisons.

Post hoc contrasts are formulated such that the researcher provides no advance specification of the actual contrasts to be tested. This type of contrast is done following a significant omnibus F test. Post hoc is Latin for "after the fact," referring to contrasts tested after a significant F in the ANOVA. Here the researcher may want to take the family-wise error rate into account somehow for purposes of overall protection. Post hoc contrasts are also known as unplanned, a posteriori, or postmortem contrasts. It should be noted that most MCPs are not derived or based on finding a significant F in the ANOVA.

2.1.3   The Type I Error Rate

How does the researcher deal with the family-wise Type I error rate? Depending on the multiple comparison procedure selected, one may either set α for each contrast or set α for a family of contrasts. In the former category, α is set for each individual contrast. The MCPs in this category are known as **contrast-based**. We designate the α level for contrast-based procedures as α_{pc}, as it represents the **per contrast** Type I error rate. Thus α_{pc} represents the probability of making a Type I error for that particular contrast. In the latter category, α is set for a family or set of contrasts. The MCPs in this category are known as **family-wise**. We designate the α level for family-wise procedures as α_{fw}, as it represents the family-wise Type I error rate. Thus α_{fw} represents the probability of making at least one Type I error in the family or set of contrasts. For orthogonal (or independent) contrasts, the following property holds:

$$\alpha_{fw} = 1 - (1 - \alpha_{pc})^c$$

where $c = J - 1$ orthogonal contrasts (as defined in the next section). For nonorthogonal contrasts, this property is more complicated in that

$$\alpha_{fw} \le c\,\alpha_{pc}$$

These properties should be familiar from the discussion in chapter 1, where we were looking at the probability of a Type I error in the use of multiple independent t tests.

2.1.4   Orthogonal Contrasts

Let us begin this section by defining orthogonal contrasts. A set of contrasts is orthogonal if they represent nonredundant and independent (if the usual ANOVA assumptions are met) sources of variation. For J groups, you will only be able to construct $J - 1$ orthogonal contrasts. However, more than one set of orthogonal contrasts may exist; although the contrasts within each set are orthogonal, contrasts across such sets may not be.

For purposes of simplicity, we first consider the equal n's or balanced case. With equal observations per group, two contrasts are defined to be orthogonal if the products of their contrast coefficients sum to zero. That is, two contrasts are orthogonal if

$$\sum_{j=1}^{J} (c_j c_{j'}) = c_1 c_{1'} + c_2 c_{2'} + \ldots + c_j c_{j'} = 0$$

where j and j' represent two distinct contrasts. Thus we see that orthogonality depends on the contrast coefficients, the c_j, and not the group means, the $\mu_{.j}$. For example, if $J = 3$, then we can form a set of two orthogonal contrasts. One such set is

$$
\begin{array}{lccc}
 & c_1 & c_2 & c_3 \\
\psi_1: \mu_{.1} - \mu_{.2} = 0 & +1 & -1 & 0 \\
\psi_2: \tfrac{1}{2}\mu_{.1} + \tfrac{1}{2}\mu_{.2} - \mu_{.3} = 0 & +\tfrac{1}{2} & +\tfrac{1}{2} & -1 \\
\hline
 & +\tfrac{1}{2} + -\tfrac{1}{2} + & 0 = 0
\end{array}
$$

If the sum of the contrast coefficient products for a set of contrasts is equal to zero, then we define this as an orthogonal set of contrasts. A set of two contrasts that are not orthogonal is

$$
\begin{array}{lccc}
 & c_1 & c_2 & c_3 \\
\psi_3: \mu_{.1} - \mu_{.2} = 0 & +1 & -1 & 0 \\
\psi_4: \mu_{.1} - \mu_{.3} = 0 & +1 & 0 & -1 \\
\hline
 & +1 & + \; 0 \; + & 0 = +1
\end{array}
$$

Consider a situation where there are three groups and we decide to form three pairwise contrasts, knowing full well that they cannot all be orthogonal. The contrasts we form are

$$
\begin{array}{lccc}
 & c_1 & c_2 & c_3 \\
\psi_1: \mu_{.1} - \mu_{.2} = 0 & +1 & -1 & 0 \\
\psi_2: \mu_{.2} - \mu_{.3} = 0 & 0 & +1 & -1 \\
\psi_3: \mu_{.1} - \mu_{.3} = 0 & +1 & 0 & -1
\end{array}
$$

Say that the group means are $\mu_{.1} = 30$, $\mu_{.2} = 24$, and $\mu_{.3} = 20$. We find $\psi_1 = 6$ for the first contrast, and $\psi_2 = 4$ for the second contrast. Because these three contrasts are not orthogonal and contain totally redundant information about the means, $\psi_3 = 10$ for the third contrast by definition. Thus the third contrast contains no additional information to that contained in the first two contrasts.

Finally, for the unequal n's or unbalanced case, two contrasts are orthogonal if

$$
\sum_{j=1}^{J} \left[\frac{(c_j c_{j'})}{n_j} \right] = 0
$$

The denominator n_j makes it more difficult to find an orthogonal set of contrasts that is of any interest to the researcher (see Pedhazur, 1997, for an example).

2.2 SELECTED MULTIPLE COMPARISON PROCEDURES

This section considers a selection of multiple comparison procedures (MCP). These represent the "best" procedures in some sense, in terms of ease of utility, popularity, and control of Type I and II error rates. Other procedures are briefly mentioned. In the interest of consistency, each procedure is discussed in the hypothesis testing situation based on a test statistic. Most, but not all, of the procedures can also be formulated as confidence intervals (sometimes called a **critical difference**), although not discussed here. The first few procedures discussed are for planned comparisons, whereas the remainder of the section is devoted to post hoc comparisons. For each MCP, we describe its major characteristics, and present the test statistic with an example using the example data from chapter 1.

Unless otherwise specified, each MCP makes the standard assumptions of normality, homogeneity of variance, and independence of observations. Some of the procedures do make additional assumptions, such as equal n's per group. Throughout this section we also assume that a two-tailed alternative hypothesis is of interest, although some of the MCPs can also be used with a one-tailed alternative. In general, the MCPs are fairly robust to nonnormality (but not for extreme cases), but are not as robust to departures from homogeneity of variance or from independence (see Pavur, 1988).

2.2.1   Planned Analysis of Trend

Trend analysis is a planned MCP useful when the groups represent different quantitative levels of a factor (i.e., an interval or ratio level independent variable). Examples of such a factor might be age, drug dosage, and different amounts of instruction, practice, or trials. Here the researcher is interested in whether the sample means vary with a change in the amount of the independent variable. We define **trend analysis** in the form of orthogonal polynomials, and assume that the levels of the independent variable are equally spaced and the number of observations per group are equal. This is the standard case; other cases are briefly discussed at the end of this section.

Orthogonal polynomial contrasts use the standard t test statistic, which is compared to the critical values of $\pm_{\alpha/2} t_{\mathrm{df(error)}}$ obtained from the t table in Appendix Table 2. The form of the contrasts is a bit different and requires a bit of discussion. Orthogonal polynomial contrasts incorporate two concepts, orthogonal contrasts and polynomial regression. For J groups, there can be only $J - 1$ orthogonal contrasts in the set. In polynomial regression, we have terms in the model for a linear trend, a quadratic trend, a cubic trend, and so on. For example, linear trend is represented by a straight line (no bends), quadratic trend by a curve with one bend (U or upside-down U shapes), and cubic trend by a curve with two bends (S shape).

Now put those two ideas together. A set of orthogonal contrasts can be formed where the first contrast evaluates a linear trend, the second a quadratic trend, the third a cubic trend, and so forth. Thus for J groups, the highest order polynomial that could be formed is $J - 1$. With four groups, for example, one could form a set of orthogonal contrasts to assess linear, quadratic, and cubic trend.

You may be wondering just how these contrasts are formed? For $J = 4$ groups, the contrast coefficients for the linear, quadratic, and cubic trends are

	c_1	c_2	c_3	c_4
ψ_{linear}	-3	-1	$+1$	$+3$
$\psi_{\text{quadratic}}$	$+1$	-1	-1	$+1$
ψ_{cubic}	-1	$+3$	-3	$+1$

where the contrasts can be written out as

$$\psi_{\text{linear}} = (-3)\mu_{.1} + (-1)\mu_{.2} + (+1)\mu_{.3} + (+3)\mu_{.4}$$

$$\psi_{\text{quadratic}} = (+1)\mu_{.1} + (-1)\mu_{.2} + (-1)\mu_{.3} + (+1)\mu_{.4}$$

$$\psi_{\text{cubic}} = (-1)\mu_{.1} + (+3)\mu_{.2} + (-3)\mu_{.3} + (+1)\mu_{.4}$$

These contrast coefficients can be found in Appendix Table 6, for a number of different values of J. If you look in the table of contrast coefficients for values of J greater than 6, you see that the coefficients for the higher-order polynomials are not included. As an example, for $J = 7$, coefficients only up through a quintic trend are included. Although they could easily be derived and tested, these higher-order polynomials are usually not of interest to the researcher. In fact, it is rare to find anyone interested in polynomials beyond the cubic because they are difficult to understand and interpret (although statistically sophisticated, they say little to the applied researcher). The contrasts are typically tested sequentially beginning with the linear trend and proceeding to higher-order trends.

Using the example data on the attractiveness of the lab instructors from Chapter 1, let us test for linear, quadratic, and cubic trends. Trend analysis may be relevant for this data because the groups do represent different quantitative levels of an attractiveness factor. Because $J = 4$, we can use the contrast coefficients given previously. The following are the computations:

Critical values: $\pm_{\alpha/2} t_{\text{df(error)}} = \pm_{.025} t_{28} = \pm 2.048$

Standard error for linear trend:

$$s_{\psi'} = \sqrt{MS_{error} \sum_{j=1}^{J} \left(\frac{c_j^2}{n_j} \right)} = \sqrt{36.1116(9/8 + 1/8 + 1/8 + 9/8)} = 9.5015$$

Standard error for quadratic trend:

$$s_{\psi'} = \sqrt{MS_{error} \sum_{j=1}^{J} \left(\frac{c_j^2}{n_j} \right)} = \sqrt{36.1116(1/8 + 1/8 + 1/8 + 1/8)} = 4.2492$$

Standard error for cubic trend:

$$s_{\psi'} = \sqrt{MS_{error} \sum_{j=1}^{J} \left(\frac{c_j^2}{n_j} \right)} = \sqrt{36.1116(1/8 + 9/8 + 9/8 + 1/8)} = 9.5015$$

Test statistics:

$$t_{linear} = \frac{-3\overline{Y}_{.1} - 1\overline{Y}_{.2} + 1\overline{Y}_{.3} + 3\overline{Y}_{.4}}{s_{\psi'}}$$

$$= \frac{-3(11.1250) - 1(17.8750) + 1(20.2500) + 3(24.3750)}{9.5015} = 4.4335 \, (significant)$$

$$t_{quadratic} = \frac{1\overline{Y}_{.1} - 1\overline{Y}_{.2} - 1\overline{Y}_{.3} + 1\overline{Y}_{.4}}{s_{\psi'}}$$

$$= \frac{1(11.1250) - 1(17.8750) - 1(20.2500) + 1(24.3750)}{4.2492} = -0.6178 \, (nonsignificant)$$

$$t_{cubic} = \frac{-1\overline{Y}_{.1} + 3\overline{Y}_{.2} - 3\overline{Y}_{.3} + 1\overline{Y}_{.4}}{s_{\psi'}}$$

$$= \frac{-1(11.1250) + 3(17.8750) - 3(20.2500) + 1(24.3750)}{9.5015} = 0.6446 \, (nonsignificant)$$

Thus we see that there is a significant linear trend in the means, but no higher-order trend. This should not be surprising when we plot the means, as shown in Fig. 2.1, where there is a very strong linear trend, and that is about it. In other words, there is a steady increase in mean attendance as the level of attractiveness of the instructor increases. Always plot the means so that you can interpret the results of the contrasts.

Let us make some final points about orthogonal polynomial contrasts. First, be particularly careful about extrapolating beyond the range of the levels investigated. The trend may or may not be the same outside of this range; given only those sample means, we have no way of knowing what the trend is outside of the range. Second, in the unequal n's or unbalanced case, it becomes difficult to formulate a set of orthogonal contrasts that make any sense to the researcher. See the discussion in the next section on planned orthogonal contrasts, as well as

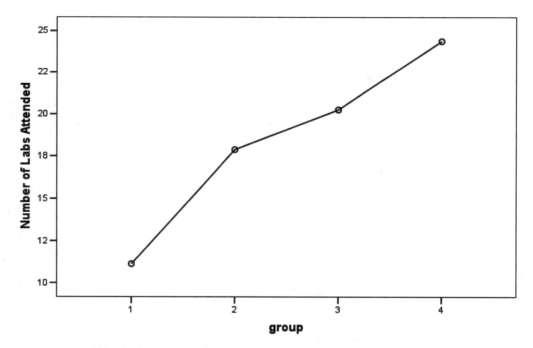

FIG. 2.1   Profile plot for statistics lab example.

Kirk (1982). Third, when the levels are not equally spaced, this needs to be taken into account in the contrast coefficients (see Kirk, 1982).

2.2.2 Planned Orthogonal Contrasts

Planned orthogonal contrasts (POC) are a MCP where the contrasts are defined ahead of time by the researcher (i.e., planned) and the set of contrasts are orthogonal. The POC method is a contrast-based procedure where the researcher is not concerned with control of the family-wise error rate. The set of contrasts are orthogonal, so the number of contrasts should be small.

Computationally, planned orthogonal contrasts use the standard t test statistic that is compared to the critical values of $\pm_{\alpha/2} t_{\text{df(error)}}$ obtained from the t table in Appendix Table 2. Using the example data set from Chapter 1, let us find a set of orthogonal contrasts and complete the computations. Since $J = 4$, we can find at most a set of three (or $J - 1$) orthogonal contrasts. One orthogonal set that seems reasonable for these data is

	c_1	c_2	c_3	c_4
ψ_1:	$+\frac{1}{2}$	$+\frac{1}{2}$	$-\frac{1}{2}$	$-\frac{1}{2}$
ψ_2:	$+1$	-1	0	0
ψ_3:	0	0	$+1$	-1

Here we see that the first contrast compares the average of the two least attractive groups with the average of the two most attractive groups, the second contrast compares the two least attractive groups, and the third contrast compares the two most attractive groups. Note that the design is balanced (i.e., the equal n's case). The following are the computations:

Critical values: $\pm_{\alpha/2} t_{\text{df(error)}} = \pm_{.025} t_{28} = \pm 2.048$

Standard error for contrast 1:

$$s_{\psi'} = \sqrt{MS_{error} \sum_{j=1}^{J} \left(\frac{c_j^2}{n_j} \right)} = \sqrt{36.1116(.25/8 + .25/8 + .25/8 + .25/8)} = 2.1246$$

Standard error for contrasts 2 and 3:

$$s_{\psi'} = \sqrt{MS_{error} \left[\frac{1}{n_j} + \frac{1}{n_{j'}} \right]} = \sqrt{36.1116(1/8 + 1/8)} = 3.0046$$

Test statistics:

$$t_1 = \frac{+\frac{1}{2}\overline{Y}_{.1} + \frac{1}{2}\overline{Y}_{.2} - \frac{1}{2}\overline{Y}_{.3} - \frac{1}{2}\overline{Y}_{.4}}{s_{\psi'}}$$

$$= \frac{+\frac{1}{2}(11.1250) + \frac{1}{2}(17.8750) - \frac{1}{2}(20.2500) - \frac{1}{2}(24.3750)}{2.1246} = -3.6772 \ (significant)$$

$$t_2 = \frac{\overline{Y}_{.1} - \overline{Y}_{.2}}{s_{\psi'}} = \frac{11.1250 - 17.8750}{3.0046} = -2.2466 \, (nonsignific\text{\i}$$

$$t_3 = \frac{\overline{Y}_{.3} - \overline{Y}_{.4}}{s_{\psi'}} = \frac{20.2500 - 24.3750}{3.0046} = -1.3729 \, (nonsignificant)$$

These results indicate that the less attractive groups have significantly lower attendance than the more attractive groups, the two less attractive groups are different, but the two more attractive groups are not different.

There is a practical problem with this procedure because the contrasts of interest may not be orthogonal, or the researcher may not be interested in all of the contrasts of an orthogonal set. Another problem already mentioned occurs when the design is unbalanced, where an orthogonal set of contrasts may be constructed at the expense of meaningful contrasts. My advice is simple. If the contrasts you are interested in are not orthogonal, then use another MCP. If you are not interested in all of the contrasts of an orthogonal set, then use another MCP. If your design is not balanced and the orthogonal contrasts formed are not meaningful, then use another MCP. In each case, if you desire a planned MCP, then we recommend either the Dunnett, Dunn (Bonferroni), or Dunn-Sidak procedure.

We defined the POC as a contrast-based procedure. One could also consider an alternative family-wise method where the α_{pc} level is divided among the contrasts in the set. This procedure is defined by $\alpha_{pc} = \alpha_{fw}/c$, where c is the number of orthogonal contrasts in the set (i.e., $c = J - 1$). As shown later, this borrows a concept from the Dunn (Bonferroni) procedure. If the variances are not equal across the groups, several approximate solutions have been proposed that take the individual group variances into account (see Kirk, 1982).

2.2.3   Planned Contrasts with Reference Group: Dunnett Method

A third method of planned comparisons is due to Dunnett (1955). It is designed to test pairwise contrasts where a reference group (e.g., a control or baseline group) is compared to each of the other $J - 1$ groups. Thus a family of prespecified pairwise contrasts is to be evaluated. The Dunnett method is a family-wise MCP and is slightly more powerful than the Dunn procedure (another planned family-wise MCP). The test statistic is the standard t except that the standard error is simplified as follows:

$$s_{\psi'} = \sqrt{MS_{error}\left[\frac{1}{n_j} + \frac{1}{n_c}\right]}$$

where c is the reference group and j is the group to which it is being compared. The test statistic is compared to the critical values $\pm_{\alpha/2} \, t_{df(error),J-1}$ obtained from the Dunnett table located in Appendix Table 7.

Using the example data set, compare the unattractive group (used as a reference or baseline group) to each of the other three groups. The following are the computations:

Critical values: $\pm_{\alpha/2} \, t_{df(error),J-1} = \pm_{.025} \, t_{28,3} \approx \pm 2.48$

Standard error:

$$s_{\psi'} = \sqrt{MS_{error}\left[\frac{1}{n_j}+\frac{1}{n_c}\right]} = \sqrt{36.1116\,[1/8+1/8]} = 3.0046$$

Test statistics:

$$t_1 = \frac{\bar{Y}_{.1}-\bar{Y}_{.2}}{s_{\psi'}} = \frac{11.1250-17.8750}{3.0046} = -2.2466 \ (nonsignificant)$$

$$t_2 = \frac{\bar{Y}_{.1}-\bar{Y}_{.3}}{s_{\psi'}} = \frac{11.1250-20.2500}{3.0046} = -3.0370 \ (significant)$$

$$t_3 = \frac{\bar{Y}_{.1}-\bar{Y}_{.4}}{s_{\psi'}} = \frac{11.1250-24.3750}{3.0046} = -4.4099 \ (significant)$$

Here we see that the second group (i.e., slightly attractive) is not significantly different from the baseline group (i.e., unattractive), but the third and fourth more attractive groups do differ from the baseline.

If the variance of the reference group is different from the variances of the other $J-1$ groups, a modification of this method is described in Dunnett (1964). For related procedures that are less sensitive to unequal group variances, see Wilcox (1987) or Wilcox (1996) (e.g., variation of Dunnett T3 procedure).

2.2.4   Other Planned Contrasts: Dunn (or Bonferroni) and Dunn-Sidak Methods

The Dunn (1961) procedure (commonly attributed to Dunn as the developer is unknown), also often called the Bonferroni procedure (because it is based on the Bonferroni inequality), is a planned family-wise MCP. It is designed to test either pairwise or complex contrasts for balanced or unbalanced designs. Thus this MCP is very flexible and may be used to test any planned contrast of interest. Dunn's method uses the standard t test statistic with one important exception. The α level is split up among the set of planned contrasts. Typically the per contrast α level is set at α/c, where c is the number of contrasts. That is, $\alpha_{pc} = \alpha_{fw}/c$. According to this rationale, the family-wise Type I error rate will be maintained at α. For example, if $\alpha_{fw} = .05$ is desired and there are five contrasts to be tested, then each contrast would be tested at the .01 level of significance. We are reminded that α need not be distributed equally among the set of contrasts, as long as the sum of the individual α_{pc} terms is equal to α_{fw} (Rosenthal & Rosnow, 1985; Keppel & Wickens, 2004).

Computationally, the Dunn method uses the standard t test statistic, which is compared to the critical values of $\pm_{\alpha/c}\, t_{\text{df(error)}}$ for a two-tailed test obtained from the table in Appendix Table 8. The table takes the number of contrasts into account without requiring you to split up the α. Using the example data set from Chapter 1, for comparison purposes let us test the same set of three orthogonal contrasts that we evaluated with the POC method. These contrasts are

	c_1	c_2	c_3	c_4
$\psi_1:$	$+\frac{1}{2}$	$+\frac{1}{2}$	$-\frac{1}{2}$	$-\frac{1}{2}$
$\psi_2:$	$+1$	-1	0	0
$\psi_3:$	0	0	$+1$	-1

The following are the computations:

Critical values: $\pm_{\alpha/c}\, t_{df(error)} = \pm_{.05/3}\, t_{28} \approx \pm\, 2.539$

Standard error for contrast 1:

$$s_{\psi'} = \sqrt{MS_{error} \sum_{j=1}^{J}\left(\frac{c_j^2}{n_j}\right)} = \sqrt{36.1116(.25/8 + .25/8 + .25/8 + .25/8)} = 2.1246$$

Standard error for contrasts 2 and 3:

$$s_{\psi'} = \sqrt{MS_{error}\left[\frac{1}{n_j} + \frac{1}{n_{j'}}\right]} = \sqrt{36.1116(1/8 + 1/8)} = 3.0046$$

Test statistics:

$$t_1 = \frac{+\frac{1}{2}\overline{Y}_{.1} + \frac{1}{2}\overline{Y}_{.2} - \frac{1}{2}\overline{Y}_{.3} - \frac{1}{2}\overline{Y}_{.4}}{s_{\psi'}}$$

$$= \frac{+\frac{1}{2}(11.1250) + \frac{1}{2}(17.8750) - \frac{1}{2}(20.2500) - \frac{1}{2}(24.3750)}{2.1246} = -3.6772 \,(significant)$$

$$t_2 = \frac{\overline{Y}_{.1} - \overline{Y}_{.2}}{s_{\psi'}} = \frac{11.1250 - 17.8750}{3.0046} = -2.2466 \,(nonsignificant)$$

$$t_3 = \frac{\overline{Y}_{.3} - \overline{Y}_{.4}}{s_{\psi'}} = \frac{20.2500 - 24.3750}{3.0046} = -1.3729 \,(nonsignificant)$$

For this set of contrasts then, we see the same results as were obtained via the POC procedure with the exception of contrast 2, which is now nonsignificant. The reason for this difference lies in the critical values used, which were ± 2.048 for the POC method and ± 2.539 for the Dunn method. Here we see the conservative nature of the Dunn procedure because the critical value is larger than with the POC method, thus making it a bit more difficult to reject H_0.

The Dunn procedure is slightly conservative (i.e., not as powerful) in that the true α_{fw} may be less than the specified nominal α level. A less conservative (i.e., more powerful) modification is known as the Dunn—Sidak procedure (Dunn, 1974; Sidak, 1967), and uses slightly different critical values. For more information see Kirk (1982), Wilcox (1987), and Keppel and Wickens (2004). The Bonferroni modification can also be applied to other MCPs.

2.2.5 Complex Post Hoc Contrasts: Scheffe' and Kaiser-Bowden Methods

Another early MCP due to Scheffe' (1953) is quite versatile. The Scheffe' procedure can be used for any possible type of comparison, orthogonal or nonorthogonal, pairwise or complex, planned or post hoc, where the family-wise error rate is controlled. The Scheffe' method is so general that the tests are quite conservative (i.e., less powerful), particularly for the pairwise contrasts. This is so because the family of contrasts for the Scheffe' method consists of all possible linear comparisons. To control the Type I error rate for such a large family, the procedure has to be conservative. Thus we recommend the Scheffe' method for complex post hoc comparisons.

The Scheffe' procedure is the only MCP that is necessarily consistent with the results of the F ratio in the analysis of variance. If the F is significant, then at least one contrast from the family of linear contrasts, when tested by the Scheffe' method, will also be significant. Do not forget, however, that this family is infinitely large and you may not even be interested in the significant contrasts. If the F is not significant, then none of the contrasts in the family, when tested by the Scheffe' method, will be significant.

The test statistic for the Scheffe' method is the standard t again. This is compared to the critical value $\sqrt{(J-1)}\ _\alpha F_{J-1,df(error)}$ taken from the F table in Appendix Table 4. In other words, the square root of the F critical value is adjusted by $J-1$, which serves to increase the Scheffe' critical value and make the procedure a more conservative one.

Consider a few example contrasts with the Scheffe' method. Using the example data set from chapter 1, for comparison purposes test the same set of three orthogonal contrasts that were evaluated with the POC method. These contrasts are again as follows

	c_1	c_2	c_3	c_4
ψ_1:	$+\frac{1}{2}$	$+\frac{1}{2}$	$-\frac{1}{2}$	$-\frac{1}{2}$
ψ_2:	$+1$	-1	0	0
ψ_3:	0	0	$+1$	-1

The following are the computations:

Critical value:

$$\sqrt{(J-1)\ _\alpha F_{J-1,df(error)}} = \sqrt{(3)\ _{.05}F_{3,28}} = \sqrt{(3)2.95} = 2.97$$

Standard error for contrast 1:

$$s_{\psi'} = \sqrt{MS_{error}\sum_{j=1}^{J}\left(\frac{c_j^2}{n_j}\right)} = \sqrt{36.1116(.25/8 + .25/8 + .25/8 + .25/8)} = 2.1246$$

Standard error for contrasts 2 and 3:

$$s_{\psi'} = \sqrt{MS_{error}\left[\frac{1}{n_j} + \frac{1}{n_{j'}}\right]} = \sqrt{36.1116(1/8 + 1/8)} = 3.0046$$

Test statistics:

$$t_1 = \frac{+\frac{1}{2}\overline{Y}_{.1} + \frac{1}{2}\overline{Y}_{.2} - \frac{1}{2}\overline{Y}_{.3} - \frac{1}{2}\overline{Y}_{.4}}{s_{\psi'}}$$

$$= \frac{+\frac{1}{2}(11.1250) + \frac{1}{2}(17.8750) - \frac{1}{2}(20.2500) - \frac{1}{2}(24.3750)}{2.1246} = -3.6772 \ (significant)$$

$$t_2 = \frac{\overline{Y}_{.1} - \overline{Y}_{.2}}{s_{\psi'}} = \frac{11.1250 - 17.8750}{3.0046} = -2.2466 \ (nonsignificant)$$

$$t_3 = \frac{\overline{Y}_{.3} - \overline{Y}_{.4}}{s_{\psi'}} = \frac{20.2500 - 24.3750}{3.0046} = -1.3729 \ (nonsignificant)$$

Using the Scheffe' method, these results are precisely the same as those obtained via the Dunn procedure. There is somewhat of a difference in the critical values, which were 2.97 for the Scheffe' method, 2.539 for the Dunn method, and 2.048 for the POC method. Here we see that the Scheffe' procedure is even more conservative than the Dunn procedure, thus making it a bit more difficult to reject H_0.

For situations where the group variances are unequal, a modification of the Scheffe' method that is less sensitive to unequal variances has been proposed by Brown and Forsythe (1974). Kaiser and Bowden (1983) found that the Brown-Forsythe procedure may cause the actual α level to exceed the nominal α level and thus we recommend the Kaiser-Bowden modification. For more information see Kirk (1982), Wilcox (1987), and Wilcox (1996).

2.2.6 Simple Post Hoc Contrasts: Tukey HSD, Tukey-Kramer, Fisher LSD and Hayter Tests

Tukey's (1953) honestly significant difference (HSD) test is one of the most popular post hoc MCPs. The HSD test is a family-wise procedure and is most appropriate for considering all pair-wise contrasts with equal n's per group (i.e., a balanced design). The HSD test is sometimes referred to as the **studentized range test** because it is based on the sampling distribution of the studentized range statistic developed by William Sealy Gossett (forced to use the pseudonym "Student" by his employer, the Guinness brewery). For one approach, the first step in the analysis is to rank order the means from largest ($\overline{Y}_{.1}$) to smallest ($\overline{Y}_{.J}$). The test statistic, or studentized range statistic, is

$$q_i = \frac{\overline{Y}_{.j} - \overline{Y}_{.j'}}{s_{\psi'}}$$

where

$$s_{\psi'} = \sqrt{\frac{MS_{error}}{n}}$$

and i identifies the specific contrast, j and j' designate the two group means to be compared, and n represents the number of observations per group (equal n's per group is required). The test statistic is compared to the critical value $_\alpha q_{df\,(error),J}$, where df_{error} is equal to $J(n-1)$. A table for these critical values is given in Appendix Table 9.

The first contrast involves a test of the largest pairwise difference in the set of J means (q_1). If these means are not significantly different, then the analysis stops because no other pairwise difference would be significant. If these means are different, then we proceed to test the second pairwise difference involving group 1 (i.e., q_2). Contrasts involving the largest mean are continued until a nonsignificant difference is found. Then the analysis picks up with the second largest mean and compares it with the smallest mean. Contrasts involving the second largest mean are continued until a nonsignificant difference is detected. The analysis continues with the next largest mean and the smallest mean, and so on, until it is obvious that no other pairwise contrast would be significant.

Finally, consider an example using the HSD procedure with the attractiveness data. The following are the computations:

Critical value: $_\alpha q_{df(error),J} = {_{.05}}q_{28,4} \approx 3.87$

Standard error:

$$s_{\psi'} = \sqrt{\frac{MS_{error}}{n}} = \sqrt{\frac{36.1116}{8}} = 2.1246$$

Test statistics:

$$q_1 = \frac{\bar{Y}_{.4} - \bar{Y}_{.1}}{s_{\psi'}} = \frac{24.3750 - 11.1250}{2.1246} = 6.2365 \ (significant)$$

$$q_2 = \frac{\bar{Y}_{.4} - \bar{Y}_{.2}}{s_{\psi'}} = \frac{24.3750 - 17.8750}{2.1246} = 3.0594 \ (nonsignificant)$$

$$q_3 = \frac{\bar{Y}_{.3} - \bar{Y}_{.1}}{s_{\psi'}} = \frac{20.2500 - 11.1250}{2.1246} = 4.2949 \ (significant)$$

$$q_4 = \frac{\bar{Y}_{.3} - \bar{Y}_{.2}}{s_{\psi'}} = \frac{20.2500 - 17.8750}{2.1246} = 1.1179 \ (nonsignificant)$$

$$q_5 = \frac{\bar{Y}_{.2} - \bar{Y}_{.1}}{s_{\psi'}} = \frac{17.8750 - 11.1250}{2.1246} = 3.1771 \ (nonsignificant)$$

These results indicate that the group means are significantly different for Groups 1 and 4, and for Groups 1 and 3. Just for completeness, we examine the final possible pairwise contrast involving Groups 3 and 4. However, we already know from the results of previous contrasts that these means cannot possibly be significantly different. The results for this contrast are as follows:

$$q_6 = \frac{\bar{Y}_{.4} - \bar{Y}_{.3}}{s_{\psi'}} = \frac{24.3750 - 20.2500}{2.1246} = 1.9415 \, (nonsignificant)$$

Occasionally researchers need to summarize the results of their pairwise comparisons. Table 2.1 shows the results of Tukey's HSD contrasts for the example data. For ease of interpretation, the means are ordered from lowest to highest. The first row consists of the results for those contrasts that involve Group 1. Thus the mean for Group 1 is different from those of Groups 3 and 4 only. None of the other pairwise contrasts were shown to be significant. Such a table could also be developed for other pairwise MCPs.

The HSD test has exact control of the family-wise error rate assuming normality, homogeneity, and equal n's (better than Dunn or Dunn-Sidak). The HSD procedure is more powerful than the Dunn or Scheffe' procedures for testing all possible pairwise contrasts, although Dunn is more powerful for less than all possible pairwise contrasts. The HSD technique is the recommended MCP as a pairwise method in the equal n's situation. The HSD test is reasonably robust to nonnormality, but not in extreme cases, and not as robust as the Scheffe' MCP.

There are several alternatives to the HSD for the unequal n's case. These include the Tukey-Kramer modification (Tukey, 1953; Kramer, 1956), which assumes normality and homogeneity.

The Tukey-Kramer test statistic is the same as the Tukey HSD except that

$$s_{\psi'} = \sqrt{MS_{error} \left[\frac{1}{2} \left(\frac{1}{n_1} + \frac{1}{n_2} \right) \right]}$$

The critical value is the same as with the Tukey HSD procedure.

Fisher's (1949) least significant difference (LSD) test, also known as the protected t test, was the first MCP developed and is a pairwise post hoc procedure. It is a sequential procedure where a significant ANOVA F is followed by the LSD test in which all (or perhaps some) pairwise t tests are examined. The standard t test statistic is compared with the critical values of $\pm_{\alpha/2}t_{df(error)}$. The LSD test has precise control of the family-wise error rate for the three group situation, assuming normality and homogeneity, but for more than three groups the protection deteriorates. In that case, a modification due to Hayter (1986) is suggested for more adequate protection. Hayter's test

TABLE 2.1
Test Statistics and Results of Tukey HSD Contrasts

	Group 1	Group 2	Group 3	Group 4
Group 1 (mean = 11.1250)	—	3.1771	4.2949*	6.2365*
Group 2 (mean = 17.8750)		—	1.1179	3.0594
Group 3 (mean = 20.2500)			—	1.9415
Group 4 (mean = 24.3750)				—

*$p < .05$; $_{.05}q_{28,4} = 3.87$

appears to have more power than Tukey HSD and excellent control of family-wise error (Keppel & Wickens, 2004).

2.2.7 Simple Post Hoc Contrasts for Unequal Variances: Games-Howell, Dunnett T3 and C Tests

When the group variances are unequal, several alternative procedures are available. These alternatives include the Games-Howell (1976), and Dunnett T3 and C (1980) procedures. According to Wilcox (1996, 2003), T3 is recommended for $n < 50$, Games-Howell for $n > 50$, and C performs about the same as Games-Howell. For further details on these methods, see Kirk (1982), Wilcox (1987, 1996, 2003), Hochberg (1988), and Benjamini and Hochberg (1995).

2.2.8 Follow-up Tests to Kruskal-Wallis

Recall from chapter 1 the nonparametric equivalent to the analysis of variance, the Kruskal-Wallis test. Several post hoc procedures are available to follow up a significant Kruskal-Wallis test. The procedures discussed here are the nonparametric equivalents to the Scheffe' and Tukey HSD methods. One may form pairwise or complex contrasts as in the parametric case. The test statistic is Z and given as

$$Z = \frac{\psi_i'}{s_{\psi'}}$$

where

$$s_{\psi'} = \sqrt{\frac{N(N+1)}{12} \sum_{j=1}^{J} \left(\frac{c_j^2}{n_j} \right)}$$

and where N is the total number of observations. For the Scheffe' method, the test statistic Z is compared to the critical value $\sqrt{_\alpha \chi_{J-1}^2}$ obtained from the χ^2 table in Appendix Table 3. For the Tukey procedure, the test statistic Z is compared to the critical value $[_\alpha q_{df(error),J}]/\sqrt{2}$ obtained from the table of critical values for the studentized range statistic in Appendix Table 9.

Let us use the attractiveness data to illustrate. Do not forget that we use the ranked data as described in chapter 1. The rank means for the groups are as follows: Group 1 = 7.7500; Group 2 = 15.2500; Group 3 = 18.7500; Group 4 = 24.2500. Here we only examine two contrasts and then compare the results for both the Scheffe' and Tukey methods. The first contrast compares the two low-attractiveness groups (i.e., Groups 1 and 2), whereas the second contrast compares the two low-attractiveness groups with the two high-attractiveness groups (i.e., Groups 3 and 4). In other words, we examine a pairwise contrast and a complex contrast, respectively. The results are given here.

Critical values:

$$\text{Scheffe'} - \sqrt{_\alpha \chi_{J-1}^2} = \sqrt{_{.05}\chi_3^2} = \sqrt{7.8147} = 2.7955$$

$$\text{Tukey} - [_\alpha q_{df(error),J}]/\sqrt{2} = {_{.05}}q_{28.4} / \sqrt{2} \approx 3.87 / \sqrt{2} \approx 2.7365$$

Standard error for contrast 1:

$$s_{\psi'} = \sqrt{\frac{N(N+1)}{12} \sum_{j=1}^{J} \left(\frac{c_j^2}{n_j} \right)} = \sqrt{\left[\frac{32(33)}{12} \right] \left[\frac{1}{8} + \frac{1}{8} \right]} = 4.6904$$

Standard error for contrast 2:

$$s_{\psi'} = \sqrt{\frac{N(N+1)}{12} \sum_{j=1}^{J} \left(\frac{c_j^2}{n_j} \right)} = \sqrt{\left[\frac{32(33)}{12} \right] \left[\frac{.25}{8} + \frac{.25}{8} + \frac{.25}{8} + \frac{.25}{8} \right]} = 3.3166$$

Test statistics:

$$Z_1 = \frac{\overline{Y}_{.1} - \overline{Y}_{.2}}{s_{\psi'}} = \frac{7.75 - 15.25}{4.6904} = -1.5990 \ (nonsignificant \ for \ both \ procedures)$$

$$Z_2 = \frac{\frac{1}{2}\overline{Y}_{.1} + \frac{1}{2}\overline{Y}_{.2} - \frac{1}{2}\overline{Y}_{.3} - \frac{1}{2}Y_{.4}}{s_{\psi'}} = \frac{\frac{1}{2}(7.75) + \frac{1}{2}(15.25) - \frac{1}{2}(18.75) - \frac{1}{2}(24.25)}{3.3166}$$

$$= -3.0151 \ (significant \ for \ both \ procedures)$$

These results agree with most of the other parametric procedures for these particular contrasts. That is, the less attractive groups are not significantly different (only significant with POC), whereas the two less attractive groups are significantly different from the two more attractive groups (significant with all procedures). One could conceivably devise nonparametric equivalent MCPs for methods other than the Scheffe' and Tukey procedures.

2.3 SPSS

In our last section we examine what SPSS has to offer in terms of MCPs, including an APA type paragraph of our example findings. Using the GLM module (although the One-Way ANOVA module can also used), go to the "Analyze" pulldown, into "General Linear Model," and then into the "Univariate" procedure. Check the dependent and fixed-effects variables into the appropriate boxes as we did in chapter 1. Click on the "Post Hoc" button, then move the "Factor" variable into the box labelled "Post Hoc Tests for:." There you see numerous MCPs available. Check an appropriate MCP for your situation, click "Continue" to return to the previous screen, then click "OK." Results from the Tukey HSD procedure, just as one example MCP, are shown in Table 2.2. Note that confidence intervals around a mean difference of zero are given to the right for each contrast. To obtain trend analysis contrasts, click the "Contrasts" button. On the resulting screen, click the "Contrasts:" pulldown and scroll down to "Polynomial." Then click "Change," then "Continue" to return to the main screen. Other specific planned contrasts are also available.

The MCP results for the statistics lab example are as follows. After a significant ANOVA F, Tukey HSD tests were conducted on all possible pairwise contrasts. The following pairs of groups were found to be significantly different ($p < .05$) (depicted by asterisks next to the mean differences and by significance values less than .05): Groups 1 and 3; Groups 1 and 4. In

TABLE 2.2

Tukey HSD SPSS Results for the Statistics Lab Example

Multiple Comparisons

Dependent Variable: dv
Tukey HSD

(I) group	(J) group	Mean Difference (I–J)	Std. Error	Sig.	95% Confidence Interval	
					Lower Bound	Upper Bound
1.00000	2.00000	−6.7500000	3.004647	.135	−14.9536217	1.4536217
	3.00000	−9.1250000*	3.004647	.025	−17.3286217	−.9213783
	4.00000	−13.250000*	3.004647	.001	−21.4536217	−5.0463783
2.00000	1.00000	6.7500000	3.004647	.135	−1.4536217	14.9536217
	3.00000	−2.3750000	3.004647	.858	−10.5786217	5.8286217
	4.00000	−6.5000000	3.004647	.158	−14.7036217	1.7036217
3.00000	1.00000	9.1250000*	3.004647	.025	.9213783	17.3286217
	2.00000	2.3750000	3.004647	.858	−5.8286217	10.5786217
	4.00000	−4.1250000	3.004647	.526	−12.3286217	4.0786217
4.00000	1.00000	13.2500000*	3.004647	.001	5.0463783	21.4536217
	2.00000	6.5000000	3.004647	.158	−1.7036217	14.7036217
	3.00000	4.1250000	3.004647	.526	−4.0786217	12.3286217

Based on observed means.

*The mean difference is significant at the .05 level.

other words, the least attractive instructor group attended significantly fewer labs than either of the two most attractive instructor groups. Feel free to examine other MCPs for this dataset.

2.4 SUMMARY

In this chapter methods involving the comparison of multiple group means for a single independent variable were considered. The chapter began with a look at the characteristics of multiple comparisons including: (a) the definition of a contrast; (b) planned and post hoc comparisons; (c) contrast-based and family-wise Type I error rates; and (d) orthogonal contrasts. Next, we moved into a lengthy discussion of recommended multiple comparison procedures.

Figure 2.2 is a flowchart to assist you in making decisions about which MCP to use. Not every statistician will agree with every decision on the flowchart as there is not a consensus about which MCP is appropriate in every single situation. Nonetheless, this is simply a guide. Whether you use it in its present form, or adapt it for your own needs, we hope you find the figure to be useful in your own research.

At this point you should have met the following objectives: (a) be able to understand the concepts underlying the MCPs, (b) be able to select the appropriate MCP for a given research situation, and (c) be able to determine and interpret the results of MCPs. Chapter 3 returns to the analysis of variance again and discusses models for which there is more than one independent variable.

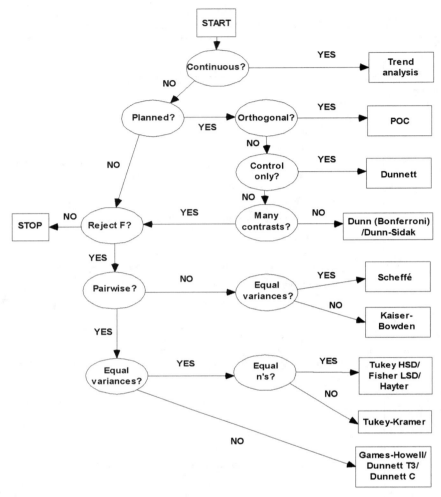

FIG. 2.2   Flowchart of recommended MCPs.

PROBLEMS

Conceptual Problems

1.   The Tukey HSD procedure requires equal n's and equal means. True or false?

2.   Which of the following linear combinations of population means is not a legitimate contrast?

    a. $(\mu_{.1} + \mu_{.2} + \mu_{.3})/3 - \mu_{.4}$

    b. $\mu_{.1} - \mu_{.4}$

    c. $(\mu_{.1} + \mu_{.2})/2 - (\mu_{.3} + \mu_{.4})$

    d. $\mu_{.1} - \mu_{.2} + \mu_{.3} - \mu_{.4}$

3. When a one-factor fixed-effects ANOVA results in a significant F ratio for $J = 2$, one should follow the ANOVA with the
    a. Tukey HSD method
    b. Scheffe' method
    c. Hayter method
    d. none of the above

4. If a family-based error rate for α is desired, and hypotheses involving all pairs of means are to be tested, which method of multiple comparisons should be selected?
    a. Tukey HSD
    b. Scheffe'
    c. POC
    d. Trend analysis
    e. none of the above

5. A priori comparisons
    a. are planned in advance of the research.
    b. often arise out of theory and prior research.
    c. may be done without examining the F ratio.
    d. all of the above

6. For planned contrasts involving the control group, the Dunn procedure is most appropriate. True or false?

7. Which is not a property of planned orthogonal contrasts?
    a. The contrasts are independent.
    b. The contrasts are post hoc.
    c. The sum of the cross-products of the contrast coefficients $= 0$.
    d. If there are J groups, there are $J - 1$ orthogonal contrasts.

8. Which multiple comparison procedure is most flexible in the contrasts that can be tested?
    a. planned orthogonal contrasts
    b. Newman-Keuls
    c. Dunnett
    d. Tukey HSD
    e. Scheffe'

9. Post hoc tests are necessary after an ANOVA whenever
    a. H_0 is rejected.
    b. there are more than two groups.
    c. H_0 is rejected and there are more than two groups.
    d. you should always do post hoc tests after an ANOVA.

10. Post hoc tests are done after ANOVA to determine why H_0 was not rejected. True or False?

11. Holding the α level and the number of groups constant, as the df_{with} increases, the critical value of the q decreases. True or False?

12. The Tukey HSD procedure maintains the family Type I error rate at α. True or False?

13. The Dunnett procedure assumes equal numbers of observations per group. True or False?

14. For complex post hoc contrasts with unequal group variances, which of the following MCPs is most appropriate?
    a. Kaiser-Bowden
    b. Dunnett
    c. Tukey HSD
    d. Scheffe'

15. A researcher is interested in testing the following contrasts in a $J = 6$ study: Group 1 vs. 2; Group 3 vs. 4; and Group 5 vs. 6. I assert that these contrasts are orthogonal. Am I correct?

16. I assert that rejecting H_0 in a one-factor fixed-effects ANOVA with $J = 3$ indicates that all 3 pairs of group means are necessarily significant using the Scheffe' procedure. Am I correct?

17. For complex post hoc contrasts with equal group variances, which of the following MCPs is most appropriate?
    a. planned orthogonal contrasts
    b. Dunnett
    c. Tukey HSD
    d. Scheffe'

18. If the difference between two sample means is 10, I assert that H_0 will necessarily be rejected with Tukey's HSD. Am I correct?

19. Suppose all $J = 4$ of the sample means are equal to 100. I assert that it is possible to find a significant contrast with some MCP. Am I correct?

Computational Problems

1. A one-factor fixed-effects analysis of variance is performed on data for 10 groups of unequal sizes and H_0 is rejected at the .01 level of significance. Using the Scheffe' procedure, test the contrast that

$$\overline{Y}_{.2} - \overline{Y}_{.5} = 0$$

at the .01 level of significance given the following information: $df_{with} = 40$, $\overline{Y}_{.2} = 10.8$, $n_2 = 8$, $\overline{Y}_{.5} = 15.8$, $n_5 = 8$, and $MS_{with} = 4$.

2. A one-factor fixed-effects ANOVA is performed on data from three groups of equal size ($n = 10$) and H_0 is rejected at the .01 level. The following values were computed: $MS_{with} = 40$ and the sample means are $\overline{Y}_{.1} = 4.5$, $\overline{Y}_{.2} = 12.5$, and $\overline{Y}_{.3} = 13.0$. Use the Tukey HSD method to test all possible pairwise contrasts.

3. Using the data from Chapter 1, Computational Problem 4, conduct a trend analysis at the .05 level.

4. Consider the situation where there are $J = 4$ groups of subjects. Answer the following questions:

    a. Construct a set of orthogonal contrasts and show that they are orthogonal.

    b. Is the following contrast legitimate? Why or why not?

    $$H_0: \mu_{.1} - (\mu_{.2} + \mu_{.3} + \mu_{.4}).$$

    c. How might the contrast in part (b) be altered to yield a legitimate contrast?

Interpretive Problem

For the interpretive problem you selected in chapter 1 (using the statistics survey CD dataset), select an appropriate MCP, apply it using SPSS, and write a paragraph describing the results.

3

FACTORIAL ANALYSIS OF VARIANCE— FIXED-EFFECTS MODEL

Chapter Outline

Key Concepts

1. Main effects
2. Interaction effects
3. Partitioning the sums of squares
4. The ANOVA model
5. Main effects contrasts, simple and complex interaction contrasts
6. Nonorthogonal designs

The last two chapters have dealt with the one-factor analysis of variance (ANOVA) model and various multiple comparison procedures (MCPs) for that model. In this chapter we continue our discussion of analysis of variance models by extending the one-factor case to the two- and three-factor models. This chapter seeks an answer to the question, what should we do if we have multiple factors for which we want to make comparisons of the means? In other words, the researcher is interested in the effect of two or more independent variables or factors on the dependent (or criterion) variable. This chapter is most concerned with two- and three-factor models, but the extension to more than three factors, when warranted, is fairly simple.

For example, suppose that a researcher is interested in the effects of textbook choice and time of day on statistics achievement. Thus one independent variable would be the textbook selected for the course, and the second independent variable would be the time of day the course was offered. The researcher hypothesizes that certain texts may be more effective in terms of achievement than others, and that student learning may be greater at certain times of the day. For the time-of-day variable, one might expect that students would not do as well in an early morning section or a late evening section. In the example study, say that the researcher is interested in comparing three textbooks (A, B, and C) and three times of the day (early morning, mid-afternoon, and evening sections). Students would be randomly assigned to sections of statistics based on a combination of textbook and time of day. One group of students might be assigned to the section offered in the evening using textbook A. These results would be of interest to statistics instructors for selecting a textbook and optimal time of the day.

Most of the concepts used in this chapter are the same as those covered in Chapters 1 and 2. In addition, new concepts include main effects, interaction effects, multiple comparison procedures for main and interaction effects, and nonorthogonal designs. Our objectives are that by the end of this chapter, you will be able to (a) understand the characteristics and concepts underlying factorial ANOVA, (b) determine and interpret the results of factorial ANOVA, and (c) understand and evaluate the assumptions of factorial ANOVA.

3.1   THE TWO-FACTOR ANOVA MODEL

This section describes the distinguishing characteristics of the two-factor ANOVA model, the layout of the data, the linear model, main effects and interactions, assumptions of the model and their violation, partitioning the sums of squares, the ANOVA summary table, multiple comparison procedures, effect size measures, confidence intervals, and power, and an example.

3.1.1   Characteristics of the Model

The first characteristic of the two-factor ANOVA model should be obvious by now, which considers the effect of two factors or independent variables on a dependent variable. Each factor consists of two or more levels. This yields what we call a **factorial design** because more than a single factor is included. We see then that the two-factor ANOVA is an extension of the one-factor ANOVA. Why would a researcher want to complicate things by considering a second factor? Three reasons come to mind. First, the researcher may have a genuine interest in studying the second factor. Rather than studying each factor separately in two analyses, the researcher includes both factors in the same analysis. This allows a test not only of the effect of each individual factor, but of the effect of both factors collectively. This latter effect is known as an **interaction** effect and provides information about whether the two factors are operating independent of one another (i.e., no interaction exists) or whether the two factors are operating together to produce some additional impact (i.e., an interaction exists). If two separate analyses were conducted, one for each independent variable, no information would be obtained about the interaction effect. As becomes evident, the researcher will test three hypotheses, one for each factor individually, and a third for the interaction between the factors. This chapter spends considerable time discussing interactions.

A second reason for including an additional factor is an attempt to reduce the error (or within groups) variation, which is variation that is unexplained by the first factor. The use of a second factor provides a more precise estimate of error variance. For this reason, a two-factor design is generally more powerful than two one-factor designs, as the second factor serves to control for additional extraneous variability. A third reason for considering two factors simultaneously is to provide greater generalizability of results and to provide a more efficient and economical use of observations and resources. Thus the results can be generalized to more situations, and the study will be more cost efficient in terms of time and money.

In addition, for the two-factor ANOVA every level of the first factor (hereafter known as factor A) is paired with every level of the second factor (hereafter known as factor B). In other words, every combination of factors A and B is included in the design of the study, yielding what is referred to as a **fully crossed design**. If some combinations are not included, then the design is not fully crossed and may form some sort of a nested design (see chap. 16). Individuals (or objects or subjects) are randomly assigned to one combination of the two factors. In other words, each individual responds to only one combination of the factors. If individuals respond to more than one combination of the factors, this would be some sort of repeated measures design, which we examine in chapter 15. In this chapter we only consider models where all factors are fixed. Thus the overall design is known as a fixed-effects model. If one or both factors are random, then the design is not a fixed-effects model, which we discuss in chapter 15. It is also assumed that the dependent variable is measured at least at the interval level.

In this section of the chapter, we assume the same number of observations are made for each factor combination. This yields what is known as an orthogonal design, where the effects due to the factors (separately and collectively) are independent. We leave the discussion of the unequal n's factorial ANOVA until later in this chapter. In addition, we assume there are at least two observations per factor combination so as to have within groups variation.

In summary, the characteristics of the two-factor analysis of variance fixed-effects model are as follows: (a) two independent variables each with two or more levels, (b) the levels of both independent variables are fixed by the researcher, (c) subjects are randomly assigned to only one combination of these levels, (d) the two factors are fully crossed, and (e) the dependent variable is measured at least at the interval level. In the context of experimental design, the two-factor analysis of variance is often referred to as the **completely randomized factorial design**.

3.1.2 The Layout of the Data

Before we get into the theory and analysis of the data, let us examine one form in which the data can be placed, known as the layout of the data. We designate each observation as Y_{ijk}, where the j subscript tells us what level of factor A (e.g., textbook) the observation belongs to, the k subscript tells us what level of factor B (e.g., time of day) the observation belongs to, and the i subscript tells us the observation or identification number within that combination of factor A and factor B. For instance, Y_{321} would mean that this is the third observation in the second level of factor A and the first level of factor B. The first subscript ranges over $i = 1, ..., n$, the second subscript ranges over $j = 1, ..., J$, and the third subscript ranges over $k = 1, ..., K$. Note also that the latter two subscripts denote the cell of an observation. Using the same example, we are referring to the third observation in the 21 cell. Thus there are J levels of factor A, K levels of factor B, and n subjects in each cell, for a total of $JKn = N$ observations. For now we assume there are n subjects in each cell in order to simplify matters; this is referred to as the equal n's case. Later in this chapter, we consider the unequal n's case.

The layout of the sample data is shown in Table 3.1. Here we see that each row represents the observations for a particular level of factor A (textbook), and that each column represents the observations for a particular level of factor B (time). At the bottom of each column are the column means ($\overline{Y}_{.k}$), to the right of each row are the row means ($\overline{Y}s_{.j.}$), and in the lower right-hand corner is the overall mean ($\overline{Y}_{...}$). We also need the cell means ($\overline{Y}_{.jk}$), which are shown at the bottom of each cell. Thus the layout is one form in which to think about the data.

3.1.3 The ANOVA Model

This section introduces the analysis of variance linear model, as well as estimation of the parameters of the model. The two-factor analysis of variance model is a form of the general linear model like the one-factor ANOVA model of chapter 1. The two-factor ANOVA fixed-effects model can be written in terms of population parameters as

$$Y_{ijk} = \mu + \alpha_j + \beta_k + (\alpha\beta)_{jk} + \varepsilon_{ijk}$$

where Y_{ijk} is the observed score on the criterion variable for individual i in level j of factor A (text) and level k of factor B (time) (or in the jk cell), μ is the overall or grand population mean

TABLE 3.1
Layout for the Two-Factor ANOVA

Level of Factor A	Level of Factor B				Row Mean
	1	*2*	...	*K*	
1	Y_{111}	Y_{112}	...	Y_{11K}	
	.	.	...	.	
	.	.	...	.	$\bar{Y}_{.1.}$
	.	.	...	.	
	Y_{n11}	Y_{n12}	...	Y_{n1K}	
	$\bar{Y}_{.11}$	$\bar{Y}_{.12}$	...	$\bar{Y}_{.1K}$	
2	Y_{121}	Y_{122}	...	Y_{12K}	
	.	.	...	.	
	.	.	...	.	$\bar{Y}_{.2.}$
	.	.	...	.	
	Y_{n21}	Y_{n22}	...	Y_{n2K}	
	$\bar{Y}_{.21}$	$\bar{Y}_{.22}$	...	$\bar{Y}_{.2K}$	
.	.	.	...	.	.
.	.	.	...	.	.
.	.	.	...	.	.
J	Y_{1J1}	Y_{1J2}	...	Y_{1JK}	
	.	.	...	.	
	.	.	...	.	$\bar{Y}_{.J.}$
	.	.	...	.	
	Y_{nJ1}	Y_{nJ2}	...	Y_{nJK}	
	$\bar{Y}_{.J1}$	$\bar{Y}_{.J2}$	...	$\bar{Y}_{.JK}$	
Column Mean	$\bar{Y}_{..1}$	$\bar{Y}_{..2}$	...	$\bar{Y}_{..K}$	$\bar{Y}_{...}$

(i.e., regardless of cell designation), α_j is the main effect for level j of factor A (row or text effect), β_k is the main effect for level k of factor B (column or time effect), $(\alpha\beta)_{jk}$ is the interaction effect for the combination of level j of factor A and level k of factor B, and ε_{ijk} is the random residual error for individual i in cell jk. The residual error can be due to individual differences, measurement error, and/or other factors not under investigation.

The population effects and residual error are computed as follows:

$$\alpha_j = \mu_{j.} - \mu$$
$$\beta_k = \mu_{..k} - \mu$$

$$(\alpha\beta)_{jk} = \mu_{.jk} - (\mu_{.j.} + \mu_{..k} - \mu)$$

$$\varepsilon_{ijk} = Y_{ijk} - \mu_{.jk}$$

That is, the row effect is equal to the difference between the population mean of level j of factor A (a particular text) and the overall population mean, the column effect is equal to the difference between the population mean of level k of factor B (a particular time) and the overall population mean, the interaction effect is the effect of being in a certain combination of the levels of factor A and B (a particular text used at a particular time), whereas the residual error is equal to the difference between an individual's observed score and the population mean of cell jk. The row, column, and interaction effects can also be thought of as the average effect of being a member of a particular row, column, or cell, respectively. It should also be noted that the sum of the row effects is equal to zero, the sum of the column effects is equal to zero, and the sum of the interaction effects is equal to zero (both across rows and across columns). This implies, for example, that if there are any nonzero row effects, then the row effects will balance out around zero with some positive and some negative effects.

You may be wondering why the interaction effect looks a little different than the main effects. I have given you the version that is solely a function of population means. A more intuitively convincing conceptual version of this effect is

$$(\alpha\beta)_{jk} = \mu_{.jk} - \alpha_j - \beta_k - \mu$$

which is written in similar fashion to the row and column effects. Here we see that the interaction effect is equal to the population cell mean minus (a) the row effect, (b) the column effect, and (c) the overall population mean. In other words, the interaction is solely a function of cell means without regard to its row effect, column effect, or the overall mean.

To estimate the parameters of the model μ, α_j, β_k, $(\alpha\beta)_{jk}$, and ε_{ijk}, the least squares method of estimation is used as most appropriate for general linear models (e.g., regression, ANOVA). These sample estimates are represented as $\overline{Y}_{...}$, a_j, b_k, $(ab)_{jk}$, and e_{ijk}, respectively, where the latter four are computed as follows, respectively:

$$a_j = \overline{Y}_{.j.} - \overline{Y}_{...}$$

$$b_k = \overline{Y}_{..k} - \overline{Y}_{...}$$

$$(ab)_{jk} = \overline{Y}_{.jk} - (\overline{Y}_{.j.} + \overline{Y}_{..k} - \overline{Y}_{...})$$

$$e_{ijk} = Y_{ijk} - \overline{Y}_{.jk}$$

Note that $\overline{Y}_{...}$ represents the overall sample mean, $\overline{Y}_{.j.}$ represents the sample mean for level j of factor A (a particular text), $\overline{Y}_{..k}$ represents the sample mean for level k of factor B (a particular time), and $\overline{Y}_{.jk}$ represents the sample mean for cell jk (a particular text at a particular time).

For the two-factor ANOVA model there are three sets of hypotheses, one for each of the main effects, and one for the interaction effect. The null and alternative hypotheses, respectively, for testing the main effect of factor A (text) are

$$H_{01}: \mu_{.1.} = \mu_{.2.} = ... = \mu_{.J.}$$

$$H_{11}: \text{not all the } \mu_{.j.} \text{ are equal}$$

The hypotheses for testing the main effect of factor B (time) are

$$H_{02}: \mu_{..1} = \mu_{..2} = ... = \mu_{..K}$$

$$H_{12}: \text{not all the } \mu_{..k} \text{ are equal}$$

Finally, the hypotheses for testing the interaction effect (text with time) are

$$H_{03}: (\mu_{.jk} - \mu_{.j.} - \mu_{..k} + \mu) = 0 \text{ for all } j \text{ and } k$$

$$H_{13}: \text{not all the } (\mu_{.jk} - \mu_{.j.} - \mu_{..k} + \mu) = 0$$

The null hypotheses can also be written in terms of row, column and interaction effects (which may make more intuitive sense) as

$$H_{01}: \alpha_1 = \alpha_2 = ... = \alpha_J = 0$$

$$H_{02}: \beta_1 = \beta_2 = ... = \beta_K = 0$$

$$H_{03}: (\alpha\beta)_{jk} = 0 \text{ for all } j \text{ and } k$$

As in the one-factor model, all of the alternative hypotheses are written in a general form to cover the multitude of possible mean differences that could arise. These range from only two of the means being different to all of the means being different from one another. Also, because of the way the alternative hypotheses have been written, only a nondirectional alternative is appropriate. If one of the null hypotheses is rejected, then consider a multiple comparison procedure so as to determine which means or combination of means are significantly different (discussed later).

3.1.4 Main Effects and Interaction Effects

Finally we come to a formal discussion of main effects and interaction effects. A **main effect** of factor A (text) is defined as the effect of factor A, averaged across the levels of factor B (time), on the dependent variable Y (achievement). More precisely, it represents the unique effect of factor A on Y, controlling statistically for factor B. A similar statement may be made for the main effect of factor B.

As far as the concept of interaction is concerned, things are a bit more complex. An **interaction** can be defined in any of the following ways: An interaction is said to exist if (a) certain combinations of the two factors produce effects beyond the effects of the two factors when considered separately; (b) the mean differences among the levels of factor A are not constant across (and thus depend on) the levels of factor B; (c) there is a joint effect of factors A and B on Y; or (d) there is a unique effect that could not be predicted from knowledge of only the main effects. Let me mention two fairly common examples of interaction effects. The first is known as an aptitude–treatment interaction (ATI). This means that the effectiveness of a particular treatment depends on the aptitude of the individual. In other words, some treatments are more effective for individuals with a high aptitude, and other treatments are more effective for those with a low aptitude. A second example is an interaction between treatment and gender. Here some treatments may be more effective for males and others may be more effective for females. This is often considered in gender studies research.

For some graphical examples of main and interaction effects, take a look at the various plots in Fig. 3.1. Each plot represents the graph of a particular set of cell means, sometimes referred to as a **profile plot**. On the X axis are the levels of factor A (text), the Y axis provides the cell means on the dependent variable Y (achievement), and the lines in the body of the plot represent the levels of factor B (time) (although the specific placement of the two factors here is arbitrary; alternatively factor B could be plotted on the X axis and factor A as the lines). Profile plots provide information about the possible existence of a main effect for A, a main effect for B, and/or an interaction effect. A main effect for factor A, for example, can be examined by taking the means for each level of A and averaging them across the levels of B. If these marginal means for the levels of A are the same or nearly so, this would indicate no main effect for factor A. A main effect for factor B would be assessed by taking the means for each level of B and averaging them across the levels of A. If these marginal means for the levels of B are the same or nearly so, this would imply no main effect for factor B. An interaction effect is determined by whether the cell means for the levels of A are constant across the levels of B (or vice versa). This is easily viewed in a profile plot by checking to see whether or not the lines are parallel. Parallel lines indicate no interaction, whereas nonparallel lines suggest that an interaction may exist. Of course the statistical significance of the main and interaction effects is a matter to be determined by the F statistics. The profile plots only give you a rough idea as to the possible existence of the effects. For instance, lines that are nearly parallel will probably not show up as a significant interaction. It is suggested that the plot can be simplified if the factor with the most levels is shown on the X axis. This cuts down on the number of lines drawn.

The plots shown in Fig. 3.1 represent the eight different sets of results possible for a two-factor design. To simplify matters, only two levels of each factor are used. Figure 3.1 (a) indicates that there is no main effect either for factor A or B, and there is no interaction effect. The lines are horizontal (no A effect), lie nearly on top of one another (no B effect), and are parallel (no interaction effect). Figure 3.1 (b) suggests the presence of an effect due to factor A only (the lines are not horizontal because the mean for A_1 is greater than the mean for A_2), but are nearly on top of one another (no B effect), and are parallel (no interaction). In Fig. 3.1 (c) we see a separation between the lines for the levels of B (B_1 being greater than B_2); thus a main effect for B is likely, but the lines are horizontal (no A effect), and are parallel (no interaction).

For Fig. 3.1 (d) there are no main effects (the means for the levels of A are the same, and the means for the levels of B are the same), but an interaction is indicated by the lack of parallel lines. Figure 3.1 (e) suggests a main effect for both factors as shown by mean differences (A_1 less than A_2, and B_1 greater than B_2), but no interaction (the lines are parallel). In Fig. 3.1 (f) we see a main effect for A (A_1 less than A_2) and an interaction are likely, but no main effect for B (little separation between the lines for factor B). For Fig. 3.1 (g) there appears to be a main effect for B (B_1 greater than B_2) and an interaction, but no main effect for A. Finally, in Fig. 3.1 (h) we see the likelihood of two main effects (A_1 less than A_2, and B_1 greater than B_2), and an interaction. Although these are clearly the only possible outcomes from a two-factor design, the precise pattern will differ depending on the obtained cell means. In other words, if your study yields a significant effect only for factor A, your profile plot need not look exactly like Fig. 3.1 (b), but it will retain the same general pattern and interpretation.

In many statistics texts, a big deal is made about the type of interaction shown in the profile plot. A distinction is made between an ordinal interaction and a disordinal interaction. An ordinal

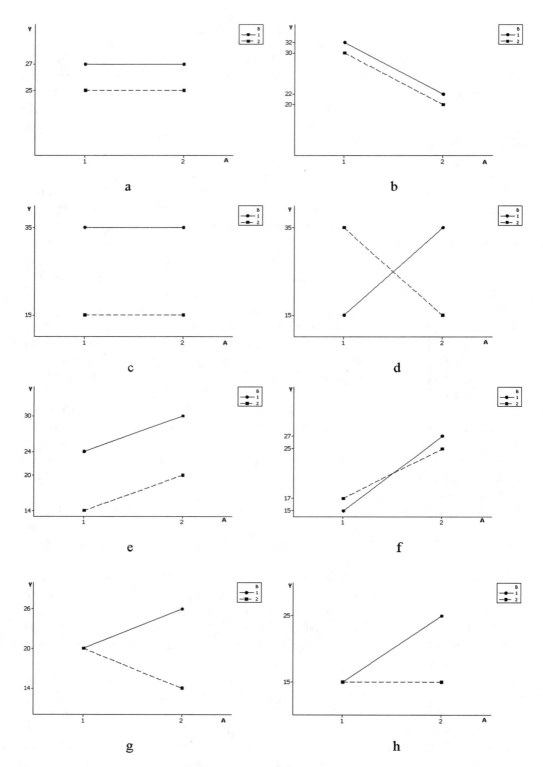

FIG. 3.1   Display of possible two-factor ANOVA effects.

interaction is said to exist when the lines are not parallel and they do not cross; ordinal here means the same relative order of the cell means is maintained across the levels of one of the factors. For example, the means for level 1 of factor B are always greater than the means for level 2 of B, regardless of the level of factor A. A disordinal interaction is said to exist when the lines are not parallel and they do cross. For example, the mean for B_1 is greater than the mean for B_2 at A_1, but the opposite is true at A_2. Dwelling on the distinction between the two types of interaction is not recommended as it can depend on which factor is plotted on the X axis. That is, when factor A is plotted on the X axis a disordinal interaction may be shown, and when factor B is plotted on the X axis an ordinal interaction may be shown. The purpose of the profile plot is to simplify interpretation of the results; worrying about the type of interaction may merely serve to confuse that interpretation.

Now for a Lomax commercial about dealing with the interaction effect. Let us consider two possible situations, one where there is a significant interaction effect and one where there is no such effect. If there is no significant interaction effect, then the findings regarding the main effects can be generalized with greater confidence. In this situation, the main effects are known as **additive effects** and an additive linear model with no interaction term could actually be used to describe the data. For example, the results might be that for factor A, the level 1 means always exceed those of level 2 by 10 points, across all levels of factor B. Thus we can make a blanket statement about the constant added benefits of A_1 over A_2, regardless of the level of factor B. In addition, for the no interaction situation, the main effects are statistically independent of one another; that is, each of the main effects serve as an independent predictor of Y.

If there is a significant interaction effect, then the findings regarding the main effects cannot be generalized with such confidence. In this situation, the main effects are not additive and the interaction term must be included in the linear model. For example, the results might be that (a) the mean for A_1 is greater than A_2 when considering B_1, but (b) the mean for A_1 is less than A_2 when considering B_2. Thus we cannot make a blanket statement about the constant added benefits of A_1 over A_2, because it depends on the level of factor B. In addition, for the interaction situation, the main effects are not statistically independent of one another; that is, each of the main effects does not serve as an independent predictor of Y. In order to predict Y well, information is necessary about the levels of factors A and B. Thus in the presence of a significant interaction, generalizations about the main effects must be qualified. A profile plot should be examined so that a proper graphical interpretation of the interaction and main effects can be made. A significant interaction serves as a warning that one cannot generalize statements about a main effect for A over all levels of B. If you obtain a significant interaction, this is an important result. Do not ignore it and go ahead to interpret the main effects.

3.1.5 Assumptions and Violation of Assumptions

In chapter 1 we described in detail the assumptions for the one-factor analysis of variance. In the two-factor model, the assumptions are again concerned with independence, homogeneity of variance, and normality. A summary of the effects of their violation is provided in Table 3.2. The same methods for detecting violations described in chapter 1 can be used for this model.

There are only two different wrinkles for the two-factor model as compared to the one-factor model. First, as the effect of heterogeneity is small with balanced designs (equal n's per cell) or nearly balanced designs, and/or with larger n's, this is a reason to strive for such a design.

TABLE 3.2
Assumptions and Effects of Violations—Two-Factor Design

Assumption	Effect of Assumption Violation
1. Independence	Increased likelihood of a Type I and/or Type II error in the F statistic; influences standard errors of means and thus inferences about those means
2. Homogeneity of variance	Bias in SS_{with}; increased likelihood of a Type I and/or Type II error; less effect with balanced or nearly balanced design; effect decreases as n increases
3. Normality	Minimal effect with moderate violation; minimal effect with balanced or nearly balanced design; effect decreases as n increases

Unfortunately, there is very little research on this problem, except the classic Box (1954b) article for a no-interaction model with one observation per cell. There are limited solutions for dealing with a violation of the homogeneity assumption, such as the Welch (1951) test, the Johansen (1980) procedure, and variations described by Wilcox (1996, 2003). Transformations are not usually used, as they may destroy an additive linear model and create interactions that did not previously exist. Nonparametric techniques are not commonly used with the two-factor model, although see the description of the Brunner, Dette, and Munk (1997) procedure in Wilcox (2003). Second, the effect of nonnormality seems to be the same as heterogeneity (Miller, 1997).

3.1.6   Partitioning the Sums of Squares

As pointed out in chapter 1, partitioning the sums of squares is an important concept in the analysis of variance. Let us begin with the total sum of squares in Y, denoted here as SS_{total}. The term SS_{total} represents the amount of total variation among all of the observations without regard to cell membership. The next step is to partition the total variation into variation between the levels of factor A (denoted by SS_A), variation between the levels of factor B (denoted by SS_B), variation due to the interaction of the levels of factors A and B (denoted by SS_{AB}), and variation within the cells combined across cells (denoted by SS_{with}). In the two-factor analysis of variance, then, we can partition SS_{total} into

$$SS_{total} = SS_A + SS_B + SS_{AB} + SS_{with}$$

Then computational formulas are used by statistical software to compute these sums of squares.

3.1.7   The ANOVA Summary Table

The next step is to assemble the ANOVA summary table. The purpose of the summary table is to simply summarize the analysis of variance. A general form of the summary table for the two-factor case is shown in Table 3.3. The first column lists the sources of variation in the model. We note that the total variation is divided into a within groups source, and a general

TABLE 3.3
Two-Factor Analysis of Variance Summary Table

Source	SS	df	MS	F
Between:				
A	SS_A	$J - 1$	MS_A	MS_A/MS_{with}
B	SS_B	$K - 1$	MS_B	MS_B/MS_{with}
AB	SS_{AB}	$(J - 1)(K - 1)$	MS_{AB}	MS_{AB}/MS_{with}
Within	SS_{with}	$N - JK$	MS_{with}	
Total	SS_{total}	$N - 1$		

between groups source, which is subdivided into sources due to A, B, and the AB interaction. This is in keeping with the spirit of the one-factor model, where total variation was divided into a between groups source (just one because there is only one factor and no interaction term) and a within groups source. The second column provides the computed sums of squares.

The third column gives the degrees of freedom for each source. As always, degrees of freedom have to do with the number of observations that are free to vary in a particular context. Because there are J levels of factor A, then the number of degrees of freedom for the A source is equal to $J - 1$. As there are J means and we know the overall mean, then only $J - 1$ of the means are free to vary. This is the same rationale we have been using throughout this text. As there are K levels of factor B, there are then $K - 1$ degrees of freedom for the B source. For the AB interaction source, we take the product of the degrees of freedom for the main effects. Thus we have as degrees of freedom for AB the product $(J - 1)(K - 1)$. The degrees of freedom within groups is equal to the total number of observations minus the number of cells, $N - JK$. Finally, the degrees of freedom total can be written simply as $N - 1$.

Next, the sum of squares terms are weighted by the appropriate degrees of freedom to generate the mean squares terms. Thus, for instance, $MS_A = SS_A/df_A$. Finally, in the last column of the ANOVA summary table, we have the F values, which represent the summary statistics for the analysis of variance. There are three hypotheses that we are interested in testing, so there will be three F test statistics, for the two main effects and the interaction effect. For the factorial fixed-effects model, each F value is computed by taking the MS for the source that you are interested in testing and dividing it by MS_{with}. Thus for each hypothesis, the same error term is used in forming the F ratio (i.e., MS_{with}). We return to the two-factor model for cases where the effects are not fixed in chapter 5.

Each of the F test statistics is then compared with the appropriate F critical value so as to make a decision about the relevant null hypothesis. These critical values are found in the F table of Appendix Table 4 as follows: for the test of factor A as $_\alpha F_{J-1,N-JK}$; for the test of factor B as $_\alpha F_{K-1,N-JK}$; and for the test of the interaction as $_\alpha F_{(J-1)(K-1),N-JK}$. Each significance test is a one-tailed test so as to be consistent with the alternative hypothesis. The null hypothesis is rejected if the F test statistic exceeds the F critical value

If the F test statistic does exceed the F critical value, and there is more than one degree of freedom for the source being tested, then it is not clear precisely why the null hypothesis was rejected. For example, if there are three levels of factor A and the null hypothesis for A is rejected, then we are not sure where the mean differences lie among the levels of A. In this case, some multiple comparison procedure should be used to determine where the mean differences are; this is the topic of the next section.

3.1.8   Multiple Comparison Procedures

In this section, we extend the concepts related to multiple comparison procedures (MCPs) covered in chapter 2 to the two-factor ANOVA model. This model includes main and interaction effects; consequently you can examine contrasts of both main and interaction effects. In general, the procedures described in chapter 2 can be applied to the two-factor situation. Things become more complicated as we have row and column means (or marginal means), and cell means. Thus we have to be careful about which means are being considered.

Let us begin with contrasts of the main effects. If the effect for factor A is significant, and there are more than two levels of factor A, we can form contrasts that compare the levels of factor A ignoring factor B. Here we would be comparing the means for the levels of factor A, which are marginal means as opposed to cell means. Considering each factor separately is strongly advised; considering the factors simultaneously is to be avoided. Some statistics texts suggest that you consider the design as a one-factor model with JK levels when using MCPs to examine main effects. This is inconsistent with the design and the intent of separating effects, and is not recommended.

For contrasts involving the interaction, my recommendation is to begin with a complex interaction contrast if there are more than four cells in the model. Thus for a 4×4 design that consists of four levels of A (method of instruction) and four levels of B (instructor), one possibility is to test both 4×2 complex interaction contrasts. An example of one such contrast is

$$\psi' = \frac{(\overline{Y}_{.11} + \overline{Y}_{.21} + \overline{Y}_{.31} + \overline{Y}_{.41})}{4} - \frac{(\overline{Y}_{.12} + \overline{Y}_{.22} + \overline{Y}_{.32} + \overline{Y}_{.42})}{4}$$

with a standard error of

$$s_{\psi'} = \sqrt{MS_{\text{with}}\left(\sum_{j=1}^{J}\sum_{k=1}^{K}\frac{c_{jk}^2}{n_{jk}}\right)}$$

where n_{jk} is the number of observations in cell jk. This contrast would examine the interaction between the four methods of instruction and the first two instructors. A second complex interaction contrast could consider the interaction between the four methods of instruction and the other two instructors.

If the complex interaction contrast is significant, then follow this up with a simple interaction contrast that involves only four cell means. This is a single degree of freedom contrast because it involves only two levels of each factor (known as a **tetrad difference**). An example of such a contrast is

$$\psi' = (\overline{Y}_{.11} - \overline{Y}_{.21}) - (\overline{Y}_{.12} - \overline{Y}_{.22})$$

with a similar standard error term. Using the same example, this contrast would examine the interaction between the first two methods of instruction and the first two instructors.

Most of the MCPs described in chapter 2 can be used for testing main effects and interaction effects (although there is some debate about the appropriate use of interaction contrasts; see Boik, 1979; Marascuilo & Levin, 1970, 1976). Keppel and Wickens (2004) consider interaction contrasts in much detail. Finally, some statistics texts suggest the use of simple main effects in testing a significant interaction. These involve comparing, for example, the levels of factor A at a particular level of factor B, and are generally conducted by further partitioning the sums of squares. However, the simple main effects sums of squares represent a portion of a main effect plus the interaction effect. Thus the simple main effect does not really help us to understand the interaction, and is not recommended here.

3.1.9 Effect Size Measures, Confidence Intervals, and Power

Various measures of effect size have been proposed. Let us examine two commonly-used measures, which assume equal variances across the cells. First is partial η^2, which represents the proportion of variation in Y explained by the effect of interest (i.e., by factor A, or factor B, or the AB interaction). We determine partial η^2 as follows:

$$\eta_A^2 = SS_A/(SS_A + SS_{with})$$

$$\eta_B^2 = SS_B/(SS_B + SS_{with})$$

$$\eta_{AB}^2 = SS_{AB}/(SS_{AB} + SS_{with})$$

Another effect size measure is the statistic ω^2. We can determine ω^2 as follows:

$$\omega_A^2 = \frac{SS_A - (J-1)\,MS_{with}}{SS_{total} + MS_{with}}$$

$$\omega_B^2 = \frac{SS_B - (K-1)MS_{with}}{SS_{total} + MS_{with}}$$

$$\omega_{AB}^2 = \frac{SS_{AB} - (J-1)(K-1)MS_{with}}{SS_{total} + MS_{with}}$$

Using Cohen's (1988) subjective standards, these effect sizes can be interpreted as follows: small effect, η^2 or $\omega^2 = .01$; medium effect, η^2 or $\omega^2 = .06$; large effect, η^2 or $\omega^2 = .14$. For futher discussion, see Keppel (1982), O'Grady (1982), Wilcox (1987), Cohen (1988), Fidler and Thompson (2001), Keppel and Wickens (2004), and Murphy and Myors (2004; with software).

As mentioned in chapter 1, confidence intervals can be used for providing interval estimates of a population mean or mean difference; this gives us information about the accuracy of a sample estimate. In the case of the two-factor model, we can form confidence intervals for row means, column means, cell means, the overall mean, as well as any possible contrast formed through a multiple comparison procedure. Note also that confidence intervals have been developed for η^2 and ω^2 (Fidler & Thompson, 2001; Smithson, 2001).

As also mentioned in chapter 1, power can be determined either in the planned or observed (post hoc) power context. For planned power we typically use tables or power charts (e.g., Cohen, 1988 or Murphy & Myors, 2004) or software (e.g., Power and Precision, Ex-Sample, Gpower, or Murphy & Myers software, 2004). These are particularly useful in terms of determining adequate sample sizes when designing a study. Observed power is reported by statistics software, such as SPSS, to indicate the actual power in a given study.

3.1.10 An Example

Consider the following illustration of the two-factor design. Here we expand on the example presented in chapter 1 by adding a second factor to the model. Our dependent variable will again be the number of times a student attends statistics lab during one semester (or quarter), factor A is the attractiveness of the lab instructor (assuming each instructor is of the same gender and is equally competent), and factor B is the time of day the lab is offered. Thus the researcher is interested in whether the attractiveness of the instructor, the time of day, or the interaction of attractiveness and time influences student attendance in the statistics lab. The attractiveness levels are defined as (a) unattractive, (b) slightly attractive, (c) moderately attractive, and (d) very attractive. The time of day levels are defined as (a) afternoon lab and (b) evening lab. Students were randomly assigned to a combination of lab instructor and lab time at the beginning of the semester, and attendance was taken by the instructor. There were four students in each cell and eight cells (combinations of instructor and time) for a total of 32 observations. Students could attend a maximum of 30 lab sessions. Table 3.4 depicts the raw data and sample means for each cell (given beneath each cell), column, row, and overall.

The results are summarized in the ANOVA summary table as shown in Table 3.5. The F test statistics are compared to the following critical values obtained from Appendix Table 4 ($\alpha = .05$): $_{.05}F_{3,24} = 3.01$ for the A and AB effects; $_{.05}F_{1,24} = 4.26$ for the B effect. The test statistics exceed the critical values for the A and B effects only, so we reject these H_0 and conclude that both the level of attractiveness and the time of day are related to mean differences in statistics lab attendance. The interaction was shown not to be a significant effect. If you would like to see an example of a two-factor design where the interaction is significant, take a look at the end of chapter problems, computational problem 5.

Next we estimate the main and interaction effects. The main effects for the levels of A are estimated to be:

$$a_1 = \overline{Y}_{.1.} - \overline{Y}_{...} = 11.1250 - 18.4063 = -7.2813$$

$$a_2 = \overline{Y}_{.2.} - \overline{Y}_{...} = 17.8750 - 18.4063 = -0.5313$$

$$a_3 = \overline{Y}_{.3.} - \overline{Y}_{...} = 20.2500 - 18.4063 = 1.8437$$

$$a_4 = \overline{Y}_{.4.} - \overline{Y}_{...} = 24.3750 - 18.4063 = 5.9687$$

The main effects for the levels of B are estimated to be:

$$b_1 = \overline{Y}_{..1} - \overline{Y}_{...} = 23.1250 - 18.4063 = 4.7187$$

$$b_2 = \overline{Y}_{..2} - \overline{Y}_{...} = 13.6875 - 18.4063 = -4.7188$$

TABLE 3.4
Data for the Statistics Lab Example: Number of Statistics Labs Attended,
by Level of Attractiveness and Time of Day

| Level of Attractiveness | Time of Day | | Row Mean |
	Time 1	Time 2	
Attractiveness 1	15	10	11.1250
	12	8	
	21	7	
	13	3	
	15.2500	7.0000	
Attractiveness 2	20	13	17.8750
	22	9	
	24	18	
	25	12	
	22.7500	13.0000	
Attractiveness 3	24	10	20.2500
	29	12	
	27	21	
	25	14	
	26.2500	14.2500	
Attractiveness 4	30	22	24.3750
	26	20	
	29	25	
	28	15	
	28.2500	20.2500	
Column mean	23.1250	13.6875	18.4063 *(Overall mean)*

TABLE 3.5
Two-Factor Analysis of Variance Summary Table—Statistics Lab Example

Source	SS	df	MS	F
Between:				
A	738.5938	3	246.1979	21.3504*
B	712.5313	1	712.5313	61.7911**
AB	21.8438	3	7.2813	0.6314*
Within	276.7500	24	11.5313	
Total	1749.7188	31		

* $_{.05}F_{3,24} = 3.01$.

** $_{.05}F_{1,24} = 4.26$.

Finally, the interaction effects for the various combinations of the levels of factors A and B are estimated to be:

$$(ab)_{11} = \overline{Y}_{.11} - (\overline{Y}_{.1.} + \overline{Y}_{..1} - \overline{Y}_{...}) = 15.2500 - (11.1250 + 23.1250 - 18.4063) = -0.5937$$

$$(ab)_{12} = \overline{Y}_{.12} - (\overline{Y}_{.1.} + \overline{Y}_{..2} - \overline{Y}_{...}) = 7.0000 - (11.1250 + 13.6875 - 18.4063) = 0.5938$$

$$(ab)_{21} = \overline{Y}_{.21} - (\overline{Y}_{.2.} + \overline{Y}_{..1} - \overline{Y}_{...}) = 22.7500 - (17.875 + 23.1250 - 18.4063) = 0.1563$$

$$(ab)_{22} = \overline{Y}_{.22} - (\overline{Y}_{.2.} + \overline{Y}_{..2} - \overline{Y}_{...}) = 13.000 - (17.8750 + 13.6875 - 18.4063) = -0.1562$$

$$(ab)_{31} = \overline{Y}_{.31} - (\overline{Y}_{.3.} + \overline{Y}_{..1} - \overline{Y}_{...}) = 26.2500 - (20.2500 + 23.1250 - 18.4063) = 1.2813$$

$$(ab)_{32} = \overline{Y}_{.32} - (\overline{Y}_{.3.} + \overline{Y}_{..2} - \overline{Y}_{...}) = 14.2500 - (20.2500 + 13.6875 - 18.4063) = -1.2812$$

$$(ab)_{41} = \overline{Y}_{.41} - (\overline{Y}_{.4.} + \overline{Y}_{..1} - \overline{Y}_{...}) = 28.2500 - (24.3750 + 23.1250 - 18.4063) = -0.8437$$

$$(ab)_{42} = \overline{Y}_{.42} - (\overline{Y}_{.4.} + \overline{Y}_{..2} - \overline{Y}_{...}) = 20.5000 - (24.3750 + 13.6875 - 18.4063) = 0.8438$$

The profile plot shown in Fig. 3.2 graphically depicts these effects. The A effect was significant and has more than two levels, so let us consider one example of a multiple comparison procedure, Tukey's HSD test. Recall from chapter 2 that the HSD test is a family-wise procedure

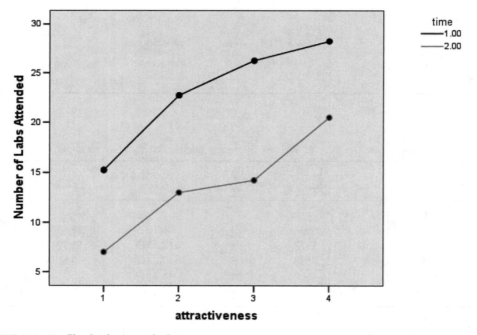

FIG. 3.2   Profile plot for example data.

most appropriate for considering all pairwise contrasts with a balanced design (which is the case for these data). The following are the computations:

Critical value (obtained from Appendix Table 9):

$$_\alpha q_{df(with),J} = {}_{.05}q_{24,4} = 3.901$$

Standard error:

$$s_{\psi'} = \sqrt{\frac{MS_{with}}{n_j}} = \sqrt{\frac{11.5313}{8}} = 1.2006$$

Test statistics:

$$q_1 = \frac{\overline{Y}_{.4.} - \overline{Y}_{.1.}}{s_{\psi'}} = \frac{24.3750 - 11.1250}{1.2006} = 11.0361 \, (significant)$$

$$q_2 = \frac{\overline{Y}_{.4.} - \overline{Y}_{.2.}}{s_{\psi'}} = \frac{24.3750 - 17.8750}{1.2006} = 5.4140 \, (significant)$$

$$q_3 = \frac{\overline{Y}_{.4.} - \overline{Y}_{.3.}}{s_{\psi'}} = \frac{24.3750 - 20.2500}{1.2006} = 3.4358 \, (nonsignificant)$$

$$q_4 = \frac{\overline{Y}_{.3.} - \overline{Y}_{.1.}}{s_{\psi'}} = \frac{20.2500 - 11.1250}{1.2006} = 7.6004 \, (significant)$$

$$q_5 = \frac{\overline{Y}_{.3.} - \overline{Y}_{.2.}}{s_{\psi'}} = \frac{20.2500 - 17.8750}{1.2006} = 1.9782 \, (nonsignificant)$$

$$q_6 = \frac{\overline{Y}_{.2.} - \overline{Y}_{.1.}}{s_{\psi'}} = \frac{17.8750 - 11.1250}{1.2006} = 5.6222 \, (significant)$$

These results indicate that the means for the levels of factor A are significantly different for levels 1 and 4, 2 and 4, 1 and 3, and 1 and 2. Thus level 1 (unattractive) is significantly different from the other three levels of attractiveness, and levels 2 and 4 (slightly unattractive vs. very attractive) are also significantly different.

These results are somewhat different than those found with the one-factor model in chapters 1 and 2 (where levels 1 and 4 as well as 1 and 3 were different). The MS_{with} has been reduced with the introduction of the second factor from 36.1116 to 11.5313 because SS_{with} has been reduced from 1,011.1250 to 276.7500. Although the SS and MS for the attractiveness factor remain unchanged, this resulted in the F test statistic being considerably larger (increased from 6.8177 to 21.3504), although observed power was quite high in both models. Recall that this is one of the benefits we mentioned earlier about the use of additional factors in the model. Also, although the B effect was significant, there are only two levels of the B factor, and thus we need not carry out any multiple comparisons (attendance is better in the afternoon section). Finally, since the interaction was not significant, it is not necessary to consider any related contrasts.

Finally we can estimate the effect size measures. The partial η^2 are determined to be

$$\eta_A^2 = \frac{SS_A}{SS_A + SS_{with}} = \frac{738.5938}{738.5938 + 276.75} = 0.7274$$

$$\eta_B^2 = \frac{SS_B}{SS_B + SS_{with}} = \frac{712.5313}{712.5313 + 276.75} = 0.7203$$

$$\eta_{AB}^2 = \frac{SS_{AB}}{SS_{AB} + SS_{with}} = \frac{21.8438}{21.8438 + 276.75} = 0.0732$$

We determine the ω^2 to be

$$\omega_A^2 = \frac{SS_A - (J-1)MS_{with}}{SS_{total} + MS_{with}} = \frac{738.5938 - (3)11.5313}{1,749.7188 + 11.5313} = 0.3997$$

$$\omega_B^2 = \frac{SS_B - (K-1)MS_{with}}{SS_{total} + MS_{with}} = \frac{712.5313 - (1)11.5313}{1,749.7188 + 11.5313} = 0.3980$$

$$\omega_{AB}^2 = \frac{SS_{AB} - (J-1)(K-1)MS_{with}}{SS_{total} + MS_{with}} = \frac{21.8438 - (3)11.5313}{1,749.7188 + 11.5313} = 0$$

Based on these effect size measures, one would conclude that there is a large effect for instructor attractiveness and for time of day, but no effect for the time-attractiveness interaction.

3.2   THREE-FACTOR AND HIGHER-ORDER ANOVA

3.2.1   Characteristics of the Model

All of the characteristics we discussed for the two-factor model apply to the three-factor model, with one obvious exception. There are three factors rather than two. This will result in three main effects (one for each factor, known as A, B, and C), three two-way interactions (known as AB, AC, and BC), and one three-way interaction (known as ABC). Here the only new concept is the three-way interaction, which may be stated as follows: "Is the AB interaction constant across all levels of factor C?" This may also be stated as "AC across the levels of B" or as "BC across the levels of A." These each have the same interpretation as there is only one way of testing the three-way interaction. In short, the three-way interaction can thought of as the two-way interaction is behaving differently across the levels of the third factor.

We do not explicitly consider models with more than three factors (Marascuilo & Serlin, 1988; Myers & Well, 1995; Keppel & Wickens, 2004). However, be warned that such models do exist, and that they will necessitate more main effects, more two-way interactions, more three-way interactions, as well as higher-order interactions. Conceptually, the only change is to add these additional effects to the model.

3.2.2 The ANOVA Model

The model for the three factor design is

$$Y_{ijkl} = \mu + \alpha_j + \beta_k + \gamma_l + (\alpha\beta)_{jk} + (\alpha\gamma)_{jl} + (\beta\gamma)_{kl} + (\alpha\beta\gamma)_{jkl} + \varepsilon_{ijkl}$$

where Y_{ijkl} is the observed score on the criterion variable for individual i in level j of factor A, level k of factor B, and level l of factor C (or in the jkl cell), μ is the overall or grand population mean (i.e., regardless of cell designation), α_j is the effect for level j of factor A, β_k is the effect for level k of factor B, γ_l is the effect for level l of factor C, $(\alpha\beta)_{jk}$ is the interaction effect for the combination of level j of factor A and level k of factor B, $(\alpha\gamma)_{jl}$ is the interaction effect for the combination of level j of factor A and level l of factor C, $(\beta\gamma)_{kl}$ is the interaction effect for the combination of level k of factor B and level l of factor C, $(\alpha\beta\gamma)_{jkl}$ is the interaction effect for the combination of level j of factor A, level k of factor B, and level l of factor C, and ε_{ijkl} is the random residual error for individual i in cell jkl. Given that there are three main effects, three two-way interactions, and a three-way interaction, there will be an accompanying null and alternative hypothesis for each of these effects. At this point in your statistics career, the hypotheses should be obvious (simply expand on the hypotheses at the beginning of this chapter).

3.2.3 The ANOVA Summary Table

The ANOVA summary table for the three-factor model is shown in Table 3.6, with the usual columns for sources of variation, sums of squares, degrees of freedom, mean squares, and F.

3.2.4 The Triple Interaction

Everything else about the three-factor design follows from the two-factor model. The assumptions are the same, MS_{with} is the error term used for testing each of the hypotheses in the fixed-

TABLE 3.6
Three-Factor Analysis of Variance Summary Table

Source	SS	df	MS	F
Between:				
A	SS_A	$J - 1$	MS_A	MS_A/MS_{with}
B	SS_B	$K - 1$	MS_B	MS_B/MS_{with}
C	SS_C	$L - 1$	MS_C	MS_C/MS_{with}
AB	SS_{AB}	$(J - 1)(K - 1)$	MS_{AB}	MS_{AB}/MS_{with}
AC	SS_{AC}	$(J - 1)(L - 1)$	MS_{AC}	MS_{AC}/MS_{with}
BC	SS_{BC}	$(K - 1)(L - 1)$	MS_{BC}	MS_{BC}/MS_{with}
ABC	SS_{ABC}	$(J - 1)(K - 1)(L - 1)$	MS_{ABC}	$MS_{ABC}/MS_{\text{with}}$
Within	SS_{with}	$N - JKL$	MS_{with}	
Total	SS_{total}	$N - 1$		

effects model, and the multiple comparison procedures are easily utilized. The main new feature is the three-way interaction. If this interaction is significant, then this means that the two-way interaction is different across the levels of the third factor. This result will need to be taken into account prior to interpreting the two-way interactions and the main effects.

Although the inclusion of additional factors in the design should result in a reduction in MS_{with}, there is a price to pay for the study of additional factors. Although the analysis is simple for the computer, you must consider the possibility of significant higher-order interactions. If you find, for example, that the four-way interaction is significant, how do you deal with it? First you have to interpret this interaction, which could be difficult if it is unexpected. Then you may have difficulty in dealing with the interpretation of your other effects. My advice is simple. Do not include additional factors just because they sound interesting. Only include those factors that are theoretically or empirically important. Then if a significant higher-order interaction occurs, you will be in a better position to understand it because you have already thought about its consequences. Reporting that an interaction is significant but not interpretable is not sound research (for additional discussion on this topic, see Keppel & Wickens, 2004).

3.3   FACTORIAL ANOVA WITH UNEQUAL *n*'s

Up until this point in the chapter, we have only considered the equal *n*'s or balanced case. That is, the model used was where the number of observations in each cell was equal. This served to make the formulas and equations easier to deal with. However, we need not assume that the *n*'s are equal. In this section we discuss ways to deal with the unequal *n*'s (or unbalanced) case for the two-factor model, although these notions can be transferred to higher-order models as well.

When *n*'s are unequal, things become a bit trickier as the main effects and the interaction effect are not orthogonal. In other words, the sums of squares cannot be partitioned into independent effects. As a result, several computational approaches have been developed. In the old days, prior to the availability of high-speed computers, the standard approach was to use unweighted means analysis. This is essentially an analysis of means, rather than raw scores, which are unweighted by cell size. This approach is only an approximate procedure. Due to the availability of quality statistical software, the unweighted means approach is no longer necessary. Another silly approach is to delete enough data until you have an equal *n*'s model.

There are three more modern approaches. Each of these approaches really test different hypotheses and thus may result in different conclusions: (a) the **sequential approach** (also known as the hierarchical sums of squares approach), (b) the **partially sequential approach** (also known as the partially hierarchical, or experimental design, or method of fitting constants approach), and (c) the **regression approach** (also known as the marginal means or unique approach). There has been considerable debate over the years about the relative merits of each approach (e.g., Applebaum & Cramer, 1974; Carlson & Timm, 1974; Cramer & Applebaum, 1980; Overall, Lee, & Hornick, 1981; Overall & Spiegel, 1969; Timm & Carlson, 1975).

Here is what each approach tests. In the sequential approach, the effects being tested are:

$$\alpha \mid \mu$$

$$\beta \mid \mu, \alpha$$

$$\alpha\beta \mid \mu, \alpha, \beta$$

This indicates, for example, that the effect for factor B is adjusted for (as denoted by the vertical line) the overall mean (μ) and the effect due to factor A (α). Thus, each effect is adjusted for prior effects in the sequential order given. Here the α effect is given theoretical or practical priority over the β effect. In SAS and SPSS this is the Type I sum of squares method.

In the partially sequential approach, the effects being tested are:

$$\alpha \mid \mu, \beta$$

$$\beta \mid \mu, \alpha$$

$$\alpha\beta \mid \mu, \alpha, \beta$$

There is difference here because each main effect controls for the other main effect, but not for the interaction effect. In SAS and SPSS this is the Type II sum of squares method. This is the only one of the three methods where the sums of squares add up to the total sum of squares. Notice in the sequential and partially sequential approaches that the interaction is not taken into account in estimating the main effects, which is only fine if there is no interaction effect.

In the regression approach, the effects being tested are:

$$\alpha \mid \mu, \beta, \alpha\beta$$

$$\beta \mid \mu, \alpha, \alpha\beta$$

$$\alpha\beta \mid \mu, \alpha, \beta$$

In this approach each effect controls for each of the other effects. In SAS and SPSS this is the Type III sum of squares method. Many statisticians (e.g., Glass & Hopkins, 1996; Keppel & Wickens, 2004; Mickey, Dunn, & Clark, 2004), including myself, recommend exclusive use of the regression approach because each effect is estimated taking the other effects into account. The hypotheses tested in the sequential and partially sequential approaches are seldom of interest and are difficult to interpret (Carlson & Timm, 1974; Kirk, 1982; Overall, Lee, & Hornick, 1981; Timm & Carlson, 1975). The regression approach seems to be conceptually closest to the traditional analysis of variance. When the n's are equal, each of these three approaches tests the same hypotheses and yields the same results.

3.4   SPSS

In the last section we look at SPSS for the statistics lab example, as well as an APA paragraph of the results. As already noted in chapter 1, SPSS needs the data to be in a specific form for the analysis to proceeed, which is different from the layout of the data in Table 3.1. For a two-factor ANOVA, the dataset must consist of three variables or columns, one for the level of factor A, one for the level of factor B, and the third for the dependent variable. Each row still represents one individual, indicating the level of factors A and B that individual is a member of, and their score on the dependent variable.

To conduct a parametric ANOVA through the GLM module, go to the "Analyze" pulldown, into "General Linear Model," and then into the "Univariate" procedure. Click the dependent variable (e.g., labs attended) into the "Dependent Variable" box, and click both fixed-effects factor variables into the "Fixed Factor(s)" box. Click on the "Options" button to obtain such information as "Descriptive Statistics," "Estimates of effect size," "Observed power," and "Homogeneity tests" (i.e., Levene's test). Click on "Continue" to return to the original dialog box. To obtain a profile plot of means, click on the "Plots" button, move one factor variable name into the "Horizontal Axis" box, move the other factor variable name into the "Separate Lines" box, click on "Add" to generate the plot, and finally click on "Continue" to return to the original dialog box. To obtain multiple comparison procedures, proceed as you did in chapter 2 by clicking the "Post Hoc" button, then move the "Factor" variables into the "Post Hoc Tests for:" box, check the box for an appropriate procedure, then click "Continue" to return to the previous screen. Then click on "OK" to run the analyses. Selected results are shown in the panels of Table 3.7 (ANOVA summary table, information about different types of means <with confidence intervals>, and Tukey's HSD procedure <with confidence intervals>) and the profile plot is shown in Fig. 3.2. In order to test interaction contrasts in SPSS, syntax is required rather than the use of point-and-click (c.f., Page, Braver, & MacKinnon, 2003). Note also that the SPSS ANOVA summary table will include additional sources of variation that I find not to be useful (i.e., corrected model, intercept, total); thus they are not shown in Table 3.7.

Finally we come to an example paragraph of the results for the statistics lab example. From Table 3.7 we see that the interaction is not significant, there are significant main effects for both attractiveness and time ($F_{attract} = 21.350$, $df = 3,24$, $p = .001$; $F_{time} = 61.791$, $df = 1,24$, $p = .001$), with attendance being significantly higher in the afternoon, effect sizes are rather large for attractiveness and time (partial $\eta^2_{attract} = .727$; partial $\eta^2_{time} = .720$), and observed power for attractiveness and time is maximal. Tukey HSD post hoc comparisons revealed that the unattractive level had significantly lower attendance than the other levels, and that the slightly attractive level had significantly lower attendance than the very attractive level. The profile plot (Fig. 3.2) summarizes these differences. From the residual plot, skewness and kurtosis statistics, and Levene's homogeneity of variance test ($p = .766$), the assumptions were satisfied.

3.5 SUMMARY

This chapter considered methods involving the comparison of means for multiple independent variables. The chapter began with a look at the characteristics of the factorial analysis of variance, including (1) two or more independent variables each with two or more fixed levels; (2) subjects are randomly assigned to cells and then exposed to only one combination of the independent variables; (3) the factors are fully crossed such that all possible combinations of the factors' levels are included in the design; and (4) the dependent variable is at least measured at the interval level. The ANOVA model was examined and followed by a discussion of main effects and, in particular, the interaction effect. Some discussion was also devoted to the ANOVA assumptions. The ANOVA summary table was shown along with partitioning the sums of squares. Multiple comparison procedures were then extended to factorial models. Then effect size measures, confidence intervals, and power were considered. Finally, several approaches were given for the unequal n's case with factorial models. At this point you should have met the following objectives: (a) be able to understand the characteristics and concepts underlying factorial ANOVA, (b) be able to determine and interpret the results of factorial ANOVA, and (c) be able to understand and evaluate the assumptions of factorial ANOVA. In chapter 4 we introduce the analysis of covariance.

TABLE 3.7
Selected SPSS Results for the Statistics Lab Example

Tests of Between-Subjects Effects

Dependent Variable: dv

Source	Type III Sum of Squares	df	Mean Square	F	Sig.	Partial Eta Squared	Observed Power[a]
attract	738.594	3	246.198	21.350	.000	.727	1.000
time	712.531	1	712.531	61.791	.000	.720	1.000
attract * time	21.844	3	7.281	.631	.602	.073	.162
Error	276.750	24	11.531				
Corrected Total	1749.719	31					

[a]Computed using alpha = .05

1. Grand Mean

Dependent Variable: dv

Mean	Std. Error	95% Confidence Interval	
		Lower Bound	Upper Bound
18.406	.600	17.167	19.645

2. attract

Dependent Variable: dv

attract	Mean	Std. Error	95% Confidence Interval	
			Lower Bound	Upper Bound
1.00000	11.125	1.201	8.647	13.603
2.00000	17.875	1.201	15.397	20.353
3.00000	20.250	1.201	17.772	22.728
4.00000	24.375	1.201	21.897	26.853

3. time

Dependent Variable: dv

time	Mean	Std. Error	95% Confidence Interval	
			Lower Bound	Upper Bound
1.00	23.125	.849	21.373	24.877
2.00	13.688	.849	11.935	15.440

(continued)

TABLE 3.7 (*Continued*)
Selected SPSS Results for the Statistics Lab Example

*4. attract * time*

Dependent Variable: dv

				95% Confidence Interval	
attract	*time*	*Mean*	*Std. Error*	*Lower Bound*	*Upper Bound*
1.00000	1.00	15.250	1.698	11.746	18.754
	2.00	7.000	1.698	3.496	10.504
2.00000	1.00	22.750	1.698	19.246	26.254
	2.00	13.000	1.698	9.496	16.504
3.00000	1.00	26.250	1.698	22.746	29.754
	2.00	14.250	1.698	10.746	17.754
4.00000	1.00	28.250	1.698	24.746	31.754
	2.00	20.500	1.698	16.996	24.004

Multiple Comparisons

Dependent Variable: dv
Tukey HSD

(I) attract	(J) attract	Mean Difference (I–J)	Std. Error	Sig.	95% Confidence Interval	
					Lower Bound	Upper Bound
1.00000	2.00000	−6.7500000*	1.697885	.003	−11.4338000	−2.0662000
	3.00000	−9.1250000*	1.697885	.000	−13.8088000	−4.4412000
	4.00000	−13.250000*	1.697885	.000	−17.9338000	−8.5662000
2.00000	1.00000	6.7500000*	1.697885	.003	2.0662000	11.4338000
	3.00000	−2.3750000	1.697885	.512	−7.0588000	2.3088000
	4.00000	−6.5000000*	1.697885	.004	−11.1838000	−1.8162000
3.00000	1.00000	9.1250000*	1.697885	.000	4.4412000	13.8088000
	2.00000	2.3750000	1.697885	.512	−2.3088000	7.0588000
	4.00000	−4.1250000	1.697885	.098	−8.8088000	.5588000
4.00000	1.00000	13.2500000*	1.697885	.000	8.5662000	17.9338000
	2.00000	6.5000000*	1.697885	.004	1.8162000	11.1838000
	3.00000	4.1250000	1.697885	.098	−.5588000	8.8088000

Based on observed means.

*The mean difference is significant at the .05 level.

PROBLEMS

Conceptual Problems

1. You are given a two-factor design with the following cell means (cell 11 = 25; cell 12 = 75; cell 21 = 50; cell 22 = 50; cell 31 = 75; cell 32 = 25). Assume that the within cell variation is small. Which one of the following conclusions seems most probable?

   a. The row means are significantly different.

   b. The column means are significantly different.

   c. The interaction is significant.

   d. All of the above.

2. In a two-factor ANOVA, one independent variable has five levels and the second has four levels. If each cell has seven observations, what is df_{with}?

   a. 20

   b. 120

   c. 139

   d. 140

3. Which of the following conclusions would result in the greatest generalizability of the main effect for factor A across the levels of factor B? The interaction between the independent variables A and B was

   a. not significant at the .25 level.

   b. significant at the .10 level.

   c. significant at the .05 level.

   d. significant at the .01 level.

   e. significant at the .001 level.

4. In a two-factor fixed-effects ANOVA, $F_A = 2$, $df_A = 3$, $df_B = 6$, $df_{AB} = 18$, $df_{with} = 56$. The null hypothesis for factor A can be rejected

   a. at the .01 level.

   b. at the .05 level but not at the .01 level.

   c. at the .10 level but not at the .05 level.

   d. none of the above

5. In ANOVA the interaction of two factors is certainly present when

   a. the two factors are positively correlated.

   b. the two factors are negatively correlated.

   c. row effects are not consistent across columns.

   d. main effects do not account for all of the variation in Y.

   e. main effects do account for all of the variation in Y.

Questions 6 through 9 are based on the following ANOVA summary table (fixed-effects):

Source	df	MS	F
A	2	45	4.5
B	1	70	7.0
AB	2	170	17.0
Within	60	10	

6. For which source of variation is the null hypothesis rejected at the .01 level of significance?
   a. A
   b. B
   c. AB
   d. all of the above

7. How many cells are there in the design?
   a. 1
   b. 2
   c. 3
   d. 5
   e. none of the above

8. The total sample size for the design is
   a. 66
   b. 68
   c. 70
   d. none of the above

9. SS_{AB} is equal to
   a. 170
   b. 340
   c. 510
   d. 1,020
   e. none of the above

10. In a design with four factors, how many interactions will there be?
    a. 4
    b. 8
    c. 11
    d. 12
    e. 16

11. Degrees of freedom for the AB interaction are equal to
   a. $df_A - df_B$
   b. $(df_A)(df_B)$
   c. $df_{with} - (df_A + df_B)$
   d. $df_{tot} - df_{with}$

12. A two-factor experiment means that the design includes
   a. two independent variables.
   b. two dependent variables.
   c. an interaction between independent and dependent variables.
   d. exactly two separate groups of subjects.

13. Two independent variables are said to interact when
   a. both variables are equally influenced by a third variable.
   b. the variables are differentially affected by a third variable.
   c. each factor produces a change in the subjects' scores.
   d. the effect of one variable depends on the second variable.

14. If there is an interaction between the independent variables textbook and time of day, this means that the textbook used has the same effect at different times of the day. True or False?

15. If the AB interaction is significant, then at least one of the two main effects must be significant. True or False?

16. I assert that a two-factor experiment (factors A and B) yields no more information than two one-factor experiments (factor A in experiment 1 and factor B in experiment 2). Am I correct?

17. For a two-factor fixed-effects model, if the degrees of freedom for testing factor A = 2,24, then I assert that the degrees of freedom for testing factor B will necessarily be = 2,24. Am I correct?

Computational Problems

1. Complete the following ANOVA summary table for a two-factor fixed-effects analysis of variance, where there are two levels of factor A (drug) and three levels of factor B (dosage). Each cell includes 26 students. Complete the summary table below where $\alpha = .05$.

Source	SS	df	MS	F	Critical Value	Decision
A	6.15	—	—	—	—	—
B	10.60	—	—	—	—	—
AB	9.10	—	—	—	—	—
Within	—	—	—			
Total	250.85	—				

2. Complete the following ANOVA summary table for a two-factor fixed-effects analysis of variance, where there are three levels of factor A (program) and two levels of factor B (gender). Each cell includes four students. Complete the summary table below where $\alpha = .01$.

Source	SS	df	MS	F	Critical Value	Decision
A	3.64	—	—	—	—	—
B	.57	—	—	—	—	—
AB	2.07	—	—	—	—	—
Within	—	—	—			
Total	8.18	—				

3. Conduct a two-factor fixed-effects ANOVA to determine if there are any effects due to A (task type), B (task difficulty), or the AB interaction ($\alpha = .01$). Conduct Tukey HSD post hoc comparisons, if necessary. The following are the scores for the individual cells of the model:

    A_1B_1: 41, 39, 25, 25, 37, 51, 39, 101
    A_1B_2: 46, 54, 97, 93, 51, 36, 29, 69
    A_1B_3: 113, 135, 109, 96, 47, 49, 68, 38
    A_2B_1: 86, 38, 45, 45, 60, 106, 106, 31
    A_2B_2: 74, 96, 101, 124, 48, 113, 139, 131
    A_2B_3: 152, 79, 135, 144, 52, 102, 166, 155

4. An experimenter is interested in the effects of strength of reinforcement (factor A), type of reinforcement (factor B), and sex of the adult administering the reinforcement (factor C) on children's behavior. Each factor consists of two levels. Thirty-two children are randomly assigned to 8 cells (i.e., 4 per cell), one for each of the factor combinations. Using the scores for the individual cells of the model that follow, conduct an three-factor fixed-effects analysis of variance ($\alpha = .05$). If there are any significant interactions, graph and interpret the interactions.

    $A_1B_1C_1$: 3, 6, 3, 3
    $A_1B_1C_2$: 4, 5, 4, 3
    $A_1B_2C_1$: 7, 8, 7, 6
    $A_1B_2C_2$: 7, 8, 9, 8
    $A_2B_1C_1$: 1, 2, 2, 2
    $A_2B_1C_2$: 2, 3, 4, 3
    $A_2B_2C_1$: 5, 6, 5, 6
    $A_2B_2C_2$: 10, 10, 9, 11

5. A revised version of the example data from this chapter is given below (A = attractiveness, B = time, same levels). Using the scores for the individual cells of the model that follow, conduct a two-factor fixed-effects analysis of variance ($\alpha = .05$). Are the results different?

    A_1B_1: 10, 8, 7, 3
    A_1B_2: 15, 12, 21, 13

A_2B_1: 13, 9, 18, 12
A_2B_2: 20, 22, 24, 25
A_3B_1: 24, 29, 27, 25
A_3B_2: 10, 12, 21, 14
A_4B_1: 30, 26, 29, 28
A_4B_2: 22, 20, 25, 15

Interpretive Problem

Building on the interpretive problem from chapter 1, utilize the statistics survey dataset from the CD. Use SPSS to conduct a two-factor fixed-effects ANOVA, where political view is factor A (as in chapter 1), gender is factor B (a new factor), and the dependent variable is the same one you used previously in chapter 1. Then write an APA style paragraph summarizing the results.

CHAPTER

4

INTRODUCTION TO ANALYSIS OF COVARIANCE: THE ONE-FACTOR FIXED-EFFECTS MODEL WITH A SINGLE COVARIATE

Chapter Outline

Key Concepts

1. Statistical adjustment
2. Covariate
3. Adjusted means
4. Homogeneity of regression slopes
5. Independence of the covariate and the independent variable

We have now considered several different analysis of variance (ANOVA) models. As we moved through chapter 3, we saw that the inclusion of additional factors helped to reduce the residual or uncontrolled variation. These additional factors served as "experimental design controls" in that their inclusion in the design helped to reduce the uncontrolled variation. In fact, this could be the reason an additional factor is included in a factorial design.

In this chapter a new type of variable, known as the covariate, is incorporated into the analysis. Rather than serving as an "experimental design control," the covariate serves as a "statistical control" where uncontrolled variation is reduced statistically in the analysis. Thus a model where a covariate is used is known as **analysis of covariance** (ANCOVA). We are most concerned with the one-factor fixed-effects model, although this model can be generalized to any of the other ANOVA designs considered in this text. That is, any of the ANOVA models discussed in the text can also include a covariate, and thus become an ANCOVA model.

Most of the concepts used in this chapter have already been covered in the text. In addition, new concepts include statistical adjustment, covariate, adjusted means, and two new assumptions, homogeneity of regression slopes and independence of the covariate and the independent variable. Our objectives are that by the end of this chapter, you will be able to (a) understand the characteristics and concepts underlying ANCOVA; (b) determine and interpret the results of ANCOVA, including adjusted means and multiple comparison procedures; and (c) understand and evaluate the assumptions of ANCOVA.

4.1 CHARACTERISTICS OF THE MODEL

In this section, we describe the distinguishing characteristics of the one-factor fixed-effects ANCOVA model. However, before we begin an extended discussion of these characteristics, consider the following example. Imagine a situation where a statistics professor is scheduled to teach two sections of introductory statistics. The professor, being a cunning researcher, decides to perform a little experiment where Section 1 is taught using the traditional lecture method and Section 2 is taught using extensive graphics, computer simulations, and computer-assisted and calculator-based instruction, using mostly small-group and self-directed instruction. The professor is interested in which section performs better.

Before the study/course begins, the professor thinks about whether there are other variables related to statistics performance that should somehow be taken into account. An obvious one is ability in quantitative methods. From previous research and experience, the professor knows that ability in quantitative methods is highly correlated with performance in statistics and decides to give a measure of quantitative ability in the first class and use that as a covariate in the analysis. A **covariate** (i.e., quantitative ability) is defined as a source of variation not controlled for in the design of the experiment, but that the researcher believes to affect the dependent variable (i.e., course performance). The covariate is used to statistically adjust the dependent variable. For instance, if Section 1 has higher quantitative ability than Section 2, it would be wise to take this into account in the analysis. Otherwise Secction 1 might outperform Section 2 due to their higher quantitative ability rather than due to the method of instruction. This is precisely the point of the analysis of covariance. Some of the more typical examples of covariates in education and the behavioral sciences are pretest (where the dependent variable is the posttest), prior achievement, weight, IQ, aptitude, age, experience, previous training, motivation, and grade point average.

Let us now begin with the characteristics of the ANCOVA model. The first set of characteristics is obvious because they carry over from the one-factor fixed-effects ANOVA model. There is a single independent variable or factor with two or more levels. The levels are fixed by the researcher rather than randomly sampled from a population of levels. Once the levels of the independent variable are selected, subjects or individuals are somehow assigned to these levels or groups. Each subject is then exposed to only one level of the independent variable (although ANCOVA with repeated measures is also possible, but is not discussed here). In our example, method of statistics instruction is the independent variable with two levels or groups, the traditional lecture method and the cutting-edge method.

Situations where the researcher is able to randomly assign subjects to groups are known as **true experimental designs**. Situations where the researcher does not have control over which level a subject is assigned to are known as **quasi-experimental designs**. This lack of control may occur for one of two reasons. First, the groups may be already in place when the researcher arrives on the scene; these groups are referred to as **intact groups** (e.g., based on classroom assignments). Second, it may be theoretically impossible for the researcher to assign subjects to groups (e.g., income level). Thus a distinction is typically made about whether or not the researcher can control the assignment of subjects to groups. The distinction about the use of ANCOVA in true and quasi-experimental situations has been quite controversial over the past few decades; we look at it in more detail later in this chapter. For further information on true experimental designs and quasi-experimental designs, see Campbell and Stanley (1966) and Cook and Campbell (1979). In our example again, if assignment of students to sections is random, then we have a true experimental design. If assignment of students to sections is not random, perhaps already assigned at registration, then we have a quasi-experimental design.

One final item in the first set of characteristics has to do with the measurement scales of the variables. In the analysis of covariance, it is assumed the dependent variable is measured at the interval level or better. If the dependent variable is measured at the ordinal level, then alternative nonparametric procedures described toward the end of this chapter should be considered. It is also assumed the covariate is measured at the interval level or better. No assumption is made about the independent variable as it is a grouping or categorical variable.

The remaining characteristics have to do with the uniqueness of the analysis of covariance. As already mentioned, the analysis of covariance is a form of statistical control developed specifically to reduce unexplained error variation. The covariate (sometimes known as a concomitant variable) is a source of variation not controlled for in the design of the experiment, but believed to affect the dependent variable. In a factorial design, for example, a factor could be included to reduce error variation. However, this represents an experimental design form of control as it is included as a factor in the model.

In ANCOVA, the dependent variable is adjusted statistically to remove the effects of the portion of uncontrolled variation represented by the covariate. The group means on the dependent variable are adjusted so that they represent groups with the same means on the covariate. The analysis of covariance is essentially an analysis of variance on these "adjusted means." This needs further explanation. Consider first the situation of the true experiment involving randomization where there are two groups. Here it is unlikely that the two groups will be statistically different on any variable related to the dependent measure. The two groups should have roughly equivalent means on the covariate, although 5% of the time we would expect a significant difference due to chance at $\alpha = .05$. Thus we typically do not see preexisting differences between the two groups on the covariate in a true experiment. However, the relationship between the covariate and the dependent variable is important. If these variables are linearly related (discussed later), then the use of the covariate in the analysis will serve to reduce the unexplained variation in the model. The greater the magnitude of the correlation, the more uncontrolled variation can be removed, as shown by a reduction in mean square error.

Consider next the situation of the quasi-experiment, that is, without randomization. Here it is more likely that the two groups will be statistically different on the covariate as well as other variables related to the dependent variable. Thus there may indeed be a preexisting difference between the two groups on the covariate. If the groups do differ on the covariate and we ignore it by conducting an ANOVA, our ability to get a precise estimate of the group effects will be reduced as the group effect will be confounded with the effect of the covariate. For instance, if a significant group difference is revealed by the ANOVA, we would not be certain if there was truly a group effect or whether the effect was due to preexisting differences on the covariate, or some combination of group and covariate effects. The analysis of covariance takes the covariate mean difference into account as well as the linear relationship between the covariate and the dependent variable.

Thus, the covariate is used to (a) reduce error variation, (b) take any preexisting group mean difference on the covariate into account, (c) take into account the relationship between the covariate and the dependent variable, and (d) yield a more precise and less biased estimate of the group effects. If error variation is reduced, the analysis of covariance will be more powerful and require smaller sample sizes than the analysis of variance (Keppel & Wickens, 2004; Mickey, Dunn, & Clark, 2004; Myers & Well, 1995). If error variation is not reduced, the analysis of variance is more powerful. A more extensive comparison of ANOVA versus ANCOVA is given in chapter 6. In addition, as shown later, one degree of freedom is lost from the error term for each covariate used. This results in a larger critical value for the F test and makes it a bit more difficult to find a significant F test statistic. This is the major cost of using a covariate. If the covariate is not effective in reducing error variance, then we are worse off than if we had ignored the covariate. Importance references on ANCOVA include Elashoff (1969) and Huitema (1980).

4.2   THE LAYOUT OF THE DATA

Before we get into the theory and subsequent analysis of the data, let us examine the layout of the data. We designate each observation on the dependent or criterion variable as Y_{ij}, where the j subscript tells us what group or level the observation belongs to and the i subscript tells us the observation or identification number within that group. The first subscript ranges over $i = 1, ..., n_j$ and the second subscript ranges over $j = 1, ..., J$. Thus there are J levels of the independent variable and n_j subjects in group j. We designate each observation on the covariate as X_{ij}, where the subscripts have the same meaning.

The layout of the data is shown in Table 4.1. Here we see that each pair of columns represents the observations for a particular group or level of the independent variable on the dependent variable and the covariate. At the bottom of the pair of columns for each group j are the group means $(\overline{Y}_{.j}, \overline{X}_{.j})$. Although the table shows there are n observations for each group, we need not make such a restriction, as this was done only for purposes of simplifying the table.

4.3   THE ANCOVA MODEL

The analysis of covariance model is a form of the general linear model much like the models shown in the last few chapters of this text. The one-factor ANCOVA fixed-effects model can be written in terms of population parameters as

$$Y_{ij} = \mu_Y + \alpha_j + \beta_w(X_{ij} - \mu_X) + \varepsilon_{ij}$$

where Y_{ij} is the observed score on the dependent variable for individual i in group j, μ_Y is the overall or grand population mean (i.e., regardless of group designation) for the dependent variable Y, α_j is the group effect for group j, β_w is the within groups regression slope from the regression of Y on X, X_{ij} is the observed score on the covariate for individual i in group j, μ_X is the overall or grand population mean (i.e., regardless of group designation) for the covariate X, and ε_{ij} is the random residual error for individual i in group j. The residual error can be due to individual differences, measurement error, and/or other factors not under investigation. As you would expect, the least squares sample estimators for each of these parameters are as follows: $\overline{Y}$ for μ_Y, $\overline{X}$ for μ_X, a_j for α_j, b_w for β_w, and e_{ij} for ε_{ij}. The sum of the group effects is equal to

TABLE 4.1
Layout for the One-Factor ANCOVA

Level of the Independent Variable						
1		*2*		...	*J*	
Y_{11}	X_{11}	Y_{12}	X_{12}	...	Y_{1J}	X_{1J}
Y_{21}	X_{21}	Y_{22}	X_{22}	...	Y_{2J}	X_{2J}
...	...	...	...	...	...	...
Y_{n1}	X_{n1}	Y_{n2}	X_{n2}	...	Y_{nJ}	X_{nJ}
$\overline{Y}_{.1}$	$\overline{X}_{.1}$	$\overline{Y}_{.2}$	$\overline{X}_{.2}$	...	$\overline{Y}_{.J}$	$\overline{X}_{.J}$

zero. This implies that if there are any nonzero group effects, then the group effects will balance out around zero with some positive and some negative effects.

The hypotheses consist of testing the equality of the adjusted means (defined by $\mu'_{.j}$ and discussed later) as follows:

$$H_0: \mu'_{.1} = \mu'_{.2} = \ldots = \mu'_{.J}$$

$$H_1: \text{not all the } \mu'_{.j} \text{ are equal}$$

4.4 THE ANCOVA SUMMARY TABLE

We turn our attention to the familiar summary table, this time for the one-factor ANCOVA model. A general form of the summary table is shown in Table 4.2. Under the first column you see the following sources: adjusted between groups variation, adjusted within groups variation, variation due to the covariate, and total variation. The second column notes the sums of squares terms for each source (i.e., $SS_{\text{betw(adj)}}$, $SS_{\text{with(adj)}}$, SS_{cov}, and SS_{total}).

The third column gives the degrees of freedom for each source. For the adjusted between groups source, because there are J group means, the $df_{\text{betw(adj)}}$ is $J - 1$, the same as in the one-factor ANOVA model. For the adjusted within groups source, because there are N total observations and J groups, we would expect the degrees of freedom within to be $N - J$, because this was the case in the one-factor ANOVA model. However, as we pointed out in the characteristics of the ANCOVA model, a price is paid for the use of a covariate. There is a price here because we lose one degree of freedom from the within term for the covariate, so that $df_{\text{with(adj)}}$ is $N - J - 1$. For multiple covariates, we lose one degree of freedom for each covariate used (see later discussion). This degree of freedom has gone to the covariate source such that df_{cov} is equal to 1. Finally, for the total source, because there are N total observations, the df_{total} is the usual $N - 1$.

The fourth column gives the mean squares for each source of variation. As always, the mean squares represent the sum of squares weighted by their respective degrees of freedom. Thus $MS_{\text{betw(adj)}} = SS_{\text{betw(adj)}}/(J - 1)$, $MS_{\text{with(adj)}} = SS_{\text{with(adj)}}/(N - J - 1)$, and $MS_{\text{cov}} = SS_{\text{cov}}/1$. The last column in the ANCOVA summary table is for the F values. Thus for the one-factor fixed-effects ANCOVA model, the F value to test for differences between the adjusted means is computed as $F = MS_{\text{betw(adj)}}/ MS_{\text{with(adj)}}$. A second F value, which is obviously not included in the ANOVA model, is the test of the covariate. To be specific, this F is actually testing the

TABLE 4.2
One-Factor Analysis of Covariance Summary Table

Source	SS	df	MS	F
Adjusted between	$SS_{\text{betw(adj)}}$	$J - 1$	$MS_{\text{betw(adj)}}$	$MS_{\text{betw(adj)}}/MS_{\text{with(adj)}}$
Adjusted within	$SS_{\text{with(adj)}}$	$N - J - 1$	$MS_{\text{with(adj)}}$	
Covariate	SS_{cov}	1	MS_{cov}	$MS_{\text{cov}}/MS_{\text{with(adj)}}$
Total	SS_{total}	$N - 1$		

hypothesis of H_0: $\beta_w = 0$. If the slope is equal to zero, then the covariate and the dependent variable are uncorrelated. This F value is equal to $F = MS_{cov}/MS_{with(adj)}$.

The critical value for the test of difference between the adjusted means is $_\alpha F_{J-1,N-J-1}$. The critical value for the test of the covariate is $_\alpha F_{1,N-J-1}$. The null hypotheses in each case are rejected if the F test statistic exceeds the F critical value. The critical values are found in the F table of Appendix Table 4.

If the F test statistic for the adjusted means exceeds the F critical value, and there are more than two groups, then it is not clear exactly how the means are different. In this case, some multiple comparison procedure may be used to determine where the mean differences are (see later discussion). For the test of the covariate (or within groups regression slope), we hope that the F test statistic does exceed the F critical value. Otherwise the power and precision of the test of the adjusted means in ANCOVA will be lower than the test of the unadjusted means in ANOVA because the covariate is not significantly related to the dependent variable.

4.5   PARTITIONING THE SUMS OF SQUARES

As seen already, the partitioning of the sums of squares is the backbone of all general linear models, whether we are dealing with an ANOVA model, a linear regression model, or an ANCOVA model. As always, the first step is to partition the total variation into its relevant sources of variation. As we have learned from the previous section, the sources of variation for the one-factor ANCOVA model are adjusted between groups, adjusted within groups, and the covariate. This is written as

$$SS_{total} = SS_{betw(adj)} + SS_{with(adj)} + SS_{cov}$$

From this point the statistical software is used to handle the remaining computations.

4.6   ADJUSTED MEANS AND RELATED PROCEDURES

In this section we formally define the adjusted mean, briefly examine several multiple comparison procedures, and consider power, confidence intervals, and effect size measures.

We have spent considerable time already discussing the analysis of the adjusted means. Now it is time to define them. The adjusted mean is denoted by $\overline{Y}'_j$ and estimated by

$$\overline{Y}'_j = \overline{Y}_j - b_w(\overline{X}_j - \overline{X}_{..})$$

Here it should be noted that the adjusted mean is equal to the unadjusted mean minus the adjustment. The adjustment is a function of the within groups regression slope and the difference between the group mean and the overall mean for the covariate. No adjustment will be made if (a) $b_w = 0$ (i.e., X and Y are unrelated), or (b) the group means on the covariate are all the same. Thus, in both of these cases $\overline{Y}_j = \overline{Y}'_j$. In all other cases, at least some adjustment will be made for some of the group means (although not necessarily for all of the group means).

You may be wondering how this adjustment actually works. Let us assume the covariate and the dependent variable are positively correlated such that b_w is also positive, and there are two treatment groups with equal n's that differ on the covariate. If Group 1 has a higher mean on both the covariate and the dependent variable than Group 2, then the adjusted means will be closer together than the unadjusted means. For our first example, if $b_w = 1$, $\overline{Y}_{.1} = 50$, $\overline{Y}_{.2} = 30$, $\overline{X}_{.1} = 20$, $\overline{X}_{.2} = 10$, $\overline{X}_{..} = 15$, then the adjusted means are equal to the following:

$$\overline{Y}'_{.1} = \overline{Y}_{.1} - b_w(\overline{X}_{.1} - \overline{X}_{..}) = 50 - 1(20 - 15) = 45$$

$$\overline{Y}'_{.2} = \overline{Y}_{.2} - b_w(\overline{X}_{.2} - \overline{X}_{..}) = 30 - 1(10 - 15) = 35$$

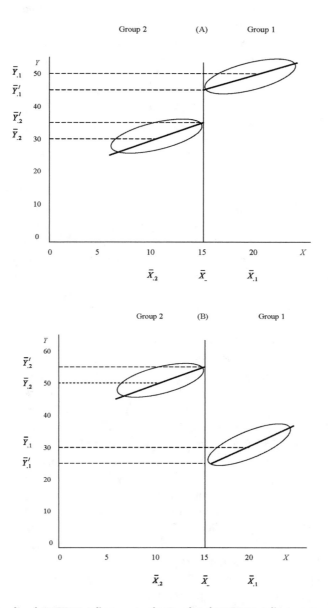

FIG. 4.1   (a) Graphs of ANCOVA Adjustments. (b) Graphs of ANCOVA Adjustments.

This is shown graphically in Fig. 4.1(a). In looking at the covariate X, we see that Group 1 has a higher mean ($\overline{X}_{.1} = 20$) than Group 2 ($\overline{X}_{.2} = 10$) by 10 points. The vertical line represents the overall mean on the covariate ($\overline{X}_{..} = 15$). In looking at the dependent variable Y, we see that Group 1 has a higher mean ($\overline{Y}_{.1} = 50$) than Group 2 ($\overline{Y}_{.2} = 30$) by 20 points. The diagonal lines represent the regression lines for each group with $b_w = 1.0$. The points at which the regression lines intersect (or cross) the vertical line ($\overline{X}_{..} = 15$) represent on the Y scale the values of the adjusted means. Here we see that the adjusted mean for Group 1 ($\overline{Y}'_{.1} = 45$) is larger than the adjusted mean for Group 2 ($\overline{Y}'_{.2} = 35$) by 10 points. Thus, because of the preexisting difference on the covariate, the adjusted means here are somewhat closer together than the unadjusted means (10 points vs. 20 points, respectively).

If Group 1 has a higher mean on the covariate and a lower mean on the dependent variable than Group 2, then the adjusted means will be further apart than the unadjusted means. As a second example, if $b_w = 1$, $\overline{Y}_{.1} = 30$, $\overline{Y}_{.2} = 50$, $\overline{X}_{.1} = 20$, $\overline{X}_{.2} = 10$, $\overline{X}_{..} = 15$, then the adjusted means are

$$\overline{Y}'_{.1} = \overline{Y}_{.1} - b_w(\overline{X}_{.1} - \overline{X}_{..}) = 30 - 1(20 - 15) = 25$$
$$\overline{Y}'_{.2} = \overline{Y}_{.2} - b_w(\overline{X}_{.2} - \overline{X}_{..}) = 50 - 1(10 - 15) = 55$$

This is shown graphically in Fig. 4.1(b) where the unadjusted means differ by 20 points and the adjusted means differ by 30 points. There are obviously other possible situations.

Let us briefly examine multiple comparison procedures (MCPs) for use in the analysis of covariance situation. Most of the procedures described in chapter 2 can be adapted for use with a covariate, although a few procedures are not mentioned here as critical values do not currently exist. The adapted procedures involve a different form of the standard error of a contrast. The contrasts are formed based on adjusted means, of course. Let me briefly outline just a few procedures. Each of the test statistics has as its numerator the contrast ψ', such as $\psi' = \overline{Y}'_{.1} - \overline{Y}'_{.2}$. The standard errors do differ somewhat depending on the specific MCP.

The example procedures briefly described here are easily translated from the ANOVA into the ANCOVA context. Dunn's (or Bonferroni) method is appropriate to use for a small number of planned contrasts (still utilizing the critical values from Appendix Table 8). Scheffe's procedure can be used for unplanned complex contrasts with equal group variances (again based on the F table in Appendix Table 4). Tukey's HSD test is most desirous for unplanned pairwise contrasts with equal n's per group. There has been some discussion in the literature about the appropriateness of this test in ANCOVA. Most statisticians currently argue that the procedure is only appropriate when the covariate is fixed, when in fact it is almost always random. As a result the Bryant-Paulson (1976) generalization of the Tukey procedure has been developed for the random covariate case. The test statistic is compared to the critical value $_\alpha q_{X, df(error), J}$ taken from Appendix Table 11, where X is the number of covariates. If the group sizes are unequal, the harmonic mean can be used in ANCOVA (Huitema, 1980). A generalization of the Tukey-Bryant procedure for unequal n's ANCOVA was developed by Hochberg and Varon-Salomon (1984) (also see Hochberg & Tamhane, 1987; Miller, 1997).

Finally a comment about power, confidence intervals, and effect size measures for the one-factor ANCOVA model. In short, these procedures work the same as in the one factor-ANOVA model, except that they are based on adjusted means (Cohen, 1988). Nothing more than that.

4.7 ASSUMPTIONS AND VIOLATION OF ASSUMPTIONS

The introduction of a covariate requires several assumptions beyond the traditional ANOVA assumptions. For the familiar assumptions, the discussion is kept to a minimum as these have already been described in chapters 1 and 3. The new assumptions are as follows: (a) linearity, (b) independence of the covariate and the independent variable, (c) the covariate is measured without error, and (d) homogeneity of the regression slopes. In this section, we describe each assumption, how each assumption can be evaluated, the effects that a violation of the assumption might have, and how one might deal with a serious violation.

4.7.1 Independence

As in previous ANOVA models, in ANCOVA it is assumed that each sample is randomly drawn from their respective populations and observations are independent of one another (both within and across samples). The use of independent random samples is also crucial in the analysis of covariance. The F ratio is very sensitive to violation of the independence assumption in terms of increased likelihood of a Type I and/or Type II error. A violation of the independence assumption may affect the standard errors of the sample adjusted means and thus influence any inferences made about those means. One purpose of random assignment of individuals to groups is to achieve independence. If each individual is only observed once and individuals are randomly assigned to groups, then the independence assumption is usually met. Random assignment is important for valid interpretation of the F test and of multiple comparison procedures. Otherwise, the F test and adjusted means may be biased.

The simplest procedure for assessing independence is to examine residual plots by group. If the independence assumption is satisfied, then the residuals should fall into a random display of points. If the assumption is violated, then the residuals will fall into some type of cyclical pattern. As discussed in chapter 1, the Durbin-Watson statistic (1950, 1951, 1971) can be used to test for autocorrelation. Violations of the independence assumption generally occur in the three situations we mentioned in chapter 1: time series data, observations within blocks, or replication. For severe violations of the independence assumption, there is no simple "fix" such as the use of transformations or nonparametric tests (see Scariana & Davenport, 1987).

4.7.2 Homogeneity of Variance

The second assumption is that the variances of each population are the same, the homogeneity of variance assumption. A violation of the homogeneity assumption may lead to bias in the SS_{with} term, as well as an increase in the Type I error rate and possibly an increase in the Type II error rate. A summary of Monte Carlo research on ANCOVA assumption violations by Harwell (2003) indicates that the effect of the violation is negligible with equal or nearly equal n's across the groups. There is a more serious problem if the larger n's are associated with the smaller variances (actual $\alpha >$ nominal α, which is a liberal result), or if the larger n's are associated with the larger variances (actual $\alpha <$ nominal α, which is a conservative result).

In a plot of Y versus the covariate X for each group, the variability of the distributions may be examined. Another method for detecting violation of the homogeneity assumption is the use of formal statistical tests, as discussed in chapter 1. Several solutions are available for dealing with a violation of the homogeneity assumption. These include the use of variance stabilizing transformations, or other ANCOVA models that are less sensitive to unequal variances, such as nonparametric ANCOVA procedures (described at the end of this chapter).

4.7.3   Normality

The third assumption is that each of the populations follows the normal distribution. Based on the classic work by Box and Anderson (1962) and Atiqullah (1964), as well as the summarization of modern Monte Carlo work by Harwell (2003), the F test is relatively robust to nonnormal Y distributions, "minimizing the role of a normally distributed X" (Harwell, 2003, p. 62). Thus we need only really be concerned with serious nonnormality.

The following graphical techniques can be used to detect violation of the normality assumption: (a) frequency distributions (such as stem-and-leaf plots, box plots, or histograms), or (b) normal probability plots. There are also several statistical procedures available for the detection of nonnormality (such as the Shapiro-Wilk test, 1965). Transformations can also be used to normalize the data, as previously discussed in chapter 1. In addition, one can use one of the rank ANCOVA procedures previously mentioned.

4.7.4   Linearity

The next assumption holds that the regression of Y on X is linear. If the relationship between X and Y is not linear, the use of the usual ANCOVA procedure is not appropriate, just as linear regression (see chapter 7) would not be appropriate. In ANCOVA (and correlation and linear regression), we fit a straight line to the data points. When the relationship is nonlinear, a straight line will not fit the data particularly well. In addition, the magnitude of the linear correlation will be smaller. If the relationship is not linear, the estimate of the group effects will be biased, and the adjustments made in SS_{with} and SS_{betw} will be smaller.

Violations of the linearity assumption can generally be detected by looking at plots of Y versus X, overall and for each group. Once a serious violation of the linearity assumption has been detected, there are two alternatives that one can use, transformations and nonlinear ANCOVA. Transformations on one or both variables can be used to achieve linearity (Keppel & Wickens, 2004). The second option is to use nonlinear ANCOVA methods as described by Huitema (1980) and Keppel and Wickens (2004).

4.7.5   Fixed Independent Variable

The fifth assumption states that the levels of the independent variable are fixed by the researcher. This results in a fixed-effects model rather than a random-effects model. As in the one-factor ANOVA model, the one-factor ANCOVA model is the same computationally in the fixed- and random-effects cases. The summary of Monte Carlo research by Harwell (2003) indicates that the impact of a random-effect on the F test is minimal.

4.7.6 Independence of the Covariate and the Independent Variable

A condition of the ANCOVA model (although not an assumption) requires that the covariate and the independent variable be independent. That is, the covariate is not influenced by the independent or treatment variable. If the covariate is affected by the treatment itself, then the use of the covariate in the analysis either (a) may remove part of the treatment effect or produce a spurious (inflated) treatment effect, or (b) may alter the covariate scores as a result of the treatment being administered prior to obtaining the covariate data. The obvious solution to this potential problem is to obtain the covariate scores prior to the administration of the treatment. In other words, be alert prior to the study for possible covariate candidates.

Let us consider an example where this condition is obviously violated. A psychologist is interested in which of several hypnosis treatments is most successful in reducing or eliminating cigarette smoking. A group of heavy smokers is randomly assigned to the hypnosis treatments. After the treatments have been completed, the researcher suspects that some patients are more susceptible to hypnosis (i.e., more suggestible) than others. By using suggestibility as a covariate, the researcher would not be able to determine whether group differences were a result of hypnosis treatment, suggestibility, or some combination. Thus, the measurement of suggestibility after the hypnosis treatments have been administered would be ill-advised. An extended discussion of this condition is given in Maxwell and Delaney (1990).

4.7.7 Covariate Measured Without Error

An assumption that we have not yet encountered in this text purports that the covariate is measured without error. This is of special concern in education and the behavioral sciences where variables are often measured with considerable measurement error. In randomized experiments, b_w will be underestimated so that less of the covariate effect is removed from the dependent variable (i.e., the adjustments will be smaller). In addition, the reduction in the unexplained variation will not be as great and the F test will not be as powerful. The F test is generally conservative in terms of Type I error (the actual α will be less than the nominal α). However, the treatment effects will not be biased. In quasi-experimental designs, b_w will also be underestimated with similar effects. However, the treatment effects may be seriously biased. A method by Porter (1967) is suggested for this situation.

There is considerable discussion about the effects of measurement error (e.g., Cohen & Cohen, 1983; Huitema, 1980; Keppel & Wickens, 2004; Lord, 1960, 1967, 1969; Mickey, Dunn, & Clark, 2004; Pedhazur, 1997; Porter, 1967; Reichardt, 1979; Weisberg, 1979). Obvious violations of this assumption can be detected by computing the reliability of the covariate prior to the study or from previous research. This is the minimum that should be done. One may also want to consider the validity of the covariate as well, where validity may be defined as the extent to which an instrument measures what it was intended to measure.

4.7.8 Homogeneity of Regression Slopes

The final assumption puts forth that the slopes of the regression lines are the same for each group. Here we assume that $\beta_1 = \beta_2 = \ldots = \beta_J$. This is an important assumption because it allows us to use b_w, the sample estimator of β_w, as the within groups regression slope. Assuming that the group slopes are parallel allows us to test for group intercept differences, which is all we are really doing when we test for differences among the adjusted means. Without this assumption, groups can differ on both the regression slope and intercept, and β_w cannot legitimately be used. If the slopes differ, then the regression lines interact in some way. As a result the size of the group differences in Y will depend on the value of X. For example, Treatment 1 may be most effective for low values of the covariate, Treatment 2 may be most effective for middle values of the covariate, and Treatment 3 may be most effective for high values of the covariate. Thus, we do not have constant differences between the groups across the values of the covariate. A straightforward interpretation is not possible, which is the same situation in factorial ANOVA when the interaction between factor A and factor B is found to be significant. Thus unequal slopes in ANCOVA represent a type of interaction.

There are other potential outcomes if this assumption is violated. Without homogeneous regression slopes, the use of β_w can yield biased adjusted means and can affect the F test. Earlier simulation studies by Peckham (1968) and Glass, Peckham and Sanders (1972) suggests that for the one-factor fixed-effects model the effects will be minimal. Later analytical research by Rogosa (1980) suggests that there is little effect on the F test for balanced designs with equal variances, but is less robust for mild heterogeneity. However, a summary of modern Monte Carlo work by Harwell (2003) indicates that the effect of slope heterogeneity on the F test is (a) negligible with equal n's and equal covariate means (randomized studies), (b) modest with equal n's and unequal covariate means (non-randomized studies), and (c) modest with unequal n's.

A formal statistical procedure is often conducted to test for homogeneity of slopes using statistical software such as SPSS (discussed later in this chapter), although the eyeball method (i.e., see if the slopes look about the same) can be a good starting point. Some alternative tests for equality of slopes when the variances are unequal is provided by Tabatabai and Tan (1985).

Several alternatives are available if the homogeneity of slopes assumption is violated. The first is to use the concomitant variable, not as a covariate, but as a blocking variable. This will work because this assumption is not made for the randomized block design (see chap. 6). A second option, and not a very desirable one, is to analyze each group separately with its own slope or subsets of the groups having equal slopes. A third possibility is to use interaction terms between the covariate and the independent variable and conduct a regression analysis (see Agresti & Finlay, 1986). A fourth option is to use the Johnson-Neyman (1936) technique, whose purpose is to determine the values of X that are related to significant group differences on Y. This procedure is beyond the scope of this text, and the interested reader is referred to Huitema (1980) or Wilcox (1987). A fifth option is use more modern robust methods (e.g., Maxwell & Delaney, 1990; Wilcox, 2003).

A summary of the ANCOVA assumptions is presented in Table 4.3.

4.8   AN EXAMPLE

Consider the following illustration of what we have covered in this chapter. Our dependent variable is the score on a statistics quiz (with a maximum possible score of 6), the covariate is the score on an aptitude test for statistics taken at the beginning of the course (with a maximum possible score of 10), and the independent variable is the section of statistics taken (where Group

TABLE 4.3

Assumptions and Effects of Violations—One-Factor ANCOVA

Assumption	Effect of Assumption Violation
1. Independence	Increased likelihood of a Type I and/or Type II error in F; affects standard errors of means and inferences about those means.
2. Homogeneity of variance	Bias in SS_{with}; increased likelihood of a Type I and/or Type II error; negligible effect with equal or nearly equal n's; otherwise more serious problem if the larger n's are associated with the smaller variances (increased α) or larger variances (decreased α).
3. Normality	F test relatively robust to nonnormal Y, minimizing the role of nonnormal X.
4. Linearity	Reduced magnitude of r_{XY}; straight line will not fit data well; estimate of group effects biased; adjustments made in SS smaller.
5. Fixed-effect	Minimal impact.
6. Independence of covariate and independent variable	May reduce or increase group effects; may alter covariate scores.
7. Covariate measured without error	True experiment: b_w underestimated; adjustments smaller; reduction in unexplained variation smaller; F less powerful; reduced likelihood of Type I error.
	Quasi-experiment: b_w underestimated; adjustments smaller; group effects seriously biased.
8. Homogeneity of slopes	Negligible effect with equal n's in true experiment; modest effect with equal n's in quasi-experiment; modest effect with unequal n's.

1 receives the traditional lecture method and Group 2 receives the modern innovative method). Thus the researcher is interested in whether the method of instruction influences student performance in statistics, controlling for statistics aptitude (assume we have developed a measure that is relatively error-free). Students are randomly assigned to one of the two groups at the beginning of the semester when the measure of statistics aptitude is administered. There are 6 students in each group for a total of 12. The layout of the data is shown in Table 4.4, where we see the data and sample statistics (means, variances, slopes, and correlations).

The results are summarized in the ANCOVA summary table as shown in the top panel of Table 4.5. The ANCOVA test statistics are compared to the critical value $_{.05}F_{1,9} = 5.12$ obtained from Appendix Table 4, using the .05 level of significance. Both test statistics exceed the critical value, so we reject H_0 in each case. We conclude that the quiz score means do differ for the two statistics groups when adjusted for aptitude in statistics, and the slope of the regression of Y on X is significantly different from zero (i.e., the test of the covariate). Just to be complete, the results for the analysis of variance on Y are shown in the bottom panel of Table 4.5. We see that in the analysis of the unadjusted means (i.e., the ANOVA), there is no significant group difference. Thus the adjustment yielded a different statistical result. The covariate also "did its thing" in that a reduction in MS_{with} resulted due to the strong relationship between the covariate and the dependent variable (i.e., $r_{XY} = 0.7203$ overall).

TABLE 4.4
Data and Summary Statistics for the Statistics Instruction Example

Statistic	Group 1		Group 2		Overall	
	Quiz (Y)	Aptitude (X)	Quiz (Y)	Aptitude (X)	Quiz (Y)	Aptitude (X)
	1	4	1	1		
	2	3	2	3		
	3	5	4	2		
	4	6	5	4		
	5	7	6	5		
	6	9	6	7		
Means	3.5000	5.6667	4.0000	3.6667	3.7500	4.6667
Variances	3.5000	4.6667	4.4000	4.6667	3.6591	5.3333
b_{YX}	0.8143		0.8143		0.5966	
r_{XY}	0.9403		0.8386		0.7203	
Adjusted means	2.6857		4.8143			

TABLE 4.5
One-Factor ANCOVA and ANOVA Summary Tables—Statistics Instruction Example

Source	SS	df	MS	F
ANCOVA				
Adjusted between	10.8127	1	10.8127	11.3734*
Adjusted within	8.5560	9	0.9507	
Covariate	20.8813	1	20.8813	21.9641*
Total	40.2500	11		
ANOVA				
Between	0.7500	1	0.7500	0.1899**
Within	39.5000	10	3.9500	
Total	40.2500	11		

* $_{.05}F_{1,9} = 5.12$
** $_{.05}F_{1,10} = 4.96$

Let us next examine the adjusted means, as shown in Table 4.4. Here we see that with the unadjusted means, there is a 0.5000 point difference in favor of Group 2, whereas for the adjusted means there is a 2.1286 point difference in favor of Group 2. In other words, the adjustment in this case resulted in a greater difference between the adjusted means than between the unadjusted means. Since there are only two groups, a multiple comparison procedure is unnecessary (although we consider this in the SPSS section).

4.9   ANCOVA WITHOUT RANDOMIZATION

There is a great deal of discussion and controversy, particularly in education and the behavioral sciences, about the use of the analysis of covariance in situations where randomization is not conducted. **Randomization** is defined as an experiment where individuals are randomly assigned to groups (or cells in a factorial design). In the Campbell and Stanley (1966) system of experimental design, these designs are known as **true experiments**.

In certain situations, randomization either has not occurred or is not possible due to the circumstances. The best example is the situation where there are **intact groups**, which are groups that have been formed prior to the researcher arriving on the scene. Either the researcher chooses not to randomly assign these individuals to groups through a reassignment (e.g., it is just easier to keep the groups in their current form) or the researcher cannot randomly assign them (legally, ethically, or otherwise). When randomization does not occur, the resulting designs are known as **quasi-experimental**. For instance, in classroom research the researcher is almost never able to come into a school district and randomly assign students to groups. Once students are given their classroom assignments at the beginning of the year, that is that. On occasion, the researcher might be able to pull a few students out of several classrooms, randomly assign them to groups, and conduct a true experiment. In general, this is possible only on a very small scale and for short periods of time.

Let me briefly consider the issues here as not all statisticians agree. In true experiments (i.e., with randomization), there is no cause for concern (except for dealing with the statistical assumptions). The analysis of covariance is more powerful and has greater precision for true experiments than for quasi-experiments. So if you have a choice, go with a true experimental situation (which is a big if). In a true experiment, the probability that the groups differ on the covariate or any other concomitant variable is equal to α. That is, the likelihood that the group means will be different on the covariate is small, and thus the adjustment in the group means may be small. The payoff is in the possibility that the error term will be greatly reduced.

In quasi-experiments, there are several possible causes for concern. Although this is the situation where the researcher needs the most help, this is also the situation where less help is available. Here it is more likely that there will be significant differences among the group means on the covariate. Thus the adjustment in the group means can be substantial (assuming that b_w is different from zero). Because there are significant mean differences on the covariate, any of the following may occur: (a) it is likely that the groups may be different on other important characteristics as well, which have not been controlled for either statistically or experimentally; (b) the homogeneity of regression slopes assumption is less likely to be met; (c) adjusting for the covariate may remove part of the treatment effect; (d) equating groups on the covariate may be an extrapolation beyond the range of possible values that occur for a particular group (e.g., see the examples by Lord, 1967, 1969, on trying to equate men and women, or by Ferguson & Takane, 1989, on trying to equate mice and elephants; these groups should not be equated on the covariate because their distributions on the covariate do not overlap); (e) although the slopes may be equal for the range of X's obtained, when extrapolating beyond the range of scores the slopes may not be equal; (f) the standard errors of the adjusted means may increase, making tests of the adjusted means not significant; and (g) there may be differential growth in the groups confounding the results (e.g., adult vs. child groups). Although one should be cautious about the use of ANCOVA in quasi-experiments, this is not to suggest that ANCOVA should never be used in such situations. Just be extra careful and do not go too far in terms of interpreting your results. If at all possible, replicate your study. For further discussion see Huitema (1980), or Porter and Raudenbush (1987).

4.10 MORE COMPLEX ANCOVA MODELS

The one-factor ANCOVA model can be extended to more complex models in much the same way as we expanded the one-factor ANOVA model. Thus one can evaluate ANCOVA designs that involve any of the following characteristics: (a) factorial designs (i.e., having more than one factor); (b) fixed-, random- and mixed-effects designs; (c) repeated measures and split-plot (mixed) designs; (d) hierarchical designs; and (e) randomized block designs. Conceptually there is nothing new for these types of ANCOVA designs, and you should have no trouble getting a statistical package to do such analyses. For further information on these designs see Huitema (1980), Keppel (1982), Kirk (1982), Myers and Well (1995), Page, Braver and MacKinnon (2003), or Keppel and Wickens (2004). One can also utilize multiple covariates in an analysis of covariance design; for further information see Huitema (1980), Kirk (1982), Myers and Well (1995), Page, Braver and MacKinnon (2003), or Keppel and Wickens (2004).

4.11 NONPARAMETRIC ANCOVA PROCEDURES

In situations where the assumptions of normality, homogeneity of variance, and/or linearity have been seriously violated, one alternative is to consider nonparametric ANCOVA procedures. Some rank ANCOVA procedures have been proposed by Quade (1967), Puri and Sen (1969), Conover and Iman (1982), and Rutherford (1992). For a description of such procedures, see these references as well as Huitema (1980), Harwell (2003), or Wilcox (2003).

4.12 SPSS

Finally we consider SPSS for the statistics instruction example, including an APA paragraph of the results. As noted in previous chapters, SPSS needs the data to be in a specific form for the analysis to proceeed, which is different from the layout of the data in Table 4.1. For a one-factor ANCOVA with a single covariate, the dataset must contain three variables or columns, one for the level of the factor or independent variable, one for the covariate, and a third for the dependent variable. Each row still represents one individual, displaying the level of the factor they are a member of, as well as their scores on the covariate and dependent variables.

To conduct an ANCOVA through the GLM module, go to the "Analyze" pulldown, into "General Linear Model," and then into the "Univariate" procedure. Click the dependent variable (e.g., quiz) into the "Dependent Variable" box, click the fixed-effects factor variable (e.g., group) into the "Fixed Factor(s)" box, and click the covariate (e.g., aptitude) into the "Covariate(s)" box. Click on the "Options" button to obtain such information as "Descriptive Statistics" (unadjusted means), "Estimates of effect size," "Observed power," and "Homogeneity tests." While there, move the listings in the "Factor(s) and Factor Interactions:" box into the "Display Means for:" box to generate adjusted means. Also check the box called "Compare Main Effects," then open the pulldown for "Confidence interval adjustment" to chose among the LSD, Bonferroni, or Sidak multiple comparison procedures of the adjusted means. Click on "Continue" to return to the original dialog box.

Notice that the "Post Hoc" option button is not active, thus you are restricted to the three MCPs just mentioned. To obtain a profile plot of adjusted means, click on the "Plots" button, move the factor variable name into the "Horizontal Axis" box, click on "Add" to generate the plot, and finally click on "Continue" to return to the original dialog box. Finally, in order to generate the appropriate sources of variation and results as recommended in this chapter, you need to click on the "Model" button, then select "Type I" from the "Sum of squares" pulldown, and click on "Continue" to go back to the main dialog box. Then click on "OK" to run the analysis.

In order the test the homogeneity of slopes assumption, you will need to rerun the analysis. Keep every screen the same as before, with one exception. Return to the "Model" screen. Click on the "Custom" button to build a custom model to include the interaction between the independent and covariate variables. To do this, under the "Build Terms" pulldown, make sure that "Main effects" is showing. Click first the independent variable, then the covariate into the righthand "Model" box using the arrow. Then change the "Build Terms" pulldown to "Interaction" and click both variables at the same time (e.g., using the shift key) into the righthand "Model" box. There should be three terms in that box, the interaction and two main effects. Then click "Continue" to return to the main screen and "OK" to generate the analysis.

Selected results are shown in the panels of Table 4.6. The top panel shows the ANCOVA summary table for the homogeneity of slopes test. Here the only thing that we care about is the test of the interaction, which we want to be nonsignificant. The middle panel shows the ANCOVA summary table for the main analysis, while the bottom panel displays the unadjusted means, the adjusted means (with confidence intervals), and the results of the Bonferroni test (with confidence intervals). From the summary tables I have again deleted additional sources of variation that I find not to be useful.

Finally we come to an example paragraph of the results for the statistics lab example. From the top panel of Table 4.6, we see that the interaction between the covariate and the independent variable is not significant, thus the homogeneity of slopes assumption has been satisfied. In the middel panel of the table, the slope is significantly different from zero ($F_{\text{aptitude}} = 21.961$, $df = 1,9$, $p = .001$), while the adjusted group effect is significant ($F_{\text{group}} = 11.372$, $df = 1,9$, $p = .008$) with a strong effect size and power (partial $\eta^2_{\text{group}} = .558$, observed power $= .850$). The bottom panel shows that while the unadjusted group mean was larger for the innovative instruction group by only .50, the adjusted mean for that group was larger by 2.128. Thus the use of the covariate resulted in a large significant difference between the instructional groups.

4.13 SUMMARY

In this chapter methods involving the comparison of adjusted group means for a single independent variable were considered. The chapter began with a look at the unique characteristics of the analysis of covariance, including: (a) statistical control through the use of a covariate; (b) the dependent variable means adjusted by the covariate; (c) the covariate used to reduce error variation; (d) the relationship between the covariate and the dependent variable taken into account in the adjustment; and (e) the covariate measured at least at the interval level. The layout of the data was shown, followed by an examination of the ANCOVA model, and the ANCOVA summary table. Next the estimation of the adjusted means was considered along with several different multiple comparison procedures. Some discussion was also devoted to the ANCOVA assumptions, their assessment, and how to deal with assumption violations. We illustrated the

TABLE 4.6
Selected SPSS Results for the Statistics Instruction Example

Homogeneity of Slopes Test

Dependent Variable: quiz

Source	Type I Sum of Squares	df	Mean Square	F	Sig.	Partial Eta Squared	Observed Power[a]
group	.750	1	.750	.701	.427	.081	.115
aptitude	30.943	1	30.943	28.928	.001	.783	.997
group* aptitude	.000	1	.000	.000	1.000	.000	.050
Error	8.557	8	1.070				
Corrected Total	40.250	11					

[a]Computed using alpha = .05

ANCOVA Summary Table

Dependent Variable: quiz

Source	Type I Sum of Squares	df	Mean Square	F	Sig.	Partial Eta Squared	Observed Power[a]
aptitude	20.881	1	20.881	21.961	.001	.709	.986
group	10.812	1	10.812	11.372	.008	.558	.850
Error	8.557	9	.951				
Corrected Total	40.250	11					

[a]Computed using alpha = .05

Descriptive Statistics (unadjusted means)

Dependent Variable: quiz

group	Mean	Std. Deviation	N
1.00	3.5000	1.87083	6
2.00	4.0000	2.09762	6
Total	3.7500	1.91288	12

Estimates (adjusted means)

Dependent Variable: quiz

group	Mean	Std. Error	95% Confidence Interval	
			Lower Bound	Upper Bound
1.00	2.686_3	.423	1.729	3.642
2.00	4.814[a]	.423	3.858	5.771

[a]Covariates appearing in the model are evaluated at the following values: aptitude = 4.6667.

(continued)

TABLE 4.6 (*continued*)
Selected SPSS Results for the Statistics Instruction Example

Pairwise Comparisons

Dependent Variable: quiz

(I) group	(J) group	Mean Difference (I–J)	Std. Error	Sig.[a]	95% Confidence Interval for Difference[a]	
					Lower Bound	Upper Bound
1.00	2.00	−2.129*	.631	.008	−3.556	−.701
2.00	1.00	2.129*	.631	.008	.701	3.556

Based on estimated marginal means

*The mean difference is significant at the .05 level.

[a]Adjustment for multiple comparisons: Bonferroni.

use of the analysis of covariance by looking at an example. Finally, we finished off the chapter by briefly examining (a) some cautions about the use of ANCOVA in situations without randomization; (b) ANCOVA for models having multiple factors and/or multiple covariates; (c) nonparametric ANCOVA procedures; and (d) SPSS. At this point you should have met the following objectives: (a) be able to understand the characteristics and concepts underlying ANCOVA, (b) be able to determine and interpret the results of ANCOVA, including adjusted means and multiple comparison procedures, and (c) be able to understand and evaluate the assumptions of ANCOVA. Chapter 5 goes beyond the fixed-effects models we have discussed thus far and considers random- and mixed-effects models.

PROBLEMS

Conceptual Problems

1. If the correlation between the covariate X and the dependent variable Y differs markedly in the two treatment groups, it seems likely that

   a. the assumption of normality is suspect.

   b. the assumption of parallel regression lines is suspect.

   c. a nonlinear relation exists between X and Y.

   d. the adjusted means for Y differ significantly.

2. If for both the treatment and control groups the correlation between the covariate X and the dependent variable Y is substantial but negative, the error variation for ANCOVA as compared to that for ANOVA is

   a. less.

   b. about the same.

    c.   greater.

    d.   unpredictably different.

3.   An experiment was conducted to compare three different instructional strategies. Fifteen subjects were included in each group. The same test was administered prior to and after the treatments. If both pretest and IQ are used as covariates, what is the degrees of freedom for the error term?

    a.   2

    b.   40

    c.   41

    d.   42

4.   The effects of a training program concerned with educating heart attack patients to the benefits of moderate exercise was examined. A group of recent heart attack patients was randomly divided into two groups; one group received the training program and the other did not. The dependent variable was the amount of time taken to jog three laps, with the weight of the patient after the program used as a covariate. Examination of the data after the study revealed that the covariate means of the two groups differed. Which of the following assumptions is most clearly violated?

    a.   linearity

    b.   homogeneity of regression coefficients

    c.   independence of the treatment and the covariate

    d.   normality

5.   In ANCOVA, the covariate is a variable which should have a

    a.   low positive correlation with the dependent variable.

    b.   high positive correlation with the independent variable.

    c.   high positive correlation with the dependent variable.

    d.   zero correlation with the dependent variable.

6.   In ANCOVA how will the correlation of zero between the covariate and the dependent variable appear?

    a.   unequal group means on the dependent variable.

    b.   unequal group means on the covariate.

    c.   regression of the dependent variable on the covariate with $b = 0$.

    d.   regression of the dependent variable on the covariate with $b = 1$.

7.   Which of the following is not a necessary requirement for using ANCOVA?

    a.   Covariate scores are not affected by the treatment.

    b.   There is a linear relationship between the covariate and the dependent variable.

    c.   The covariate variable is the same measure as the dependent variable.

    d.   Regression slopes for the groups are similar.

8.   Which of the following is the most desirable situation to use ANCOVA?

   a.   The slope of the regression line equals zero.

   b.   The variance of the dependent variable for a specific covariate score is relatively large.

   c.   The correlation between the covariate and the dependent variable is −.95.

   d.   The correlation between the covariate and the dependent variable is .60.

9.   A group of students was randomly assigned to one of three instructional strategies. Data from the study indicated an interaction between slope and treatment group. It seems likely that

   a.   the assumption of normality is suspect.

   b.   the assumption of homogeneity of regression lines is suspect.

   c.   a nonlinear relation exists between X and Y.

   d.   the covariate is not independent of the treatment.

10.   If the mean on the dependent variable GPA (Y) for persons of middle social class (X) is higher than for persons of lower and higher social classes, one would expect that

   a.   the relationship between X and Y is curvilinear.

   b.   the covariate X contains substantial measurement error.

   c.   GPA is not normally distributed.

   d.   social class is not related to GPA.

11.   If both the covariate and the dependent variable are assessed after the treatment has been concluded, and if both are affected by the treatment, the use of ANCOVA for these data would likely result in

   a.   an inflated F ratio for the treatment effect.

   b.   an exaggerated difference in the adjusted means.

   c.   an underestimate of the treatment effect.

   d.   an inflated value of the correlation r_w.

12.   When the covariate correlates +.5 with the dependent variable, I assert that the adjusted MS_{with} from the ANCOVA will be less than the MS_{with} from the ANOVA. Am I correct?

13.   For each of two groups, the correlation between the covariate and the dependent variable is substantial, but negative in direction. I assert that the error variance for ANCOVA, as compared to that for ANOVA, is greater. Am I correct?

14.   In ANCOVA, X is known as a factor. True or false?

15.   A study was conducted to compare 6 types of diets. Twelve subjects were included in each group. Their weights were taken prior to and after treatment. If pre-weight is used as a covariate, what is the degrees of freedom for the error term?

    a.   5

    b.   65

    c.   66

    d.   71

16.   A researcher conducts both a one-factor ANOVA and a one-factor ANCOVA on the same data. In comparing the adjusted group means to the unadjusted group means, they find that for each group, the adjusted mean is equal to the unadjusted mean. I assert that the researcher must have made a computational error. Am I correct?

17.   The correlation between the covariate and the dependent variable is zero. I assert that ANCOVA is still preferred over ANOVA. Am I correct?

18.   If there is a nonlinear relationship between the covariate X and the dependent variable Y, then it is very likely that

    a.   there will be less reduction in SS_{with}.

    b.   the group effects will be biased.

    c.   the correlation between X and Y will be smaller in magnitude.

    d.   all of the above

Computational Problems

1.   Consider the analysis of covariance situation where the dependent variable Y is the posttest of an achievement test and the covariate X is the pretest of the same test. Given the data that follow, where there are three groups, (a) calculate the adjusted Y values assuming that $b_w = 1.00$, and (b) determine what effects the adjustment had on the posttest results.

Group	X	$\overline{X}$	Y	$\overline{Y}$
1	40		120	
	50	50	125	125
	60		130	
2	70		140	
	75	75	150	150
	80		160	
3	90		160	
	100	100	175	175
	110		190	

2.   Below are four independent random samples (different methods of instruction) of paired values of the covariate IQ (X) and the dependent variable essay score (Y). Conduct an analysis of variance on Y, an analysis of covariance on Y using X as a covariate, and compare the results ($\alpha = .05$). Determine the unadjusted and adjusted means.

Group 1		Group 2		Group 3		Group 4	
X	Y	X	Y	X	Y	X	Y
94	14	80	38	92	55	94	24
96	19	84	34	96	53	94	37
98	17	90	43	99	55	98	22
100	38	97	43	101	52	100	43
102	40	97	61	102	35	103	49
105	26	112	63	104	46	104	24
109	41	115	93	107	57	104	41
110	28	118	74	110	55	108	26
111	36	120	76	111	42	113	70
130	66	120	79	118	81	115	63

3. A communication researcher wants to know which of five versions of commercials for a new television show is most effective in terms of viewing likelihood. Each commercial is viewed by 6 students. A one-factor ANCOVA was used to analyze these data where the covariate was amount of television viewed per week. Complete the ANCOVA summary table below ($\alpha = .05$).

Source	SS	df	MS	F	Critical Value and Decision
Between adjusted	96	—	—	—	—
Within adjusted	192	—	—		
Covariate	—	—	—	—	—
Total	328	—			

Interpretive Problem

For the interpretive problem you selected in chapter 1 (using the statistics survey CD dataset), select an appropriate covariate. Use SPSS to run a one-factor ANOVA, a one-factor ANCOVA, and then compare and contrast the results. Which method would you select and why?

5

RANDOM- AND MIXED-EFFECTS ANALYSIS OF VARIANCE MODELS

Chapter Outline

1. The one-factor random-effects model
   Characteristics of the model
   The ANOVA model
   ANOVA summary table
   Assumptions and violation of assumptions
   Multiple comparison procedures
2. The two-factor random-effects model
   Characteristics of the model
   The ANOVA model
   ANOVA summary table
   Assumptions and violation of assumptions
   Multiple comparison procedures
3. The two-factor mixed-effects model
   Characteristics of the model
   The ANOVA model
   ANOVA summary table
   Assumptions and violation of assumptions
   Multiple comparison procedures
4. The one-factor repeated measures design
   Characteristics of the model
   The layout of the data

Key Concepts

1.   Fixed-, random-, and mixed-effects models
2.   Repeated measures models
3.   Compound symmetry/sphericity assumption
4.   Friedman repeated measures test based on ranks
5.   Split-plot or mixed designs (i.e., both between and within subjects factors)

In this chapter we continue our discussion of the analysis of variance (ANOVA) by considering models in which there is a random-effects factor, previously discussed in chapter 1. These models include the one-factor and factorial designs, as well as repeated measures designs. As becomes evident, repeated measures designs are used when there is at least one factor where each individual is exposed to all levels of that factor. This factor is referred to as a **repeated factor**, for obvious reasons. This chapter is most concerned with one- and two-factor random-effects models, the two-factor mixed-effects model, and one- and two-factor repeated measures designs.

It should be noted that effect size measures, power, and confidence intervals can be determined in the same fashion for the models in this chapter as for previously described ANOVA models. The standard effect size measures already described are applicable (i.e., ω^2 and η^2), although the intraclass correlation coefficient, ρ_I, can be utilized for random effects (similarly interpreted). For additional discussion of these issues in the context of this chapter, see Cohen (1988), Fidler and Thompson (2001), Keppel and Wickens (2004), Murphy and Myors (2004), and Wilcox (1996, 2003).

Many of the concepts used in this chapter are the same as those covered in chapters 1 through 4. In addition, the following new concepts are addressed: random- and mixed-effects factors, repeated measures factors, the compound symmetry/sphericity assumption, and mixed designs. Our objectives are that by the end of this chapter, you will be able to (a) understand the characteristics and concepts underlying random- and mixed-effects ANOVA models, (b) determine and interpret the results of random- and mixed-effects ANOVA models, and (c) understand and evaluate the assumptions of random- and mixed-effects ANOVA models.

5.1 THE ONE-FACTOR RANDOM-EFFECTS MODEL

This section describes the distinguishing characteristics of the one-factor random-effects ANOVA model, the linear model, the ANOVA summary table, assumptions and their violation, and multiple comparison procedures.

5.1.1 Characteristics of the Model

The characteristics of the one-factor fixed-effects ANOVA model have already been covered in chapter 1. These characteristics include (a) one factor (or independent variable) with two or more levels, (b) all levels of the factor of interest are included in the design (i.e., a fixed-effects factor), (c) subjects are randomly assigned to one level of the factor, and (d) the dependent variable is measured at least at the interval level. Thus the overall design is a fixed-effects model, where there is one factor and the individuals respond to only one level of the factor. If individuals respond to more than one level of the factor, then this is a repeated measures design, as shown later in this chapter.

The characteristics of the one-factor random-effects ANOVA model are the same with one obvious exception. This has to do with the selection of the levels of the factor. In the fixed-effects case, researchers select all of the levels of interest, because they are only interested in making generalizations (or inferences) about those particular levels. Thus in replications of the design, each replicate would use precisely the same levels. Examples of factors that are typically fixed include SES, gender, specific types of drug treatment, age group, weight, or marital status.

In the random-effects case, researchers randomly select levels from the population of levels, because they are interested in making generalizations (or inferences) about the entire population of levels, not merely those that have been sampled. Thus in replications of the design, each replicate need not have the same levels included. The concept of random selection of factor levels from the population of levels is the same as the random selection of subjects from the population. Here the researcher is making an inference from the sampled levels to the population of levels, instead of making an inference from the sample of individuals to the population of individuals. In a random-effects design then, a random sample of factor levels is selected in the same way as a random sample of individuals is selected.

For instance, a researcher interested in teacher effectiveness may have randomly sampled history teachers (i.e., the independent variable) from the population of history teachers in a particular school district. Generalizations can then be made about other history teachers in that school district not actually sampled. Other examples of factors that are typically random include randomly selected classrooms, types of medication, observers or raters, time (seconds, minutes, hours, days, weeks, etc.), animals, students, or schools. It should be noted that in educational settings, the random selection of schools, classes, teachers, and/or students is not often possible. Here we would need to consider such factors as fixed rather than random effects.

5.1.2 The ANOVA Model

The one-factor ANOVA random-effects model is written in terms of population parameters as

$$Y_{ij} = \mu + a_j + \varepsilon_{ij}$$

where Y_{ij} is the observed score on the dependent variable for individual i in level j of factor A, μ is the overall or grand population mean, a_j is the random effect for level j of factor A, and ε_{ij} is the random residual error for individual i for level j. The residual error can be due to individual differences, measurement error, and/or other factors not under investigation. Note that we use a_j to designate the random effects to differentiate them from α_j in the fixed-effects model.

Because the random-effects model consists of only a sample of the effects from the population, the sum of the sampled effects is not necessarily zero. For instance, we may select a sample having only positive effects (e.g., all very effective teachers). If the entire population of effects were examined, then the sum of these effects would indeed be zero.

For the one-factor random-effects ANOVA model, the hypotheses for testing the effect of factor A are

$$H_0: \sigma_a^2 = 0$$
$$H_1: \sigma_a^2 > 0$$

Recall for the one-factor fixed-effects ANOVA model that the hypotheses for testing the effect of factor A are

$$H_0: \mu_{.1} = \mu_{.2} = ... = \mu_{.J}$$
$$H_1: \text{ not all the } \mu_{.j} \text{ are equal}$$

This reflects the difference in the inferences made in the random- and fixed-effects models. In the fixed-effects case the null hypothesis is about specific means, whereas in the random-effects case the null hypothesis is about variation among the population of means. As becomes evident, the difference in the models is also reflected in the multiple comparison procedures.

5.1.3 ANOVA Summary Table

Here there are very few differences between the one-factor random-effects and one-factor fixed-effects models. The sources of variation are still A (or between), within, and total. The sums of squares, degrees of freedom, mean squares, F test statistic, and critical value are determined in the same way as in the fixed-effects case. Obviously then, the ANOVA summary table looks the same as well. Using the example from chapter 1, assuming the model is now a random-effects model, we again obtain a test statistic $F = 6.8177$, which is significant at the .05 level.

5.1.4   Assumptions and Violation of Assumptions

In chapter 1 we described the assumptions for the one-factor fixed-effects model. The assumptions are nearly the same for the one-factor random-effects model and we need not devote much attention to them here. In short, the assumptions are again concerned with the distribution of the dependent variable scores, specifically that scores are random and independent, coming from normally distributed populations with equal population variances. The effect of assumption violations and how to deal with them have been thoroughly discussed in chapter 1 (although see Wilcox, 1996, 2003, for alternative procedures when variances are unequal).

Additional assumptions must be made for the random-effects model. These assumptions deal with the effects for the levels of the independent variable, the a_j. First, here are a few words about the a_j. The random group effects a_j are computed, in the population, by the following:

$$a_j = \mu_{.j} - \mu_{..}$$

For example, a_3 represents the effect for being a member of Group 3. If the overall mean $\mu_{..}$ is 60 and $\mu_{.3}$ is 100, then the group effect would be

$$a_3 = \mu_{.3} - \mu_{..} = 100 - 60 = 40$$

Thus, the effect for being a member of Group 3 is an increase of 40 points.

The assumptions are that the a_j group effects are randomly and independently sampled from the normally distributed population of group effects, with a population mean of zero and a population variance of σ_a^2. Stated another way, there is a population of group effects out there from which we are taking a random sample. For example, with teacher as the factor of interest, we are interested in examining the effectiveness of teachers. We take a random sample from the population of second-grade teachers. For these teachers we measure their effectiveness in the classroom and generate an effect for each teacher (i.e., the a_j). These effects indicate the extent to which a particular teacher is more or less effective than the population of teachers. Their effects are known as random effects because the teachers are randomly selected. In selecting teachers, each teacher is selected independently of all other teachers to prevent a biased sample.

The effects of the violation of the assumptions about the a_j are the same as with the dependent variable scores. The F test is quite robust to nonnormality of the a_j terms, and unequal variances of the a_j terms. However, the F test is quite sensitive to nonindependence among the a_j terms, with no known solutions. A summary of the assumptions and the effects of their violation for the one-factor random-effects model is presented in Table 5.1.

5.1.5   Multiple Comparison Procedures

Let us think for a moment about the use of multiple comparison procedures for the random-effects model. In general, the researcher is not usually interested in making inferences about just the levels of A that were sampled. Thus, estimation of the a_j terms does not provide us with

TABLE 5.1
Assumptions and Effects of Violations—One-Factor Random-Effects Model

Assumption	Effect of Assumption Violation
1. Independence	Increased likelihood of a Type I and/or Type II error in F; affects standard errors of means and inferences about those means.
2. Homogeneity of variance	Bias in SS_{with}; increased likelihood of a Type I and/or Type II error; small effect with equal or nearly equal n's; otherwise effect decreases as n increases.
3. Normality	Minimal effect with equal or nearly equal n's.

any information about the a_j terms that were not sampled. Also, the a_j terms cannot be summarized by their mean, as they do not necessarily sum to zero for the levels sampled, only for the population of levels.

5.2 THE TWO-FACTOR RANDOM-EFFECTS MODEL

In this section, we describe the distinguishing characteristics of the two-factor random-effects ANOVA model, the linear model, the ANOVA summary table, assumptions of the model and their violation, and multiple comparison procedures.

5.2.1 Characteristics of the Model

The characteristics of the one-factor random-effects ANOVA model have already been covered in this chapter, and of the two-factor fixed-effects model in chapter 3. Here we extend and combine these characteristics to form the two-factor random-effects model. These characteristics include (a) two factors (or independent variables) each with two or more levels, (b) the levels of each of the factors are randomly sampled from the population of levels (i.e., two random-effects factors), (c) subjects are randomly assigned to one combination of the levels of the two factors, and (d) the dependent variable is measured at least at the interval level. Thus the overall design is a random-effects model, with two factors, and the individuals respond to only one combination of the levels of the two factors (not a popular model in education and the behavioral sciences). If individuals respond to more than one combination of the levels of the two factors, then this is a repeated measures design (discussed later in this chapter).

5.2.2 The ANOVA Model

The two-factor ANOVA random-effects model is written in terms of population parameters as

$$Y_{ijk} = \mu + a_j + b_k + (ab)_{jk} + \varepsilon_{ijk}$$

where Y_{ijk} is the observed score on the dependent variable for individual i in level j of factor A and level k of factor B (or in the jk cell), μ is the overall or grand population mean (i.e., regardless of cell designation), a_j is the random effect for level j of factor A (row effect), b_k is the random effect for level k of factor B (column effect), $(ab)_{jk}$ is the interaction random effect for the combination of level j of factor A and level k of factor B, and ε_{ijk} is the random residual error for individual i in cell jk. The residual error can be due to individual differences, measurement error, and/or other factors not under investigation. Note that we use a_j, b_k, and $(ab)_{jk}$ to designate the random effects to differentiate them from the α_j, β_k, and $(\alpha\beta)_{jk}$ in the fixed-effects model. Finally, there is no requirement that the sum of the main or interaction effects is equal to zero as only a sample of these effects are taken from the population of effects.

There are three sets of hypotheses, one for each main effect and one for the interaction effect. The null and alternative hypotheses, respectively, for testing the effect of factor A are

$$H_{01}: \sigma_a^2 = 0$$
$$H_{11}: \sigma_a^2 > 0$$

The hypotheses for testing the effect of factor B are

$$H_{02}: \sigma_b^2 = 0$$
$$H_{12}: \sigma_b^2 > 0$$

Finally, the hypotheses for testing the interaction effect are

$$H_{03}: \sigma_{ab}^2 = 0$$
$$H_{13}: \sigma_{ab}^2 > 0$$

These hypotheses again reflect the difference in the inferences made in the random- and fixed-effects models. In the fixed-effects case the null hypotheses are about means, whereas in the random-effects case the null hypotheses are about variation among the means.

5.2.3   ANOVA Summary Table

Here there are very few differences between the two-factor fixed-effects and random-effects models. The sources of variation are still A, B, AB, within, and total. The sums of squares, degrees of freedom, and mean squares are determined the same as in the fixed-effects case. However, the F test statistics are different, as well as the critical values used. The F test statistics are formed for the test of factor A as

$$F_A = \frac{MS_A}{MS_{AB}}$$

for the test of factor B as

$$F_B = \frac{MS_B}{MS_{AB}}$$

and for the test of the AB interaction as

$$F_{AB} = \frac{MS_{AB}}{MS_{with}}$$

Recall that in the fixed-effects model, the MS_{with} was used as the error term for all three hypotheses. However, in the random-effects model, the MS_{with} is used as the error term only for the test of the interaction. The MS_{AB} is used as the error term for the tests of the main effects. The critical values used are those based on the degrees of freedom for the numerator and denominator of each hypothesis tested. Thus using the example from chapter 3, assuming that the model is now a random-effects model, we obtain as our test statistic for the test of factor A

$$F_A = \frac{MS_A}{MS_{AB}} = \frac{246.1979}{7.2813} = 33.8124$$

for the test of factor B

$$F_B = \frac{MS_B}{MS_{AB}} = \frac{712.5313}{7.2813} = 97.8577$$

and for the test of the AB interaction

$$F_{AB} = \frac{MS_{AB}}{MS_{\text{with}}} = \frac{7.2813}{11.5313} = 0.6314$$

The critical value for the test of factor A is found in the F table of Appendix Table 4 as $_\alpha F_{J-1,(J-1)(K-1)}$, which for the example is $_{.05}F_{3,3} = 9.28$, and is significant at the .05 level. The critical value for the test of factor B is found in the F table as $_\alpha F_{K-1,(J-1)(K-1)}$, which for the example is $_{.05}F_{1,3} = 10.13$, and is significant at the .05 level. The critical value for the test of the interaction is found in the F table as $_\alpha F_{(J-1)(K-1),N-JK}$, which for the example is $_{.05}F_{3,24} = 3.01$, and is not significant at the .05 level. It just so happens for the example data that the results for the random- and fixed-effects models are the same. This will not always be the case.

5.2.4   Assumptions and Violation of Assumptions

Previously we described the assumptions for the one-factor random-effects model. The assumptions are nearly the same for the two-factor random-effects model and we need not devote much attention to them here. As before, the assumptions are concerned with the distribution of the dependent variable scores, and of the random-effects (sampled levels of the independent variables, the a_j, b_k, and their interaction $(ab)_{jk}$). However, there are a few new wrinkles. Little is known about the effect of unequal variances (i.e., heteroscedasticity) or dependence for the random-effects model. For violation of the normality assumption, effects are known to be substantial. A summary of the assumptions and the effects of their violation for the two-factor random-effects model is presented in Table 5.2.

5.2.5   Multiple Comparison Procedures

The story of multiple comparisons for the two-factor random-effects model is the same as that for the one-factor random-effects model. In general, the researcher is not usually interested in making inferences about just the levels of A, B, or AB that were sampled. Thus, estimation of the a_j, b_k, or $(ab)_{jk}$ terms do not provide us with any information about the a_j, b_k, or $(ab)_{jk}$ terms that were not sampled. Also, the a_j, b_k, or $(ab)_{jk}$ terms cannot be summarized by their

TABLE 5.2
Assumptions and Effects of Violations—Two-Factor Random-Effects Model

Assumption	Effect of Assumption Violation
1. Independence	Little is known about the effects of dependence; however, based on the fixed-effects model, we might expect the following: increased likelihood of a Type I and/or Type II error in F; affects standard errors of means and inferences about those means.
2. Homogeneity of variance	Little is known about the effects of heteroscedasticity; however, based on the fixed-effects model, we might expect the following: bias in SS_{with}; increased likelihood of a Type I and/or Type II error; small effect with equal or nearly equal n's; otherwise effect decreases as n increases.
3. Normality	Minimal effect with equal or nearly equal n's; otherwise substantial effects.

means, as they will not necessarily sum to zero for the levels sampled, only for the population of levels.

5.3   THE TWO-FACTOR MIXED-EFFECTS MODEL

This section describes the distinguishing characteristics of the two-factor mixed-effects ANOVA model, the linear model, the ANOVA summary table, assumptions of the model and their violation, and multiple comparison procedures.

5.3.1   Characteristics of the Model

The characteristics of the two-factor random-effects ANOVA model have already been covered in the preceding section, and of the two-factor fixed-effects model in chapter 3. Here we combine these characteristics to form the two-factor mixed-effects model. These characteristics include (a) two factors (or independent variables) each with two or more levels, (b) the levels for one of the factors are randomly sampled from the population of levels (i.e., the random-effects factor) and all of the levels of interest for the second factor are included in the design (i.e., the fixed-effects factor), (c) subjects are randomly selected and assigned to one combination of the levels of the two factors, and (d) the dependent variable is measured at least at the interval level. Thus the overall design is a mixed-effects model, with one fixed-effects factor and one random-effects factor, and individuals respond to only one combination of the levels of the two factors. If individuals respond to more than one combination, then this is a repeated measures design.

5.3.2   The ANOVA Model

There are actually two variations of the two-factor mixed-effects model, one where factor A is fixed and factor B is random, and the other where factor A is random and factor B is fixed. The labeling of a factor as A or B is arbitrary, so we only consider the former variation where A is fixed and B is random. For the latter variation merely switch the labels of the factors. The two-factor ANOVA mixed-effects model is written in terms of population parameters as

$$Y_{ijk} = \mu + \alpha_j + b_k + (\alpha b)_{jk} + \varepsilon_{ijk}$$

where Y_{ijk} is the observed score on the dependent variable for individual i in level j of factor A and level k of factor B (or in the jk cell), μ is the overall or grand population mean (i.e., regardless of cell designation), α_j is the fixed effect for level j of factor A (row effect), b_k is the random effect for level k of factor B (column effect), $(\alpha b)_{jk}$ is the interaction mixed effect for the combination of level j of factor A and level k of factor B, and ε_{ijk} is the random residual error for individual i in cell jk. The residual error can be due to individual differences, measurement error, and/or other factors not under investigation. Note that we use b_k and $(\alpha b)_{jk}$ to designate the random and mixed effects to differentiate them from β_k and $(\alpha\beta)_{jk}$ in the fixed-effects model.

As shown in Fig. 5.1, due to the nature of the mixed-effects model, only some of the columns are randomly selected for inclusion in the design. Each cell of the design will include row (α), column (b), and interaction (αb) effects. With an equal n's model, if we sum these effects for a given column, then the effects will sum to zero. However, if we sum these effects for a given row, then the effects will not sum to zero, as some columns were not sampled.

The null and alternative hypotheses, respectively, for testing the effect of factor A are

$$H_{01}: \mu_{.1.} = \mu_{.2.} = ... = \mu_{.J.}$$
$$H_{11}: \text{not all the } \mu_{.j.} \text{ are equal}$$

The hypotheses for testing the effect of factor B are

$$H_{02}: \sigma_b^2 = 0$$
$$H_{12}: \sigma_b^2 > 0$$

	b_1	b_2	b_3	b_4	b_5	b_6
α_1	■		■			■
α_2	■		■			■
α_3	■		■			■
α_4	■		■			■

FIG. 5.1. Conditions for the two-factor mixed-effects model. Although all four levels of factor A are selected by the researcher (A is fixed), only three of the six levels of factor B are selected (B is random). If the levels of B selected are 1, 3, and 6, then the design will only consist of the shaded cells. In each cell of the design are row, column, and cell effects. If we sum these effects for a given column, then the effects will sum to zero. If we sum these effects for a given row, then the effects will not sum to zero (due to missing cells).

Finally, the hypotheses for testing the interaction effect are

$$H_{03}: \sigma_{\alpha b}^2 = 0$$
$$H_{13}: \sigma_{\alpha b}^2 > 0$$

These hypotheses reflect the difference in the inferences made in the mixed-effects model. Here we see that the hypotheses about the fixed-effect A (the main effect of A) are about means, whereas the hypotheses involving the random-effect B (the main effect of B and the interaction effect AB) are about variation among the means.

5.3.3   ANOVA Summary Table

Here there are very few differences between the two-factor fixed-effects, random-effects, and mixed-effects models. The sources of variation are again A, B, AB, within, and total. The sums of squares, degrees of freedom, and mean squares are determined the same as in the fixed-effects case. However, the F test statistics are different, as well as the critical values used. The F test statistics are formed for the test of factor A, the fixed effect, as

$$F_A = \frac{MS_A}{MS_{AB}}$$

for the test of factor B, the random effect, as

$$F_B = \frac{MS_B}{MS_{with}}$$

and for the test of the AB interaction, the mixed effect, as

$$F_{AB} = \frac{MS_{AB}}{MS_{with}}$$

Recall that in the fixed-effects model, the MS_{with} is used as the error term for all three hypotheses. However, in the random-effects model, the MS_{with} is used as the error term only for the test of the interaction, and the MS_{AB} is used as the error term for the tests of the main effects. Finally, in the mixed-effects model, the MS_{with} is used as the error term for the test of B and the interaction, whereas the MS_{AB} is used as the error term for the test of A. The critical values used are those based on the degrees of freedom for the numerator and denominator of each hypothesis tested.

Thus using the example from chapter 3, assuming the model is now a mixed-effects model, we obtain as our test statistic for the test of factor A

$$F_A = \frac{MS_A}{MS_{AB}} = \frac{246.1979}{7.2813} = 33.8124$$

for the test of factor B

$$F_B = \frac{MS_B}{MS_{with}} = \frac{712.5313}{11.5313} = 61.7911$$

and for the test of the AB interaction

$$F_{AB} = \frac{MS_{AB}}{MS_{with}} = \frac{7.2813}{11.5313} = 0.6314$$

The critical value for the test of factor A is found in the F table as $_\alpha F_{J-1,(J-1)(K-1)}$, which for the example is $_{.05}F_{3,3} = 9.28$, and is significant at the .05 level. The critical value for the test of factor B is found in the F table as $_\alpha F_{K-1,N-JK}$, which for the example is $_{.05}F_{1,24} = 4.26$, and is significant at the .05 level. The critical value for the test of the interaction is found in the F table as $_\alpha F_{(J-1)(K-1),N-JK}$, which for the example is $_{.05}F_{3,24} = 3.01$, and is not significant at the .05 level. It just so happens for the example data that the results for the mixed-, random-, and fixed-effects models are the same. This is not always the case.

5.3.4 Assumptions and Violation of Assumptions

Previously we described the assumptions for the two-factor random-effects model. The assumptions are nearly the same for the two-factor mixed-effects model and we need not devote much attention to them here. As before, the assumptions are concerned with the distribution of the dependent variable scores and of the random effects. However, note that not much is known about the effects of dependence or heteroscedasticity for random effects, although we expect the effects are the same as for the fixed-effects case. A summary of the assumptions and the effects of their violation for the two-factor mixed-effects model are presented in Table 5.3.

5.3.5 Multiple Comparison Procedures

For multiple comparisons of the two-factor mixed-effects model, the researcher is not usually interested in making inferences about just the levels of B or AB that were randomly sampled. Thus, estimation of the b_k or $(\alpha b)_{jk}$ terms does not provide us with any information about the

TABLE 5.3
Assumptions and Effects of Violations—Two-Factor Mixed-Effects Model

Assumption	Effect of Assumption Violation
1. Independence	Little is known about the effects of dependence; however, based on the fixed-effects model, we might expect the following: increased likelihood of a Type I and/or Type II error in F; affects standard errors of means and inferences about those means.
2. Homogeneity of variance	Little is known about the effects of heteroscedasticity; however, based on the fixed-effects model, we might expect the following: bias in SS_{with}; increased likelihood of a Type I and/or Type II error; small effect with equal or nearly equal n's; otherwise effect decreases as n increases.
3. Normality	Minimal effect with equal or nearly equal n's; otherwise substantial effects.

b_k or $(\alpha b)_{jk}$ terms not sampled. Also, the b_k or $(\alpha b)_{jk}$ terms cannot be summarized by their means as they will not necessarily sum to zero for the levels sampled, only for the population of levels. However, inferences about the fixed-factor A can be made in the same way they were made for the two-factor fixed-effects model. We have already used the example data to look at some multiple comparison procedures in chapter 3.

This concludes our discussion of random- and mixed-effects models for the one- and two-factor designs. For three-factor designs see Keppel (1982) or Keppel and Wickens (2004). In the major statistical software, the analysis of random effects can be treated as follows: in SAS PROC GLM, use the RANDOM statement to designate random effects; in SPSS GLM, random effects can also be designated.

5.4 THE ONE-FACTOR REPEATED MEASURES DESIGN

In this section, we describe the distinguishing characteristics of the one-factor repeated measures ANOVA model, the layout of the data, the linear model, assumptions of the model and their violation, the ANOVA summary table, multiple comparison procedures, alternative ANOVA procedures, and an example.

5.4.1 Characteristics of the Model

The characteristics of the one-factor repeated measures ANOVA model are somewhat similar to the one-factor fixed-effects model, yet there are a number of obvious exceptions. The first unique characteristic has to do with the fact that each subject responds to each level of factor A. This is in contrast to the nonrepeated case where each subject is exposed to only one level of factor A. The one-factor repeated measures model is the logical extension to the dependent t test. Although in the dependent t test there are only two levels of the independent variable, in the one-factor repeated measures model two or more levels of the independent variable are utilized.

This design is often referred to as a **within subjects design**, as each subject responds to each level of factor A. Thus subjects serve as their own controls such that individual differences are taken into account. This was not the case in any of the previously discussed models. As a result subjects' scores are not independent across the levels of factor A. Compare this design to the one-factor fixed-effects model where total variation was decomposed into variation due to A and due to the residual. In the one-factor repeated measures design, residual variation is further decomposed into variation due to subjects and variation due to the interaction between A and subjects. The reduction in the residual sum of squares yields a more powerful design and more precision in terms of estimating the effects of A, and thus is more economical in that less subjects are necessary than in previously discussed models (Murphy & Myors, 2004).

The one-factor repeated measures design is also a mixed model. The subjects factor is a random effect, whereas the A factor is almost always a fixed effect. If time is the fixed effect, then the researcher can examine phenomena over time. Finally, the one-factor repeated measures design is similar in some ways to the two-factor mixed-effects design except with one subject per cell. In other words, the one-factor repeated measures design is really a special case of the two-factor mixed-effects design with $n = 1$ per cell. Unequal n's can only happen when subjects miss the administration of one or more levels of factor A.

On the down side, the repeated measures design includes some risk of carry-over effects from one level of A to another because each subject responds to all levels of A. As examples of the carry-over effect, subjects' performance may be altered due to fatigue (decreased performance), practice (increased performance), and sensitization (increased performance) effects. These effects may be minimized by (a) counterbalancing the order of administration of the levels of A so that each subject does not receive the same order of the levels of A (this can also minimize problems with the compound symmetry assumption; see later discussion), (b) allowing some time to pass between the administration of the levels of A, or (c) matching or blocking similar subjects with the assumption of subjects within a block being randomly assigned to a level of A. This last method is a type of randomized block design (see chap. 6).

5.4.2 The Layout of the Data

The layout of the data for the one-factor repeated measures model is shown in Table 5.4. Here we see the columns designated as the levels of factor A and the rows as the subjects. Row, column and overall means are also shown, although the subject means are seldom of any utility (and thus are not reported in research studies). Here you see that the layout of the data looks the same as the two-factor model, although there is only one observation per cell.

5.4.3 The ANOVA Model

The one-factor repeated measures ANOVA model is written in terms of population parameters as

$$Y_{ij} = \mu + \alpha_j + s_i + (s\alpha)_{ij} + \varepsilon_{ij}$$

where Y_{ij} is the observed score on the dependent variable for individual i responding to level j of factor A, μ is the overall or grand population mean, α_j is the fixed effect for level j of factor A, s_i is the random effect for subject i of the subject factor, $(s\alpha)_{ij}$ is the interaction between subject i and level j, and ε_{ij} is the random residual error for individual i in level j. The residual

TABLE 5.4
Layout for the One-Factor Repeated Measures ANOVA

Level of Factor S	Level of Factor A (Repeated Factor)				Row Mean
	1	2	...	J	
1	Y_{11}	Y_{12}	...	Y_{1J}	$\overline{Y}_{1.}$
2	Y_{21}	Y_{22}	...	Y_{2J}	$\overline{Y}_{2.}$
...	...	...	...	...	...
n	Y_{n1}	Y_{n2}	...	Y_{nJ}	$\overline{Y}_{n.}$
Column mean	$\overline{Y}_{.1}$	$\overline{Y}_{.2}$	...	$\overline{Y}_{.J}$	$\overline{Y}_{..}$

error can be due to measurement error, and/or other factors not under investigation. From the model you can see this is similar to the two-factor model with one observation per cell. Also, the fixed effect is denoted by α and the random effect by s; thus we have a mixed-effects model. Finally, for the equal n's model, the effects for α and $s\alpha$ sum to zero for each subject (or row).

The hypotheses for testing the effect of factor A are

$$H_{01}: \mu_{.1} = \mu_{.2} = ... = \mu_{.J}$$
$$H_{11}: \text{ not all the } \mu_{.j} \text{ are equal}$$

The hypotheses are written in terms of means because factor A is a fixed effect.

5.4.4   Assumptions and Violation of Assumptions

Previously we described the assumptions for the two-factor mixed-effects model. The assumptions are nearly the same for the one-factor repeated measures model and are again mainly concerned with the distribution of the dependent variable scores and of the random effects.

A new assumption is known as **compound symmetry** and states that the covariances between the scores of the subjects across the levels of the repeated factor A are constant. In other words, the covariances for all pairs of levels of the fixed factor are the same across the population of random effects (i.e., the subjects). The analysis of variance is not particularly robust to a violation of this assumption. In particular, the assumption is often violated when factor A is time, as the relationship between adjacent levels of A is strongest. If the assumption is violated, three alternative procedures are available. The first is to limit the levels of factor A either to those that meet the assumption, or to two (in which case there would be only one covariance). The second, and more plausible, alternative is to use adjusted F tests. These are reported shortly. The third is to use multivariate analysis of variance, which has no compound symmetry assumption, but is slightly less powerful.

Huynh and Feldt (1970) showed that the compound symmetry assumption is a sufficient but not necessary condition for the validity of the F test. Thus the F test may also be valid under less stringent conditions. The necessary and sufficient condition for the validity of the F test is known as **sphericity**. This assumes that the variance of the difference scores for each pair of factor levels is the same. Further discussion of sphericity is beyond the scope of this text (see Keppel, 1982, Kirk, 1982, or Myers & Well, 1995). A summary of the assumptions and the effects of their violation for the one-factor repeated measures design is presented in Table 5.5.

5.4.5   ANOVA Summary Table

The sources of variation for this model are similar to those for the two-factor model, except that there is no within cell variation. The ANOVA summary table is shown in Table 5.6, where we see the following sources of variation: A, subjects (denoted by S), the SA interaction, and total. The test of subject differences is of no real interest. Quite naturally, we expect there to be variation among the subjects. From the table we see that although three mean square terms can be computed, only one F ratio results for the test of factor A; thus the subjects effect cannot be tested anyway as there is no appropriate error term.

TABLE 5.5
Assumptions and Effects of Violations—One-Factor Repeated Measures Model

Assumption	Effect of Assumption Violation
1. Independence	Little is known about the effects of dependence; however, based on the fixed-effects model, we might expect the following: increased likelihood of a Type I and/or Type II error in F; affects standard errors of means and inferences about those means.
2. Homogeneity of variance	Little is known about the effects of heteroscedasticity; however, based on the fixed-effects model, we might expect the following: bias in SS_{SA}; increased likelihood of a Type I and/or Type II error; small effect with equal or nearly equal n's; otherwise effect decreases as n increases.
3. Normality	Minimal effect with equal or nearly equal n's; otherwise substantial effects.
4. Sphericity	F not particularly robust; consider usual F test, Geisser-Greenhouse conservative F test, and adjusted (Box) F test, if necessary.

TABLE 5.6
One-Factor Repeated Measures ANOVA Summary Table

Source	SS	df	MS	F
A	SS_A	$J - 1$	MS_A	MS_A/MS_{SA}
S	SS_S	$n - 1$	MS_S	
SA	SS_{SA}	$(J - 1)(n - 1)$	MS_{SA}	
Total	SS_{total}	$N - 1$		

Next we need to consider the sums of squares for the one-factor repeated measures model. If we take the total sum of squares and decompose it, we have

$$SS_{total} = SS_A + SS_S + SS_{SA}$$

These three terms can then be computed by statistical software. The degrees of freedom, mean squares, and F ratio are determined as shown in Table 5.6.

As noted earlier in the discussion of assumptions for this model, the F test is not very robust to violation of the compound symmetry assumption. This assumption is often violated in education and the behavioral sciences; consequently, statisticians have spent considerable time studying this problem. Research suggests that the following sequential procedure be used in the test of factor A. First, do the usual F test that is quite liberal in terms of rejecting H_0 too often. If H_0 is not rejected, then stop. If H_0 is rejected, then continue with step 2, which is to use the Geisser-Greenhouse (1958) conservative F test. For the model being considered here, the degrees of freedom for the F critical value are adjusted to be 1 and $n - 1$. If H_0 is rejected, then stop. This would indicate that both the liberal and conservative tests reached the same conclusion to reject H_0. If H_0 is not rejected, then the two tests did not reach the same conclusion, and a further test (a tie-breaker) should be undertaken. Thus in step 3 an adjusted F test is conducted. The adjustment is known as Box's (1954b) correction (usually referred to as the Huynh & Feldt [1970] procedure). Here the numerator degrees of freedom are $(J - 1)\varepsilon$, and the denominator degrees of freedom are $(J - 1)(n - 1)\varepsilon$, where ε is the correction factor (not to be confused with the residual term ε). The correction factor is quite complex and is not shown here (see Keppel & Wickens, 2004, Myers, 1979, Myers & Well, 1995, or Wilcox, 1987). Most major statistical software conducts the Geisser-Greenhouse and Huynh and Feldt tests. The Huynh and Feldt test is recommended due to greater power (Keppel & Wickens, 2004; Myers & Well, 1995); thus when available, you can simply use the Huynh and Feldt procedure rather than the previously recommended sequence.

5.4.6   Multiple Comparison Procedures

If the null hypothesis for the A factor is rejected and there are more than two levels of the factor, then the researcher may be interested in which means or combinations of means are different. This could be assessed, as we have seen in previous chapters, by the use of some multiple comparison procedure (MCP). In general, most of the MCPs outlined in chapter 2 can be used in the one-factor repeated measures model (additional discussion in Keppel & Wickens, 2004, and Mickey, Dunn, & Clark, 2004).

It has been shown that these MCPs are seriously affected by a violation of the compound symmetry assumption. In this situation two alternatives are recommended. The first alternative is, rather than using the same error term for each contrast (i.e., MS_{SA}), to use a separate error term for each contrast tested. Then many of the MCPs previously covered in chapter 2 can be used. This complicates matters considerably (see Keppel, 1982, Keppel & Wickens, 2004, or Kirk, 1982). A second alternative, recommended by Maxwell (1980) and Wilcox (1987), involves the use of multiple dependent t tests where the α level is adjusted much like the Bonferroni procedure. Maxwell concluded that this procedure is better than many of the other MCPs. For other similar procedures, see Hochberg and Tamhane (1987).

5.4.7   Alternative ANOVA Procedures

There are several alternative procedures to the one-factor repeated measures ANOVA model. These include the Friedman (1937) test, as well as others, such as the Agresti and Pendergast (1986) test. The Friedman test, like the Kruskal-Wallis test, is a nonparametric procedure based on ranks. However, the Kruskal-Wallis test cannot be used in a repeated measures model as it assumes that the individual scores are independent. This is obviously not the case in the one-factor repeated measures model where each individual is exposed to all levels of factor A.

Let me outline how the Friedman test is conducted. First, scores are ranked within subject. For instance, if there are $J = 4$ levels of factor A, then each subjects' scores would be ranked from 1 to 4. From this, one can compute a mean ranking for each level of factor A. The null hypothesis essentially becomes a test of whether the mean rankings for each of the levels of A are equal. The test statistic is a χ^2 statistic. In the case of tied ranks, either the available ranks can be averaged, or a correction factor can be used as done with the Kruskal-Wallis test (see chap. 1).

The test statistic is compared to the critical value of $_\alpha\chi^2_{J-1}$ (see Appendix Table 3). The null hypothesis that the mean rankings are the same for the levels of factor A is rejected if the test statistic exceeds the critical value.

You may also recall from the Kruskal-Wallis test the problem with small n's in terms of the test statistic not being precisely a χ^2. The same problem exists with the Friedman test when $J < 6$ and $n < 6$, so I suggest you consult the table of critical values in Marascuilo and McSweeney (1977, Table A-22, p. 521). The Friedman test, like the Kruskal-Wallis test, assumes that the population distributions have the same shape (although not necessarily normal) and variability, and that the dependent measure is continuous. For a discussion of other alternative nonparametric procedures, see Agresti and Pendergast (1986), Myers and Well (1995), and Wilcox (1987, 1996, 2003). For information on more advanced within subjects ANOVA models, see Cotton (1998), Keppel and Wickens (2004), and Myers and Well (1995).

Various multiple comparison procedures (MCPs) can be used for the Friedman test. For the most part these MCPs are analogs to their parametric equivalents. In the case of planned (or a priori) pairwise comparisons, one may use multiple matched-pair Wilcoxon tests (i.e., a form of the Kruskal-Wallis test for two groups) in a Bonferroni form (i.e., taking the number of contrasts into account through an adjustment of the α level). For post hoc comparisons, numerous parametric analogs are available. For additional discussion on MCPs for this model, see Marascuilo and McSweeney (1977).

5.4.8   An Example

Let us consider an example to illustrate the procedures used in this section. The data are shown in Table 5.7 where there are eight subjects, each of whom has been evaluated by four raters on a task of writing assessment. First, let us take a look at the results for the parametric ANOVA model, as shown in Table 5.8. The F test statistic is compared to the usual F test critical value

TABLE 5.7

Data for the Writing Assessment Example—One-Factor Design: Raw Scores
and Rank Scores on the Writing Assessment Task by Subject and Rater

Subject	Rater 1 Raw	Rater 1 Rank	Rater 2 Raw	Rater 2 Rank	Rater 3 Raw	Rater 3 Rank	Rater 4 Raw	Rater 4 Rank
1	3	1	4	2	7	3	8	4
2	6	2	5	1	8	3	9	4
3	3	1	4	2	7	3	9	4
4	3	1	4	2	6	3	8	4
5	1	1	2	2	5	3	10	4
6	2	1	3	2	6	3	10	4
7	2	1	4	2	5	3	9	4
8	2	1	3	2	6	3	10	4

TABLE 5.8
One-Factor Repeated Measures ANOVA Summary Table for the Writing Assessment Example

Source	SS	df	MS	F
Within subjects:				
Rater (A)	198.125	3	66.042	73.477*
Error (SA)	18.875	21	0.899	
Between subjects:				
Error (S)	14.875	7	2.125	
Total	231.875	31		

*$_{.05}F_{3,21} = 3.07$

of $_{.05}F_{3,21} = 3.07$, which is significant. For the Geisser-Greenhouse conservative procedure, the test statistic is compared to the critical value of $_{.05}F_{1,7} = 5.59$, which is also significant. The two procedures both yield a statistically significant result; thus we need not be concerned with a violation of the compound symmetry assumption. As an example MCP, the Bonferroni procedure determined that all pairs of raters are significantly different from one another except for Rater 1 versus Rater 2.

Finally, let us take a look at the Friedman test. The test statistic is $\chi^2 = 22.9500$. This test statistic is compared to the critical value $_{.05}\chi_3^2 = 7.8147$, which is significant. Thus the conclusions for the parametric ANOVA and nonparametric Friedman tests are the same here. This will not always be the case, particularly when ANOVA assumptions are violated.

5.5 THE TWO-FACTOR SPLIT-PLOT OR MIXED DESIGN

In this section, we describe the distinguishing characteristics of the two-factor split-plot or mixed ANOVA design, the layout of the data, the linear model, assumptions and their violation, the ANOVA summary table, multiple comparison procedures, and an example.

5.5.1 Characteristics of the Model

The characteristics of the two-factor split-plot or mixed ANOVA design are a combination of the characteristics of the one-factor repeated measures and the two-factor fixed-effects models. It is unique because there are two factors, only one of which is repeated. For this reason the design is often called a **mixed design**. Thus, one of the factors is a between subjects factor, the other is a within subjects factor, and the result is known as a **split-plot design** (from agricultural research). Each subject then responds to every level of the repeated factor, but to only one level of the nonrepeated factor. Subjects then serve as their own controls for the repeated factor, but not for the nonrepeated factor. The other characteristics carry over from the one-factor repeated measures model and the two-factor model.

5.5.2 The Layout of the Data

The layout of the data for the two-factor split-plot or mixed design is shown in Table 5.9. Here we see the rows designated as the levels of factor A, the between subjects or nonrepeated factor, and the columns as the levels of factor B, the within subjects or repeated factor. Within

TABLE 5.9
Layout for the Two-Factor Split-Plot or Mixed ANOVA

Level of Factor A (Nonrepeated Factor)	Level of Factor B (Repeated Factor)				Row Mean
	1	2	...	K	
1	Y_{111}	Y_{112}	...	Y_{11K}	
	.	.	...	.	
	.	.	...	.	$\overline{Y}_{.1.}$
	.	.	...	.	
	Y_{n11}	Y_{n12}	...	Y_{n1K}	
	$\overline{Y}_{.11}$	$\overline{Y}_{.12}$	...	$\overline{Y}_{.1K}$	
2	Y_{121}	Y_{122}	...	Y_{12K}	
	.	.	...	.	
	.	.	...	.	$\overline{Y}_{.2.}$
	.	.	...	.	
	Y_{n21}	Y_{n22}	...	Y_{n2K}	
	$\overline{Y}_{.21}$	$\overline{Y}_{.22}$	...	$\overline{Y}_{.2K}$	
.	.	.	...	.	.
.	.	.	...	.	.
.	.	.	...	.	.
J	Y_{1J1}	Y_{1J2}	...	Y_{1JK}	
	.	.	...	.	
	.	.	...	.	$\overline{Y}_{.J.}$
	.	.	...	.	
	Y_{nJ1}	Y_{nJ2}	...	Y_{nJK}	
	$\overline{Y}_{.J1}$	$\overline{Y}_{.J2}$	...	$\overline{Y}_{.JK}$	
Column Mean	$\overline{Y}_{..1}$	$\overline{Y}_{..2}$	...	$\overline{Y}_{..K}$	$\overline{Y}_{...}$

Note: Each subject is measured at all levels of factor B, but at only one level of factor A.

each factor level combination or cell are the subjects. Notice that the same subjects appear at all levels of factor B, but only at one level of factor A. Row, column, cell, and overall means are also shown. Here you see that the layout of the data looks the same as the two-factor model.

5.5.3   The ANOVA Model

The two factor split-plot model can be written in terms of population parameters as

$$Y_{ijk} = \mu + \alpha_j + s_{i(j)} + \beta_k + (\alpha\beta)_{jk} + (\beta s)_{ki(j)} + \varepsilon_{ijk}$$

where Y_{ijk} is the observed score on the dependent variable for individual i in level j of factor A and level k of factor B (i.e., the jk cell), μ is the overall or grand population mean (i.e., regardless of cell designation), α_j is the effect for level j of factor A (row effect for the nonrepeated factor), $s_{i(j)}$ is the effect of subject i that is nested within level j of factor A (i.e., $i(j)$ denotes that i is nested within j), β_k is the effect for level k of factor B (column effect for the repeated factor), $(\alpha\beta)_{jk}$ is the interaction effect for the combination of level j of factor A and level k of factor B, $(\beta s)_{ki(j)}$ is the interaction effect for the combination of level k of factor B and subject i that is nested within level j of factor A, and ε_{ijk} is the random residual error for individual i in cell jk.

We use the terminology "subjects are nested within factor A" to indicate that a particular subject s_i is only exposed to one level of factor A, level j. This observation is then denoted in the subjects effect by $s_{i(j)}$ and in the interaction effect by $(\beta s)_{ki(j)}$. This is due to the fact that not all possible combinations of subject with the levels of factor A are included in the model. A more extended discussion of designs with nested factors is given in chapter 6. The residual error can be due to individual differences, measurement error, and/or other factors not under investigation. We assume for now that A and B are fixed-effects factors and that S is a random-effects factor.

It should be mentioned that for the equal n's model, the sum of the row effects, the sum of the column effects, and the sum of the interaction effects are all equal to zero, both across rows and across columns. This implies, for example, that if there are any nonzero row effects, then the row effects will balance out around zero with some positive and some negative effects.

The hypotheses to be tested here are exactly the same as in the nonrepeated two-factor ANOVA model (see chap. 3). If one of the null hypotheses is rejected, then the researcher may want to consider a multiple comparison procedure so as to determine which means or combination of means are significantly different (discussed later in this chapter).

5.5.4   Assumptions and Violation of Assumptions

Previously we described the assumptions for the two-factor models and the one-factor repeated measures model. The assumptions for the two-factor split-plot or mixed design are actually a combination of these two sets of assumptions.

The assumptions can be divided into two sets of assumptions, one for the between subjects factor, and one for the within subjects factor. For the between subjects factor, we have the usual assumptions of population scores being random, independent, and normally distributed with equal variances. For the within subjects factor, the assumption is the already familiar compound symmetry assumption. For this design, the assumption involves the population covariances for all pairs of the levels of the within subjects factor (i.e., k and k') being equal, at each level of the between subjects factor (for all levels j). To deal with this assumption, we look at alternative F tests in the next section. A summary of the assumptions and the effects of their violation for the two-factor split-plot or mixed design are presented in Table 5.10.

5.5.5   ANOVA Summary Table

The ANOVA summary table is shown in Table 5.11, where we see the following sources of variation: A, S, B, AB, BS, and total. The table is divided into within subjects sources and between subjects sources. The between subjects sources are A and S, where S will be used as the error term for the test of factor A. The within subjects sources are B, AB, and BS, where BS will be used as the error term for the test of factor B and of the AB interaction.

TABLE 5.10

Assumptions and Effects of Violations—Two-Factor Split-Plot or Mixed Model

Assumption	Effect of Assumption Violation
1. Independence	Increased likelihood of a Type I and/or Type II error in F; affects standard errors of means and inferences about those means.
2. Homogeneity of variance	Bias in error terms; increased likelihood of a Type I and/or Type II error; small effect with equal or nearly equal n's; otherwise effect decreases as n increases.
3. Normality	Minimal effect with equal or nearly equal n's; otherwise substantial effects.
4. Sphericity	F not particularly robust; consider usual F test, Geisser-Greenhouse conservative F test, and adjusted (Box) F test, if necessary.

TABLE 5.11

Two-Factor Split-Plot or Mixed Model ANOVA Summary Table

Source	SS	df	MS	F
Between subjects:				
A	SS_A	$J - 1$	MS_A	MS_A/MS_S
S	SS_S	$J(n - 1)$	MS_S	
Within subjects:				
B	SS_B	$K - 1$	MS_B	MS_B/MS_{BS}
AB	SS_{AB}	$(J - 1)(K - 1)$	MS_{AB}	MS_{AB}/MS_{BS}
BS	SS_{BS}	$(K - 1)J(n - 1)$	MS_{BS}	
Total	SS_{total}	$N - 1$		

Next we need to consider the sums of squares for the two-factor mixed design. Taking the total sum of squares and decomposing it yields

$$SS_{total} = SS_A + SS_S + SS_B + SS_{AB} + SS_{BS}$$

We leave the computation of these five terms for statistical software. The degrees of freedom, mean squares, and F ratios are computed as shown in Table 5.11.

As the compound symmetry assumption is often violated, we again suggest the following sequential procedure to test for B and for AB. First, do the usual F test, which is quite liberal in terms of rejecting H_0 too often. If H_0 is not rejected, then stop. If H_0 is rejected, then continue with step 2, which is to use the Geisser-Greenhouse (1958) conservative F test. For the model under consideration here, the degrees of freedom for the F critical values are adjusted to be 1 and $J(n-1)$ for the test of B, and $J-1$ and $J(n-1)$ for the test of the AB interaction. There is no conservative test necessary for factor A, the nonrepeated factor. If H_0 is rejected, then stop. This would indicate that both the liberal and conservative tests reached the same conclusion to reject H_0. If H_0 is not rejected, then the two tests did not yield the same conclusion, and an adjusted F test is conducted. The adjustment is known as Box's (1954b) correction (or the Huynh & Feldt [1970] procedure). Most major statistical software conducts the Geisser-Greenhouse and Huynh and Feldt tests.

5.5.6   Multiple Comparison Procedures

Consider the situation where the null hypothesis for any of the three hypotheses is rejected (i.e., for A, B, and/or AB). If there is more than one degree of freedom for any of these hypotheses, then the researcher may be interested in which means or combinations of means are different. This could be assessed again by the use of some multiple comparison procedure (MCP). Thus the procedures outlined in chapter 3 (i.e., main effects, simple and complex interaction contrasts) for the regular two-factor ANOVA model can be adapted to this model.

However, it has been shown that the MCPs involving the repeated factor are seriously affected by a violation of the compound symmetry assumption. In this situation, two alternatives are recommended. The first alternative is, rather than using the same error term for each contrast involving the repeated factor (i.e., MS_B or MS_{AB}), to use a separate error term for each contrast tested. Then many of the MCPs previously covered in chapter 2 can be used. This complicates matters considerably (see Keppel, 1982, Keppel & Wickens, 2004, or Kirk, 1982). The second and simpler alternative is suggested by Shavelson (1988). He recommended that the appropriate error terms be used in MCPs involving the main effects, but for interaction contrasts both error terms be pooled together (this procedure is conservative, yet simpler than the first alternative).

5.5.7   An Example

Consider now an example problem to illustrate the two-factor mixed design. Here we expand on the example presented earlier in this chapter by adding a second factor to the model. The data are shown in Table 5.12 where there are eight subjects, each of whom has been evaluated by four raters on a task of writing assessment. The possible ratings range from 1 (lowest rating) to 10

TABLE 5.12
Data for the Writing Assessment Example—Two-Factor Design: Raw Scores
on the Writing Assessment Task by Instructor and Rater

Factor A (Non-(repeated factor):		Factor B (Repeated factor)			
Instructor	Subject	Rater 1	Rater 2	Rater 3	Rater 4
1	1	3	4	7	8
	2	6	5	8	9
	3	3	4	7	9
	4	3	4	6	8
2	5	1	2	5	10
	6	2	3	6	10
	7	2	4	5	9
	8	2	3	6	10

(highest rating). Factor A represents the instructors of English composition, where the first four subjects are randomly assigned to level 1 of factor A (i.e., instructor 1) and the last four to level 2 of factor A (i.e., instructor 2). Thus factor B (i.e., rater) is repeated and factor A (i.e., instructor) is not repeated. The ANOVA summary table is shown in Table 5.13.

The test statistics are compared to the following usual F test critical values: for A, $_{.05}F_{1,6} = 5.99$, which is not significant; for B, $_{.05}F_{3,18} = 3.16$, which is significant; and for AB, $_{.05}F_{3,18} = 3.16$, which is significant. For the Geisser-Greenhouse conservative procedure, the test statistics are compared to the following critical values: for A no conservative procedure is necessary; for B, $_{.05}F_{1,6} = 5.99$, which is also significant; and for AB, $_{.05}F_{1,6} = 5.99$, which is also significant. The two procedures both yield a statistically significant result for B and for AB; thus we need not be concerned with a violation of the compound symmetry assumption. A profile plot of the interaction is shown in Figure 5.2.

There is a significant AB interaction, so we should follow this up with simple interaction contrasts, each involving only four cell means. As an example of a MCP, consider the contrast

$$\psi' = \frac{(\overline{Y}_{.11} - \overline{Y}_{.21}) - (\overline{Y}_{.14} - \overline{Y}_{.24})}{4} = \frac{(3.7500 - 1.7500) - (8.5000 - 9.7500)}{4} = 0.8125$$

with a standard error of

$$se_{\psi'} = \sqrt{MS_{BS} \left(\frac{\displaystyle\sum_{j=1}^{J} \sum_{k=1}^{K} c_{jk}^2}{n_{jk}} \right)} = \sqrt{0.3472 \frac{(1/16 + 1/16 + 1/16 + 1/16)}{4}} = 0.1473$$

TABLE 5.13
Two-Factor Split-plot ANOVA Summary Table for the Writing Assessment Example

Source	SS	df	MS	F
Within subjects:				
Rater (B)	198.125	3	66.042	190.200*
Instructor x Rater	12.625	3	4.208	12.120*
Error (BS)	6.250	18	0.347	
Between subjects:				
Instructor (A)	6.125	1	6.125	4.200**
Error (S)	8.750	6	1.458	
Total	231.875	31		

$*_{.05}F_{3,18} = 3.16$
$**_{.05}F_{1,6} = 5.99$

Using the Scheffe' procedure we formulate as the test statistic

$$t = \frac{\psi'}{se_{\psi'}} = \frac{0.8125}{0.1473} = 5.5160$$

This is compared with the critical value of

$$\sqrt{(J-1)(K-1)} {}_\alpha F_{(J-1)(K-1),(K-1)J(n-1)} = \sqrt{3({}_{.05}F_{3,18})} = \sqrt{3(3.16)} = 3.0790$$

Thus we may conclude that the tetrad difference between the first and second levels of factor A (instructor) and the first and fourth levels of factor B (rater) is significant. In other words, Rater 1 finds better writing among the students of Instructor 1 than Instructor 2, whereas Rater 4 finds better writing among the students of Instructor 2 than Instructor 1.

Although we have only considered the basic repeated measures designs here, more complex repeated measures designs also exist. For further information see Myers (1979), Keppel (1982), Kirk (1982), Myers and Well (1995), Glass and Hopkins (1996), Cotton (1998), Keppel and Wickens (2004), as well as alternative ANOVA procedures described by Wilcox (2003) and McCulloch (2005). To analyze repeated measures designs in SAS, use the GLM procedure with the REPEATED statement. In SPSS GLM use the repeated measures program.

5.6 SPSS

Finally we consider SPSS for the models presented in this chapter, as well as an APA paragraph of selected results. Note that all of the designs in this chapter are discussed in the SPSS context by Page, Braver, and MacKinnon (2003). To conduct a one-factor random-effects ANOVA, there are only two differences from the one-factor fixed-effects ANOVA. Otherwise, the form of the data and the conduct of the analyses are exactly the same. First, on the GLM main screen click the factor name into the "Random Factor(s)" box rather than the "Fixed Factor(s)" box. Second, on the same screen notice that the "Post hoc" option button is not active.

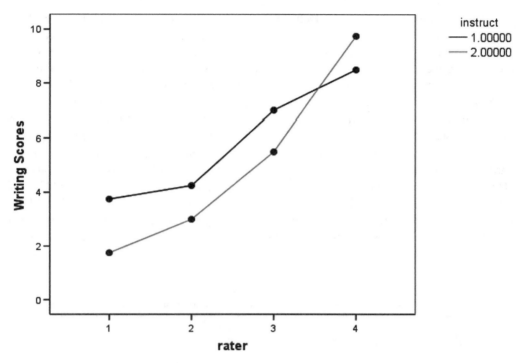

FIG. 5.2. Profile plot for example writing data.

Posthoc MCPs are only available from the "Options" screen, where you go to the "Compare main effects" pulldown to reveal the Tukey LSD, Bonferroni, and Sidak procedures. However, we have already mentioned that MCPs are not generally of interest for this model.

To run a two-factor random-effects ANOVA, there are the same two differences from the two-factor fixed-effects ANOVA. First, on the GLM screen, click both factor names into the "Random Factor(s)" box rather than the "Fixed Factor(s)" box. Second, the same situation exists with MCPs.

To conduct a two-factor mixed-effects ANOVA, there are three differences from the two-factor fixed-effects ANOVA. First, on the GLM screen, click the appropriate factors into the "Random Factor(s)" and "Fixed Factor(s)" boxes. Second, posthoc MCPs for the fixed-effects factor are available from either the "Post Hoc" or "Options" screens, while for the random-effects factor they are only available from the "Options" screen. Third, the F statistics for the main effects of mixed-effects models are incorrect in SPSS as the wrong error terms are used (when using the point-and-click features). As described in Lomax and Surman (2007), you either need to (a) compute the F statistics by hand from the MS values (which are correct), (b) use SPSS syntax to indicate the correct error terms, or (c) use a different software package.

In order to run a one-factor repeated measures ANOVA, the data have to be in the following form. All of the scores for each subject must be in one row of the dataset. For example, if there are four raters who assess each student's essay, there will be variables for each rater (e.g., Rater1 through Rater4; example dataset on the CD).

To conduct a parametric one-factor repeated measures ANOVA through the GLM module, go into the "Repeated Measures" procedure rather than the "Univariate" procedure. A screen will come up called "Repeated Measures Define Factor(s)." First input into the "Within-Subject Factor Name:" box the name you wish to give the repeated factor. This is necessary as there is no single variable representing this factor, only variables representing each level of the factor. In our example there are four levels of rater and thus four variables. Let us call the within subjects factor "rater." Then type in the number of levels of the factor (e.g., 4), click "Add," then click on "Define" to move to the main screen called "Repeated Measures." Here you see a heading called "Within-Subject Variables:" with the newly defined factor rater in parentheses. Inside the box are spaces for each of the levels of that factor with question marks. Move the appropriate variables from the dataset into that box, which then attaches a particular variable with a particular level. The "Plots" box can be used as always, the "Post Hoc" box is not active, and the "Options" box can also be used as before (this is the proper place to obtain posthoc MCPs of Tukey LSD, Bonferroni, and Sidak). These results are shown in the top panel of Table 5.14. To perform Friedman's test, go to the "Analyze" pulldown, into "Nonparametric Tests," and then into "K Related Samples." Click the variables representing the levels of the repeated factor

TABLE 5.14
Selected SPSS Results for the Writing Assessment Example

One-Factor Repeated Measures ANOVA:

Descriptive Statistics

	Mean	Std. Deviation	N
rater1	2.7500000	1.48804762	8
rater2	3.6250000	.91612538	8
rater3	6.2500000	1.03509834	8
rater4	9.1250000	.83452296	8

Tests of Within-Subjects Effects

Measure: MEASURE 1

Source		Type III Sum of Squares	df	Mean Square	F	Sig.	Partial Eta Squared	Observed Power[a]
rater	Sphericity Assumed	198.125	3	66.042	73.477	.000	.913	1.000
	Greenhouse-Geisser	198.125	1.428	138.760	73.477	.000	.913	1.000
	Huynh-Feldt	198.125	1.691	117.163	73.477	.000	.913	1.000
Error(rater)	Sphericity Assumed	18.875	21	.899				
	Greenhouse-Geisser	18.875	9.995	1.888				
	Huynh-Feldt	18.875	11.837	1.595				

[a]Computed using alpha = .05

(*continued*)

TABLE 5.14 (*continued*)
Selected SPSS Results for the Writing Assessment Example

Tests of Between-Subjects Effects

Measure: MEASURE 1
Transformed Variable: Average

Source	Type III Sum of Squares	df	Mean Square
Error	14.875	7	2.125

[a]Computed using alpha = .05

Pairwise Comparisons

Measure: MEASURE 1

(I)rater	(J)rater	Mean Difference (I–J)	Std. Error	Sig.[a]	95% Confidence Interval for Difference[a]	
					Lower Bound	Upper Bound
1	2	−.875	.295	.126	−1.948	.198
	3	−3.500*	.267	.000	−4.472	−2.528
	4	−6.375*	.706	.000	−8.940	−3.810
2	1	.875	.295	.126	−.198	1.948
	3	−2.625*	.263	.000	−3.581	−1.669
	4	−5.500*	.567	.000	−7.561	−3.439
3	1	3.500*	.267	.000	2.528	4.472
	2	2.625*	.263	.000	1.669	3.581
	4	−2.875*	.549	.007	−4.871	−.879
4	1	6.375*	.706	.000	3.810	8.940
	2	5.500*	.567	.000	3.439	7.561
	3	2.875*	.549	.007	.879	4.871

Based on estimated marginal means
*The mean difference is significant at the .05 level.
[a]Adjustment for multiple comparisons: Bonferroni.

Friedman Test:

Ranks

	Mean Rank
rater1	1.13
rater2	1.88
rater3	3.00
rater4	4.00

Test Statistics$_a$

N	8
Chi-Square	22.950
Df	3
Asymp. Sig.	.000

[a]Friedman Test

TABLE 5.14 (*continued*)
Selected SPSS Results for the Writing Assessment Example

Two-factor Split-plot ANOVA:

Descriptive Statistics

	Instruct	Mean	Std. Deviation	N
rater1	1.00000	3.7500000	1.50000000	4
	2.00000	1.7500000	.50000000	4
	Total	2.7500000	1.48804762	8
rater2	1.00000	4.2500000	.50000000	4
	2.00000	3.0000000	.81649658	4
	Total	3.6250000	.91612538	8
rater3	1.00000	7.0000000	.81649658	4
	2.00000	5.5000000	.57735027	4
	Total	6.2500000	1.03509834	8
rater4	1.0000	8.5000000	.57735027	4
	2.00000	9.7500000	.50000000	4
	Total	9.1250000	.83452296	8

Tests of Within-Subjects Effects

Measure: MEASURE 1

Source		Type III Sum of Squares	df	Mean Square	F	Sig.	Partial Eta Squared	Observed Power[a]
rater	Sphericity Assumed	198.125	3	66.042	190.200	.000	.969	1.000
	Greenhouse-Geisser	198.125	2.119	93.515	190.200	.000	.969	1.000
	Huynh-Feldt	198.125	3.000	66.042	190.200	.000	.969	1.000
rater* instruct	Sphericity Assumed	12.625	3	4.208	12.120	.000	.669	.998
	Greenhouse-Geisser	12.625	2.119	5.959	12.120	.001	.669	.983
	Huynh-Feldt	12.625	3.000	4.208	12.120	.000	.669	.998
Error(rater)	Sphericity Assumed	6.250	18	.347				
	Greenhouse-Geisser	6.250	12.712	.492				
	Huynh-Feldt	6.250	18.000	.347				

[a]Computed using alpha = .05

TABLE 5.14

(*Continued*)

Tests of Between-Subjects Effects

Measure: MEASURE 1
Transformed Variable: Average

Source	Type III Sum of Squares	df	Mean Square	F	Sig.	Partial Eta Squared	Observed Power[a]
Instruct	6.125	1	6.125	4.200	.086	.412	.407
Error	8.750	6	1.458				

[a]Computed using alpha = .05

Pairwise Comparisons

Measure: MEASURE 1

(I)rater	(J)rater	Mean Difference (I–J)	Std. Error	Sig.[a]	95% Confidence Interval for Difference[a]	
					Lower Bound	Upper Bound
1	2	−.875	.280	.122	−1.955	.205
	3	−3.500*	.270	.000	−4.543	−2.457
	4	−6.375*	.375	.000	−7.824	−4.926
2	1	.875	.280	.122	−.205	1.955
	3	−2.625*	.280	.000	−3.705	−1.545
	4	−5.500*	.339	.000	−6.808	−4.192
3	1	3.500*	.270	.000	2.457	4.543
	2	2.625*	.280	.000	1.545	3.705
	4	−2.875*	.191	.000	−3.613	−2.137
4	1	6.375*	.375	.000	4.926	7.824
	2	5.500*	.339	.000	4.192	6.808
	3	2.875*	.191	.000	2.137	3.613

Based on estimated marginal means

*The mean difference is significant at the .05 level.

[a]Adjustment for multiple comparisons: Bonferroni.

into the "Test Variables:" box, check Friedman as "Test Type," and click on "OK" to generate the output. These results are shown in the middle panel of Table 5.14.

To conduct the two-factor split-plot ANOVA, the dataset must include variables for each level of the repeated factor (as in the one-factor repeated measures ANOVA), and an additional variable for the nonrepeated factor (example dataset on CD). Return to the "Repeated Measures" program and generate the repeated factor. From the main screen, the one addition is to click the nonrepeated factor variable name into the "Between-Subjects Factor(s):" box. Otherwise, the options work as before. These results are shown in the bottom panel of Table 5.14.

Finally, here is an example paragraph of the results for the two-factor split-plot design (feel free to write similar paragraphs for the other models in this chapter). From Table 5.14 we see that there is a significant main effect for rater (F_{rater} = 190.200, df = 3,18, p = .001), a significant interaction between rater and instructor ($F_{rater \times instructor}$ = 12.120, df = 3,18, p = .001), but the main effect for instructor is not significant. The sphericity assumption was upheld in that the same results were obtained for the usual, Geisser-Greenhouse, and Huynh and Feldt F tests. Effect sizes were rather large for the significant effects (partial η^2_{rater} = .969; partial $\eta^2_{rater \times instructor}$ = .669) with maximum observed power, but less so for the nonsignificant effect (partial $\eta^2_{instructor}$ = .412, power = .407). The raters were quite inconsistent in that Bonferroni MCPs revealed significant differences among all pairs of raters except for rater 1 versus rater 2. From the profile plot in Figure 5.2, we see that while rater 4 found the students of instructor 2 to have better essays, the other raters liked the essays written by the students of instructor 1. It is suggested that a more detailed plan for evaluating essays, including rater training, be inplemented in the future.

5.7 SUMMARY

In this chapter methods involving the comparision of means for random- and mixed-effects models were considered. Five different models were examined; these included the one-factor random-effects model, the two-factor random- and mixed-effects models, the one-factor repeated measures model, and the two-factor split-plot or mixed design. Included for each design were the usual topics of model characteristics, the linear model, assumptions of the model and the effects of their violation, the ANOVA summary table, and multiple comparison procedures. Also included for particular designs was a discussion of the compound symmetry assumption, and alternative ANOVA procedures. At this point you should have met the following objectives: (a) be able to understand the characteristics and concepts underlying random- and mixed-effects ANOVA models, (b) be able to determine and interpret the results of random- and mixed-effects ANOVA models, and (c) be able to understand and evaluate the assumptions of random- and mixed-effects ANOVA models. In chapter 6, we continue our extended tour of the analysis of variance by looking at hierarchical designs that involve a factor nested within another factor, and randomized block designs, which we have very briefly introduced in this chapter.

PROBLEMS

Conceptual Problems

1. When an ANOVA design includes a random factor that is crossed with a fixed factor, the design illustrates which type of model?

    a. fixed

    b. mixed

    c. random

    d. crossed

2. The denominator of the F ratio used to test the interaction in a two-factor ANOVA is MS_{with} in

    a. the fixed-effects model.

    b. the random-effects model.

    c. the mixed-effects model.

    d. All of the above.

3. A course consists of five units, the order of presentation of which is varied. A researcher used a 5×2 ANOVA design with order (five different randomly selected orders) and gender serving as factors. Which ANOVA model is illustrated by this design?

    a. the fixed-effects model

    b. the random-effects model

    c. the mixed-effects model

    d. the nested model

4. If a given set of data were analyzed with both a one-factor fixed-effects ANOVA and a one-factor random-effects ANOVA, the F ratio for the random-effects model will be greater than the F ratio for the fixed-effects model. True or False?

5. A repeated measures design is necessarily an example of the random-effects model. True or False?

6. Suppose researchers A and B perform a two-factor ANOVA on the same data, but that A assumes a fixed-effects model and B assumes a random-effects model. I assert that if A finds the interaction significant at the .05 level, B will also find the interaction significant at the .05 level. Am I correct?

7. I assert that MS_{with} should always be used as the denominator for all F ratios in any two-factor analysis of variance. Am I correct?

8. I assert that in a one-factor repeated measures ANOVA and a two-factor split-plot ANOVA, the SS_{total} will be exactly the same when using the same data. Am I correct?

9. Football players are each exposed to all three different counterbalanced coaching strategies, one per month. This is an example of which type of model?

    a. one-factor fixed-effects ANOVA model

    b. one-factor repeated-measures ANOVA model

    c. one-factor random-effects ANOVA model

    d. one-factor fixed-effects ANCOVA model

10. A two-factor split-plot design involves which of the following?

    a. two repeated factors

    b. two nonrepeated factors

    c. one repeated factor and one nonrepeated factor

    d. farmers splitting up their land

11. The interaction between factors L and M can be assessed only if

    a. both factors are crossed.

    b. both factors are random.

    c. both factors are fixed.

    d. factor L is a repeated factor.

12. A student factor is almost always random. True or false?

13. In a two-factor split-plot design, there are two interaction terms. Hypotheses can actually be tested for how many interactions?

    a. 0

    b. 1

    c. 2

    d. cannot be determined

14. In a one-factor repeated measures ANOVA, the F test is quite robust to violation of the sphericity assumption, and thus we never need to worry about it. True or false?

Computational Problems

1. Complete the following summary table for a two-factor analysis of variance, where there are three levels of factor A (fixed method effect) and two levels of factor B (random teacher effect). Each cell of the design includes 4 students. Complete the following summary table ($\alpha = .01$).

Source	SS	df	MS	F	Critical Value and Decision	
A	3.64	—	—	—	—	—
B	0.57	—	—	—	—	—
AB	2.07	—	—	—	—	—
Within	—	—	—			
Total	8.18	—				

2. A researcher tested whether aerobics increased the fitness level of eight undergraduate students participating over a four-month period. Students were measured at the end of each month using a ten-point fitness measure (10 being most fit). The data are shown here. Conduct an ANOVA to determine the effectiveness of the program, using $\alpha = .05$. Use the Bonferroni method to detect exactly where the differences are among the time points (if they are different).

Subject	Time 1	Time 2	Time 3	Time 4
1	3	4	6	9
2	4	7	5	10
3	5	7	7	8
4	1	3	5	7
5	3	4	7	9
6	2	5	6	7
7	1	4	6	9
8	2	4	5	6

3. Using the same data as in Computational Problem #2, conduct a two-factor split-plot ANOVA, where the first four subjects participate in a step aerobics problem and the last four subjects participate in a spinning program ($\alpha = 05$).

4. As a statistical consultant, a researcher comes to you with the following partial SPSS output (sphericity assumed). In a two-factor split-plot ANOVA design, rater is the repeated factor, gender of the rater is the nonrepeated factor, and the dependent variable is history exam scores. (a) Are the effects significant (which you must determine, as significance is missing, using $\alpha = .05$)? (b) What are the implications of these results in terms of rating the history exam?

Tests of Within-Subjects Effects

Source	Type III SS	df	MS	F
RATER	298.38	3	99.46	30.47
RATER * GENDER	184.38	3	61.46	18.83
ERROR(RATER)	58.75	18	3.26	

Tests of Between-Subjects Effects

Source	Type III SS	df	MS	F
GENDER	153.13	1	153.13	20.76
Error	44.25	6	7.38	

Interpretive Problem

Using the same interpretive problem you developed in Chapter 3, conduct two-factor ANOVAs using the fixed-effects, random-effects, and mixed-effects designs. Determine whether the nature of the factors makes any difference in the results

6

HIERARCHICAL AND RANDOMIZED BLOCK ANALYSIS OF VARIANCE MODELS

Chapter Outline

Key Concepts

1. Crossed designs and nested designs
2. Confounding
3. Randomized block designs
4. Methods of blocking

In the last several chapters our discussion has dealt with different analysis of variance (ANOVA) models. In this chapter we complete our discussion of the analysis of variance by considering models in which there are multiple factors, but where at least one of the factors is either a nested factor or a blocking factor. As becomes evident when we define these models, this results in a nested or hierarchical design and a blocking design, respectively. In this chapter we are most concerned with the two-factor nested model and the two-factor randomized block model, although these models can be generalized to designs with more than two factors. Most of the concepts used in this chapter are the same as those covered in previous chapters. In addition, new concepts include crossed and nested factors, confounding, blocking factors, and methods of blocking. Our objectives are that by the end of this chapter, you will be able to (a) understand the characteristics and concepts underlying hierarchical and randomized block ANOVA models, (b) determine and interpret the results of hierarchical and randomized block ANOVA models, (c) understand and evaluate the assumptions of hierarchical and randomized block ANOVA models, and (d) compare different ANOVA models and select an appropriate model.

6.1 THE TWO-FACTOR HIERARCHICAL MODEL

In this section, we describe the distinguishing characteristics of the two-factor hierarchical ANOVA model, the layout of the data, the linear model, the ANOVA summary table, and multiple comparison procedures.

6.1.1 Characteristics of the Model

The characteristics of the two-factor fixed-, random-, and mixed-effects models have already been covered in chapters 3 and 5. Here we consider a special form of the two-factor model where one factor is nested within another factor. An example is the best introduction to this model. Suppose you are interested in which of several different major teaching pedagogies (e.g., worksheet, math manipulative, and computer-based approaches) results in the highest level of achievement in mathematics among second-grade students. Thus math achievement is the dependent variable and teaching pedagogy is one factor. A second factor is teacher. That is, you may also believe that some teachers are more effective than others, which results in different levels of student achievement. However, each teacher has only one class of students and thus only one major teaching pedagogy. In other words, all combinations of the pedagogy and teacher factors are not possible. This design is known as a **nested** or **hierarchical design** because the teacher factor is nested within the pedagogy factor. This is in contrast to a two-factor **crossed design** where all possible combinations of the two factors are included. The two-factor designs described in chapters 3 and 5 were all crossed designs.

Let me give a more precise definition of crossed and nested designs. A two-factor completely crossed design (or **complete factorial design**) is one where every level of factor A occurs in combination with every level of factor B. A two-factor nested design (or **incomplete factorial design**) of factor B being nested within factor A is one where the levels of factor B occur for only one level of factor A. We denote this particular nested design as B(A), which is read as factor B being nested within factor A (in other references you may see this written as B : A or as B|A). To return to our example, the teacher factor (factor B) is nested within the method factor (factor A) because each teacher utilizes only one major teaching pedagogy.

These models are shown graphically in Fig. 6.1. In Fig. 6.1(a) a completely crossed or complete factorial design is shown where there are 2 levels of factor A and 6 levels of factor B. Thus, there are 12 possible factor combinations that would all be included in a completely crossed design. The shaded region indicates the combinations that might be included in a nested or incomplete factorial design where factor B is nested within factor A. Although the number of

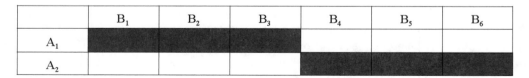

Part (a)

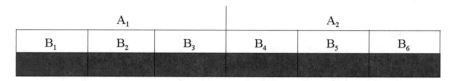

Part (b)

Fig. 6.1 Two-factor completely crossed versus nested designs. (a) The completely crossed design. The shaded region indicates the cells that would be included in a nested design where factor B is nested within factor A. In the nested design, factor A has two levels and factor B has three levels within each level of factor A. You see that only 6 of the 12 possible cells are filled in the nested design. (b) The same nested design in traditional form. The shaded region indicates the cells included in the nested design (i.e., the same 6 as shown in the first part).

levels of each factor remains the same, factor B now has only three levels within each level of factor A. For A_1 we see only B_1, B_2, and B_3, whereas for A_2 we see only B_4, B_5, and B_6. Thus, only 6 of the possible 12 factor combinations are included in the nested design. For example, level 1 of factor B occurs only with level 1 of factor A. In summary, Fig. 6.1(a) shows that the nested or incomplete factorial design consists of only a portion of the completely crossed design (the shaded regions). In Fig. 6.1(b) we see the nested design depicted in its more traditional form. Here you see that the 6 factor combinations not included are not even shown (e.g., A_1 with B_4). Other examples of the two-factor nested design are where (a) school is nested within school district, (b) faculty member is nested within department, (c) individual is nested within gender, and (d) county is nested within state.

Thus with this design, one factor is nested within another factor, rather than the two factors being crossed. As is shown in more detail later in this chapter, the nesting characteristic has some interesting and distinct outcomes. For now some mention should be made of these outcomes. **Nesting** is a particular type of confounding among the factors being investigated, where the AB interaction is part of the B effect (or is **confounded** with B) and therefore cannot be investigated. In the ANOVA model and the ANOVA summary table, there will not be an interaction term or source of variation. This is due to the fact that each level of factor B occurs in combination with only one level of factor A. We cannot compare for a particular level of B all levels of factor A, as a level of B only occurs with one level of A.

Confounding may occur for two reasons. First, the confounding may be intentional due to practical reasons, such as a reduction in the number of individuals to be observed. Fewer individuals would be necessary in a nested design, as compared to a crossed design, due to the fact that there are fewer cells in the model. Second, the confounding may be absolutely necessary because crossing may not be possible. For example, school is nested within school district because a particular school can only be a member of one school district. The nested factor (here factor B) may be a nuisance variable that the researcher wants to take into account in terms of explaining or predicting the dependent variable Y. An error commonly made is to ignore the nuisance variable B and go ahead with a one-factor design using only factor A. This design may result in a biased test of factor A such that the F ratio is inflated. Thus H_0 would be rejected more often that it should be, serving to increase the actual α level over that specified by the researcher and thereby increase the likelihood of a Type I error. The F test is then too liberal.

Let me make two further points about this first characteristic. First, in the one-factor design discussed in chapter 1, we have already seen nesting going on in a different way. Here subjects were nested within factor A because each subject only responded to one level of factor A. It was only when we got to repeated measures designs in chapter 5 that individuals were allowed to respond to more than one level of a factor. For the repeated measures design we actually had a completely crossed design of subjects by factor A. Second, Glass and Hopkins (1996) give a nice example of a nested design with teachers being nested within schools, where each school is like a nest having multiple eggs or teachers.

The remaining characteristics should be familiar. These include the following: (a) two factors (or independent variables), each with two or more levels; (b) the levels of each of the factors may be either randomly sampled from the population of levels or fixed by the researcher (i.e., the model may be fixed, mixed, or random); (c) subjects are randomly assigned to one combination of the levels of the two factors; and (d) the dependent variable is measured at least at the interval level. If individuals respond to more than one combination of the levels of the two factors, then this is a repeated measures design (see chap. 5).

For simplicity we again assume the design is balanced. For the two-factor nested design, a design is balanced if (a) the number of observations within each factor combination are equal, and (b) the number of levels of the nested factor within each level of the other factor are equal. The first portion of this statement should be quite familiar from factorial designs, so no further explanation is necessary. The second portion of this statement is unique to this design and requires a brief explanation. As an example, say factor B is nested within factor A and factor A has two levels. On the one hand, factor B may have the same number of levels for each level of factor A. This occurs if there are three levels of factor B under level 1 of factor A (i.e., A_1) and also three levels of factor B under level 2 of factor A (i.e., A_2). On the other hand, factor B may not have the same number of levels for each level of factor A. This occurs if there are three levels of factor B under A_1 and only two levels of factor B under A_2. If the design is unbalanced, see the discussion in Kirk (1982) and Dunn and Clark (1987), although most statistical software can deal with this type of unbalanced design.

6.1.2 The Layout of the Data

The layout of the data for the two-factor nested design is shown in Table 6.1. To simplify matters, I have limited the number of levels of the factors to two levels of factor A and three levels of factor B. This only serves as an example layout because many other possibilities obviously exist. Here we see the major set of columns designated as the levels of factor A, the nonnested factor, and for each level of A the minor set of columns are the levels of factor B, the nested factor. Within each factor level combination or cell are the subjects. Means are shown for each cell, for the levels of factor A, and overall. Note that the means for the levels of factor B need not be shown, as they are the same as the cell means. For instance $\overline{Y}_{.11}$ is the same as $\overline{Y}_{..1}$ (not shown) as B_1 only occurs once. This is another result of the nesting.

Table 6.1
Layout for the Two-Factor Nested Design

	A_1			A_2		
	B_1	B_2	B_3	B_4	B_5	B_6
	Y_{111}	Y_{112}	Y_{113}	Y_{124}	Y_{125}	Y_{126}
	.	.	.	.	.	.
	.	.	.	.	.	.
	.	.	.	.	.	.
	Y_{n11}	Y_{n12}	Y_{n13}	Y_{n24}	Y_{n25}	Y_{n26}
Cell means	$\overline{Y}_{.11}$	$\overline{Y}_{.12}$	$\overline{Y}_{.13}$	$\overline{Y}_{.24}$	$\overline{Y}_{.25}$	$\overline{Y}_{.26}$
A means		$\overline{Y}_{.1.}$			$\overline{Y}_{.2.}$	
Overall mean			$\overline{Y}_{...}$			

6.1.3   The ANOVA Model

The nested factor is almost always random (Glass & Hopkins, 1996; Keppel & Wickens, 2004; Mickey, Dunn, & Clark, 2004; Page, Braver, & MacKinnon, 2003). As a result, the two-factor nested ANOVA is usually a mixed-effects model where the nonnested factor is fixed and the nested factor is random. Thus the two-factor mixed-effects nested ANOVA model is written in terms of population parameters as

$$Y_{ijk} = \mu + \alpha_j + b_{k(j)} + \varepsilon_{ijk}$$

where Y_{ijk} is the observed score on the dependent variable for individual i in level j of factor A and level k of factor B (or in the jk cell), μ is the overall or grand population mean (i.e., regardless of cell designation), α_j is the fixed effect for level j of factor A, $b_{k(j)}$ is the random effect for level k of factor B, and ε_{ijk} is the random residual error for individual i in cell jk. Notice that there is no interaction term in the model, and also that the effect for factor B is denoted by $b_{k(j)}$. This tells us that factor B is nested within factor A. The residual error can be due to individual differences, measurement error, and/or other factors not under investigation. We consider the fixed-, mixed-, and random-effects cases later in this chapter.

For the two-factor mixed-effects nested ANOVA model, there are only two sets of hypotheses, one for each of the main effects, because there is no interaction effect. The null and alternative hypotheses, respectively, for testing the effect of factor A are

$$H_{01}: \mu_{.1.} = \mu_{.2.} = ... = \mu_{.J.}$$
$$H_{11}: \text{not all the } \mu_{.j.} \text{ are equal}$$

The hypotheses for testing the effect of factor B are

$$H_{02}: \sigma_b^2 = 0$$
$$H_{12}: \sigma_b^2 > 0$$

These hypotheses reflect the inferences made in the fixed-, mixed-, and random-effects models (as fully described in chap. 5). For fixed main effects the null hypotheses are about means, whereas for random main effects the null hypotheses are about variation among the means. As we already know, the difference in the models is also reflected in the multiple comparison procedures. As before, we do need to pay particular attention to whether the model is fixed, mixed, or random. The assumptions about the two-factor nested model are exactly the same as with the two-factor crossed model, and thus we need not provide any additional discussion. In addition, procedures for determining power, confidence intervals, and effect size are the same as with the two-factor crossed model.

6.1.4   ANOVA Summary Table

The computations of the two-factor mixed-effects nested model are somewhat similar to those of the two-factor mixed-effects crossed model. The main difference lies in the fact that there is no interaction term. The ANOVA summary table is shown in Table 6.2, where we see the following

Table 6.2

Two-Factor Nested Design ANOVA Summary Table—Mixed Effects Model

Source	SS	df	MS	F
A	SS_A	$J-1$	MS_A	$MS_A/MS_{B(A)}$
B(A)	$SS_{B(A)}$	$J(K_{(j)}-1)$	$MS_{B(A)}$	$MS_{B(A)}/MS_{with}$
Within	SS_{with}	$JK_{(j)}(n-1)$	MS_{with}	
Total	SS_{total}	$N-1$		

sources of variation: A, B(A), within cells, and total. There we see that only two F ratios can be formed, one for each of the two main effects, because no interaction term is estimated.

If we take the total sum of squares and decompose it, we have

$$SS_{total} = SS_A + SS_{B(A)} + SS_{with}$$

We leave the computations involving these terms to the statistical software. The degrees of freedom, mean squares, and F ratios are determined as shown in Table 6.2, assuming a mixed-effects model. The critical value for the test of factor A is $_\alpha F_{J-1, J(K(j)-1)}$ and for the test of factor B is $_\alpha F_{J(K(j)-1), JK(j)(n-1)}$. Let me explain something about the degrees of freedom. The degrees of freedom for B(A) are equal to $J(K_{(j)}-1)$. This means that for a design with two levels of factor A and three levels of factor B within each level of A (for a total of six levels of B), the degrees of freedom are equal to $2(3-1)=4$. This is not the same as the degrees of freedom for a completely crossed design where df_B would be 5. The degrees of freedom for within are equal to $JK_{(j)}(n-1)$. For this same design with $n=10$, then the degrees of freedom within are equal to $(2)(3)(10-1)=54$ (i.e., 6 cells with 9 degrees of freedom per cell).

The appropriate error terms for each of the fixed-, random-, and mixed-effects models are as follows. For the fixed-effects model, both F ratios use the within source as the error term. For the random-effects model, the appropriate error term for the test of A is $MS_{B(A)}$ and for the test of B is MS_{with}. For the mixed-effects model where A is fixed and B is random, the appropriate error term for the test of A is $MS_{B(A)}$ and for the test of B is MS_{with}. As already mentioned, this is the predominant model in education and the behavioral sciences. Finally, for the mixed-effects model where A is random and B is fixed, both F ratios use the within source as the error term.

6.1.5   Multiple Comparison Procedures

This section considers multiple comparison procedures (MCPs) for the two-factor nested design. First of all, the researcher is usually not interested in making inferences about random effects. Second, for MCPs based on the levels of factor A (the nonnested factor), there is nothing new to report. Third, for MCPs based on the levels of factor B (the nested factor), this is a different situation. The researcher is not usually as interested in MCPs about the nested factor as compared to the nonnested factor because inferences about the levels of factor B are not even generalizable across the levels of factor A, due to the nesting. If you are nonetheless interested in MCPs for factor B, by necessity you have to look within a level of A to formulate a contrast. Otherwise MCPs are conducted as before. For more complex nested designs, see Myers (1979), Kirk (1982), Dunn and Clark (1987), Myers and Well (1995), or Keppel and Wickens (2004).

6.1.6   An Example

Let us consider an example to illustrate the procedures in this section. The data are shown in Table 6.3. Factor A is approach to the teaching of reading (basal vs. whole language approaches), and factor B is teacher. Thus there are two teachers using the basal approach and two different teachers using the whole language approach. The researcher is interested in the effects these factors have on student's reading comprehension in the first grade. Thus the dependent variable is a measure of reading comprehension. Six students are randomly assigned to each approach-teacher combination for small-group instruction. This particular example is a mixed model, where factor A (teaching method) is a fixed effect and factor B (teacher) is a random effect. The results are shown in the ANOVA summary table of Table 6.4.

From Appendix Table 4, the critical value for the test of factor A is $_\alpha F_{J-1,J(K(j)-1)} = _{.05}F_{1,2} = 18.51$, and the critical value for the test of factor B is $_\alpha F_{J(K(j)-1),JK(j)(n-1)} = _{.05}F_{2,20} = 3.49$. Thus there is a significant difference between the two approaches to reading instruction at the .05 level of significance, and there is no significant difference between the teachers. When we look at the means for the levels of factor A, we see that the mean comprehension score for the whole language approach ($\overline{Y}_{.2.} = 10.8333$) is greater than the mean for the basal approach ($\overline{Y}_{.1.} = 3.3333$). No post hoc multiple comparisons are really necessary here given the results obtained.

Table 6.3
Data for the Teaching Reading Example—Two-Factor Nested Design

	Reading Approaches:			
	A_1 (Basal)		A_2 (Whole Language)	
	Teacher B_1	Teacher B_2	Teacher B_3	Teacher B_4
	1	1	7	8
	1	3	8	9
	2	3	8	11
	4	4	10	13
	4	6	12	14
	5	6	15	15
Cell means	2.8333	3.8333	10.0000	11.6667
A means	3.3333		10.8333	
Overall mean	7.0833			

Table 6.4

Two-Factor Nested Design ANOVA Summary Table—Teaching Reading Example

Source	SS	df	MS	F
A	337.5000	1	337.5000	59.5585*
B(A)	11.3333	2	5.6667	0.9524**
Within	119.0000	20	5.9500	
Total	467.8333	23		

$*_{.05}F_{1,2} = 18.51$

$**_{.05}F_{2,20} = 3.49$

6.2 THE TWO-FACTOR RANDOMIZED BLOCK DESIGN FOR $n = 1$

In this section, we describe the distinguishing characteristics of the two-factor randomized block ANOVA model for one observation per cell, the layout of the data, the linear model, assumptions and their violation, the ANOVA summary table, multiple comparison procedures, and methods of block formation.

6.2.1 Characteristics of the Model

The characteristics of the two-factor randomized block ANOVA model are quite similar to those of the regular two-factor model, as well as sharing a few characteristics with the one-factor repeated measures design. There is one obvious exception, which has to do with the nature of the factors being used. Here there will be two factors, each with at least two levels. One factor is known as the **treatment factor** and is referred to as factor A (a treatment factor is what we have been considering in the last five chapters). The second factor is known as the **blocking factor** and is referred to as factor B. A blocking factor is a new concept and requires some discussion.

Take an ordinary one-factor design, where the single factor is a treatment factor (e.g., method of exercising) and the researcher is interested in its effect on some dependent variable (e.g., % body fat). Despite individuals being randomly assigned to a treatment group, the groups may be different due to a nuisance variable operating in a nonrandom way. For instance, Group 1 may have mostly older adults and Group 2 may have mostly younger adults. Thus, it is likely that Group 2 will be favored over Group 1 because age, the nuisance variable, has not been properly balanced out across the groups by randomization.

One way to deal with this problem is to control the effect of the nuisance variable by incorporating it into the design of the study. Including the blocking or nuisance variable as a factor in the design will result in a reduction in residual variation (due to some portion of individual differences being explained) and an increase in power (Glass & Hopkins, 1996; Keppel & Wickens, 2004). The blocking factor is selected based on the strength of its relationship to the dependent variable, where an unrelated blocking variable would not reduce residual variation. It would be reasonable to expect, then, that variability among individuals within a block (e.g., within younger adults) should be less than variability among individuals between blocks (e.g., between younger and older adults). Thus each block represents the formation of a matched set of individuals, that is, matched on the blocking variable, but not necessarily matched on any other nuisance variable. Using our example, we expect that in general, adults within a particular age block (i.e., older or younger blocks) will be more similar in terms of variables related to body fat than adults across blocks.

Let us consider several examples of blocking factors. Some blocking factors are naturally occurring blocks such as siblings, friends, neighbors, plots of land, and time. Other blocking factors are not naturally occurring, but can be formed by the researcher. Examples of this type include grade point average, age, weight, aptitude test scores, intelligence test scores, socio-economic status, and school or district size.

Let me make some summary statements about characteristics of blocking designs. First, designs that include one or more blocking factors are known as **randomized block designs**, also known as matching designs or treatment by block designs. The researcher's main interest is in the treatment factor. The purpose of the blocking factor is to reduce residual variation. Thus the researcher is not as much interested in the test of the blocking factor (possibly not at all) as compared to the treatment factor. Thus there is at least one blocking factor and one treatment factor, each with two or more levels. Second, each subject falls into only one block in the design and is subsequently randomly assigned to one level of the treatment factor within that block. Thus subjects within a block serve as their own controls such that some portion of their individual differences is taken into account. As a result, subjects' scores are not independent within a particular block. Third, for purposes of this section, we assume there is only one subject for each treatment-block level combination. As a result, the model does not include an interaction term. Later we consider the multiple observations case, where there is an interaction term in the model. Finally, the dependent variable is measured at least at the interval level.

6.2.2 The Layout of the Data

The layout of the data for the two-factor randomized block model is shown in Table 6.5. Here we see the columns designated as the levels of blocking factor B and the rows as the levels of treatment factor A. Row, block, and overall means are also shown. Here you see that the layout of the data looks the same as the two-factor model, but with a single observation per cell.

6.2.3 The ANOVA Model

The two-factor fixed-effects randomized block ANOVA model is written in terms of population parameters as

$$Y_{jk} = \mu + \alpha_j + \beta_k + \varepsilon_{jk}$$

where Y_{jk} is the observed score on the dependent variable for the individual responding to level j of factor A and level k of block B, μ is the overall or grand population mean, α_j is the fixed effect for level j of factor A, β_k is the fixed effect for level k of the block B, and ε_{jk} is the random residual error for the individual in cell jk. The residual error can be due to measurement error, individual differences, and/or other factors not under investigation. You can see this is

Table 6.5
Layout for the Two-Factor Randomized Block Design

Level of Factor A	Level of Factor B				Row mean
	1	2	...	K	
1	Y_{11}	Y_{12}	...	Y_{1K}	$\overline{Y}_{1.}$
2	Y_{21}	Y_{22}	...	Y_{2K}	$\overline{Y}_{2.}$
.	.	.	...	.	.
.	.	.	...	.	.
.	.	.	...	.	.
J	Y_{J1}	Y_{J2}	...	Y_{JK}	$\overline{Y}_{J.}$
Block mean	$\overline{Y}_{.1}$	$\overline{Y}_{.2}$	...	$\overline{Y}_{.K}$	$\overline{Y}_{..}$

similar to the two-factor fully-crossed model with one observation per cell (i.e., $i = 1$ making the i subscript unnecessary), and with no interaction term included. Also, the effects are denoted by α and β given we have a fixed-effects model. Note that the row and column effects both sum to zero in the fixed-effects model.

The hypotheses for testing the effect of factor A are

$$H_{01}: \mu_{1.} = \mu_{2.} = ... = \mu_{J.}$$
$$H_{11}: \text{not all the } \mu_{j.} \text{ are equal}$$

and for testing the effect of factor B are

$$H_{02}: \mu_{.1} = \mu_{.2} = ... = \mu_{.K}$$
$$H_{12}: \text{not all the } \mu_{.k} \text{ are equal}$$

The factors are both fixed, so the hypotheses are written in terms of means.

6.2.4   Assumptions and Violation of Assumptions

In chapter 5 we described the assumptions for the one-factor repeated measures model. The assumptions are nearly the same for the two-factor randomized block model and we need not devote much attention to them here. As before, the assumptions are mainly concerned with independence, normality, and homogeneity of variance of the population scores on the dependent variable.

Another assumption is **compound symmetry** and is necessary because the observations within a block are not independent. The assumption states that the population covariances for all pairs of the levels of the treatment factor A (i.e., j and j') are equal. The analysis of variance is not particularly robust to a violation of this assumption. If the assumption is violated, three alternative procedures are available. The first is to limit the levels of factor A either to those that meet the assumption or to two levels (in which case there is only one covariance). The second, and more plausible, alternative is to use adjusted F tests. These are reported shortly. The third is to use multivariate analysis of variance, which has no compound symmetry assumption, but is slightly less powerful.

Huynh and Feldt (1970) showed that the compound symmetry assumption is a sufficient but unnecessary condition for the test of treatment factor A to be F distributed. Thus the F test may also be valid under less stringent conditions. The necessary and sufficient condition for the validity of the F test of A is known as **sphericity**. This assumes that the variance of the difference scores for each pair of factor levels is the same. Further discussion of sphericity is beyond the scope of this text (see Keppel, 1982, or Kirk, 1982).

A final assumption purports that there is no interaction between the treatment and blocking factors. This is obviously an assumption of the model because no interaction term is included. Such a model is often referred to as an **additive model**. As was mentioned previously, in this model the interaction is confounded with the error term. Violation of the additivity assumption allows the test of factor A to be negatively biased; this means an increased probability of committing a Type II error. In other words, if H_0 is rejected, then we are confident that H_0 is really false. If H_0 is not rejected, then our interpretation is ambiguous as H_0 may or may not be really true. Here you would not know whether H_0 was true or not, as there might really be a difference, but the test may not be powerful enough to detect it. Also, the power of the test of factor A is reduced by a violation of the additivity assumption. The assumption may be tested by Tukey's (1949) test of additivity (see Hays, 1988; Kirk, 1982; Timm, 2002), which generates an F test statistic that is compared to the critical value of $_\alpha F_{1,[(J-1)(K-1)-1]}$. If the test is nonsignificant, then the model is additive and the assumption has been met. If the test is significant, then the model is not additive and the assumption has not been met. A summary of the assumptions and the effects of their violation for this model are presented in Table 6.6.

6.2.5 ANOVA Summary Table

The sources of variation for this model are similar to those of the regular two-factor model, except there is no interaction term. The ANOVA summary table is shown in Table 6.7, where we

Table 6.6
Assumptions and Effects of Violations—Two-Factor Randomized Block ANOVA

Assumption	Effect of Assumption Violation
1. Independence	Increased likelihood of a Type I and/or Type II error in F; affects standard errors of means and inferences about those means.
2. Homogeneity of variance	Small effect with equal or nearly equal n's; otherwise effect decreases as n increases.
3. Normality	Minimal effect with equal or nearly equal n's.
4. Sphericity	Fairly serious effect.
5. No interaction between treatment and blocks	Increased likelihood of a Type II error for the test of factor A and thus reduced power.

Table 6.7

Two-Factor Randomized Block Design ANOVA Summary Table

Source	SS	df	MS	F
A	SS_A	$J - 1$	MS_A	MS_A/MS_{res}
B	SS_B	$K - 1$	MS_B	MS_B/MS_{res}
Residual	SS_{res}	$(J - 1)(K - 1)$	MS_{res}	
Total	SS_{total}	$N - 1$		

see the following sources of variation: A (treatments), B (blocks), residual, and total. The test of block differences is usually of no real interest. In general, we expect there to be differences between the blocks. From the table we see that two F ratios can be formed.

If we take the total sum of squares and decompose it, we have

$$SS_{total} = SS_A + SS_B + SS_{res}$$

The remaining computations are determined by statistical software. The degrees of freedom, mean squares, and F ratios are also shown in Table 6.7.

Earlier in the discussion on the two-factor randomized block design, I mentioned that the F test is not very robust to a violation of the sphericity assumption. We again recommend the following sequential procedure be used in the test of factor A. First, do the usual F test, which is quite liberal in terms of rejecting H_0 too often, where the degrees of freedom are $J - 1$ and $(J - 1)(K - 1)$. If H_0 is not rejected, then stop. If H_0 is rejected, then continue with step 2, which is to use the Geisser-Greenhouse (1958) conservative F test. For the model we are considering, the degrees of freedom for the F critical value are adjusted to be 1 and $K - 1$. If H_0 is rejected, then stop. This would indicate that both the liberal and conservative tests reached the same conclusion, that is, to reject H_0. If H_0 is not rejected, then the two tests did not reach the same conclusion, and a further test should be undertaken. Thus in step 3 an adjusted F test is conducted. The adjustment is known as Box's (1954b) correction (the Huynh & Feldt [1970] procedure). Here the degrees of freedom are equal to $(J - 1) \varepsilon$ and $(J - 1) (K - 1)\varepsilon$, where ε is the correction factor (see Kirk, 1982). It is now fairly routine for the major statistical software to conduct the Geisser—Greenhouse and Huynh and Feldt tests.

Note that the residual is the proper error term for the fixed-, random-, and mixed-effects models. One may also be interested in an assessment of the effect size for the treatment factor A (the effect size of the blocking factor B is usually not of interest). As in previously presented ANOVA models, effect size measures such as ω^2 and η^2 should be considered. Finally, the procedures for determing confidence intervals and power are the same as in previous models.

6.2.6   Multiple Comparison Procedures

If the null hypothesis for either the A or B factor is rejected and there are more than two levels of the factor, then the researcher may be interested in which means or combinations of means are different. This could be assessed, as put forth in previous chapters, by the use of some multiple comparison procedure (MCP). In general, the use of MCPs outlined in chapter 2 is unchanged if the sphericity assumption is met. If the assumption is not met, then MS_{res} is not the appropriate error term, and the alternatives recommended in chapter 5 should be considered (see Boik, 1981; Kirk, 1982; or Maxwell, 1980).

6.2.7   Methods of Block Formation

There are different methods available for the formation of blocks. This discussion borrows heavily from the work of Pingel (1969) in defining five such methods. The first method is the **predefined value blocking method**, where the blocking factor is an ordinal variable. Here the researcher specifies K different population values of the blocking variable. For each of these values (i.e., a fixed effect), individuals are randomly assigned to the levels of the treatment factor. Thus individuals within a block have the same value on the blocking variable. For example, if class rank is the blocking variable, the levels might be the top third, middle third, and bottom third of the class.

The second method is the **predefined range blocking method**, where the blocking factor is an interval variable. Here the researcher specifies K mutually exclusive ranges in the population distribution of the blocking variable, where the probability of obtaining a value of the blocking variable in each range may be specified as $\frac{1}{K}$. For each of these ranges (i.e., a fixed effect), individuals are randomly assigned to the levels of the treatment factor. Thus individuals within a block are in the same range on the blocking variable. For example, if the Graduate Record Exam-Verbal score is the blocking variable, the levels might be 200–400, 401–600, and 601–800.

The third method is the **sampled value blocking method**, where the blocking variable is an ordinal variable. Here the researcher randomly samples K population values of the blocking variable (i.e., a random effect). For each of these values, individuals are randomly assigned to the levels of the treatment factor. Thus individuals within a block have the same value on the blocking variable. For example, if class rank is again the blocking variable, only this time measured in tenths, the researcher might randomly select 3 levels from the population of 10.

The fourth method is the **sampled range blocking method**, where the blocking variable is an interval variable. Here the researcher randomly samples N individuals from the population, such that $N = JK$, where K is the number of blocks desired (i.e., a fixed effect) and J is the number of treatment groups. These individuals are ranked according to their values on the blocking variable from 1 to N. The first block consists of those individuals ranked from 1 to J, the second block of those ranked from $J + 1$ to $2J$, and so on. Finally individuals within a block are randomly assigned to the J treatment groups. For example, consider the GRE–Verbal again as the blocking variable, where there are $J = 4$ treatment groups, $K = 10$ blocks, and thus $N = JK = 40$ individuals. The top 4 ranked individuals on the GRE–Verbal would constitute the first block and they would be randomly assigned to the four groups. The next 4 ranked individuals would constitute the second block, and so on.

The fifth method is the **post hoc blocking method**. Here the researcher has already designed the study and collected the data, without the benefit of a blocking variable. After the fact, a blocking variable is identified and incorporated into the analysis. It is possible to implement any of the four preceding procedures on a post hoc basis.

Based on the research of Pingel (1969), some statements can be made about the precision of these methods in terms of a reduction in residual variability and better estimation of the treatment effect. In general, for an ordinal blocking variable, the predefined value blocking method is more precise than the sampled value blocking method. Likewise, for an interval blocking variable, the predefined range blocking method is more precise than the sampled range blocking method. Finally, the post hoc blocking method is the least precise of the methods discussed. For a discussion of selecting the optimal number of blocks, see Feldt (1958) (highly recommended), as well as Myers (1979), Myers and Well (1995), or Keppel and Wickens (2004). They make the following recommendations about the optimal number of blocks: if $r_{xy} = .2$, then use five blocks; if $r_{xy} = .4$, then use four blocks, if $r_{xy} = .6$, then use three blocks, and if $r_{xy} = .8$, then use two blocks.

6.2.8   An Example

Let us consider an example to illustrate the procedures in this section. The data are shown in Table 6.8. The blocking factor is age (i.e., 20, 30, 40, and 50 years of age), the treatment factor is number of workouts per week (i.e., 1, 2, 3, and 4), and the dependent variable is amount of weight lost during the first month. Assume we have a fixed-effects model. Table 6.9 contains the resultant ANOVA summary table.

Table 6.8
Data for the Exercise Example—Two-Factor Randomized Block Design

		Age			
Exercise Program	20	30	40	50	Row Means
1/week	3	2	1	0	1.5000
2/week	6	5	4	2	4.2500
3/week	10	8	7	6	7.7500
4/week	9	7	8	7	7.7500
Block means	7.0000	5.5000	5.0000	3.7500	5.3125
					(Overall mean)

Table 6.9
Two-Factor Randomized Block Design ANOVA Summary Table—Exercise Example

Source	SS	df	MS	F
A	21.6875	3	7.2292	18.2648*
B	110.1875	3	36.7292	92.7974*
Residual	3.5625	9	0.3958	
Total	135.4375	15		

*${}_{.05}F_{3,9} = 3.86$.

The test statistics are both compared to the usual F test critical value of $_{.05}F_{3,9} = 3.86$ (from Appendix Table 4), so that both tests are significant. The Geisser-Greenhouse conservative procedure is necessary for the test of factor A; here the test statistic is compared to the critical value of $_{.05}F_{1,3} = 10.13$, which is also significant. The two procedures both yield a statistically significant result, so we need not be concerned with a violation of the sphericity assumption for the test of A. In summary, the effects of amount of exercise undertaken and age on amount of weight lost are both statistically significant beyond the .05 level of significance.

Next we need to test the additivity assumption using Tukey's (1949) test of additivity. The F test statistic is equal to 0.1010, which is compared to the critical value of $_{.05}F_{1,8} = 5.32$ from Appendix Table 4. The test is nonsignificant, so the model is additive and the assumption has been met.

As an example of a MCP, the Tukey HSD procedure is used to test for the equivalence of exercising once a week ($j = 1$) and four times a week ($j = 4$), where the contrast is written as $\overline{Y}_{4.} - \overline{Y}_{1.}$. The means for these groups are 1.5000 for the once a week program and 7.7500 for the four times a week program. The standard error is

$$s_{\psi'} = \sqrt{\frac{MS_{res}}{J}} = \sqrt{\frac{0.3958}{4}} = 0.3146$$

and the studentized range statistic is

$$q = \frac{\overline{Y}_{4.} - \overline{Y}_{1.}}{s_{\psi'}} = \frac{7.7500 - 1.5000}{0.3146} = 19.8665$$

The critical value is $_{.05}q_{9,4} = 4.415$ (from Appendix Table 9). The test statistic exceeds the critical value; thus we conclude that the means for groups 1 and 4 are significantly different at the .05 level (i.e., more frequent exercise helps one to lose more weight).

6.3   THE TWO-FACTOR RANDOMIZED BLOCK DESIGN FOR $n > 1$

For two-factor randomized block designs with more than one observation per cell, there is little that we have not already covered. First, the characteristics are exactly the same as with the $n = 1$ model, with the obvious exception that when $n > 1$, an interaction term exists. Second, the layout of the data, the model, the ANOVA summary table, and the multiple comparison procedures are the same as in the regular two-factor model. The assumptions are the same as with the $n = 1$ model, except the assumption of additivity is not necessary, because an interaction term exists. The sphericity assumption is required for those tests that use MS_{AB} as the error term. We do not mean to minimize the importance of this popular model; however, there really is no additional information to provide. For a discussion of other randomized block designs, see Kirk (1982).

6.4   THE FRIEDMAN TEST

There is a nonparametric equivalent to the two-factor randomized block ANOVA model. The test was developed by Friedman (1937) and is based on ranks. For the case of $n = 1$, the procedure is precisely the same as the Friedman test in the one-factor repeated measures model (see chap. 5). For the case of $n > 1$, the procedure is slightly different. First, all of the scores within each block are ranked for that block. For instance, if there are $J = 4$ levels of factor A and $n = 10$ individuals per cell, then each block's scores would be ranked from 1 to 40. From this, a mean ranking can be determined for each level of factor A. The null hypothesis tests whether the mean rankings for each of the levels of A are equal. The test statistic is a χ^2, which is compared to the critical value of $_\alpha\chi^2_{J-1}$ (see Appendix Table 3), where the null hypothesis is rejected if the test statistic exceeds the critical value.

In the case of tied ranks, either the available ranks can be averaged, or a correction factor can be used (see chap. 5). You may also recall the problem with small n's in terms of the test statistic not being precisely a χ^2. For situations where $J < 6$ and $n < 6$, consult the table of critical values in Marascuilo and McSweeney (1977, Table A-22, p. 521). The Friedman test assumes that the population distributions have the same shape (although not necessarily normal) and the same variability, and the dependent measure is continuous. For alternative nonparametric procedures, see the discussion in chapter 5.

Various multiple comparison procedures (MCPs) can be used for the nonparametric two-factor randomized block model. For the most part these MCPs are analogs to their parametric equivalents. In the case of planned pairwise comparisons, one may use multiple matched-pair Wilcoxon tests in a Bonferroni form (i.e., taking the number of contrasts into account by splitting up the α level). Due to the nature of planned comparisons, these are more powerful than the Friedman test. For post hoc comparisons, two example MCPs are the Tukey HSD analog for pairwise contrasts, and the Scheffe' analog for complex contrasts. For additional discussion about the use of MCPs for this model, see Marascuilo and McSweeney (1977). For an example of the Friedman test, return to chapter 5. Finally, note that MCPs are not usually conducted on the blocking factor as they are rarely of interest to the applied researcher.

6.5   COMPARISON OF VARIOUS ANOVA MODELS

How do various ANOVA models we have considered compare in terms of power and precision? Recall again that **power** is defined as the probability of rejecting H_0 when H_0 is false, and **precision** is defined as a measure of our ability to obtain good estimates of the treatment effects. The classic literature on this topic revolves around the correlation between the dependent variable Y and the covariate or concomitant variable X (i.e., r_{xy}). First let us compare the one-factor ANOVA and one-factor ANCOVA models. If r_{xy} is not significantly different from zero, then the amount of unexplained variation will be the same in the two models, and no statistical adjustment will be made on the group means. In this situation, the ANOVA model is more powerful, as we lose one degree of freedom for each covariate used in the ANCOVA model. If r_{xy} is significantly different from zero, then the amount of unexplained variation will be smaller in the ANCOVA model as compared to the ANOVA model. Here the ANCOVA model is more powerful and is more precise as compared to the ANOVA model. According to one rule of thumb, if $r_{xy} < .2$, then ignore the covariate or concomitant variable and use the one-factor analysis of variance. Otherwise, take the concomitant variable into account somehow.

How should we take the concomitant variable into account if $r_{xy} > .2$? The two best possibilities are the analysis of covariance design (chap. 4) and the randomized block design. That is, the concomitant variable can be used either as a covariate through a statistical form of control, or as a blocking factor through an experimental form of control. As suggested by the classic work of Feldt (1958), if $.2 < r_{xy} < .4$, then use the concomitant variable as a blocking factor in a randomized block design as it is the most powerful and precise design. If $r_{xy} > .6$, then use the concomitant variable as a covariate in an ANCOVA design as it is the most powerful and precise design. If $.4 < r_{xy} < .6$, then the randomized block and ANCOVA designs are about equal in terms of power and precision.

However, Maxwell, Delaney, and Dill (1984) showed that the correlation between the covariate and dependent variable should not be the ultimate criterion in deciding whether to use an ANCOVA or randomized block design. These designs differ in two ways: (a) whether the concomitant variable is treated as continuous (ANCOVA) or categorical (randomized block), and (b) whether individuals are assigned to groups based on the concomitant variable (randomized blocks) or without regard to the concomitant variable (ANCOVA). Thus the Feldt (1958) comparison of these particular models is not a fair one in that the models differ in these two ways. The ANCOVA model makes full use of the information contained in the concomitant variable, whereas in the randomized block model some information is lost due to the categorization. In examining nine different models, Maxwell and colleagues suggest that r_{xy} should not be the sole factor in the choice of a design (given that r_{xy} is at least .3), but that two other factors be considered. The first factor is whether scores on the concomitant variable are available prior to the assignment of individuals to groups. If so, power will be increased by assigning individuals to groups based on the concomitant variable (i.e., blocking). The second factor is whether X and Y are linearly related. If so, the use of ANCOVA with a continuous concomitant variable is more powerful because linearity is an assumption of the model (Keppel & Wickens, 2004; Myers & Well, 1995). If not, either the concomitant variable should be used as a blocking variable, or some sort of nonlinear ANCOVA model should be used.

There are a few other decision criteria you may want to consider in choosing between the randomized block and ANCOVA designs. First, in some situations, blocking may be difficult to carry out. For instance, we may not be able to find enough homogeneous individuals to constitute a block. If the blocks formed are not very homogeneous, this defeats the whole purpose of blocking. Second, the interaction of the independent variable and the concomitant variable may be an important effect to study. In this case, use the randomized block design with multiple individuals per cell. If the interaction is significant, this violates the assumption of homogeneity of regression slopes in the analysis of covariance design, but does not violate any assumption in the randomized block design. Third, it should be obvious by now that the assumptions of the ANCOVA design are much more restrictive than in the randomized block design. Thus when important assumptions are likely to be seriously violated, the randomized block design is preferable.

There are other alternative designs for incorporating the concomitant variable as a pretest, such as an analysis of variance on gain (the difference between posttest and pretest), or a mixed (split-plot) design where the pretest and posttest measures are treated as the levels of a repeated factor. Based on the research of Huck and McLean (1975) and Jennings (1988), the ANCOVA model is generally preferred over these other two models. For further discussion see Reichardt (1979), Huitema (1980), or Kirk (1982).

6.6   SPSS

In this last section we examine SPSS for the models presented in this chapter, including an APA paragraph of selected results. As we see, SPSS is rather limited in terms of what it can do for hierarchical and randomized block designs. To conduct a two-factor mixed-effects hierarchical ANOVA, there are a few differences from other ANOVA models we have considered in this text. To begin, on the GLM Univariate main screen click the nested "teacher" factor name into the "Random Factor(s)" box, the nonnested "method" factor into the "Fixed Factor(s)" box, and the dependent variable "score" into the "Dependent variable" box. Second, move into the "Model" option, click the "Custom" radio button, and use the "Build Terms" arrow and pulldown to build a model on the righthand side with terms for the main effect "method" and the interaction effect "method*teacher." Thus the model should not include a main effect term for "teacher." The interaction term is necessary to trick SPSS into computing the main effect B(A) for the nested factor (which SPSS calls "method*teacher," but is actually "teacher"), and thus generate the proper ANOVA summary table. Finally, the "Posthoc" option will only allow you to obtain post hoc MCPs for the nonnested factor. For post hoc MCPs on the nested factor (although generally not of interest), go to the "Options" screen, then to the "Compare main effects" pulldown to find the Tukey LSD, Bonferroni, and Sidak procedures. Otherwise everything is the same as in other ANOVA models. Selected results are shown in the top panel of Table 6.10.

To run a two-factor fixed-effects randomized block ANOVA for $n = 1$, there a few differences from the regular two-factor fixed-effects ANOVA. First, a custom model must again be built. Here you go into the "Model" option, click the "Custom" radio button, and use the "Build Terms" arrow and pulldown to build a model on the righthand side with main effect terms for "age" and "exercise." Thus the model should not include an interaction term. This will then generate the proper ANOVA summary table. Second, the test of additivity is not available in this module of SPSS. Third, the adjusted F tests (i.e., the Geisser-Greenhouse and Huynh & Feldt procedures) are not available in this module. All other ANOVA procedures that you are familiar with will operate as before. Selected results are shown in the bottom panel of Table 6.10.

To run a two-factor randomized block ANOVA for $n > 1$, the procedures are exactly the same as with the regular two-factor ANOVA. However, the adjusted F tests are not available. Lastly, the Friedman test can be run as previously described in chapter 5.

Finally, here is an example paragraph of the results for the two-factor hierarchical example (feel free to write a similar paragraph for the two-factor randomized block example). From Table 6.10, we see that there is a significant main effect for method ($F_{\text{method}} = 59.559$, $df = 1,2$, $p = .016$), but the main effect for teacher is not significant (shown as "method*teacher" in the SPSS ANOVA summary table). Effect size is rather large for the method effect (partial $\eta^2_{\text{method}} = .968$), with high observed power (.948), but expectedly less so for the nonsignificant teacher effect (partial $\eta^2_{\text{teacher}} = .087$, power = .192). Reading comprehension scores were significantly higher for students taught by the whole language method than by the basal method.

Nested teaching reading example:

Descriptive Statistics

Dependent Variable: score

method	teacher	Mean	Std. Deviation	N
basal	1.00	2.8333	1.72240	6
	2.00	3.8333	1.94079	6
	Total	3.3333	1.82574	12
whole	3.00	10.0000	3.03315	6
	4.00	11.6667	2.80476	6
	Total	10.8333	2.91807	12
Total	1.00	2.8333	1.72240	6
	2.00	3.8333	1.94079	6
	3.00	10.0000	3.03315	6
	4.00	11.6667	2.80476	6
	Total	7.0833	4.51005	24

Tests of Between-Subjects Effects

Dependent Variable: score

Source		Type III Sum of Squares	df	Mean Square	F	Sig.	Partial Eta Squared	Observed Power[a]
method	Hypothesis	337.500	1	337.500	59.559	.016	.968	.948
	Error	11.333	2	5.667				
method*	Hypothesis	11.333	2	5.667	.952	.403	.087	192
teacher	Error	119.000	20	5.950				

[a]Computed using alpha = .05

Randomized block exercise example:

Tests of Between-Subjects Effects

Dependent Variable: wghtlost

Source	Type III Sum of Squares	df	Mean Square	F	Sig.	Partial Eta Squared	Observed Power[a]
age	21.688	3	7.229	18.263	.000	.859	.999
exercise	110.188	3	36.729	92.789	.000	.969	1.000
Error	3.563	9	.396				
Corrected Total	135.438	15					

[a]Computed using alpha = .05

(*continued*)

Estimates

Dependent Variable: wghtlost

			95% Confidence Interval	
age	Mean	Std. Error	Lower Bound	Upper Bound
20.00	7.000	.315	6.288	7.712
30.00	5.500	.315	4.788	6.212
40.00	5.000	.315	4.288	5.712
50.00	3.750	.315	3.038	4.462

Pairwise Comparisons

Dependent Variable: wghtlost

(I) age	(J) age	Mean Difference (I–J)	Std. Error	Sig.[a]	95% Confidence Interval for Difference[a]	
					Lower Bound	Upper Bound
20.00	30.00	1.500*	.445	.049	.003	2.997
	40.00	2.000*	.445	.009	.503	3.497
	50.00	3.250*	.445	.000	1.753	4.747
30.00	20.00	−1.500*	.445	.049	−2.997	−.003
	40.00	.500	.445	1.000	−.997	1.997
	50.00	1.750*	.445	.021	.253	3.247
40.00	20.00	−2.000*	.445	.009	−3.497	−.503
	30.00	−.500	.445	1.000	−1.997	.997
	50.00	1.250	.445	.122	−.247	2.747
50.00	20.00	−3.250*	.445	.000	−4.747	−1.753
	30.00	−1.750*	.445	.021	−3.247	−.253
	40.00	−1.250	.445	.122	−2.747	.247

Based on estimated marginal means

*The mean difference is significant at the .05 level.

[a]Adjustment for multiple comparisons: Bonferroni.

(*continued*)

Estimates

Dependent Variable: wghtlost

exercise	Mean	Std. Error	95% Confidence Interval	
			Lower Bound	Upper Bound
1.00	1.500	.315	.788	2.212
2.00	4.250	.315	3.538	4.962
3.00	7.750	.315	7.038	8.462
4.00	7.750	.315	7.038	8.462

Pairwise Comparisons

Dependent Variable: wghtlost

(I) exercise	(J) exercise	Mean Difference (I–J)	Std. Error	Sig.[a]	95% Confidence Interval for Difference[a]	
					Lower Bound	Upper Bound
1.00	2.00	−2.750*	.445	.001	−4.247	−1.253
	3.00	−6.250*	.445	.000	−7.747	−4.753
	4.00	−6.250*	.445	.000	−7.747	−4.753
2.00	1.00	2.750*	.445	.001	1.253	4.247
	3.00	−3.500*	.445	.000	−4.997	−2.003
	4.00	−3.500*	.445	.000	−4.997	−2.003
3.00	1.00	6.250*	.445	.000	4.753	7.747
	2.00	3.500*	.445	.000	2.003	4.997
	4.00	.000	.445	1.000	−1.497	1.497
4.00	1.00	6.250*	.445	.000	4.753	7.747
	2.00	3.500*	.445	.000	2.003	4.997
	3.00	.000	.445	1.000	−1.497	1.497

Based on estimated marginal means

*The mean difference is significant at the .05 level.

[a]Adjustment for multiple comparisons: Bonferroni.

6.7   SUMMARY

In this chapter models involving nested and blocking factors for the two-factor case were considered. Three different models were examined; these included the two-factor hierarchical design, the two-factor randomized block design with one observation per cell, and the two-factor randomized block design with multiple observations per cell. Included for each design were the usual topics of model characteristics, the layout of the data, the linear model, assumptions of the model and dealing with their violation, the ANOVA summary table, and multiple comparison procedures. Also included for particular designs was a discussion of the compound symmetry/sphericity assumption, and the Friedman test based on ranks. We concluded with a comparison of various ANOVA models on precision and power. At this point you should have met the following objectives: (a) be able to understand the characteristics and concepts underlying hierarchical and randomized block ANOVA models, (b) be able to determine and interpret the results of hierarchical and randomized block ANOVA models, (c) be able to understand and evaluate the assumptions of hierarchical and randomized block ANOVA models, and (d) be able to compare different ANOVA models and select an appropriate model. This chapter concludes our extended discussion of ANOVA models. In the remaining two chapters of the text, we discuss regression models where the dependent variable is predicted by one or more independent variables or predictors (chaps. 7 and 8, respectively).

PROBLEMS

Conceptual Problems

1. To study the effectiveness of three spelling methods, 45 subjects are randomly selected from the 4th graders in a particular elementary school. Based on the order of their IQ scores, subjects are grouped into high, middle, and low IQ groups, 15 in each. Subjects in each group are randomly assigned to one of the three methods of spelling, 5 each. Which of the following methods of blocking is employed here?
    a.   predefined value blocking
    b.   predefined range blocking
    c.   sampled value blocking
    d.   sampled range blocking

2. If three teachers employ method A and three other teachers employ method B, then
    a.   teachers are nested within method.
    b.   teachers are crossed with methods.
    c.   methods are nested within teacher.
    d.   cannot be determined.

3. The interaction of factors A and B can be assessed only if
    a.   both factors are fixed.
    b.   both factors are random.
    c.   factor A is nested within factor B.
    d.   factors A and B are crossed.

4. In a two-factor design, factor A is nested within factor B if
   a. at each level of A each level of B appears.
   b. at each level of A unique levels of B appear.
   c. at each level of B unique levels of A appear.
   d. cannot be determined

5. Five teachers use an experimental method of teaching statistics, and five other teachers use the traditional method. If factor M is method of teaching, and factor T is teacher, this design can be denoted by
   a. T(M)
   b. T × M
   c. M × T
   d. M(T)

6. If factor C is nested within factors A and B, this is denoted as AB(C). True or False?

7. A design in which all levels of each factor are found in combination with each level of every other factor is necessarily a nested design. True or False?

8. To determine if counseling method E is uniformly superior to method C for the population of counselors, of which those in the study can be considered to be a random sample, one needs a nested design with a mixed model. True or False?

9. I assert that the predefined value method of block formation is more effective than the sampled value method in reducing unexplained variability. Am I correct?

10. For the interaction to be tested in a two-factor randomized block design, it is required that
    a. both factors be fixed.
    b. both factors be random.
    c. $n = 1$.
    d. $n > 1$.

11. Five medical professors use a computer-based method of teaching and five other medical professors use a lecture-based method of teaching. This is an example of which type of design?
    a. completely crossed design
    b. repeated measures design
    c. hierarchical design
    d. randomized block design

12. In a randomized block study, the correlation between the blocking factor and the dependent variable is .35. I assert that the residual variation will be smaller when using the blocking variable than without. Am I correct?

13.   In a two-factor hierarchical design with 2 levels of factor A and 3 levels of factor B
       nested within each level of A, how many F ratios can be tested?

       a.   1

       b.   2

       c.   3

       d.   cannot be determined

14.   If the correlation between the concomitant variable and dependent variable is $-.80$,
       which of the following designs is recommended?

       a.   ANCOVA

       b.   one-factor ANOVA

       c.   randomized block ANOVA

       d.   all of the above

15.   IQ must be used as a treatment factor. True or false?

16.   Which of the following blocking methods best estimates the treatment effects?

       a.   predefined value blocking

       b.   post hoc predefined value blocking

       c.   sampled value blocking

       d.   sampled range blocking

Computational Problems

1.   An experiment was conducted to compare three types of behavior modification in
       classrooms (1, 2, and 3) using age as a blocking variable (4-, 6-, and 8-year old chil-
       dren). The mean scores on the dependent variable, number of instances of disruptive
       behavior, are listed here for each cell. The intention of the treatments is to minimize the
       number of disruptions.

| Types of behavior | Age | | |
modification	4-years	6-years	8-years
1	20	40	40
2	50	30	20
3	50	40	30

       Use these cell means to graph the interaction between type of behavior modification
       and age.

       a)   Is there an interaction between type of behavior modification and age?

       b)   What kind of recommendation would you make to teachers?

2. An experiment tested three types of perfume (or after shave)(tame, sexy, and musk) when worn by light-haired and dark-haired women (or men). Thus hair color is a blocking variable. The dependent measure was attractiveness defined as the number of times during a 2-week period that other persons complimented a subject on their perfume (or after shave). There were five subjects in each cell. Complete the summary table below, assuming a fixed-effects model, where $\alpha = .05$.

Source	SS	df	MS	F	Critical Value and Decision
Perfume (A)	200	—	—	—	— —
Hair color (B)	100	—	—	—	— —
Interaction (AB)	20	—	—	—	— —
Within	240	—	—		
Total	—	—			

3. A mathematics professor wants to know which of three approches to teaching calculus resulted in the best test performance (section 1, 2, or 3). Scores on the GRE-Quantitative portion were used as a blocking variable (block 1: 200–400; block 2: 401–600; block 3: 601–800). The data are shown here. Conduct a two-factor randomized block ANOVA ($\alpha = .05$) and Bonferroni MCPs using SPSS to determine the results of the study.

Subject	Section	GRE-Q	Test Score
1	1	1	90
2	1	2	93
3	1	3	100
4	2	1	88
5	2	2	90
6	2	3	97
7	3	1	79
8	3	2	85
9	3	3	92

Interpretive Problem

Take the one-factor ANOVA interpretive problem you developed in chapter 1. What are some reasonable blocking variables to consider? Which type of blocking would be best in your situation? Select a blocking variable from the same dataset and conduct a two-factor ANOVA. Compare these results with the one-factor ANOVA results (without the blocking factor) to determine how useful the blocking variable was in terms of reducing residual variability.

7

SIMPLE LINEAR REGRESSION

Chapter Outline

1. The concepts of simple linear regression
2. The population simple linear regression model
3. The sample simple linear regression model
   - Unstandardized regression model
   - Standardized regression model
   - Prediction errors
   - Least squares criterion
   - Proportion of predictable variation (coefficient of determination)
   - Significance tests and confidence intervals
   - Assumptions and violation of assumptions
4. SPSS

Key Concepts

1. Slope and intercept of a straight line
2. Regression model
3. Prediction errors/residuals
4. Standardized and unstandardized regression coefficients
5. Proportion of variation accounted for; coefficient of determination

Beginning in chapter 1 we examined various analysis of variance (ANOVA) models. It should be mentioned again that ANOVA and regression are both forms of the same general linear model (GLM), where the relationship between one or more independent variables and one dependent variable is evaluated. The major difference between the two procedures is that in ANOVA the independent variables are discrete variables while in regression the independent variables are continuous variables. Otherwise there is considerable overlap of these two procedures in terms of concepts and their implementation.

When considering the relationship between two variables (say X and Y), the researcher usually determines some measure of relationship between those variables, such as a correlation coefficient (e.g., r_{XY}, the Pearson product moment correlation coefficient). Another way of looking at how two variables may be related is through regression analysis, in terms of prediction. That is, we evaluate the ability of one variable to predict a second. Here we adopt the usual notation where X is defined as the **independent** or **predictor variable**, and Y as the **dependent** or **criterion variable**.

For example, an admissions officer might want to use Graduate Record Exam (GRE) scores to predict graduate-level grade point averages (GPA) to make admissions decisions for a sample of applicants to a university or college (the GRE assesses general aptitude for graduate study). The research question of interest is how well does the GRE (the independent or predictor variable) predict performance in graduate school (the dependent or criterion variable)? This is an example of simple linear regression where only a single predictor variable is included in the analysis. The use of the GRE in predicting GPA requires that these variables have a correlation different from zero. Otherwise the GRE will have little utility in predicting GPA. For education and the behavioral sciences, the use of a single predictor does not usually result in reasonable prediction. Thus chapter 8 considers the case of multiple predictor variables through multiple linear regression.

In this chapter we consider the concepts of slope, intercept, regression model, unstandardized and standardized regression coefficients, residuals, proportion of variation accounted for, tests of significance, and statistical assumptions. Our objectives are that by the end of this chapter, you will be able to (a) understand the concepts underlying simple linear regression, (b) determine and interpret the results of simple linear regression, and (c) understand and evaluate the assumptions of simple linear regression.

7.1   THE CONCEPTS OF SIMPLE LINEAR REGRESSION

Let us consider the basic concepts involved in simple linear regression. Many years ago when you had algebra, you learned about an equation used to describe a straight line,

$$Y = bX + a$$

Here the predictor variable X is used to predict the criterion variable Y. The **slope** of the line is denoted by b and indicates the number of Y units the line changes for a one-unit change in X. You may find it easier to think about the slope as measuring tilt or steepness. The Y-intercept is denoted by a and is the point at which the line intersects or crosses the Y axis. To be more specific, a is the value of Y when X is equal to zero. Hereafter we use the term **intercept** rather than Y-intercept to keep it simple.

Consider the plot of the straight line $Y = 0.5X + 1.0$ as shown in Fig. 7.1. Here we see that the line clearly intersects the Y axis at $Y = 1.0$; thus the intercept is equal to one. The slope of a line is defined, more specifically, as the change in Y divided by the change in X.

$$b = \frac{\Delta Y}{\Delta X} \text{ or } \frac{Y_2 - Y_1}{X_2 - X_1}$$

For instance, take two points shown in Fig. 7.1, (X_1, Y_1) and (X_2, Y_2), that fall on the straight line with coordinates $(0,1)$ and $(4,3)$, respectively. We compute the slope for those two points to be $(3 - 1) / (4 - 0) = 0.5$. If we were to select any other two points that fall on the straight line, then the slope for those two points would also be equal to 0.5. That is, regardless of the two points on the line that we select, the slope will always be the same, constant value of 0.5. This is true because we only need two points to define a particular straight line. That is, with the points $(0,1)$ and $(4,3)$ we can draw only one straight line that passes through both of those points, and that line has a slope of 0.5 and an intercept of 1.0.

Let us take the concepts of slope, intercept, and straight line and apply them in the context of correlation so that we can study the relationship between the variables X and Y. If the slope of the line is a positive value (e.g., Fig. 7.1), where as X increases Y increases, then the correlation will be positive. If the slope of the line is zero, where the line is parallel or horizontal to the X axis such that as X increases Y remains constant, then the correlation will be zero. If the

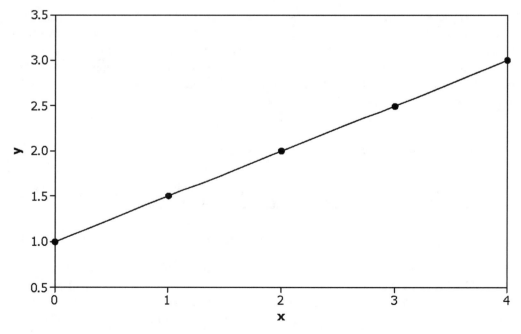

FIG. 7.1 Plot of line: $Y = 0.5X + 1.0$.

slope of the line is a negative value, where as X increases Y decreases (i.e., the line decreases from left to right), then the correlation will be negative. Thus the sign of the slope corresponds to the sign of the correlation.

7.2 THE POPULATION SIMPLE LINEAR REGRESSION MODEL

Let us take these concepts and apply them to simple linear regression. Consider the situation where we have the entire population of individuals' scores on both variables X (GRE) and Y (GPA). We define the linear regression model as the equation for a straight line. This yields an equation for the regression of Y the criterion, given X the predictor, often stated as the regression of Y on X, although more easily understood as Y being predicted by X.

The **population regression model** for Y being predicted by X is

$$Y_i = \beta_{YX}X_i + \alpha_{YX} + \varepsilon_i$$

where Y is the criterion variable, X is the predictor variable, β_{YX} is the population slope for Y predicted by X, α_{YX} is the population intercept for Y predicted by X, ε_i are the population residuals or errors of prediction (the part of Y_i not predicted from X_i), and i represents an index for a particular individual (or object). The index i can take on values from 1 to N, where N is the size of the population, written as $i = 1, ..., N$.

The **population prediction model** is

$$Y_i' = \beta_{YX} X_i + \alpha_{YX}$$

where Y_i' is the predicted value of Y given a specific value of X. That is, Y_i is the actual score obtained by individual i, while Y_i' is the predicted score based on their X score for that same individual. Thus, we see that the population prediction error is defined as

$$\varepsilon_i = Y_i - Y_i'$$

There is only one difference between the regression and prediction models. The regression model explicitly includes prediction error as ε_i whereas the prediction model includes prediction error implicitly as part of Y_i'.

Consider for a moment a practical application of the difference between the regression and prediction models. Frequently a researcher will develop a regression model for a population where X and Y are both known, and then use the prediction model to actually predict Y when only X is known (i.e., Y will not be known until later). Using the GRE example, the admissions officer first develops a regression model for a population of students currently attending the university so as to have a current measure of GPA. This yields the slope and intercept. Then the prediction model is used to predict future GPA and make admission decisions for next year's population of applicants based on their GRE scores.

A simple method for determining the population slope and intercept is as

$$\beta_{YX} = \rho_{XY} \frac{\sigma_Y}{\sigma_X}$$

and

$$\alpha_{YX} = \mu_Y - \beta_{YX}\,\mu_X$$

where σ_Y and σ_X are the population standard deviations for Y and X respectively, ρ_{XY} is the population correlation between X and Y, and μ_Y and μ_X are the population means for Y and X respectively. Note that the previously used method for determining the slope and intercept of a straight line is not appropriate in regression analysis.

7.3   THE SAMPLE SIMPLE LINEAR REGRESSION MODEL

7.3.1   Unstandardized Regression Model

Let us return to the real world of sample statistics and consider the sample simple linear regression model. As usual, Greek letters refer to population parameters and English letters refer to sample statistics. The sample regression model for predicting Y from X is

$$Y_i = b_{YX}X_i + a_{YX} + e_i$$

where Y and X are as before, b_{YX} is the sample slope for Y predicted by X, a_{YX} is the sample intercept for Y predicted by X, e_i are sample residuals or errors of prediction (the part of Y_i not predictable from X_i), and i represents an index for an individual (or object). The index i can take on values from 1 to n, where n is the size of the sample, and is written as $i = 1, ..., n$.

The sample prediction model is

$$Y_i' = b_{YX}X_i + a_{YX}$$

where Y_i' is the predicted value of Y given a specific value of X. Thus, we see that the sample prediction error is defined as

$$e_i = Y_i - Y_i'$$

The difference between the regression and prediction models is the same as previously discussed except now we are dealing with a sample rather than a population.

The sample slope and intercept can be determined by

$$b_{YX} = r_{XY}\,\frac{s_Y}{s_X}$$

and

$$a_{YX} = \overline{Y} - b_{YX}\overline{X}$$

where s_Y and s_X are the sample standard deviations for Y and X respectively, r_{XY} is the sample correlation between X and Y, and $\overline{Y}$ and $\overline{X}$ are the sample means for Y and X respectively. The sample slope is referred to alternately as (a) the expected or predicted change in Y for a one-unit change in X and (b) the unstandardized or raw regression coefficient. The sample intercept is referred to alternately as (a) the point at which the regression line intersects (or crosses) the Y axis and (b) the value of Y when X is zero.

Consider now the analysis of a realistic example to be followed throughout this chapter. Let us use the GRE-Quantitative (GRE-Q) subtest to predict midterm scores of an introductory statistics course. The GRE-Q has a possible range of 20 to 80 points (if we remove the unnecessary last digit of zero), and the statistics midterm has a possible range of 0 to 50 points. Given the sample of 10 statistics students shown in Table 7.1, let us work through a simple linear regression analysis. The observation numbers (i = 1, ..., 10), and values for the GRE-Q (X) and midterm (Y) variables are given in the first three columns of the table, respectively. The other columns are discussed as we go along.

The sample statistics for the GRE-Q are $\bar{X}$ = 55.5 and s_X = 13.1339, for the statistics midterm are $\bar{Y}$ = 38 and s_Y = 7.5130, and the correlation r_{XY} is 0.9177. The sample slope and intercept are computed as follows:

$$b_{YX} = r_{XY} \frac{s_Y}{s_X} = 0.9177 \frac{7.5130}{13.1339} = 0.5250$$

and

$$a_{YX} = \bar{Y} - b_{YX}\bar{X} = 38 - 0.5250\,(55.5) = 8.8625$$

Let us interpret the slope and intercept values. A slope of 0.5250 means that if your score on the GRE-Q is increased by one point, then your predicted score on the statistics midterm will be increased by 0.5250 points. An intercept of 8.8625 means that if your score on the GRE-Q is zero (although not possible as you receive 200 points for showing up), then your score on the statistics midterm is 8.8625. The sample simple linear regression model becomes

$$Y_i = b_{YX}X_i + a_{YX} + e_i = .5250X_i + 8.8625 + e_i$$

If your score on the GRE-Q is 63, then your predicted score on the statistics midterm is

$$Y_i' = .5250\,(63) + 8.8625 = 41.9375$$

TABLE 7.1
Statistics Midterm Example Regression Data

Student	GRE-Q (X)	Midterm (Y)	Residual (e)	Predicted Midterm (Y')
1	37	32	3.7125	28.2875
2	45	36	3.5125	32.4875
3	43	27	−4.4375	31.4375
4	50	34	−1.1125	35.1125
5	65	45	2.0125	42.9875
6	72	49	2.3375	46.6625
7	61	42	1.1125	40.8875
8	57	38	−0.7875	38.7875
9	48	30	−4.0625	34.0625
10	77	47	−2.2875	49.2875

Thus based on the prediction model developed, your predicted score on the midterm is approximately 42; however, as becomes evident, predictions are generally not perfect.

7.3.2   Standardized Regression Model

Up until now the computations in simple linear regression have involved the use of raw scores. For this reason we call this the unstandardized regression model. The slope estimate is an unstandardized or raw regression slope because it is the predicted change in Y raw score units for a one raw score unit change in X. We can also express regression in standard z score units as

$$z(X_i) = \frac{X_i - \overline{X}}{s_X} \text{ and } z(Y_i) = \frac{Y_i - \overline{Y}}{s_Y}$$

The means and variances of both standardized variables (i.e., z_X and z_Y) are 0 and 1, respectively. The sample standardized linear prediction model becomes

$$z(Y_i') = b_{YX}^* \, z(X_i) = r_{XY} z(X_i)$$

Thus the standardized regression slope b_{YX}^*, sometimes referred to as a **beta weight**, is equal to r_{XY}. No intercept term is necessary in the prediction model as the mean of the z scores for both X and Y is zero (i.e., $a_{YX}^* = \overline{z}_Y - b_{YX}^* \overline{z}_X = 0$). In summary, the standardized slope is equal to the correlation coefficient and the standardized intercept is equal to zero.

For our statistics midterm example, the sample standardized linear prediction model is

$$z(Y_i') = .9177 \, z(X_i)$$

The slope of .9177 would be interpreted as the expected increase in the statistics midterm in z score units for a one z score unit increase in the GRE-Q. A one z score unit increase is also the same as a one standard deviation increase because the standard deviation of z is equal to one.

When should you consider use of the standardized versus unstandardized regression analyses? According to Pedhazur (1997), b^* is not very stable from sample to sample. For example, at Ivy-Covered University, b^* would vary across different graduating classes (or samples) whereas b would be much more consistent across classes. Thus, in simple regression most researchers prefer the use of b. We see later that b^* has some utility in multiple regression.

7.3.3   Prediction Errors

Previously we mentioned that perfect prediction of Y from X is extremely unlikely, only occurring with a perfect correlation between X and Y (i.e., $r_{XY} = \pm 1.0$). When developing the regression model, the values of Y are known. Once the slope and intercept have been estimated, we then use the prediction model to predict Y from X when the values of Y are unknown. We have already defined the predicted values of Y as Y'. In other words, a predicted value Y' can be computed by plugging the obtained value for X into the prediction model. It can be shown that $Y_i' = Y_i$ for all i only when there is perfect prediction. However, this is extremely unlikely in reality, particularly in simple linear regression using a single predictor.

We can determine a value of Y' for each of the i individuals (objects) from the prediction model. In comparing the actual Y values to the predicted Y values, we obtain the residuals as

$$e_i = Y_i - Y_i'$$

for all $i = 1, ..., n$ individuals or objects in the sample. The e_i are also known as **errors of estimate**, or **prediction errors**, and are that portion of Y_i that is not predictable from X_i. The residual terms are random values that are unique to each individual or object.

The residuals and predicted values for the statistics midterm example are shown in the last two columns of Table 7.1, respectively. Consider observation 2, where the observed GRE-Q score is 45 and the observed midterm score is 36. The predicted midterm score is 32.4875 and the residual is $+3.5125$. This indicates that person 2 had a higher observed midterm score than was predicted using the GRE-Q as a predictor. We see that a positive residual indicates the observed criterion score is larger than the predicted criterion score, whereas a negative residual (such as in observation 3) indicates the observed criterion score is smaller than the predicted criterion score. For observation 3, the observed GRE-Q score is 43, the observed midterm score is 27, the predicted midterm score is 31.4375, and thus the residual is -4.4375. Person 2 scored higher on the midterm than we predicted, and person 3 scored lower on the midterm than we predicted.

The regression example is shown graphically in the **scatterplot** of Fig. 7.2, where the straight diagonal line represents the regression line. Individuals falling above the regression line have positive residuals (e.g., observation 2) and individuals falling below the regression line have negative residuals (e.g., observation 3). In the residual column of Table 7.1 we see that half of the residuals are positive and half negative, and in Fig. 7.2 that half of the points fall above the regression line and half below the regression line. It can be shown that the mean of the residuals is always zero (i.e., $\bar{e} = 0$) as the sum of the residuals is always zero. This results from the

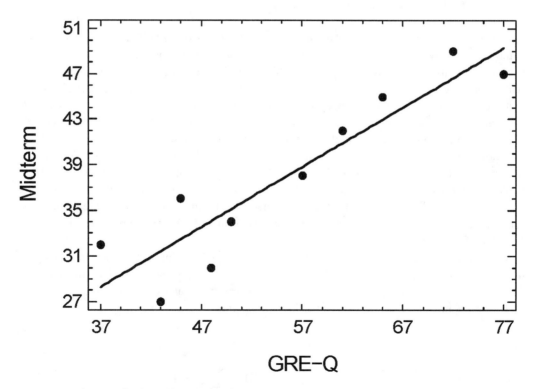

FIG. 7.2   Scatterplot for midterm example.

fact that the mean of the observed criterion scores is equal to the mean of the predicted criterion scores (i.e., $\bar{Y} = \bar{Y}'$; 38 for the example).

7.3.4   Least Squares Criterion

How was one particular method selected for determining the slope and intercept? Obviously, some standard procedure has to be used. Thus there are statistical criteria that help us decide which method to use in calculating the slope and intercept. The criterion usually used in linear regression analysis (and in all general linear models for that matter) is the **least squares criterion**. According to the least squares criterion, the sum of the squared prediction errors or residuals is smallest. That is, we want to find that regression line, defined by a particular slope and intercept, that results in the smallest sum of the squared residuals. Given the value that we place on the accuracy of prediction, this is the most logical choice of a method for estimating the slope and intercept.

In summary then, the least squares criterion gives us a particular slope and intercept, and thus a particular regression line, such that the sum of the squared residuals is smallest. We often refer to this particular method for calculating the slope and intercept as **least squares estimation**, because b and a represent sample estimates of the population parameters β and α obtained using the least squares criterion.

7.3.5   Proportion of Predictable Variation (Coefficient of Determination)

How well is the criterion variable Y predicted by the predictor variable X? For our example, we want to know how well the statistics midterm scores are predicted by the GRE-Q. Let us consider two possible situations with respect to this example. First, if the GRE-Q is found to be a really good predictor of statistics midterm scores, then instructors could use the GRE-Q information to individualize their instruction to the skill level of each student or class. They could, for example, provide special instruction to those students with low GRE-Q scores, or in general, adjust the level of instruction to fit the quantitative skills of their students. Second, if the GRE-Q is not found to be a very good predictor of statistics midterm scores, then instructors would not find very much use for the GRE-Q in terms of their preparation for the statistics course. They could search for some other more useful predictor, such as prior grades in quantitatively oriented courses or the number of years since the student had algebra. In other words, if a predictor is not found to be particularly useful in predicting the criterion variable, then other relevant predictors should be considered.

How do we determine the utility of a predictor variable? The simplest method involves partitioning the total sum of squares in Y, which we denote as SS_{total} (sometimes written as SS_Y). This process is much like partitioning the sum of squares in the analysis of variance.

In simple linear regression, we can partition SS_{total} into

$$SS_{total} = SS_{reg} + SS_{res}$$

$$\sum_{i=1}^{n}(Y - \bar{Y})^2 = \sum_{i=1}^{n}(Y' - \bar{Y})^2 + \sum_{i=1}^{n}(Y - Y')^2$$

where SS_{total} is the total sum of squares in Y, SS_{reg} is the sum of squares of the regression of Y predicted by X (sometimes written as $SS_{Y'}$), SS_{res} is the sum of squares of the residuals, and the sums are taken over all observations from $i = 1, ..., n$. Thus SS_{total} represents the total variation in the observed Y scores, SS_{reg} the variation in Y predicted by X, and SS_{res} the variation in Y not predicted by X. Let us write SS_{total}, SS_{reg}, and SS_{res} as follows:

$$SS_{total} = \frac{n \sum_{i=1}^{n} Y^2 - \left(\sum_{i=1}^{n} Y\right)^2}{n}$$

$$SS_{reg} = r_{XY}^2 SS_{total}$$

$$SS_{res} = (1 - r_{XY}^2) SS_{total}$$

where r_{XY}^2 is the squared sample correlation between X and Y, commonly referred to as the **coefficient of determination**.

There is no objective gold standard as to how large the coefficient of determination needs to be in order to say a meaningful proportion of variation has been predicted. The coefficient is determined, not just by the quality of the one predictor variable included in the model, but also by the quality of relevant predictor variables not included in the model and by the amount of total variation in Y. However, the coefficient of determination can be used both as a measure of effect size and as a test of significance (described in the next section). According to the subjective standards of Cohen (1988), a small effect size is defined as $r^2 = .02$, a medium effect size as $r^2 = .13$, and a large effect size as $r^2 = .51$. For additional information on effect size measures in regression, see Steiger and Fouladi (1992), Mendoza and Stafford (2001), and Smithson (2001; which also includes some discussion of power).

With the sample data of predicting midterm statistics scores from the GRE-Q, let us determine the sums of squares. We can write SS_{total} as follows:

$$SS_{total} = \frac{n \sum_{i=1}^{n} Y^2 - \left(\sum_{i=1}^{n} Y\right)^2}{n} = \frac{10(14,948) - (380)^2}{10} = 508.0000$$

We already know that $r_{XY} = .9177$, so squaring it we obtain $r_{XY}^2 = .8422$. Next we can determine SS_{reg} and SS_{res} as follows:

$$SS_{reg} = r_{XY}^2 SS_{total} = .8422\,(508.0000) = 427.8376$$

$$SS_{res} = (1 - r_{XY}^2) SS_{total} = (1 - .8422)\,(508.0000) = 80.1624$$

Thus the GRE-Q predicts approximately 84% of the variation in the midterm statistics exam, which is clearly a large effect size. Significance tests are discussed in the next section.

7.3.6 Significance Tests and Confidence Intervals

This section describes four procedures used in the simple linear regression context. The first two are tests of statistical significance that generally involve testing whether or not X is a significant predictor of Y. Then we consider two confidence interval techniques.

Test of Significance of r_{XY}^2.   The first test is the test of the significance of r_{XY}^2 (alternatively known as the test of the proportion of variation in Y predicted by X). It is important that r_{XY}^2 be different from zero in order to have reasonable prediction. The null and alternative hypotheses, respectively, are as follows:

$$H_0: \rho_{XY}^2 = 0$$

$$H_1: \rho_{XY}^2 > 0$$

This test is based on the following test statistic:

$$F = \frac{r^2 / m}{(1 - r^2) / (n - m - 1)}$$

where F indicates that this is an F statistic, r^2 is the coefficient of determination, $1 - r^2$ is the proportion of variation in Y that is not predicted by X, m is the number of predictors (which in the case of simple linear regression is always 1), and n is the sample size. The F test statistic is compared to the F critical value, always a one-tailed test and at the designated level of signifi-cance, with degrees of freedom m and $(n - m - 1)$, as taken from the F table in Appendix Table 4. That is, the tabled critical value is $_\alpha F_{m,(n-m-1)}$.

For the statistics midterm example, we determine the test statistic to be

$$F = \frac{r^2 / m}{(1 - r^2) / (n - m - 1)} = \frac{.8422 / 1}{(1 - .8422) / (10 - 1 - 1)} = 42.6971$$

From Appendix Table 4, the critical value, at the .05 level of significance, is $_{.05}F_{1,8} = 5.32$. The test statistic exceeds the critical value; thus we reject H_0 and conclude that ρ_{XY}^2 is not equal to zero at the .05 level of significance (i.e., GRE-Q does predict a significant proportion of the variation on the midterm exam).

Test of Significance of b_{YX}.   The second test is the test of the significance of the slope or regression coefficient, b_{YX}. In other words, is the unstandardized regression coefficient statisti-cally significantly different from zero? This is actually the same as the test of b^*, the standard-ized regression coefficient, so we need not develop a separate test for b^*. The null and alterna-tive hypotheses, respectively, are as follows:

$$H_0: \beta_{YX} = 0$$

$$H_1: \beta_{YX} \neq 0$$

To test whether the regression coefficient is equal to zero, we need a standard error for b. However, first we need to develop some new concepts. The first new concept is the **variance error of estimate**. Although this is the correct term, it is easier to consider this as the **variance of the residuals**. The variance error of estimate, or variance of the residuals, is defined as

$$s_{res}^2 = \Sigma\, e_i^2 / df_{res} = SS_{res} / df_{res} = MS_{res}$$

where the summation is taken from $i = 1, ..., n$ and $df_{res} = (n - m - 1)$ (or $n - 2$ with a single predictor). Two degrees of freedom are lost because we have to estimate the population slope and intercept, β and α, from the sample data. The variance error of estimate indicates the amount of variation among the residuals. If there are some extremely large residuals, this will result in a relatively large value of s_{res}^2, indicating poor prediction overall. If the residuals are generally small, this will result in a comparatively small value of s_{res}^2, indicating good prediction overall.

The next new concept is the **standard error of estimate** (sometimes known as the root mean square error). The standard error of estimate is simply the positive square root of the variance error of estimate, and thus is the standard deviation of the residuals or errors of estimate. We denote the standard error of estimate as s_{res}. The final new concept is the **standard error of b**. We denote the standard error of b as s_b and define it as

$$s_b = \frac{s_{res}}{\sqrt{[n\sum X^2 - (\sum X)^2]/n}} = \frac{s_{res}}{\sqrt{SS_X}}$$

where the summation is taken over $i = 1, ..., n$. We want s_b to be small to reject H_0, so we need s_{res} to be small and SS_X to be large. In other words, we want there to be a large spread of scores in X. If the variability in X is small, it is difficult for X to be a significant predictor of Y.

Now we can put these concepts together into a test statistic to test the significance of b. As in many significance tests, the test statistic is formed by the ratio of a parameter estimate divided by its respective standard error. A ratio of the parameter estimate of the slope b to its standard error s_b is formed as

$$t = \frac{b}{s_b}$$

The test statistic t is compared to the critical values of t (in Appendix Table 2), a two-tailed test for a non-directional H_1, at the designated level of significance α, and with degrees of freedom of $(n - m - 1)$. That is, the tabled critical values are $\pm_{(\alpha/2)} t_{(n-m-1)}$ for a two-tailed test.

In addition, all other things being equal (i.e., same data, same degrees of freedom, same level of significance), both of these significance tests will yield the exact same result. That is, if X is a significant predictor of Y, then H_0 will be rejected in both tests. If X is not a significant predictor of Y, then H_0 will not be rejected for either test. In simple linear regression, each of these tests is a method for testing the same general hypothesis and logically should lead the researcher to the exact same conclusion. Thus, there is no need to implement both tests.

We can also form a confidence interval around b. As in most confidence interval procedures, it follows the form of the sample estimate plus or minus the tabled critical value multiplied by the standard error. The confidence interval (CI) around b is formed as follows:

$$CI(b) = b \pm_{(\alpha/2)} t_{(n-m-1)} s_b$$

Recall that the null hypothesis was written as H_0: $\beta = 0$. Therefore, if the confidence interval contains zero, then β is not significantly different from zero at the specified α level. This is interpreted to mean that in $(1 - \alpha)\%$ of the sample confidence intervals that would be formed from multiple samples, β will be included. This procedure assumes homogeneity of variance (discussed later in this chapter); for alternative procedures see Wilcox (1996, 2003).

Now we can determine the second test statistic for the midterm statistics example. We specify H_0: $\beta = 0$ and conduct a two-tailed test. First the variance error of estimate is

$$s_{res}^2 = \sum e_i^2 / df_{res} = SS_{res} / df_{res} = MS_{res} = 80.1578 / 8 = 10.0197$$

The standard error of estimate, s_{res}, is $+\sqrt{10.0197} = 3.1654$. Next the standard error of b is

$$s_b = \frac{s_{res}}{\sqrt{[n\sum X^2 - (\sum X)^2]/n}} = \frac{s_{res}}{\sqrt{SS_X}} = \frac{3.1654}{\sqrt{1,552.5000}} = .0803$$

Finally, we determine the test statistic to be

$$t = \frac{b}{s_b} = \frac{.5250}{.0803} = 6.5380$$

To evaluate the null hypothesis, we compare this test statistic to its critical values $\pm_{.025}t_8 = \pm 2.306$. The test statistic exceeds the critical value, so H_0 is rejected in favor of H_1. We conclude that the slope is indeed significantly different from zero, at the .05 level of significance.

Finally let us determine the confidence interval for b as follows:

$$\text{CI}(b) = b \pm {}_{(\alpha/2)}t_{(n-m-1)}\, s_b = b \pm {}_{.025}t_8\,(s_b)$$
$$= 0.5250 \pm 2.306\,(0.0803) = (0.3398, 0.7102)$$

The interval does not contain zero, the value specified in H_0; thus we conclude that β is significantly different from zero, at the .05 level of significance.

Confidence Interval for the Predicted Mean Value of Y.   The third procedure is to develop a confidence interval for the predicted mean value of Y, denoted by $\overline{Y}_0'$, for a specific value of X_0. Alternatively, $\overline{Y}_0'$ is referred to as the conditional mean of Y given X_0 (more about conditional distributions in the next section). In other words, for a particular predictor score X_0, how confident we can be in the predicted mean for Y?

The standard error of $\overline{Y}_0'$ is

$$s(\overline{Y}_0') = s_{res}\sqrt{(1/n) + [(X_0 - \overline{X})^2/SS_X]}$$

In looking at this equation, the further X_0 is from $\overline{X}$, the larger the standard error. Thus, the standard error depends on the particular value of X_0 selected. In other words, we expect to make our best predictions at the center of the distribution of X scores, and to make our poorest predictions for extreme values of X. Thus, the closer the value of the predictor is to the center of the distribution of the X scores, the better the prediction will be.

A confidence interval around $\overline{Y}_0'$ is formed as follows:

$$\text{CI}(\overline{Y}_0') = \overline{Y}_0' \pm {}_{(\alpha/2)}t_{(n-2)}\, s(\overline{Y}_0')$$

Our interpretation is that in $(1 - \alpha)\%$ of the sample confidence intervals that would be formed from multiple samples, the population mean value of Y for a given value of X will be included.

Let us consider an example of this confidence interval procedure with the midterm statistics data. If we take a GRE-Q score of 50, the predicted score on the statistics midterm is 35.1125. A confidence interval for the predicted mean value of 35.1125 is as follows:

$$s(\overline{Y}_0') = s_{res}\sqrt{(1/n) + [(X_0 - \overline{X})^2/SS_X]} = 3.1654\sqrt{(1/10) + [(50 - 55)^2/1,552.5000]} = 1.0786$$

$$\mathrm{CI}(\overline{Y_0'}) = \overline{Y_0'} \pm {}_{(\alpha/2)} t_{(n-2)} s(\overline{Y_0'}) = \overline{Y_0'} \pm {}_{.025} t_8 s(\overline{Y_0'})$$

$$= 35.1125 \pm (2.306)(1.0786) = (32.6252, 37.5998)$$

In Fig. 7.3 the confidence interval around $\overline{Y_0'}$ given X_0 is plotted as the pair of curved lines closest to the regression line. Here we see graphically that the width of the confidence interval increases the further we move from $\overline{X}$ (where $\overline{X} = 55.5000$).

Prediction Interval for Individual Values of Y. The fourth and final procedure is to develop a prediction interval for an individual predicted value of Y_0' at a specific individual value of X_0. That is, the predictor score for a particular individual is known, but the criterion score for that individual has not yet been observed. This is in contrast to the confidence interval just discussed where the individual Y scores have already been observed. Thus the confidence interval deals with the mean of the predicted values, while the prediction interval deals with an individual predicted value not yet observed.

The standard error of Y_0' is

$$s(Y_0') = s_{res} \sqrt{1 + (1/n) + [(X_0 - \overline{X})^2 / SS_X]}$$

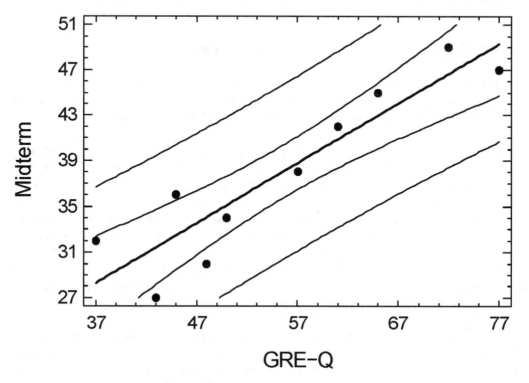

FIG. 7.3 Confidence intervals for midterm example. The curved lines closest to the regression line are for the 95% CI and the curved lines furthest from the regression line are for the 95% PI.

The standard error of Y'_0 is similar to the standard error of $\overline{Y}'_0$ with the addition of 1 to the equation. Thus the standard error of Y'_0 will always be greater than the standard error of $\overline{Y}'_0$ as there is more uncertainty about individual values than about the mean. The further X_0 is from $\overline{X}$, the larger the standard error. Thus the standard error again depends on the particular value of X, where we have more confidence in predictions for values of X close to $\overline{X}$.

The prediction interval (PI) around Y'_0 is formed as follows:

$$PI(Y'_0) = Y'_0 \pm {}_{(\alpha/2)}t_{(n-2)}\ s(Y'_0)$$

Our interpretation is that in $(1 - \alpha)\%$ of the sample prediction intervals that would be formed from multiple samples, the new observation Y_0 for a given value of X will be included.

Consider an example of this prediction interval procedure with the midterm statistics data. If we take a GRE-Q score of 50, the predicted score on the statistics midterm is 35.1125. A prediction interval for the predicted individual value of 35.1125 is as follows:

$$s(Y'_0) = s_{res}\sqrt{1 + (1/n) + \left[(X_0 - \overline{X})^2 / SS_X\right]} = 3.1654\sqrt{1 + (1/10) + [(50 - 55)^2/1,552.5000]} = 3.3441$$

$$PI\ (Y'_0) = Y'_0 \pm {}_{(\alpha/2)}t_{(n-2)}\ s(Y'_0) = Y'_0 \pm {}_{.025}t_8\ s(Y'_0)$$

$$= 35.1125 \pm (2.306)\ (3.3441) = (27.4010, 42.8240)$$

In Fig. 7.3 the prediction interval around Y'_0 given X_0 is plotted as the pair of curved lines furthest from the regression line. Here we see graphically that the prediction interval is always wider than its corresponding confidence interval.

7.3.7   Assumptions and Violation of Assumptions

In this section we consider the following assumptions involved in simple linear regression: (a) independence; (b) homogeneity; (c) normality; (d) linearity; and (e) fixed X. Some discussion is also devoted to the effects of assumption violations and how to detect them.

Independence.   The first assumption is concerned with independence of the observations. We should be familiar with this assumption from previous chapters (e.g., ANOVA). In regression analysis another way to think about this assumption is that the errors in prediction or residuals (i.e., e_i) are assumed to be random and independent. That is, there is no systematic pattern about the errors and each error is independent of the other errors. An example of a systematic pattern would be where for small values of X the residuals tended to be small, whereas for large values of X the residuals tended to be large. Thus there would be a relationship between X and e. Dependent errors occur when the error for one individual depends on or is related to the error for another individual as a result of some predictor not being included in the model. For our midterm statistics example, students similar in age might have similar residuals because age was not included as a predictor in the model.

Note that there are several different types of residuals. The e_i are known as **raw residuals** for the same reason that X_i and Y_i are called raw scores, all being in their original scale. The raw residuals are on the same raw score scale as Y with a mean of zero and a variance of s^2_{res}. Some researchers dislike raw residuals as their scale depends on the scale of Y, and therefore they must temper their interpretation of the residual values. Several different types of **standardized residuals** have been developed, including the original form of standardized residual e_i/s_{res}. These values are measured along the z score scale with a mean of 0, a variance of 1, and approximately 95% of the values are within ± 2 units of zero. Some researchers prefer these over raw residuals because they find it easier to detect large residuals. However, if you really think about it, one can easily look at the middle 95% of the raw residuals by just considering the range of ± 2 standard errors (i.e., $\pm 2 \, s_{res}$) around zero. Other types of standardized residuals will not be considered here (see Atkinson, 1985; Cook & Weisberg, 1982; Dunn & Clark, 1987; Kleinbaum, Kupper, Muller & Nizam, 1998; Weisberg, 1985).

The simplest procedure for assessing this assumption is to examine a scatterplot (Y versus X) or a residual plot (e.g., e versus X). If the independence assumption is satisfied, there should be a random display of points. If the assumption is violated, the plot will display some type of pattern; for example, the negative residuals tend to cluster together and positive residuals tend to cluster together. As we know from ANOVA, violation of the independence assumption generally occurs in the following three situations: (a) when the observations are collected over time (the independent variable is a measure of time; consider using the Durban-Watson test [1950, 1951, 1971]); (b) observations are made within blocks, such that the observations within a particular block are more similar than observations in different blocks; or (c) when observation involves replication. Lack of independence affects the estimated standard errors, being under- or overestimated. For serious violations one could consider using generalized or weighted least squares as the method of estimation.

Homogeneity.   The second assumption is **homogeneity of variance**, which should also be a familiar assumption (e.g., ANOVA). This assumption must be reframed a bit in the regression context by examining the concept of a **conditional distribution**. In regression analysis, a conditional distribution is defined as the distribution of Y for a particular value of X. For instance, in the midterm statistics example, we could consider the conditional distribution of midterm scores for GRE-Q $= 50$; in other words, what the distribution of Y looks like for $X = 50$. We call this a conditional distribution because it represents the distribution of Y conditional on a particular value of X (sometimes denoted as $Y \mid X$, read as Y given X). We could alternatively examine the conditional distribution of the prediction errors, that is, the distribution of the prediction errors conditional on a particular value of X (i.e., $e \mid X$, read as e given X). Thus the homogeneity assumption is that the conditional distributions have a constant variance for all values of X.

In a plot of the Y scores or the residuals versus X, the consistency of the variance of the conditional distributions can be examined. A common violation of this assumption occurs when the conditional residual variance increases as X increases. Here the residual plot is cone- or fan-shaped where the cone opens toward the right. An example of this violation would be where weight is predicted by age, as weight is more easily predicted for young children than it is for adults. Thus residuals would tend to be larger for adults than for children.

If the homogeneity assumption is violated, estimates of the standard errors are larger, and although the regression coefficients remain unbiased, the validity of the significance tests is affected. In fact with larger standard errors, it is more difficult to reject H_0, therefore resulting in a larger number of Type II errors. Minor violations of this assumption will have a small net effect; more serious violations occur when the variances are greatly different. In addition, nonconstant variances may also result in the conditional distributions being nonnormal in shape.

If the homogeneity assumption is seriously violated, the simplest solution is to use some sort of transformation, known as **variance stabilizing transformations** (e.g., Weisberg, 1985). Commonly used transformations are the log or square root of Y (e.g., Kleinbaum, Kupper, Muller & Nizam, 1998). These transformations can also often improve on the nonnormality of the conditional distributions. However, this complicates things in terms of dealing with transformed variables rather than the original variables. A better solution is to use generalized or weighted least squares (e.g., Weisberg, 1985). A third solution is to use a form of robust estimation (e.g., Carroll & Ruppert, 1982; Kleinbaum, Kupper, Muller & Nizam, 1998; Wilcox, 1996, 2003).

Normality. The third assumption of **normality** should also be familar. In regression the assumption is that the conditional distributions of either Y or the prediction errors are normal in shape. That is, for all values of X, the scores on Y or the prediction errors are normally distributed. Oftentimes nonnormal distributions are largely a function of one or a few extreme observations, known as **outliers**. Extreme values may cause nonnormality and seriously affect the regression results. The regression estimates are quite sensitive to outlying observations such that the precision of the estimates is affected, particularly the slope. Also the coefficient of determination can be affected. In general, the regression line will be pulled toward the outlier, because the least squares principle always attempts to find the line that best fits all of the points.

Various rules of thumb are used to crudely detect outliers from a residual plot or scatterplot. A commonly used rule is to define an outlier as an observation more than two standard errors from the mean (i.e., a large distance from the mean). The outlier observation may be a result of (a) a simple recording or data entry error, (b) an error in observation, (c) an improperly functioning instrument, (d) inappropriate use of administration instructions, or (e) a true outlier. If the outlier is the result of an error, correct the error if possible and redo the regression analysis. If the error cannot be corrected, then the observation could be deleted. If the outlier represents an accurate observation, then this observation may contain important theoretical information, and one would be more hesitant to delete it.

A simple procedure to use for single case outliers (i.e., just one outlier) is to perform two regression analyses, both with and without the outlier being included. A comparison of the regression results will provide some indication of the effects of the outlier. Other methods for detecting and dealing with outliers are available, but are not described here (e.g., Andrews & Pregibon, 1978; Barnett & Lewis, 1978; Beckman & Cook, 1983; Cook, 1977; Hawkins, 1980; Kleinbaum, Kupper, Muller & Nizam, 1998; Mickey, Dunn & Clark, 2004; Pedazur, 1997; Rousseeuw & Leroy, 1987; Wilcox, 1996, 2003).

How does one go about detecting violation of the normality assumption? There are two commonly used procedures. The simplest procedure involves checking for symmetry in a histogram, frequency distribution, boxplot, or skewness and kurtosis statistics. Although **non-zero kurtosis** (i.e., a distribution that is either flat or has a sharp peak) will have minimal effect on the regression estimates, **non-zero skewness** (i.e., a distribution that is not symmetric) will have much more impact on these estimates. Thus, finding asymmetrical distributions is a must. For the midterm statistics example, the skewness value for the raw residuals is -0.2692. One rule of thumb is to be concerned if the skewness value is larger than 1.5 or 2.0 in magnitude.

Another useful graphical technique is the normal probability plot. With normally distributed data or residuals, the points on the normal probability plot will fall along a straight diagonal line, whereas nonnormal data will not. There is a difficulty with this plot because there is no criterion with which to judge deviation from linearity. A normal probability plot of the raw residuals for the midterm statistics example is shown in Fig. 7.4. Together the skewness and normal probability plot results indicate that the normality assumption is satisfied. It is recommended that skewness and/or the normal probability plot be considered at a minimum.

There are also several statistical procedures available for the detection of nonnormality (e.g., Andrews, 1971; Belsley, Kuh & Welsch, 1980; Ruppert & Carroll, 1980; Wu, 1985). In addition, various transformations are available to transform a nonnormal distribution into a normal distribution. The most commonly used transformations in regression analysis are the log and the square root. However, again there is the problem of dealing with transformed variables measured along some other scale than that of the original variables.

Linearity. The fourth assumption is **linearity**, that there is a linear relationship between X and Y, which is also assumed for most correlations. Consider the scatterplot and regression line in Fig. 7.5 where X and Y are not linearly related. Here X and Y form a perfect curvilinear relationship as all of the points fall precisely on a curve. However, fitting a straight line to these points results in a slope of zero as indicated by the solid horizontal line, not useful at all for predicting Y from X. For example, age and performance are not linearly related.

If the relationship between X and Y is linear, then the sample slope and intercept will be unbiased estimators of the population slope and intercept, respectively. The linearity assumption is important because, regardless of the value of X_i, we always expect Y_i to increase by b_{YX} units for a one-unit increase in X_i. If a nonlinear relationship exists, this means that the expected increase

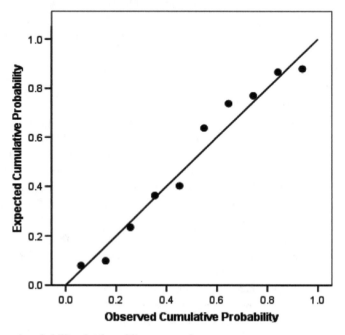

FIG. 7.4   Normal probability plot for midterm example.

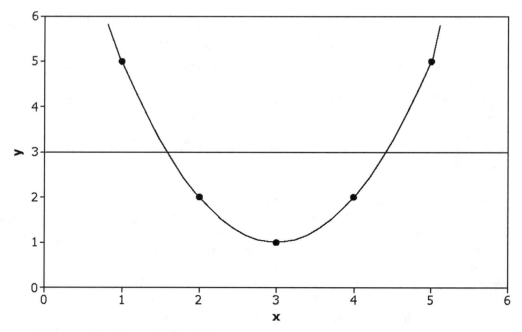

FIG. 7.5   Nonlinear regression example.

in Y_i depends on the value of X_i. Strictly speaking, linearity in a model refers to there being linearity in the parameters of the model (i.e., β and α).

Detecting violation of the linearity assumption can often be done by looking at the scatterplot of Y versus X. If the linearity assumption is met, we expect to see no systematic pattern of points. While this plot is often satisfactory in simple linear regression, less obvious violations are more easily detected in a residual plot. If the linearity assumption is met, we expect to see a horizontal band of residuals mainly contained within $\pm 2\, s_{res}$ (or standard errors) across the values of X. If the assumption is violated, we expect to see a systematic pattern between e and X. Therefore I recommend you examine both the scatterplot and the residual plot. A residual plot for the midterm statistics example is shown in Fig. 7.6. Even with a very small sample, we see a fairly random pattern of residuals, and therefore feel fairly confident that the linearity assumption has been satisfied.

If a serious violation of the linearity assumption has been detected, how should we deal with it? There are two alternative procedures that the researcher can utilize, **transformations** or **nonlinear models**. The first option is to transform either one or both of the variables to achieve linearity. That is, the researcher selects a transformation that subsequently results in a linear relationship between the transformed variables. Then the method of least squares can be used to perform a linear regression analysis on the transformed variables. However, when dealing with transformed variables measured along a different scale, results need to be described in terms of the transformed rather than the original variables. A better option is to use a nonlinear model to examine the relationship between the variables in their original scale (see Wilcox, 1996; 2003; also discussed in chapter 8).

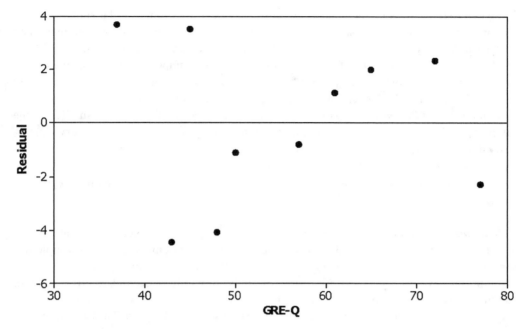

FIG. 7.6   Residual plot for midterm example.

Fixed X.   The fifth and final assumption is that the values of X are **fixed**. That is, X is a fixed variable rather than a random variable. This results in the regression model being valid only for those particular values of X that were actually observed and used in the analysis. Thus the same values of X would be used in replications or repeated samples. You may recall a similar concept in the fixed-effects analysis of variance models previously considered.

Strictly speaking, the regression model and its parameter estimates are only valid for those values of X actually sampled. The use of a prediction model, based on one sample of individuals, to predict Y for another sample of individuals may be suspect. Depending on the circumstances, the new sample of individuals may actually call for a different set of parameter estimates. Two obvious situations that come to mind are the **extrapolation** and **interpolation** of values of X. In general we may not want to make predictions about individuals having X scores outside of the range of values used in developing the prediction model; this is defined as extrapolating beyond the sample predictor data. We cannot assume that the function defined by the prediction model is the same outside of the values of X that were initially sampled. The prediction errors for the new nonsampled X values would be expected to be larger than those for the sampled X values because there is no supportive prediction data for the former.

On the other hand, we are not quite as concerned in making predictions about individuals having X scores within the range of values used in developing the prediction model; this is defined as interpolating within the range of the sample predictor data. We would feel somewhat more comfortable in assuming that the function defined by the prediction model is the same for other new values of X within the range of those initially sampled. For the most part, the fixed X assumption is satisfied if the new observations behave like those in the prediction sample. In the interpolation situation, we expect the prediction errors to be somewhat smaller as compared to the extrapolation situation because there is at least some similar supportive prediction data for the former. It has been shown that when other assumptions are met, regression analysis performs just as well when X is a random variable (e.g., Glass & Hopkins, 1996; Myers & Well, 1995; Pedhazur, 1997). There is no corresponding assumption about the nature of Y.

In our midterm statistics example, we have more confidence in our prediction for a GRE-Q value of 52 (which did not occur in the sample, but falls within the range of sampled values), than in a value of 20 (which also did not occur, but is much smaller than the smallest value sampled, 37). In fact, this is precisely the rationale underlying the prediction interval previously developed, where the width of the interval increased as an individual's score on the predictor (X_i) moved away from the predictor mean ($\overline{X}$).

A summary of the assumptions and the effects of their violation for simple linear regression is presented in Table 7.2.

Summary.   The simplest procedure for assessing assumptions is to plot the residuals and see what the plot tells you. Take the midterm statistics problem as an example. Although sample size is quite small in terms of looking at conditional distributions, it would appear that all of our assumptions have been satisfied. All of the residuals are within two standard errors of zero, and there does not seem to be any systematic pattern in the residuals. The distribution of the residuals is nearly symmetric and the normal probability plot looks good. The scatterplot also strongly suggests a linear relationship.

7.4   SPSS

Finally we consider SPSS for the simple linear regression model, including an APA paragraph of selected results. To conduct a simple linear regression analysis, go from the "Analyze" pull-down, into "Regression," and then into the "Linear" procedure. Click your dependent variable "midterm" into the "Dependent:" box and the independent variable "GRE-Q" into the "Independent(s):" box. Second, click on the "Statistics" button, where various types of statistics can be requested. At a minimum I suggest you ask for the following: estimates, confidence intervals,

TABLE 7.2

Assumptions and Violation of Assumptions—Simple Linear Regression

Assumption	Effect of Assumption Violation
1. Independence	Influences standard errors of the model
2. Homogeneity	Bias in s^2_{res}; may inflate standard errors and thus increase likelihood of a Type II error; may result in nonnormal conditional distributions
3. Normality	Less precise slope, intercept, and R^2
4. Linearity	Bias in slope and intercept; expected change in Y is not a constant and depends on value of X; reduced magnitude of coefficient of determination
5. Values of X are fixed	(a) Extrapolating beyond the range of X: prediction errors larger, may also bias slope and intercept (b) Interpolating within the range of X: smaller effects than in (a); if other assumptions met, negligible effect

model fit, and descriptives. If you click on the "Plots" button, you can generate residual plots and the normal probability plot. Finally, click on the "Save" button if you want to save various results (e.g., you can save different types of residuals as well as values from the confidence intervals into your dataset). In Chapter 8 we see other regression modules in SPSS which allow you to consider, for example, generalized or weighted least squares regression, nonlinear regression, and logistic regression. Additional information on regression analysis in SPSS is provided in texts such as Morgan and Griego (1998) and Meyers, Gamst, and Guarino (2006). Selected results for the example are shown in Table 7.3.

Lastly, here is an example paragraph of the results for the midterm statistics example. From the top panel of Table 7.3, we see that $r_{XY}^2 = .842$, indicating that 84% of the variation in midterm scores was predicted by GRE-Q scores. In the middle panel of Table 7.3, the ANOVA summary table indicates that a significant proportion of the total variation in midterm scores was predicted by GRE-Q ($F = 42.700$, $df = 1,8$, $p < .001$). In the bottom panel of Table 7.3 we see the following results: (a) the unstandardized slope (.525) and standardized slope (.918) are

TABLE 7.3
Selected SPSS Results for the Midterm Example

Model Summary[b]

Model	R	R Square	Std. Error of the Estimate
1	.918[a]	.842	3.165

[a]Predictors: (Constant), GRE-Q
[b]Dependent Variable: Midterm

ANOVA[b]

Model		Sum of Squares	df	Mean Square	F	Sig.
1	Regression	427.842	1	427.842	42.700	.000[a]
	Residual	80.158	8	10.020		
	Total	508.000	9			

[a]Predictors: (Constant), GRE-Q
[b]Dependent Variable: Midterm

Coefficients[a]

Model		Unstandardized Coefficients B	Std. Error	Standardized Coefficients Beta	t	Sig.	95% Confidence Inverval for B Lower Bound	Upper Bound
1	(Constant)	8.865	4.570		1.940	.088	−1.673	19.402
	GRE-Q	.525	.080	.918	6.535	.000	.340	.710

[a]Dependent Variable: Midterm

significantly different from zero ($t = 6.535$, $df = 8$, $p < .001$); (b) the confidence interval around the unstandardized slope does not include zero (.340, .710); and (c) the intercept was 8.865. Thus GRE-Q was shown to be a statisticially significant predictor of midterm exam scores.

7.5   SUMMARY

In this chapter the method of simple linear regression was described. First we discussed the basic concepts of regression such as the slope and intercept. Next, a formal introduction to the population simple linear regression model was given. These concepts were then extended to the sample situation where a more detailed discussion was given. In the sample context we considered unstandardized and standardized regression coefficients, errors in prediction, the least squares criterion, the coefficient of determination, tests of significance, and a discussion of statistical assumptions. At this point you should have met the following objectives: (a) be able to understand the concepts underlying simple linear regression, (b) be able to determine and interpret the results of simple linear regression, and (c) be able to understand and evaluate the assumptions of simple linear regression. Chapter 8 follows up with a description of multiple regression, where regression models are developed based on two or more predictors.

PROBLEMS

Conceptual Problems

1. A regression intercept represents
    a.   the slope of the line.
    b.   the amount of change in Y given a one unit change in X.
    c.   the value of Y when X is equal to zero.
    d.   the strength of the relationship between X and Y.

2. The regression line for predicting final exam grades in history from midterm scores in the same course is found to be $Y' = .61 X + 3.12$. If the value of X increases from 74 to 75, the value of Y will
    a.   increase .61 points.
    b.   increase 1.00 points.
    c.   increase 3.12 points.
    d.   decrease .61 points.

3. Given that $\mu_X = 14$, $\sigma_X^2 = 36$, $\mu_Y = 14$, $\sigma_Y^2 = 49$, and $Y' = 14$ is the prediction equation for predicting Y from X, the variance of the predicted values of Y' is
    a.   0.
    b.   14.
    c.   36.
    d.   49.

4. In regression analysis, the prediction of Y is *most* accurate for which of the following correlations between X and Y?
   a. −.90
   b. −.30
   c. +.20
   d. +.80

5. If the relationship between two variables is linear,
   a. all the points fall on a curved line.
   b. the relationship is best represented by a curved line.
   c. all the points must fall on a straight line.
   d. the relationship is best represented by a straight line.

6. If both X and Y are measured on a z score scale, the regression line will have a slope of
   a. 0.00.
   b. +1 or −1.
   c. r_{XY}.
   d. s_Y/s_X.

7. If the simple linear regression equation for predicting Y from X is $Y' = 25$, then the correlation between X and Y is
   a. 0.00.
   b. 0.25.
   c. 0.50.
   d. 1.00.

8. The unstandardized regression slope
   a. may never be negative.
   b. may never be greater than +1.00.
   c. may never be greater than the correlation coefficient r_{XY}.
   d. none of the above.

9. If two individuals have the same score on the predictor, their residual scores will
   a. be necessarily equal.
   b. depend *only* on their observed scores on Y.
   c. depend *only* on their predicted scores on Y.
   d. depend *only* on the number of individuals that have the same predicted score.

10. If $r_{XY} = .6$, the proportion of variation in Y that is *not* predictable from X is
    a. .36.
    b. .40.
    c. .60.
    d. .64.

11.   Homogeneity assumes that
       a.   the range of Y is the same as the range of X.
       b.   the X and Y distributions have the same mean values.
       c.   the variability of the X and the Y distributions is the same.
       d.   the conditional variability of Y is the same for all values of X.

12.   The linear regression slope b_{YX} represents the
       a.   amount of change in X expected from a one unit change in Y.
       b.   amount of change in Y expected from a one unit change in X.
       c.   correlation between X and Y.
       d.   error of estimate of Y from X.

13.   If the correlation between X and Y is zero, then the best prediction of Y that can be made is the mean of Y. True or False?

14.   If X and Y are highly nonlinear, linear regression is more useful than the situation where X and Y are highly linear. True or False?

15.   If the pretest (X) and the posttest (Y) are positively correlated, and your friend receives a pretest score below the mean, then the regression equation would predict that your friend would have a posttest score that is above the mean. True or False?

16.   Two variables are linearly related so that given X, Y can be predicted without error. I assert that r_{XY} must be equal to either $+1.0$ or -1.0. Am I correct?

17.   I assert that the simple regression model is structured so that at least two of the actual data points will fall on the regression line. Am I correct?

Computational Problems

1.   You are given the following pairs of scores on X (number of hours studied) and Y (quiz score).

X	Y
4	5
4	6
3	4
7	8
2	4

      a)   Find the linear regression model for predicting Y from X.
      b)   Use the prediction model obtained to predict the value of Y for a person who has an X value of 6.

2.   The prediction equation for predicting Y (pain indicator) from X (drug dosage) is $Y' = 2.5X + 18$. What is the observed mean for Y if $\mu_X = 40$ and $\sigma_X^2 = 81$?

3. You are given the following pairs of scores on X (# of years working) and Y (# of raises).

X	Y
2	2
2	1
1	1
1	1
3	5
4	4
5	7
5	6
7	7
6	8
4	3
3	3
6	6
6	6
8	10
9	9
10	6
9	6
4	9
4	10

Perform the following computations using $\alpha = .05$.
   a) the regression equation of Y predicted by X
   b) test of the significance of X as a predictor
   c) plot Y versus X
   d) compute the residuals
   e) plot residuals versus X

Interpretive Problem

With the class survey data on the CD, your task is to use SPSS to find a suitable single predictor of current GPA. In other words, select several potential predictors that seem reasonable, and conduct a simple linear regression analysis for each of those predictors individually. Which of those is the best predictor of current GPA?

8

MULTIPLE REGRESSION

Chapter Outline

Key Concepts

1. Partial and semipartial (part) correlations
2. Standardized and unstandardized regression coefficients
3. Coefficient of multiple determination and multiple correlation

In Chapter 7 our concern was with the prediction of a dependent or criterion variable (Y) by a single independent or predictor variable (X). However, given the types of phenomena we typically deal with in education and the behavioral sciences, the use of a single predictor variable is quite restrictive. In other words, given the complexity of most human, organizational, and animal behaviors, one predictor is usually not sufficient in terms of understanding the criterion. In order to account for a sufficient proportion of variability in the criterion, more than one predictor is necessary. This leads us to analyze the data via multiple regression where two or more predictors are used to predict the criterion variable. Here we adopt the usual notation where the X's are defined as the independent or predictor variables, and Y as the dependent or criterion variable.

For example, our admissions officer might want to use more than just Graduate Record Exam (GRE) scores to predict graduate-level grade point averages (GPA) to make admissions decisions for a sample of applicants to your favorite local university or college. Other potentially useful predictors might be undergraduate grade point average, recommendation letters, writing samples, and/or an evaluation from a personal interview. The research question of interest would now be, how well do the GRE, undergraduate GPA, recommendations, writing samples, and/or interview scores (the independent or predictor variables) predict performance in graduate school (the dependent or criterion variable)? This is an example of a situation where multiple regression using multiple predictor variables might be the method of choice.

Most of the concepts used in simple linear regression from Chapter 7 carry over to multiple regression. This chapter considers the concepts of partial, semipartial, and multiple correlations, standardized and unstandardized regression coefficients, and the coefficient of multiple determination, as well as introduces a number of other types of regression models. Our objectives are that by the end of this chapter, you will be able to (a) determine and interpret the results of partial and semipartial correlations, (b) understand the concepts underlying multiple linear regression, (c) determine and interpret the results of multiple linear regression, (d) understand and evaluate the assumptions of multiple linear regression, and (e) have a basic understanding of other types of regression models.

8.1 PARTIAL AND SEMIPARTIAL CORRELATIONS

Prior to a discussion of regression analysis, we need to consider two related concepts in correlational analysis, partial and semipartial correlations. Multiple regression involves the use of two or more predictor variables and one criterion variable; thus there are at a minimum three variables involved in the analysis. If we think about these variables in the context of the Pearson correlation, we have a problem because this correlation can only be used to relate two variables at a time. How do we incorporate additional variables into a correlational analysis? The answer is through partial and semipartial correlations, and later in this chapter, multiple correlations.

8.1.1 Partial Correlation

First we discuss the concept of **partial correlation**. The simplest situation consists of three variables, which we label X_1, X_2, and X_3. Here an example of a partial correlation would be the correlation between X_1 and X_2 where X_3 is held constant (i.e., controlled or partialled out). That is, the influence of X_3 is removed from both X_1 and X_2 (both have been adjusted for X_3).

Thus the partial correlation here represents the linear relationship between X_1 and X_2 independent of the linear influence of X_3. This particular partial correlation is denoted by $r_{12.3}$, where the X's are not shown for simplicity and the dot indicates that the variables preceding it are to be correlated and the variable(s) following it are to be partialled out. A method for computing $r_{12.3}$ is as follows:

$$r_{12.3} = \frac{r_{12} - r_{13}r_{23}}{\sqrt{\left(1 - r_{13}^2\right)\left(1 - r_{23}^2\right)}}$$

Let us take an example of a situation where a partial correlation might be computed. Say a researcher is interested in the relationship between height (X_1) and weight (X_2). The sample consists of individuals ranging in age (X_3) from 6 months to 65 years. The sample correlations are $r_{12} = .7$, $r_{13} = .1$, and $r_{23} = .6$. We compute $r_{12.3}$ as

$$r_{12.3} = \frac{r_{12} - r_{13}r_{23}}{\sqrt{\left(1 - r_{13}^2\right)\left(1 - r_{23}^2\right)}} = \frac{.7 - (.1)\,.6}{\sqrt{(1 - .01)\,(1 - .36)}} = .8040$$

We see here that the bivariate correlation between height and weight, ignoring age ($r_{12} = .7$), is smaller than the partial correlation between height and weight controlling for age ($r_{12.3} = .8040$). That is, the relationship between height and weight is stronger when age is held constant (i.e., for a particular age) than it is across all ages. Although we often talk about holding a particular variable constant, in reality variables such as age cannot be held constant artificially.

Some rather interesting partial correlation results can occur in particular situations. At one extreme, if both r_{13} and r_{23} equal zero, then $r_{12} = r_{12.3}$. That is, if the variable being partialled out is uncorrelated with each of the other two variables, then the partialling process will logically not have any effect. At the other extreme, if either r_{13} or r_{23} equals 1, then $r_{12.3}$ cannot be calculated as the denominator is equal to zero (you cannot divide by zero). Thus $r_{12.3}$ is undefined. Later in this chapter we refer to this as perfect collinearity, which is a serious problem. In between these extremes, it is possible for the partial correlation to be greater than or less than its corresponding bivariate correlation (including a change in sign), and even for the partial correlation to be equal to zero when its bivariate correlation is not. For significance tests of partial and semipartial correlations, refer to your favorite statistical software.

8.1.2 Semipartial (Part) Correlation

Next the concept of **semipartial correlation** (also called a part correlation) is discussed. The simplest situation consists again of three variables, which we label X_1, X_2, and X_3. Here an example of a semipartial correlation would be the correlation between X_1 and X_2 where X_3 is removed from X_2 only. That is, the influence of X_3 is removed from X_2 only. Thus the semipartial correlation here represents the linear relationship between X_1 and X_2 after that portion of X_2 that can be linearly predicted from X_3 has been removed from X_2. This particular semipartial correlation is denoted by $r_{1(2.3)}$, where the X's are not shown for simplicity and within the parentheses the dot indicates that the variable(s) following it are to be removed from the variable preceding it. Another use of the semipartial correlation is when we want to examine the predictive power in the prediction of Y from X_1 after removing X_2 from the prediction. A method for computing $r_{1(2.3)}$ is as follows:

$$r_{1(2.3)} = \frac{r_{12} - r_{13}r_{23}}{\sqrt{1 - r_{23}^2}}$$

Let us take an example of a situation where a semipartial correlation might be computed. Say a researcher is interested in the relationship between GPA (X_1) and GRE scores (X_2). The researcher would like to remove the influence of intelligence (IQ: X_3) from GRE scores, but not from GPA. The sample correlations are $r_{12} = .5$, $r_{13} = .3$, and $r_{23} = .7$. We compute $r_{1(2.3)}$ as

$$r_{1(2.3)} = \frac{r_{12} - r_{13}r_{23}}{\sqrt{1 - r_{23}^2}} = \frac{.5 - (.3).7}{\sqrt{1 - .49}} = .4061$$

Thus the bivariate correlation between GPA and GRE ignoring IQ ($r_{12} = .50$) is larger than the semipartial correlation between GPA and GRE controlling for IQ in GRE ($r_{1(2.3)} = .4061$). As was the case with partial correlations, various values of a semipartial correlation can be obtained depending on the combination of the bivariate correlations. For more information on partial and semipartial correlations, see Hays (1988), Glass and Hopkins (1996), or Pedhazur (1997).

Now that we have considered the correlational relationships among two or more variables (i.e., partial and semipartial correlations), let us move on to an examination of the multiple regression model where there are two or more predictor variables.

8.2   MULTIPLE LINEAR REGRESSION

Let us take the concepts we have learned in this and the previous chapter and place them into the context of multiple linear regression. For purposes of brevity, we do not consider the population situation because the sample situation is invoked 99.44% of the time. In this section we discuss the unstandardized and standardized multiple regression models, the coefficient of multiple determination, multiple correlation, tests of significance, and statistical assumptions.

8.2.1   Unstandardized Regression Model

The sample multiple linear regression model for predicting Y from m predictors $X_{1,2,...,m}$ is

$$Y_i = b_1 X_{1i} + b_2 X_{2i} + ... + b_m X_{mi} + a + e_i$$

where Y is the criterion variable, the X_k's are the predictor variables where $k = 1, ..., m$, b_k is the sample partial slope of the regression line for Y as predicted by X_k, a is the sample intercept of the regression line for Y as predicted by the set of X_k's, e_i are the residuals or errors of prediction (the part of Y not predictable from the X_k's), and i represents an index for an individual or object. The index i can take on values from 1 to n where n is the size of the sample (i.e., $i = 1, ..., n$). The term **partial slope** is used because it represents the slope of Y for a particular X_k in which we have partialled out the influence of the other X_k's, much as we did with the partial correlation.

The sample prediction model is

$$Y_i' = b_1 X_{1i} + b_2 X_{2i} + \dots + b_m X_{mi} + a$$

where Y_i' is the predicted value of Y for specific values of the X_k's, and the other terms are as before. The difference between the regression and prediction models is the same as in chapter 7. We can compute residuals, the e_i, for each of the i individuals or objects by comparing the actual Y values with the predicted Y values as

$$e_i = Y_i - Y_i'$$

for all $i = 1,\dots, n$ individuals or objects in the sample.

Determining the sample partial slopes and the intercept in the multiple predictor case is rather complicated. To keep it simple, we use a two-predictor model for illustrative purposes. Generally we rely on statistical software for implementing multiple regression. For the two-predictor case the sample partial slopes and the intercept can be determined as

$$b_1 = \frac{(r_{Y1} - r_{Y2} r_{12}) s_Y}{(1 - r_{12}^2) s_1}$$

$$b_2 = \frac{(r_{Y2} - r_{Y1} r_{12}) s_Y}{(1 - r_{12}^2) s_2}$$

$$a = \bar{Y} - b_1 \bar{X}_1 - b_2 \bar{X}_2$$

The sample partial slope b_1 is referred to alternately as (a) the expected or predicted change in Y for a one unit change in X_1 with X_2 held constant (or for individuals with the same score on X_2), and (b) the unstandardized or raw regression coefficient. Similar statements may be made for b_2. Note the similarity of the partial slope equation to the semipartial correlation. The sample intercept is referred to as the value of Y when X_1 and X_2 are both zero.

An alternative method for computing the sample partial slopes that involves the use of a partial correlation is as follows:

$$b_1 = r_{Y1.2} \frac{s_Y \sqrt{1 - r_{Y2}^2}}{s_1 \sqrt{1 - r_{12}^2}}$$

$$b_2 = r_{Y2.1} \frac{s_Y \sqrt{1 - r_{Y1}^2}}{s_2 \sqrt{1 - r_{12}^2}}$$

What statistical criterion is used to arrive at the particular values for the partial slopes and intercept? The criterion usually used in multiple linear regression analysis (and in all general linear models [GLM] for that matter) is the least squares criterion. The least squares criterion arrives at those values for the partial slopes and intercept such that the sum of the squared prediction errors or residuals is smallest. That is, we want to find that regression model, defined by a particular set of partial slopes and an intercept, that has the smallest sum of the squared residuals. We often refer to this particular method for calculating the slope and intercept as least squares estimation, because a and the b_k's represent sample estimates of the population parameters α and the β_ks obtained using the least squares criterion.

Consider now the analysis of a realistic example we will follow in this chapter. We use the GRE—Quantitative + Verbal Total (GRETOT) and undergraduate grade point average (UGPA) to predict graduate grade point average (GGPA). GRETOT has a possible range of 40 to 160 points (if we remove the unnecessary last digit of zero), and GPA is defined as having a possible range of 0.00 to 4.00 points. Given the sample of 11 statistics students as shown in Table 8.1, let us work through a multiple linear regression analysis.

As sample statistics, we compute for GRETOT (X_1 or subscript 1) that $\overline{X}_1 = 112.7273$ and $s_1^2 = 266.8182$, for UGPA (X_2 or subscript 2) that $\overline{X}_2 = 3.1091$ and $s_2^2 = 0.1609$, and for GGPA (Y) that $\overline{Y} = 3.5000$ and $s_Y^2 = 0.1100$. In addition we compute $r_{Y1} = .7845$, $r_{Y2} = .7516$, and $r_{12} = .3011$. The sample partial slopes and intercept are determined as follows:

$$b_1 = \frac{(r_{Y1} - r_{Y2}r_{12})s_Y}{(1 - r_{12}^2)s_1} = \frac{[.7845 - .7516(.3011)].3317}{(1 - .3011^2)16.3346} = .0125$$

$$b_2 = \frac{(r_{Y2} - r_{Y1}r_{12})s_Y}{(1 - r_{12}^2)s_2} = \frac{[.7516 - .7845(.3011)].3317}{(1 - .3011^2).4011} = .4687$$

$$a = \overline{Y} - b_1\overline{X}_1 - b_2\overline{X}_2 = 3.5000 - (.0125)(112.7273) - (.4687)(3.1091) = .6337$$

Let us interpret the partial slope and intercept values. A partial slope of .0125 for GRETOT would mean that if your score on the GRETOT was increased by 1 point, then your graduate grade point average would be increased by .0125 points, controlling for undergraduate grade

TABLE 8.1
GRE—GPA Example Data

Student	GRE-TOT (X_1)	UGPA (X_2)	GGPA (Y)
1	145	3.2	4.0
2	120	3.7	3.9
3	125	3.6	3.8
4	130	2.9	3.7
5	110	3.5	3.6
6	100	3.3	3.5
7	95	3.0	3.4
8	115	2.7	3.3
9	105	3.1	3.2
10	90	2.8	3.1
11	105	2.4	3.0

point average. Likewise, a partial slope of .4687 for UGPA would mean that if your undergraduate grade point average was increased by 1 point, then your graduate grade point average would be increased by .4687 points, controlling for GRETOT. An intercept of .6337 would mean that if your scores on the GRETOT and UGPA were both 0, then your graduate grade point average would be .6337. However, it is impossible to obtain a GRETOT score of 0 because you receive 40 points for putting your name on the answer sheet. In a similar way, an undergraduate student could not obtain a UGPA of 0 and be admitted to graduate school.

To put all of this together then, the sample multiple linear regression model is

$$Y_i = b_1 X_{1i} + b_2 X_{2i} + a + e_i = .0125\, X_{1i} + .4687\, X_{2i} + .6337 + e_i$$

If your score on the GRETOT was 130 and your UGPA was 3.5, then your predicted score on the GGPA would be

$$Y_i' = .0125(130) + .4687(3.5000) + .6337 = 3.8992$$

Based on the prediction equation, we predict your GGPA to be around 3.9; however, as we saw in chapter 17, predictions are usually somewhat less than perfect, even with 2 predictors.

8.2.2   Standardized Regression Model

Up until this point in the chapter, everything in multiple linear regression has involved the use of raw scores. For this reason we referred to the model as the unstandardized regression model. Often we may want to express the regression in terms of standard z score units rather than in raw score units (as in chap. 17). The means and variances of the standardized variables (e.g., z_1, z_2, z_Y) are 0 and 1, respectively. The sample standardized linear prediction model becomes

$$z(Y_i') = b_1^* z_{1i} + b_2^* z_{2i} + ... + b_m^* z_{mi}$$

where b_k^* represents a sample standardized partial slope (sometimes called beta weights) and the other terms are as before. As was the case in simple linear regression, no intercept term is necessary in the standardized prediction model, as the mean of the z scores for all variables is 0. The sample standardized partial slopes are, in general, computed by

$$b_k^* = b_k(s_k/s_Y)$$

For the two predictor case, the standardized partial slopes can be calculated by

$$b_1^* = b_1(s_1/s_Y)$$
$$\text{or} = (r_{Y1} - r_{Y2} r_{12})/(1 - r_{12}^2)$$

and

$$b_2^* = b_2(s_2/s_Y)$$
$$\text{or} = (r_{Y2} - r_{Y1} r_{12})/(1 - r_{12}^2)$$

If $r_{12} = 0$, where the two predictors are uncorrelated, then $b_1^* = r_{Y1}$ and $b_2^* = r_{Y2}$ because the rest of the equation goes away.

For our graduate grade point average example, the standardized partial slopes are equal to

$$b_1^* = b_1(s_1/s_Y) = .0125(16.3346/.3317) = .6156$$
$$b_2^* = b_2(s_2/s_Y) = .4687(.4011/.3317) = .5668$$

The prediction model is then

$$z(Y_i') = .6156\, z_{1i} + .5668\, z_{2i}$$

The standardized partial slope of .6156 for GRETOT would be interpreted as the expected increase in GGPA in z score units for a 1 z score unit increase in the GRETOT, controlling for UGPA. A similar statement may be made for the standardized partial slope of UGPA. The b_k^* can also be interpreted as the expected standard deviation change in Y associated with a 1 standard deviation change in X_k when the other X_k's are held constant.

When would you want to use the standardized versus unstandardized regression analyses? According to Pedhazur (1997), b_k^* is sample specific and is not very stable across different samples due to the variance of X_k changing (as the variance of X_k increases, the value of b_k^* also increases, all else being equal). For example, at Ivy-Covered University, b_k^* would vary across different graduating classes (or samples) while b_k would be much more consistent across classes. Thus most researchers prefer the use of b_k to compare the influence of a particular predictor variable across different samples and/or populations. Pedhazur also states that the b_k^* are of "limited value" (p. 321), but could be reported along with the b_k. As Pedhazur and others have reported, the b_k^* can be deceptive in determining the relative importance of the predictors as they are affected by the variances and covariances of both the included predictors and the predictors not included in the model. Thus we recommend the b_k for general purpose use.

8.2.3   Coefficient of Multiple Determination and Multiple Correlation

An obvious question now is, How well is the criterion variable predicted by the set of predictor variables? For our example, we are interested in how well the graduate grade point averages are predicted by the GRE total scores and the undergraduate grade point averages. In other words, what is the utility of the set of predictor variables?

The simplest method involves the partitioning of the familiar total sum of squares in Y, which we denote as SS_{total}. In multiple linear regression, we can write SS_{total} as follows:

$$SS_{total} = [n\, \Sigma Y_i^2 - (\Sigma Y_i)^2]/n$$
$$\text{or} = (n - 1)\, s_Y^2$$

where we sum over Y from $i = 1, ..., n$. Next we can conceptually partition SS_{total} as

$$SS_{total} = SS_{reg} + SS_{res}$$
$$\Sigma(Y_i - \overline{Y})^2 = \Sigma(Y_i' - \overline{Y})^2 + \Sigma(Y_i - Y_i')^2$$

where SS_{reg} is the regression sum of squares due to the prediction of Y from the X_k's (often written as $SS_{Y'}$), and SS_{res} is the sum of squares due to the residuals.

Before we consider computation of SS_{reg} and SS_{res}, let us look at the coefficient of multiple determination. Recall from chapter 7 the coefficient of determination, r^2_{XY}. Now consider the multiple predictor version of r^2_{XY}, here denoted as $R^2_{Y.1,...,m}$. The subscript tells us that Y is the criterion variable and that $X_{1,...,m}$ are the predictor variables. The simplest procedure for computing R^2 is as follows:

$$R^2_{Y.1,...,m} = b^*_1 r_{Y1} + b^*_2 r_{Y2} + ... + b^*_m r_{Ym}$$

The coefficient of multiple determination tells us the proportion of total variation in Y that is predicted from the set of predictor variables. Often we see the coefficient in terms of SS as

$$R^2_{Y.1,...,m} = SS_{reg}/SS_{total}$$

Thus one method for computing SS_{reg} and SS_{res} is from R^2 as follows:

$$SS_{reg} = R^2 SS_{total}$$
$$SS_{res} = (1 - R^2)SS_{total} = SS_{total} - SS_{reg}$$

As discussed in chapter 7, there is no objective gold standard as to how large the coefficient of determination needs to be in order to say a meaningful proportion of variation has been predicted. The coefficient is determined, not just by the quality of the predictor variables included in the model, but also by the quality of relevant predictor variables not included in the model and by the amount of total variation in Y. However, the coefficient of determination can be used as a measure of effect size. According to the subjective standards of Cohen (1988), a small effect size is defined as $R^2 = .02$, a medium effect size as $R^2 = .13$, and a large effect size as $R^2 = .51$. For additional information on effect size measures in regression, see Steiger and Fouladi (1992), Mendoza and Stafford (2001), and Smithson (2001; which also includes some discussion of power). Note also that $R_{Y.1,...,m}$ is referred to as the multiple correlation coefficient.

With the example of predicting GGPA from GRETOT and UGPA, let us examine the partitioning of the SS_{total}, as follows:

$$SS_{total} = (n - 1)s^2_Y = (10).1100 = 1.1000$$

Next we can determine R^2 as

$$R^2_{Y.12} = b^*_1 r_{Y1} + b^*_2 r_{Y2} = .6156(.7845) + .5668(.7516) = .9089$$

We can also partition SS_{total} into SS_{reg} and SS_{res}, where

$$SS_{reg} = R^2 SS_{total} = .9089(1.1000) = 0.9998$$
$$SS_{res} = (1 - R^2)SS_{total} = (1 - .9089)1.1000 = .1002$$

Finally, let us summarize these results for the example data. We found that the coefficient of multiple determination was equal to .9089. Thus the GRE total score and the undergraduate grade point average predicts around 91% of the variation in the graduate grade point average. This would be quite satisfactory for the college admissions officer in that there is little variation left to be explained, although this result is quite unlikely in actual research in education and the behavioral sciences. Obviously there is a large effect size here.

It should be noted that R^2 is sensitive to sample size and to the number of predictor variables. R is a biased estimate of the population multiple correlation due to sampling error in the bivariate correlations and in the standard deviations of X and Y. Because R systematically overestimates the population multiple correlation, an adjusted coefficient of multiple determination has been devised. The adjusted R^2 (R^2_{adj}) is calculated as follows:

$$R^2_{adj} = 1 - (1 - R^2) \left(\frac{n-1}{n-m-1} \right)$$

Thus, R^2_{adj} adjusts for sample size and for the number of predictors in the model; this allows us to compare models fitted to the same set of data with different numbers of predictors or with different samples of data. The difference between R^2 and R^2_{adj} is called **shrinkage**.

When n is small relative to m, the amount of bias can be large as R^2 can be expected to be large by chance alone. In this case the adjustment will be quite large, as it should be. In addition, with small samples, the regression coefficients (i.e., the b_k's) may not be very good estimates of the population values. When n is large relative to m, bias will be minimized and generalizations are likely to be better about the population values.

With a large number of predictors, power is reduced, and there is an increased likelihood of a Type I error across the total number of significance tests (i.e., one for each predictor and overall, as we show in the next section). In multiple regression power is a function of sample size, the number of predictors, the level of significance, and the size of the population effect (i.e., for a given predictor, or overall). To determine how large a sample you need relative to the number of predictors, consult power tables (e.g., Cohen, 1988) or power software (e.g., Murphy & Myors, 2004; Power and Precision). Simple advice is to design your research such that the ratio of n to m is large.

For the example data, we determine R^2_{adj} to be

$$R^2_{adj} = 1 - (1 - R^2) \left(\frac{n-1}{n-m-1} \right) = 1 - (1 - .9089) \left(\frac{11-1}{11-2-1} \right) = .8861$$

which in this case indicates a very small adjustment in comparison to R^2.

8.2.4   Significance Tests

Here we describe two procedures used in multiple linear regression. These involve testing the significance of the overall regression model, and of each individual partial slope (or regression coefficient).

Test of Significance of the Overall Regression Model.   The first test is the test of significance of the overall regression model, or alternatively the test of significance of the coefficient of multiple determination. This is a test of all of the b_k's simultaneously. The null and alternative hypotheses, respectively, are as follows:

$$H_0: \beta_1 = \beta_2 = \dots = \beta_k = 0$$

$$H_1: \text{not all the } \beta_k = 0$$

If H_0 is rejected, then one or more of the individual regression coefficients (i.e., the b_k) is statistically significantly different from zero (if assumptions are satisfied, as discussed later). If H_0 is not rejected, then none of the individual regression coefficients will be significantly different from zero.

The test is based on the following test statistic:

$$F = \frac{R^2 / m}{(1 - R^2)/(n - m - 1)}$$

where F indicates that this is an F statistic, m is the number of predictors, and n is the sample size. The F test statistic is compared to the F critical value, always a one-tailed test and at the designated level of significance, with degrees of freedom being m and $(n - m - 1)$, as taken from the F table in Appendix Table 4. That is, the tabled critical value is ${}_{\alpha}F_{m,(n-m-1)}$. The test statistic can also be written in equivalent form as

$$F = \frac{SS_{reg}/df_{reg}}{SS_{res}/df_{res}} = \frac{MS_{reg}}{MS_{res}}$$

where $df_{reg} = m$ and $df_{res} = (n - m - 1)$.

For the GGPA example, we compute the test statistic as

$$F = \frac{R^2 / m}{(1 - R^2)/(n - m - 1)} = \frac{.9089/2}{(1 - .9089)/(11 - 2 - 1)} = 39.9078$$

or as

$$F = \frac{SS_{reg}/df_{reg}}{SS_{res}/df_{res}} = \frac{0.9998/2}{.1002/8} = 39.9122$$

The critical value, at the .05 level of significance, is ${}_{.05}F_{2,8} = 4.46$. The test statistic exceeds the critical value, so we reject H_0 and conclude that all of the partial slopes are not equal to zero at the .05 level of significance (the two F test statistics differ slightly due to rounding error).

Test of Significance of b_k.   The second test is the test of the statistical significance of each individual partial slope or regression coefficient, b_k. That is, are the individual unstandardized regression coefficients statistically significantly different from zero? This is actually the same as the test of b_k^*, so we need not develop a separate test for b_k^*. The null and alternative hypotheses, respectively, are as follows:

$$H_0: \beta_k = 0$$

$$H_1: \beta_k \neq 0$$

where β_k is the population partial slope for X_k.

In multiple regression it is necessary to compute a standard error for each b_k. Recall from chapter 7 the variance error of estimate concept. The variance error of estimate is similarly defined for multiple linear regression as

$$s^2_{res} = SS_{res}/df_{res} = MS_{res}$$

where $df_{res} = (n - m - 1)$. Degrees of freedom are lost as we have to estimate the population partial slopes and intercept, the β_k's and α, respectively, from the sample data. The variance error of estimate indicates the amount of variation among the residuals. The standard error of estimate is simply the positive square root of the variance error of estimate, and is the standard deviation of the residuals or errors of estimate. We call it the **standard error of estimate**, denoted as s_{res}.

Finally, we need to compute a standard error for each b_k. Denote the standard error of b_k as $s(b_k)$ and define it as

$$s(b_k) = \frac{s_{res}}{\sqrt{(n-1)\, s_k^2 (1 - R_k^2)}}$$

where s_k^2 is the sample variance for predictor X_k, and R_k^2 is the squared multiple correlation between X_k and the remaining X_k's. The R_k^2 represent the overlap between that predictor (X_k) and the remaining predictors. In the case of two predictors, R_k^2 is equal to r_{12}^2.

The test statistic for testing the significance of the b_k's is as follows:

$$t = \frac{b_k}{s(b_k)}$$

The test statistic t is compared to the critical values of t, a two-tailed test for a nondirectional H_1, at the designated level of significance, and with degrees of freedom $(n - m - 1)$, as taken from the t table in Appendix Table 2. Thus the tabled critical values are $\pm_{(\alpha/2)} t_{(n-m-1)}$ for a two-tailed test.

We can also form a confidence interval around b_k as follows:

$$CI\,(b_k) = b_k \pm {}_{(\alpha/2)} t_{(n-m-1)}\, s(b_k)$$

Recall that the null hypothesis tested is H_0: $\beta_k = 0$. Therefore, if the confidence interval contains zero, then b_k is not significantly different from zero at the specified α level. This is interpreted to mean that in $(1 - \alpha)\%$ of the sample confidence intervals that would be formed from multiple samples, β_k will be included.

Let us compute the second test statistic for the GGPA example. We specify the null hypothesis to be $\beta_k = 0$ and conduct two-tailed tests. First the variance error of estimate is

$$s^2_{res} = SS_{res}/df_{res} = MS_{res} = .1002/8 = .0125$$

The standard error of estimate, s_{res}, is .1118. Next the standard errors of the b_k are found to be

$$s(b_1) = \frac{s_{res}}{\sqrt{(n-1)\, s_1^2 \left(1 - r_{12}^2\right)}} = \frac{.1118}{\sqrt{(10)\, 266.8182\, (1 - .3011^2)}} = .0023$$

$$s(b_2) = \frac{s_{res}}{\sqrt{(n-1)\,s_2^2\,(1-r_{12}^2)}} = \frac{.1118}{\sqrt{(10)\,0.1609\,(1-.3011^2)}} = .0924$$

Finally we find the t test statistics to be

$$t_1 = b_1/s(b_1) = .0125/.0023 = 5.4348$$

$$t_2 = b_2/s(b_2) = .4687/.0924 = 5.0725$$

To evaluate the null hypotheses, we compare these test statistics to the critical values of $\pm\,_{.025}t_8 = \pm 2.306$. Both test statistics exceed the critical value; consequently H_0 is rejected in favor of H_1 for both predictors. We conclude that the partial slopes are indeed significantly different from zero, at the .05 level of significance.

Finally, let us compute the confidence intervals for the b_k's as follows:

$$\text{CI}\,(b_1) = b_1 \pm {}_{(\alpha/2)}t_{(n-m-1)}\,s(b_1) = b_1 \pm {}_{.025}t_8\,s(b_1) = .0125 \pm 2.306(.0023) = (.0072, .0178)$$

$$\text{CI}\,(b_2) = b_2 \pm {}_{(\alpha/2)}t_{(n-m-1)}\,s(b_2) = b_2 \pm {}_{.025}t_8\,s(b_2) = .4687 \pm 2.306(.0924) = (.2556, .6818)$$

The intervals do not contain zero, the value specified in H_0; thus we again conclude that both b_k's are significantly different from zero, at the .05 level of significance.

Other Tests.   One can also form confidence intervals for the predicted mean of Y and the prediction intervals for individual values of Y, as we described in chapter 7.

8.2.5   Assumptions

A considerable amount of space in chapter 7 was dedicated to the assumptions of simple linear regression. For the most part, the assumptions of multiple linear regression are the same, and thus we need not devote as much space here. The assumptions are concerned with independence, homogeneity, normality, linearity, fixed X, and noncollinearity. This section also mentions those techniques appropriate for evaluating each assumption.

Independence.   The first assumption is concerned with **independence** of the observations. The simplest procedure for assessing independence is to examine residual plots of e versus Y' and of e versus each X_k (alternatively, one can look at plots of Y versus Y' and of Y versus each X_k). If the independence assumption is satisfied, the residuals should fall into a random display of points. If the assumption is violated, the residuals will fall into some sort of pattern. Lack of independence affects the estimated standard errors of the model. For serious violations one could consider generalized or weighted least squares as the method of estimation (e.g., Weisberg, 1985; Myers, 1986), or some type of transformation. The residual plots shown in Fig. 8.1 do not suggest any independence problems for the GGPA example, where Fig. 8.1(a) represents e versus Y', Fig. 8.1(b) represents e versus GRETOT, and Fig. 8.1(c) represents e versus UGPA.

Homogeneity.   The second assumption is **homogeneity of variance**, where the conditional distributions have the same constant variance for all values of X. In the residual plots the con-

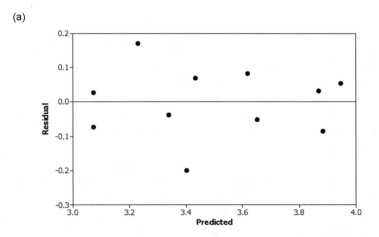

(a)

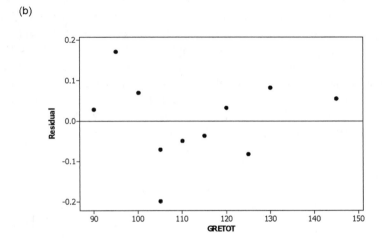

(b)

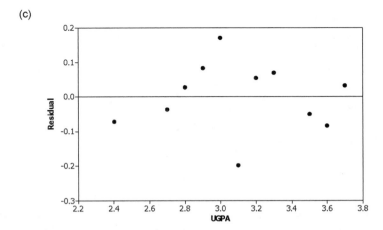

(c)

FIG. 8.1   Residual plots for GRE—GPA example: (a), (b), (c).

sistency of the variance of the conditional distributions may be examined. If the homogeneity assumption is violated, estimates of the standard errors are larger, and the conditional distributions may also be nonnormal. As described in chapter 7, solutions include variance stabilizing transformations (such as the square root or log of Y), generalized or weighted least squares (e.g., Myers, 1986; Weisberg, 1985), or robust regression (Kleinbaum, Kupper, Muller, & Nizam, 1998; Myers, 1986; Wilcox, 1996, 2003; Wu, 1985). Due to the small sample size, homogeneity cannot really be assessed for the example data.

Normality.   The third assumption is that the conditional distributions of the scores on Y, or the prediction errors, are **normal** in shape. Violation of the normality assumption may be the result of outliers. The simplest outlier detection procedure is to look for observations that are more than two standard errors from the mean. Other procedures were described in chapter 17. Several methods for dealing with outliers are available, such as conducting regression analyses with and without suspected outliers, robust regression (Kleinbaum, Kupper, Muller, & Nizam, 1998; Myers, 1986; Wilcox, 1996, 2003; Wu, 1985), and nonparametric regression (Miller, 1997; Rousseeuw & Leroy, 1987; Wu, 1985). The following can be used to detect normality violations: frequency distributions, normal probability plots, and skewness statistics. For the example data, the normal probability plot is shown in Fig. 8.2, and even with a small sample looks good. Violation can lead to imprecision in the partial slopes and the coefficient of determination. There are also several statistical procedures available for the detection of nonnormality (e.g., Andrews, 1971; Belsley, Kuh, & Welsch, 1980; D'Agostino, 1971; Ruppert & Carroll, 1980; Shapiro & Wilk, 1965; Wu, 1985); transformations can also be used to normalize the data. Review chapter 7 for more details.

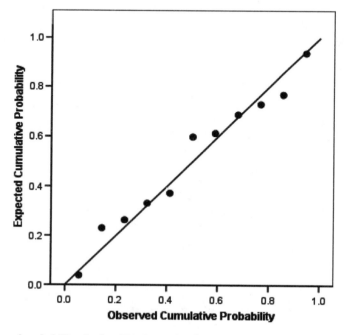

FIG. 8.2   Normal probability plot for GRE-GPA example.

Linearity. The fourth assumption is **linearity**, that there is a linear relationship between Y and the X_k's. If satisfied, then the sample partial slopes and intercept are unbiased estimators of the population partial slopes and intercept, respectively. The linearity assumption is important because regardless of the value of X_k, we always expect Y to increase by b_k units for a one unit increase in X_k, controlling for the other X_k's. If a nonlinear relationship exists, this means that the expected increase in Y depends on the value of X_k; that is, the expected increase is not a constant value. Strictly speaking, linearity in a model refers to there being linearity in the parameters of the model (i.e., α and the β_k's).

Violation of the linearity assumption can be detected through residual plots. The residuals should be located within a band of $\pm 2\, s_{res}$ (or standard errors), indicating no systematic pattern of points, as previously discussed in chapter 7. Residual plots for the GGPA example are shown in Figure 8.1. Even with a very small sample, we see a fairly random pattern of residuals, and therefore feel fairly confident that the linearity assumption has been satisfied. Note also that there are other types of residual plots developed especially for multiple regression, such as the added variable and partial residual plots (Larsen & McCleary, 1972; Mansfield & Conerly, 1987; Weisberg, 1985). Procedures to deal with nonlinearity include transformations (of one or more of the X_k's and/or of Y as described in chapter 7) and other regression models (discussed later in this chapter).

Fixed X. The fifth assumption is that the values of X_k are **fixed**, where the X_k are fixed variables rather than random variables. This results in the regression model being valid only for those particular values of X_k that were actually observed and used in the analysis. Thus, the same values of X_k would be used in replications or repeated samples.

Strictly speaking, the regression model and its parameter estimates are only valid for those values of X_k actually sampled. The use of a prediction model developed to predict Y, based on one sample of individuals, may be suspect for another sample of individuals. Depending on the circumstances, the new sample of individuals may actually call for a different set of parameter estimates. Expanding on our discussion in chapter 7, generally we may not want to make predictions about individuals having combinations of X_k scores outside of the range of values used in developing the prediction model; this is defined as extrapolating beyond the sample predictor data. On the other hand, we may not be quite as concerned in making predictions about individuals having combinations of X_k scores within the range of values used in developing the prediction model; this is defined as interpolating within the range of the sample predictor data.

It has been shown that when other assumptions are met, regression analysis performs just as well when X is a random variable (e.g., Glass & Hopkins, 1996; Myers & Well, 1995; Pedhazur, 1997; Wonnacott & Wonnacott, 1981). There is no such assumption about Y.

Noncollinearity. The final assumption is unique to multiple linear regression, being unnecessary in simple linear regression. A violation of this assumption is known as collinearity where there is a very strong linear relationship between two or more of the predictors. The presence of severe collinearity is problematic in several respects. First, it will lead to instability of the regression coefficients across samples, where the estimates will bounce around quite a bit in terms of magnitude and even occasionally result in changes in sign (perhaps opposite of expectation). This occurs because the standard errors of the regression coefficients become larger, thus making it more difficult to achieve statistical significance. Another result that may occur involves an overall regression that is significant, but none of the individual predictors are significant. Collinearity will also restrict the utility and generalizability of the estimated regression model.

Recall from earlier in the chapter the notion of partial regression coefficients, where the other predictors were held constant. In the presence of severe collinearity the other predictors cannot really be held constant because they are so highly intercorrelated. Collinearity may be indicated when there are large changes in estimated coefficients due to (a) a variable being added or deleted and/or (b) an observation being added or deleted (Chatterjee & Price, 1977). Collinearity is also likely when a composite variable as well as its component variables are used as predictors (e.g., including GRETOT, GRE-Quantitative, and GRE-Verbal as predictors).

How do we detect violations of this assumption? The simplest procedure is to conduct a series of special regression analyses, one for each X, where that predictor is predicted by all of the remaining X's (i.e., the criterion variable is not involved). If any of the resultant R_k^2 values are close to one (greater than .9 is a good rule of thumb), then there may be a collinearity problem. However, the large R^2 value may also be due to small sample size; thus more data would be useful. For the example data, $R_{12}^2 = .0907$ and therefore collinearity is not a concern.

Also, if the number of predictors is greater than or equal to n, then perfect collinearity is a possibility. Another statistical method for detecting collinearity is to compute a variance inflation factor (VIF) for each predictor, which is equal to $1/(1 - R_k^2)$. The VIF is defined as the inflation that occurs for each regression coefficient above the ideal situation of uncorrelated predictors. Many suggest that the largest VIF should be less than 10 in order to satisfy this assumption (Myers, 1990; Stevens, 2002; Wetherill, 1986).

There are several possible methods for dealing with a collinearity problem. First, one can remove one or more of the correlated predictors. Second, ridge regression techniques can be used (e.g., Hoerl & Kennard, 1970a, 1970b; Marquardt & Snee, 1975; Myers, 1986; Wetherill, 1986). Third, principal component scores resulting from principal component analysis can be utilized rather than raw scores on each variable (e.g., Kleinbaum et al., 1998; Myers, 1986; Weisberg, 1985; Wetherill, 1986). Fourth, transformations of the variables can be used to remove or reduce the extent of the problem. The final solution, and probably my last choice, is to use simple linear regression, as collinearity cannot exist with a single predictor.

Summary. For the GGPA example, although sample size is quite small in terms of looking at conditional distributions, it would appear that all of our assumptions have been satisfied. All of the residuals are within two standard errors of zero, and there does not seem to be any systematic pattern in the residuals. The distribution of the residuals is nearly symmetric and the normal probability plot looks good. A summary of the assumptions and the effects of their violation for multiple linear regression is presented in Table 8.2.

8.3   OTHER REGRESSION MODELS

The multiple predictor model we have considered thus far can be viewed as **simultaneous regression**. That is, all of the predictors to be used are entered (or selected) simultaneously, such that all of the regression parameters are estimated simultaneously; here the set of predictors has been selected a priori. There is also another class of models where the predictor variables are entered (or selected) systematically; here the set of predictors has not been selected a priori. This class of models is referred to as **sequential regression** (also known as **variable selection pro-**

TABLE 8.2

Assumptions and Violation of Assumptions—Multiple Linear Regression

Assumption	Effect of Assumption Violation
1. Independence	Influences standard errors of the model
2. Homogeneity	Bias in s^2_{res}; may inflate standard errors and thus increase likelihood of a Type II error; may result in nonnormal conditional distributions
3. Normality	Less precise slopes and R^2
4. Linearity	Bias in slopes and intercept; expected change in Y is not a constant and depends on value of X variables
5. Values of X's are fixed	(a) Extrapolating beyond the range of X combinations: prediction errors larger, may also bias slopes and intercept (b) Interpolating within the range of X combinations: smaller effects than in (a); if other assumptions met, negligible effect
6. Noncollinearity of X's	Regression coefficients can be quite unstable across samples (as standard errors are larger); R^2 may be significant, yet none of the predictors are significant; restricted generalizability of the model

cedures). This section introduces a brief description of the following sequential regression procedures: backward elimination, forward selection, stepwise selection, all possible subsets regression, and hierarchical regression. We also include introductions to dealing with nonlinear relationships and logistic regression in this section.

Backward Elimination. First consider the backward elimination procedure. Here variables are eliminated from the model based on their minimal contribution to the prediction of the criterion variable. In the first stage of the analysis, all potential predictors are included in the model. In the second stage, that predictor is deleted from the model that makes the smallest contribution to the prediction of the dependent variable. This can be done by eliminating that variable having the smallest t or F statistic such that it is making the smallest contribution to R^2_{adj}. In subsequent stages, that predictor is deleted that makes the next smallest contribution to the prediction of Y. The analysis continues until each of the remaining predictors in the model is a significant predictor of Y. This could be determined by comparing the t or F statistics for each predictor to the critical value, at a preselected level of significance. Some computer programs use as a stopping rule the maximum F-to-remove criterion, where the procedure is stopped when all of the selected predictors' F values are greater than the specified F criterion. Another stopping rule is where the researcher stops at a predetermined number of predictors (see Hocking, 1976; Thompson, 1978).

Forward Selection. In the forward selection procedure variables are added or selected into the model based on their maximal contribution to the prediction of the criterion variable. Initially, none of the potential predictors are included in the model. In the first stage, the predictor is added to the model that makes the largest contribution to the prediction of the dependent variable. This can be done by selecting that variable having the largest t or F statistic such that it is making the largest contribution to R^2_{adj}. In subsequent stages, the predictor is selected that makes the next largest contribution to the prediction of Y. The analysis continues until each of the selected predictors in the model is a significant predictor of Y, whereas none of the unselected predictors is a significant predictor. This could be determined by comparing the t or F statistics for each predictor to the critical value, at a preselected level of significance. Some computer programs use as a stopping rule the minimum F-to-enter criterion, where the procedure is stopped when all of the unselected predictors' F values are less than the specified F criterion. For the same set of data and at the same level of significance, the backward elimination and forward selection procedures may not necessarily result in the exact same final model, due to the differences in how variables are selected.

Stepwise Selection. The stepwise selection procedure is a modification of the forward selection procedure with one important difference. Predictors that have been selected into the model can at a later step be deleted from the model; thus the modification conceptually involves a backward elimination mechanism. This situation can occur for a predictor when a significant contribution at an earlier step later becomes a nonsignificant contribution given the set of other predictors in the model. Thus a predictor loses its significance due to new predictors being added to the model.

The stepwise selection procedure is as follows. Initially, none of the potential predictors are included in the model. In the first step, that predictor is added to the model that makes the largest contribution to the explanation of the dependent variable. This can be done by selecting that variable having the largest t or F statistic such that it is making the largest contribution to R^2_{adj}. In subsequent stages, the predictor is selected that makes the next largest contribution to the prediction of Y. Those predictors that have entered at earlier stages are also checked to see if their contribution remains significant. If not, then that predictor is eliminated from the model. The analysis continues until each of the predictors remaining in the model is a significant predictor of Y, while none of the other predictors is a significant predictor. This could be determined by comparing the t or F statistics for each predictor to the critical value, at a specified level of significance. Some computer programs use as stopping rules the minimum F-to-enter and maximum F-to-remove criteria, where the F-to-enter value selected is usually equal to or slightly greater than the F-to-remove value selected (to prevent a predictor from continuously being entered and removed). For the same set of data and at the same level of significance, the backward elimination, forward selection, and stepwise selection procedures may not necessarily result in the exact same final model, due to differences in how variables are selected.

All Possible Subsets Regression. Another sequential regression procedure is known as all possible subsets regression. Let us say, for example, that there are five potential predictors. In this procedure, all possible one-, two-, three-, and four-variable models are analyzed (with five predictors there is only a single five-predictor model). Thus there will be 5 one-predictor models, 10 two-predictor models, 10 three-predictor models, and 5 four-predictor models. The best k predictor model can be selected as the model that yields the largest R^2_{adj}. For example, the best three-predictor model would be that model of the 10 estimated that yields the largest R^2_{adj}. With today's powerful computers, this procedure is easier and more cost efficient than in the past. However, the researcher is not advised to consider this procedure, or for that matter any of the other sequential regression procedures, when the number of potential predictors is large. Here the researcher is allowing number crunching to take precedence over thoughtful analysis. Also, the number of models will be equal to 2^m, so that for 10 predictors there are 1,024 possible subsets. Obviously examining that number of models is not a thoughtful analysis.

Hierarchical Regression.   In hierarchical regression, the researcher specifies a priori a sequence for the individual predictor variables (not to be confused with hierarchical linear models, which is a method for analyzing data collected at multiple levels, such as child, classroom, and school). The analysis proceeds in a forward selection, backward elimination, or stepwise selection mode according to a researcher specified, theoretically-based sequence rather than an unspecified statistically-based sequence. This variable selection method is different from those previously discussed in that the researcher determines the order of entry from a careful consideration of the available research instead of the software dictating the sequence.

A type of hierarchical regression is known as **setwise regression** (also called **blockwise**, **chunkwise**, or **forced stepwise regression**). Here the researcher specifies a priori a sequence for sets of predictor variables. This procedure is similar to hierarchical regression in that the researcher determines the order of entry of the predictors. The difference is that the setwise method uses sets of predictor variables at each stage rather than one individual predictor variable at a time. The sets of variables are determined by the researcher so that variables within a set share some common theoretical ground (e.g., home background variables in one set and aptitude variables in another set). Variables within a set are selected according to one of the sequential regression procedures. The variables selected for a particular set are then entered in the specified theoretically-based sequence.

Commentary on Sequential Regression Procedures.   Let me make some comments and recommendations about the sequential regression procedures. First, numerous statisticians have noted problems with stepwise methods (i.e., backward elimination, forward selection, and stepwise selection) (e.g., Derksen & Keselman, 1992; Huberty, 1989; Mickey, Dunn, & Clark, 2004; Miller, 1984, 1990; Wilcox, 2003). These problems include the following: (a) selecting noise rather than important predictors; (b) highly inflated R^2 and R^2_{adj} values; (c) confidence intervals for partial slopes that are too narrow; (d) p values that are not trustworthy; (e) important predictors being barely edged out of the model, making it possible to miss the true model; and (f) potentially heavy capitalization on chance given the number of models analyzed. Second, theoretically-based regression models have become the norm in many disciples. Thus hierarchical regression either has or will dominate the landscape of the sequential regression procedures. Thus I strongly encourage you to consider more extended discussions of hierarchical regression (e.g., Bernstein, 1988; Cohen & Cohen, 1983; Pedhazur, 1997; Schafer, 1991; Tabachnick & Fidell, 2001).

If you are dealing in an area of inquiry where research evidence is sparce or non-existant, then you are conducting exploratory research. Thus you are probably trying to simply identify the key variables. Here hierarchical regression is not appropriate, as a theoretically-driven sequence cannot be developed. Here we recommend the use of all possible subsets regression (e.g., Kleinbaum, Kupper, Muller, & Nizam, 1998). For additional information on the sequential regression procedures, see Cohen and Cohen (1983), Weisberg (1985), Miller (1990), Pedhazur (1997), and Kleinbaum, et al. (1998).

Nonlinear Relationships.   Here we continue our discussion on how to deal with nonlinearity from chapter 7. We formally introduce several multiple regression models for when the criterion variable does not have a linear relationship with the predictor variables.

First consider polynomial regression models. In polynomial models, powers of the predictor variables are used. In general, a sample polynomial regression model is as follows:

$$Y = b_1 X + b_2 X^2 + \dots + b_m X^m + a + e$$

where the independent variable X is taken from the first power through the mth power, and the i subscript for observations has been deleted to simplify matters. If the model consists only of X taken to the first power, then this is a **simple linear regression model** (or **first-degree polynomial**; this is a straight line). A **second-degree polynomial** includes X taken to the second power (or **quadratic model**; this is a curve with one bend in it rather than a straight line). A **third-degree polynomial** includes X taken to the third power (or **cubic model**; this is a curve with two bends in it).

A polynomial model with multiple predictors can also be utilized. An example of a second-degree polynomial model with two predictors would be

$$Y = b_1 X_1 + b_2 X_1^2 + b_3 X_2 + b_4 X_2^2 + a + e$$

For more information on polynomial regression models, see Weisberg (1985), Bates and Watts (1988), Seber and Wild (1989), Pedhazur (1997), and Kleinbaum, et al. (1998). Alternatively, one might transform the criterion variable and/or the predictor variables to obtain a more linear form, as previously discussed.

A final type of model involves the use of an interaction term, as previously discussed in factorial ANOVA (chap. 3). These can be implemented in any type of regression model. We can write a simple two-predictor interaction-type model as

$$Y = b_1 X_1 + b_2 X_2 + b_3 X_1 X_2 + a + e$$

where $X_1 X_2$ represents the interaction of predictor variables 1 and 2. An interaction can be defined as occurring when the relationship between Y and X_1 depends on the level of X_2. In other words, X_2 is a **moderator variable**. For example, suppose one were to use years of education and age to predict political attitude. The relationship between education and attitude might be moderated by age. In other words, the relationship between education and attitude may be different for older versus younger individuals. If age were a moderator, we would expect there to be an interaction between age and education in a regression model. Note that if the predictors are very highly correlated, collinearity is likely. For more information on interaction models, see Cohen and Cohen (1983), Berry and Feldman (1985), Kleinbaum, et al. (1998), Weinberg and Abramowitz (2002), and Meyers, Gamst, and Guarino (2006).

Logistic Regression.   There is one final regression model to introduce. If the dependent variable is dichotomous, then none of the regression methods described in this text are appropriate. This is where the method of logistic regression becomes important. Initially used mostly in the hard sciences, this method has become more broadly popular in recent years. Some examples of dichotomous dependent variables are pass/fail, surviving surgery/not, admit/reject, vote for/against, employ/not, or purchase/not. The first condition is indicated by a value of 1 (e.g., pass), whereas a value of 0 indicates the opposite condition (e.g., fail). An important statistic in logistic regression is the odds ratio (*OR*), which is analagous to R^2. Conceptually this is the odds for one level (e.g., pass) divided by the odds for the other level (e.g., fail). The null hypothesis to be tested is that $OR = 1$, which indicates that there no relationship between a predictor variable and the dependent variable. Thus we want to find *OR* to be significantly different from 1. One can also determine OR_{adj} (adjusted *OR*) and confidence intervals for *OR*. Logistic regression utilizes maximum likelihood rather than least squares estimation, and the linear, normality, and homogeneity assumptions are not required. For more information on logistic regression, consider Wright (1995), Glass and Hopkins (1996), Christiansen (1997), Pedhazur (1997), Kleinbaum, et al. (1998), Hosmer and Lemeshow (2000), Pampel (2000), Huck (2004), and Meyers, Gamst, and Guarino (2006).

8.4 SPSS

In this section we consider the use of SPSS for the multiple linear regression model, including an APA paragraph of selected results. To conduct a multiple linear regression analysis, go from the "Analyze" pulldown, into "Regression," and then into the "Linear" procedure. Click your dependent variable "GGPA" into the "Dependent:" box and the independent variables "GRE-TOT" and "UGPA" into the "Independent(s):" box. Second, click on the "Statistics" button, where various types of statistics can be requested. At a minimum I suggest the following: estimates, confidence intervals, model fit, and descriptives. Note that part and partial correlations and collinearity diagnostics are also available there. If you click on the "Plots" button, you can generate residual plots and the normal probability plot. Finally, click on the "Save" button if you want to save various results into your dataset (e.g., different types of residuals or values from the confidence intervals). Selected results for the GRE-GPA example are shown in Table 8.3.

Lastly, here is an example paragraph of the results for the GRE-GPA example. From the top panel of Table 8.3, we see that $R^2 = .908$, indicating that 91% of the variation in GGPA was predicted by the set of GRETOT and UGPA. In the middle panel of Table 8.3, the ANOVA summary table indicates that a significant proportion of the total variation in GGPA scores was predicted by GRETOT and UGPA together ($F = 39.291, df = 2,8, p < .001$). In the bottom panel of Table 8.3 we see the following results: (a) the unstandardized partial slopes are both significantly different from zero (GRETOT: $b = .012, t = 5.447, df = 8, p = .001$; for UGPA: $b = .469, t = 5.030, df = 8, p = .001$); (b) the confidence intervals around the unstandardized partial slopes do not include zero, (c) the intercept was .638, and (d) VIF = 1.100 indicating no collinearity problems. Thus GRETOT and UGPA were shown to be statisticially significant predictors of GGPA, both individually and collectively.

Lastly we note that the more advanced regression models described in the previous section can all be conducted using SPSS. For further information on regression analysis with SPSS, see Morgan and Griego (1998), Weinberg and Abramowitz (2002), and Meyers, Gamst, and Guarino (2006),

8.5 WHAT'S NEXT?

As we conclude this text, the natural question to ask is what's next to examine in the field of statistics. There are two likely key alternatives. First, you could consider more advanced regression

TABLE 8.3

Selected SPSS Results for the GRE-GPA Example

Model Summary[b]

Model	R	R Square	Adjusted R Square	Std. Error of the Estimate
1	.953[a]	.908	.885	.11272

a. Predictors: (Constant), UGPA, GRETOT
b. Dependent Variable: GGPA

ANOVA[b]

Model	Sum of Squares	df	Mean Square	F	Sig.
1 Regression	.998	2	.499	39.291	.000[a]
Residual	.102	8	.013		
Total	1.100	10			

a. Predictors: (Constant), UGPA, GRETOT
b. Dependent Variable: GGPA

Coefficients

Model	Unstandardized Coefficients B	Std. Error	Standardized Coefficients Beta	t	Sig.	95% Confidence Interval for B Lower Bound	Upper Bound	Collinearity Statistics VIF
1 (Constant)	.638	.327		1.954	.087	−.115	1.391	
GRETOT	.012	.002	.614	5.447	.001	.007	.018	1.100
UGPA	.469	.093	.567	5.030	.001	.254	.684	1.100

a. Dependent Variable: GGPA

models, along the lines of those introduced toward the end of this chapter. These would also be covered in a regression course. In terms of regression readings, you might consider looking at Cohen and Cohen (1983), Grimm and Arnold (1995), Pedhazur (1997), Kleinbaum, et al. (1998), and Meyers, Gamst, and Guarino (2006).

Alternatively you could consider multivariate analysis methods, either in terms of readings or in a multivariate course. Briefly, the major methods of multivariate analysis include multivariate analysis of variance (MANOVA), discriminant analysis, factor and principal components analysis, canonical correlation analysis, cluster analysis, multidimensional scaling, multivariate regression, and structural equation modeling. For multivariate readings, take a look at Grimm and Arnold (1995, 2000), Marcoulides and Hershberger (1997), Johnson and Wichern (1998),

Kleinbaum, et al. (1998), Stevens (2002), Timm (2002), Manly (2004), and Meyers, Gamst, and Guarino (2006).

8.6   SUMMARY

In this chapter, methods involving multiple predictors in the regression context were considered. The chapter began with a look at partial and semipartial correlations. Next, a lengthy discussion of multiple linear regression was conducted. Here we extended many of the basic concepts of simple linear regression to the multiple predictor situation. In addition, several new concepts were introduced, including the coefficient of multiple determination, multiple correlation, and tests of the individual regression coefficients. Finally we examined a number of other regression models, such as forward selection, backward elimination, stepwise selection, all possible subsets regression, hierarchical regression, nonlinear relationship, and logistic regression. At this point you should have met the following objectives: (a) be able to determine and interpret the results of part and semipartial correlations, (b) be able to understand the concepts underlying multiple linear regression, (c) be able to determine and interpret the results of multiple linear regression, (d) be able to understand and evaluate the assumptions of multiple linear regression, and (e) be able to have a basic understanding of other types of regression models. This concludes our statistical concepts text. We wish you the best of luck in your future statistical adventures.

PROBLEMS

Conceptual Problems

1. Variable 1 is to be predicted from a combination of variable 2 and one of variables 3, 4, 5, or 6. The correlations of importance are as follows:

    $r_{13} = .8$ $r_{23} = .2$

    $r_{14} = .6$ $r_{24} = .5$

    $r_{15} = .6$ $r_{25} = .2$

    $r_{16} = .8$ $r_{26} = .5$

    Which of the following multiple correlation coefficients will have the largest value?

    a. $r_{1.23}$

    b. $r_{1.24}$

    c. $r_{1.25}$

    d. $r_{1.26}$

2. The most accurate predictions are made when the standard error of estimate equals

    a. $\overline{Y}$

    b. s_Y

    c.   0

    d.   1

3. The intercept can take on a positive value only. True or false?

4. Adding an additional predictor to a regression equation will necessarily result in an increase in R^2. True or false?

5. The best prediction in multiple regression will result when each predictor has a high correlation with the other predictor variables and a high correlation with the dependent variable. True or false?

6. Consider the following two situations:

   Situation 1 $r_{Y1} = .6$ $r_{Y2} = .5$ $r_{12} = .0$
   Situation 2 $r_{Y1} = .6$ $r_{Y2} = .5$ $r_{12} = .2$

   I assert that the value of R^2 will be greater in Situation 2. Am I correct?

7. Values of variables X_1, X_2, X_3 are available for a sample of 50 students. The value of $r_{12} = .6$. I assert that if the partial correlation $r_{12.3}$ were calculated it would be larger than .6. Am I correct?

8. I assert that the forward selection, backward elimination, and stepwise regression methods will always arrive at the same final model, given the same dataset and level of significance? Am I correct?

9. I assert the R^2_{adj} will always be larger for the most predictors in the model. Am I correct?

10. In a two-predictor regression model, if the correlation among the predictors is .95 and VIF is 20, then we should be concerned about collinearity. True or false?

Computational Problems

1. You are given the following data, where X_1 (hours of professional development) and X_2 (aptitude test scores) are used to predict Y (annual salary in thousands):

Y	X_1	X_2
40	100	10
50	200	20
50	300	10
70	400	30
65	500	20
65	600	20
80	700	30

   Determine the following values: intercept; b_1; b_2; SS_{res}; SS_{reg}; F; s^2_{res}; $s(b_1)$; $s(b_2)$; t_1; t_2.

2. Complete the missing information for this regression model ($df = 23$).

$$Y' = 25.1 + 1.2\,X_1 + 1.0\,X_2 - .50\,X_3$$

	(2.1)	(1.5)	(1.3)	(.06)	standard errors
	(11.9)	( )	( )	( )	t ratios
		( )	( )	( )	significant at .05?

3. Consider a sample of elementary school children. Given that r(strength, weight) $=$ .6, r(strength, age) $= .7$, and r(weight, age) $= .8$, what is the first-order partial correlation coefficient between strength and weight holding age constant?

4. For a sample of 100 adults, you are given that $r_{12} = .55$, $r_{13} = .80$, $r_{23} = .70$. What is the value of $r_{1(2.3)}$?

5. A researcher would like to predict salary from a set of four predictor variables for a sample of 45 subjects. Multiple linear regression was used to analyze these data. Complete the following summary table ($\alpha = .05$) for the test of significance of the overall regression model:

Source	SS	df	MS	F	Critical Value and Decision
Regression	—	—	20	—	—
Residual	400	—	—		
Total	—	—			

6. Calculate the partial correlation $r_{12.3}$ and the part correlation $r_{1(2.3)}$ from the following bivariate correlations: $r_{12} = .5$, $r_{13} = .8$, $r_{23} = .9$.

7. Calculate the partial correlation $r_{13.2}$ and the part correlation $r_{1(3.2)}$ from the following bivariate correlations: $r_{12} = .21$, $r_{13} = .40$, $r_{23} = -.38$.

8. You are given the following data, where X_1 (verbal aptitude) and X_2 (prior reading achievement) are to be used to predict Y (reading achievement):

Y	X_1	X_2
2	2	5
1	2	4
1	1	5
1	1	3
5	3	6
4	4	4
7	5	6
6	5	4
7	7	3
8	6	3

3	4	3
3	3	6
6	6	9
6	6	8
10	8	9
9	9	6
6	10	4
6	9	5
9	4	8
10	4	9

Determine the following values: intercept; b_1; b_2; SS_{res}; SS_{reg}; F; s^2_{res}; $s(b_1)$; $s(b_2)$; t_1; t_2.

Interpretive Problem

Use SPSS to develop a multiple regression model with the example survey data on the CD. Utilize current GPA as the dependent variable to find at least two strong predictors from among the continuous variables in the dataset.

References

Agresti, A. & Finlay, B. (1986). *Statistical methods for the social sciences* (2nd ed.). San Francisco: Dellen.

Agresti, A. & Pendergast, J. (1986). Comparing mean ranks for repeated measures data. *Communications in Statistics—Theory and Methods, 15*, 1417–1433.

Algina, J., Blair, R. C., & Coombs, W. T. (1995). A maximum test for scale: Type I error rates and power. *Journal of Educational and Behavioral Statistics, 20*, 27–39.

Andrews, D. F. (1971). Significance tests based on residuals. *Biometrika, 58*, 139–148.

Andrews, D. F. & Pregibon, D. (1978). Finding the outliers that matter. *Journal of the Royal Statistical Society, Series B, 40*, 85–93.

Applebaum, M. I. & Cramer, E. M. (1974). Some problems in the nonorthogonal analysis of variance. *Psychological Bulletin, 81*, 335–343.

Atiqullah, M. (1964). The robustness of the covariance analysis of a one-way classification. *Biometrika, 51*, 365–373.

Atkinson, A. C. (1985). *Plots, transformations, and regression*. Oxford: Oxford University Press.

Barnett, V. & Lewis, T. (1978). *Outliers in statistical data*. New York: Wiley.

Basu, S. & DasGupta, A. (1995). Robustness of standard confidence intervals for location parameters under departure from normality. *Annals of Statistics, 23*, 1433–1442.

Bates, D. M. & Watts, D. G. (1988). *Nonlinear regression analysis and its applications* . New York: Wiley.

Beal, S. L. (1987). Asymptotic confidence intervals for the difference between two binomial parameters for use with small samples. *Biometrics, 43*, 941–950.

Beckman, R. & Cook, R. D. (1983). Outliers . . . s. *Technometrics*, 25, 119–149.

Belsley, D. A., Kuh, E., & Welsch, R. E. (1980). *Regression diagnostics*. New York: Wiley.

Benjamini, Y. & Hochberg, Y. (1995). Controlling the false discovery rate: A practical and powerful approach to multiple testing. *Journal of the Royal Statistical Society, B, 57*, 289–300.

Bernstein, I. H. (1988). *Applied multivariate analysis*. New York: Springer-Verlag.

Berry, W. D. & Feldman, S. (1985). *Multiple regression in practice*. Beverly Hills: Sage.

Boik, R. J. (1979). Interactions, partial interactions, and interaction contrasts in the analysis of variance. *Psychological Bulletin, 86*, 1084–1089.

Boik, R. J. (1981). A priori tests in repeated measures designs: Effects of nonsphericity. *Psychometrika, 46*, 241–255.

Box, G. E. P. (1954a). Some theorems on quadratic forms applied in the study of analysis of variance problems, I: Effects of inequality of variance in the one-way model. *Annals of Mathematical Statistics, 25*, 290–302.

Box, G. E. P. (1954b). Some theorems on quadratic forms applied in the study of analysis of variance problems, II: Effects of inequality of variance and of correlation between errors in the two-way classification. *Annals of Mathematical Statistics, 25*, 484–498.

Box, G. E. P. & Anderson, S. L. (1962). *Robust tests for variances and effect of non-normality and variance heterogeneity on standard tests*. Technical Report No. 7, Ordinance Project No. TB 2-0001 (832), Dept. of Army Project No. 599-01-004.

Bradley, J. V. (1978). Robustness? *British Journal of Mathematical and Statistical Psychology, 31*, 144–152.

Brown, M. B. & Forsythe, A. (1974). The ANOVA and multiple comparisons for data with heterogeneous variances. *Biometrics, 30*, 719–724.

Brunner, E., Detta, H., & Munk, A. (1997). Box-type approximations in nonparametric factorial designs. *Journal of the American Statistical Association, 92*, 1494–1502.

Bryant, J. L. & Paulson, A. S. (1976). An extension of Tukey's method of multiple comparisons to experimental designs with random concomitant variables. *Biometrika, 63*, 631–638.

Campbell, D. T. & Stanley, J. C. (1966). *Experimental and quasi-experimental designs for research*. Chicago: Rand McNally.

Carlson, J. E. & Timm, N. H. (1974). Analysis of nonorthogonal fixed-effects designs. *Psychological Bulletin, 81*, 563–570.

Carroll, R. J. & Ruppert, D. (1982). Robust estimation in heteroscedastic linear models. *Annals of Statistics, 10*, 429–441.

Chambers, J. M., Cleveland, W. S., Kleiner, B., & Tukey, P. A. (1983). *Graphical methods for data analysis*. Belmont CA: Wadsworth.

Chatterjee, S. & Price, B. (1977). *Regression analysis by example*. New York: Wiley.

Christensen, R. (1997). *Log-linear models and logistic regression* (2nd ed.) New York: Springer-Verlag.

Cleveland, W. S. (1993). *Elements of graphing data*. New York: Chapman & Hall.

Clinch, J. J. & Keselman, H. J. (1982). Parametric alternatives to the analysis of variance. *Journal of Educational Statistics, 7*, 207–214.

Coe, P. R. & Tamhane, A. C. (1993). Small sample confidence intervals for the difference, ratio and odds ratio of two success probabilities. *Communications in Statistics—Simulation and Computation, 22*, 925–938.

Cohen, J. (1988). *Statistical power analysis for the behavioral sciences* (2nd ed.). Hillsdale NJ: Erlbaum.

Cohen, J. & Cohen, P. (1983). *Applied multiple regression/correlation analysis for the behavioral sciences* (2nd ed.). Hillsdale, NJ: Erlbaum.

Coombs, W. T., Algina, J., & Ottman, D. O. (1996). Univariate and multivariate omnibus hypothesis tests selected to control Type I error rates when population variances are not necessarily equal. *Review of Educational Research, 66*, 137–179.

Conover, W. & Iman, R. (1981). Rank transformations as a bridge between parametric and nonparametric statistics. *The American Statistician, 35*, 124–129.

Conover, W. & Iman, R. (1982). Analysis of covariance using the rank transformation. *Biometrics, 38*, 715–724.

Cotton, J. W. (1998). *Analyzing within-subjects experiments*. Mahwah NJ: Lawrence Erlbaum Associates.

Cook, R. D. (1977). Detection of influential observations in linear regression. *Technometrics, 19*, 15–18.

Cook, R. D. & Weisberg, S. (1982). *Residuals and influence in regression*. London: Chapman and Hall.

Cook, T. D. & Campbell, D. T. (1979). *Quasi-experimentation: Design and analysis issues for field settings*. Chicago: Rand McNally.

Cramer, E. M. & Applebaum, M. I. (1980). Nonorthogonal analysis of variance—Once again. *Psychological Bulletin, 87*, 51–57.

D'Agostino, R. B. (1971). An omnibus test of normality for moderate and large size samples. *Biometrika, 58*, 341–348.

Derksen, S. & Keselman, H. J. (1992). Backward, forward and stepwise automated subset selection algorithms: Frequency of obtaining authentic and noise variables. *British Journal of Mathematical and Statistical Psychology, 45*, 265–282.

Duncan, G. T. & Layard, M. W. J. (1973). A Monte-Carlo study of asymptotically robust tests for correlation coefficients. *Biometrika, 60*, 551–558.

Dunn, O. J. (1961). Multiple comparisons among means. *Journal of the American Statistical Association, 56*, 52–64.

Dunn, O. J. (1974). On multiple tests and confidence intervals. *Communications in Statistics, 3*, 101–103.

Dunn, O. J. & Clark, V. A. (1987). *Applied statistics: Analysis of variance and regression* (2nd ed.). New York: Wiley.

Dunnett, C. W. (1955). A multiple comparison procedure for comparing several treatments with a control. *Journal of the American Statistical Association, 50*, 1096–1121.

Dunnett, C. W. (1964). New tables for multiple comparisons with a control. *Biometrics, 20*, 482–491.

Dunnett, C. W. (1980). Pairwise multiple comparisons in the unequal variance case. *Journal of the American Statistical Association, 75*, 796–800.

Durbin, J. & Watson, G. S. (1950). Testing for serial correlation in least squares regression, I. *Biometrika, 37*, 409–428.

Durbin, J. & Watson, G. S. (1951). Testing for serial correlation in least squares regression, II. *Biometrika, 38*, 159–178.

Durbin, J. & Watson, G. S. (1971). Testing for serial correlation in least squares regression, III. *Biometrika, 58*, 1–19.

Educational and Psychological Measurement (October 2000). Special section: Statistical significance with comments by editors of marketing journals. *Educational and Psychological Measurement, 60*, 661–696.

Educational and Psychological Measurement (April 2001). Special section: Colloquium on effect sizes: The roles of editors, textbook authors, and the publication manual. *Educational and Psychological Measurement, 61*, 181–228.

Educational and Psychological Measurement (August 2001). Special section: Confidence intervals for effect sizes. *Educational and Psychological Measurement, 61*, 517–674.

Elashoff, J. D. (1969). Analysis of covariance: A delicate instrument. *American Educational Research Journal, 6*, 383–401.

Feldt, L. S. (1958). A comparison of the precision of three experimental designs employing a concomitant variable. *Psychometrika, 23*, 335–354.

Ferguson, G. A. & Takane, Y. (1989). *Statistical analysis in psychology and education* (6th ed.). New York: McGraw-Hill.

Fidler, F. & Thompson, B. (2001). Computing correct confidence intervals for ANOVA fixed- and random-effects effect sizes. *Educational and Psychological Measurement, 61*, 575–604.

Fink, A. (1995). *How to sample in surveys.* Thousand Oaks CA: Sage.

Fisher, R. A. (1949). *The design of experiments.* Edinburgh: Oliver & Boyd, Ltd.

Friedman, M. (1937). The use of ranks to avoid the assumption of normality implicit in the analysis of variance. *Journal of the American Statistical Association, 32*, 675–701.

Games, P. A. & Howell, J. F. (1976). Pairwise multiple comparison procedures with unequal n's and/or variances: A Monte Carlo study. *Journal of Educational Statistics, 1*, 113–125.

Geisser, S. & Greenhouse, S. (1958). Extension of Box's results on the use of the F distribution in multivariate analysis. *Annals of Mathematical Statistics, 29*, 855–891.

Ghosh, B. K. (1979). A comparison of some approximate confidence intervals for the binomial parameter. *Journal of the American Statistical Association, 74*, 894–900.

Glass, G. V. & Hopkins, K. D. (1996). *Statistical methods in education and psychology* (3rd ed.). Boston: Allyn & Bacon.

Glass, G. V., Peckham, P. D., & Sanders, J. R. (1972). Consequences of failure to meet assumptions underlying the fixed effects analyses of variance and covariance. *Review of Educational Research, 42*, 237–288.

Grimm, L. G. & Arnold, P. R. (Eds.). (1995). *Reading and understanding multivariate statistics*. Washington DC: American Psychological Association.

Grimm, L. G. & Arnold, P. R. (Eds.). (2002). *Reading and understanding more multivariate statistics*. Washington DC: American Psychological Association.

Grissom, R. J. & Kim, J. J. (2005). *Effect sizes for research: A broad practical approach*. Mahwah NJ: Lawrence Erlbaum Associates.

Harlow, L., Mulaik, S., & Steiger, J. (Eds.). (1997). *What if there were no significance tests?* Mahwah NJ: Lawrence Erlbaum Associates.

Harwell, M. (2003). Summarizing Monte Carlo results in methodological research: The single- factor, fixed-effects ANCOVA case. *Journal of Educational and Behavioral Statistics, 28*, 45–70.

Hawkins, D. M. (1980). *Identification of outliers*. London: Chapman and Hall.

Hays, W. L. (1988). *Statistics* (4th ed.). New York: Holt, Rinehart and Winston.

Hayter, A. J. (1986). The maximum familywise error rate of Fisher's least significant difference test. *Journal of the American Statistical Association, 81*, 1000–1004.

Heyde, C. C., Seneta, E., Crepel, P., Feinberg, S. E., & Gani, J. (Eds.) (2001). *Statisticians of the centuries*. New York: Springer.

Hockberg, Y. (1988). A sharper Bonferroni procedure for multiple tests of significance. *Biometrika, 75*, 800–802.

Hochberg, Y. & Tamhane, A. C. (1987). *Multiple comparison procedures*. New York: Wiley.

Hochberg, Y. & Varon-Salomon, Y. (1984). On simultaneous pairwise comparisons in analysis of covariance. *Journal of the American Statistical Association, 79*, 863–866.

Hocking, R. R. (1976). The analysis and selection of variables in linear regression. *Biometrics, 32*, 1–49.

Hoenig, J. M. & Heisey, D. M. (2001). The abuse of power: The pervasive fallacy of power calculations for data analysis. *The American Statistician, 55*, 19–24.

Hoerl, A. E. & Kennard, R. W. (1970a). Ridge regression: Biased estimation for non-orthogonal models. *Technometrics, 12*, 55–67.

Hoerl, A. E. & Kennard, R. W. (1970b). Ridge regression: Application to non-orthogonal models. *Technometrics, 12*, 591–612.

Hogg, R. V. & Craig, A. T. (1970). *Introduction to mathematical statistics*. New York: Macmillan.

Hosmer, D. W. & Lemeshow, S. (2000). *Applied logistic regression* (2nd ed.). New York: Wiley.

Huberty, C. J. (1989). Problems with stepwise methods—better alternatives. In B. Thompson (Ed.), *Advances in social science methodology, Volume 1* (pp. 43–70). Greenwich CT: JAI Press.

Huck, S. W. (2004). *Reading statistics and research* (4th ed.). Boston: Allyn and Bacon.

Huck, S. W. & McLean, R. A. (1975). Using a repeated measures ANOVA to analyze data from a pretest-posttest design: A potentially confusing task. *Psychological Bulletin, 82*, 511–518.

Huitema, B. E. (1980). *The analysis of covariance and alternatives*. New York: Wiley.

Huynh, H. & Feldt, L. S. (1970). Conditions under which mean square ratios in repeated measurement designs have exact F-distributions. *Journal of the American Statistical Association, 65*, 1582–1589.

Jaeger, R. M. (1984). *Sampling in education and the social sciences*. New York: Longman.

James, G. S. (1951). The comparison of several groups of observations when the ratios of the population variances are unknown. *Biometrika, 38*, 324–329.

Jennings, E. (1988). Models for pretest-posttest data: Repeated measures ANOVA revisited. *Journal of Educational Statistics, 13*, 273–280.

Johansen, S. (1980). The Welch-James approximation to the distribution of the residual sum of squares in a weighted linear regression. *Biometrika, 67*, 85–93.

Johnson, P. O. & Neyman, J. (1936). Tests of certain linear hypotheses and their application to some educational problems. *Statistical Research Memoirs, 1*, 57–93.

Johnson, R. A. & Wichern, D. W. (1998). *Applied multivariate statistical analysis* (4th ed.). Upper Saddle River NJ: Prentice Hall.

Kaiser, L. & Bowden, D. (1983). Simultaneous confidence intervals for all linear contrasts of means with heterogeneous variances. *Communications in Statistics—Theory and Methods, 12*, 73–88.

Kalton, G. (1983). *Introduction to survey sampling*. Thousand Oaks CA: Sage.

Keppel, G. (1982). *Design and analysis: A researcher's handbook* (2nd ed.). Englewood Cliffs, NJ: Prentice-Hall.

Keppel, G. & Wickens, T. D. (2004). *Design and analysis: A researcher's handbook* (3rd ed.). Upper Saddle River, NJ: Pearson.

Kirk, R. E. (1982). *Experimental design: Procedures for the behavioral sciences* (2nd ed.). Monterey, CA: Brooks/Cole.

Kleinbaum, D. G., Kupper, L. L., Muller, K. E., & Nizam, A. (1998). *Applied regression analysis and other multivariable methods* (3rd ed.). Pacific Grove CA: Duxbury.

Kramer, C. Y. (1956). Extension of multiple range test to group means with unequal numbers of replications. *Biometrics, 12*, 307–310.

Kruskal, W. H. & Wallis, W. A. (1952). Use of ranks on one-criterion variance analysis. *Journal of the American Statistical Association, 47*, 583–621. (with corrections in *48*, 907–911)

Lamb, G. S. (1984). What you always wanted to know about six but were afraid to ask. *The Journal of Irreproducible Results, 29*, 18–20.

Larsen, W. A. & McCleary, S. J. (1972). The use of partial residual plots in regression analysis. *Technometrics, 14*, 781–790.

Levy, P. S. & Lemeshow, S. (1999). *Sampling of populations: Methods and applications* (3rd ed.). New York: Wiley.

Lomax, R. G. & Surman, S. H. (2007). Factorial ANOVA in SPSS: Fixed-, random-, and mixed-effects models. In S. S. Sawilowsky (Ed.), *Real data analysis*. Greenwich CT: Information Age.

Lord, F. M. (1960). Large-sample covariance analysis when the control variable is fallible. *Journal of the American Statistical Association, 55*, 307–321.

Lord, F. M. (1967). A paradox in the interpretation of group comparisons. *Psychological Bulletin, 68*, 304–305.

Lord, F. M. (1969). Statistical adjustments when comparing preexisting groups. *Psychological Bulletin, 72*, 336–337.

Manly, B. F. J. (2004). *Multivariate statistical methods: A primer* (3rd ed.). London: Chapman & Hall.

Mansfield, E. R. & Conerly, M. D. (1987). Diagnostic value of residual and partial residual plots. *The American Statistician, 41*, 107–116.

Marascuilo, L. A. & Levin, J. R. (1970). Appropriate post hoc comparisons for interactions and nested hypotheses in analysis of variance designs: The elimination of type IV errors. *American Educational Research Journal, 7*, 397–421.

Marascuilo, L. A. & Levin, J. R. (1976). The simultaneous investigation of interaction and nested hypotheses in two-factor analysis of variance designs. *American Educational Research Journal, 13*, 61–65.

Marascuilo, L. A. & McSweeney, M. (1977). *Nonparametric and distribution-free methods for the social sciences*. Monterey, CA: Brooks/Cole.

Marascuilo, L. A. & Serlin, R. C. (1988). *Statistical methods for the social and behavioral sciences*. New York: Freeman.

Marcoulides, G. A. & Hershberger, S. L. (1997). *Multivariate statistical methods: A first course*. Mahwah NJ: Lawrence Erlbaum Associates.

Marquardt, D. W. & Snee, R. D. (1975). Ridge regression in practice. *The American Statistician, 29*, 3–19.

Maxwell, S. E. (1980). Pairwise multiple comparisons in repeated measures designs. *Journal of Educational Statistics, 5*, 269–287.

Maxwell, S. E. & Delaney, H. D. (1990). *Designing experiments and analyzing data: A model comparison perspective*. Belmont, CA: Wadsworth.

Maxwell, S. E., Delaney, H. D., & Dill, C. A. (1984). Another look at ANOVA versus blocking. *Psychological Bulletin, 95*, 136–147.

McCulloch, C. E. (2005). Repeated measures ANOVA, RIP? *Chance, 18*, 29–33.

Mendoza, J. L. & Stafford, K. L. (2001). Confidence intervals, power calculation, and sample size estimation for the squared multiple correlation coefficient under the fixed and random regression models: A computer program and useful standard tables. *Educational and Psychological Measurement, 61*, 650–667.

Meyers, L. S., Gamst, G., & Guarino, A. J. (2006). *Applied multivariate research: Design and interpretation*. Thousand Oaks CA: Sage.

Mickey, R. M., Dunn, O. J., & Clark, V. A. (2004). *Applied statistics: Analysis of variance and regression* (3rd ed.). Hoboken NJ: Wiley.

Miller, A. J. (1984). Selection of subsets of regression variables (with discussion). *Journal of the Royal Statistical Society, A, 147*, 389–425.

Miller, A. J. (1990). *Subset selection in regression*. New York: Chapman and Hall.

Miller, R. G. (1997). *Beyond ANOVA, basics of applied statistics*. Boca Raton, FL: CRC Press.

Morgan, G. A. & Griego, O.V. (1998). *Easy use and interpretation of SPSS for Windows: Answering research questions with statistics*. Mahwah NJ: Lawrence Erlbaum Associates.

Morgan, G. A., Leech, N. L., & Barrett, K. C. (2005). *SPSS for introductory and intermediate statistics*. Mahwah NJ: Lawrence Erlbaum Associates.

Murphy, K. R. & Myors, B. (2004). *Statistical power analysis: A simple and general model for traditional and modern hypothesis tests* (2nd ed.). Mahwah NJ: Lawrence Erlbaum Associates.

Myers, J. L. & Well, A. D. (1995). *Research design and statistical analysis*. Mahwah NJ: Lawrence Erlbaum Associates.

Myers, R. H. (1979). *Fundamentals of experimental design* (3rd ed.). Boston: Allyn and Bacon.

Myers, R. H. (1986). *Classical and modern regression with applications*. Boston: Duxbury.

Myers, R. H. (1990). *Classical and modern regression with applications* (2nd ed.). Boston: Duxbury.

Noreen, E. W. (1989). *Computer intensive methods for testing hypotheses*. New York: Wiley.

O'Grady, K. E. (1982). Measures of explained variance: Cautions and limitations. *Psychological Bulletin, 92*, 766–777.

Olejnik, S. F. & Algina, J. (1987). Type I error rates and power estimates of selected parametric and nonparametric tests of scale. *Journal of Educational Statistics, 21*, 45–61.

Overall, J. E., Lee, D. M., & Hornick, C. W. (1981). Comparison of two strategies for analysis of variance in nonorthogonal designs. *Psychological Bulletin, 90*, 367–375.

Overall, J. E. & Spiegel, D. K. (1969). Concerning least squares analysis of experimental data. *Psychological Bulletin, 72*, 311–322.

Page, M. C., Braver, S. L., & MacKinnon, D. P. (2003). *Levine's guide to SPSS for analysis of variance*. Mahwah NJ: Lawrence Erlbaum Associates.

Pampel, F. C. (2000). *Logistic regression: A primer*. Thousand Oaks CA: Sage.

Pavur, R. (1988). Type I error rates for multiple comparision procedures with dependent data. *The American Statistician, 42*, 171–173.

Pearson, E. S. (Ed.) (1978). *The history of statistics in the 17th and 18th Centuries*. New York: Macmillan.

Peckham, P. D. (1968). *An investigation of the effects of non-homogeneity of regression slopes upon the F-test of analysis of covariance* . Laboratory of Educational Research, Report No. 16, University of Colorado, Boulder.

Pedhazur, E. J. (1997). *Multiple regression in behavioral research* (3rd ed.). Fort Worth: Harcourt Brace.

Pingel, L. A. (1969). *A comparison of the effects of two methods of block formation on design precision*. Paper presented at the annual meeting of the American Educational Research Association, Los Angeles.

Porter, A. C. (1967). *The effects of using fallible variables in the analysis of covariance.* Unpublished doctoral dissertation, University of Wisconsin, Madison.

Porter, A. C. & Raudenbush, S. W. (1987). Analysis of covariance: Its model and use in psychological research. *Journal of Counseling Psychology, 34*, 383–392.

Puri, M. L. & Sen, P. K. (1969). Analysis of covariance based on general rank scores. *Annals of Mathematical Statistic, 40*, 610–618.

Quade, D. (1967). Rank analysis of covariance. *Journal of the American Statistical Association, 62*, 1187–1200.

Ramsey, P. H. (1989). Critical values of Spearman's rank order correlation. *Journal of Educational Statistics, 14*, 245–253.

Ramsey, P. H. (1994). Testing variances in psychological and educational research. *Journal of Educational Statistics, 19*, 23–42.

Reichardt, C. S. (1979). The statistical analysis of data from nonequivalent control group designs. In T. D. Cook & D. T. Campbell (eds.), *Quasi-experimentation: Design and analysis issues for field settings*. Chicago: Rand McNally.

Robbins, N. B. (2004). *Creating more effective graphs*. San Francisco: Jossey-Bass.

Rogosa, D. R. (1980). Comparing non-parallel regression lines. *Psychological Bulletin, 88*, 307–321.

Rosenthal, R. & Rosnow, R. L. (1985). *Contrast analysis: Focused comparisons in the analysis of variance*. Cambridge: Cambridge University Press.

Rousseeuw, P. J. & Leroy, A. M. (1987). *Robust regression and outlier detection*. New York: Wiley.

Rudas, T. (2004). *Probability theory: A primer*. Thousand Oaks CA: Sage.

Ruppert, D. & Carroll, R. J. (1980). Trimmed least squares estimation in the linear model. *Journal of the American Statistical Association, 75*, 828–838.

Rutherford, A. (1992). Alternatives to traditional analysis of covariance. *British Journal of Mathematical and Statistical Psychology, 45*, 197–223.

Sawilowsky, S. S. & Blair, R. C. (1992). A more realistic look at the robustness and type II error properties of the t-test to departures from population normality. *Psychological Bulletin, 111*, 352–360.

Scariano, S. M. & Davenport, J. M. (1987). The effects of violations of independence assumptions in the one-way ANOVA. *The American Statistician, 41*, 123–129.

Schafer, W. D. (1991). Reporting hierarchical regression results. *Measurement and Evaluation in Counseling and Development, 24*, 98–100.

Scheffé, H. (1953). A method for judging all contrasts in the analysis of variance. *Biometrika, 40*, 87–104.

Schmid, C. F. (1983). *Statistical graphics: Design principles and practices*. New York: Wiley.

Seber, G. A. F. & Wild, C. J. (1989). *Nonlinear regression*. New York: Wiley.

Shapiro, S. S. & Wilk, M. B. (1965). An analysis of variance test for normality (complete samples). *Biometrika, 52*, 591–611.

Shavelson, R. J. (1988). *Statistical reasoning for the behavioral sciences* (2nd ed.). Boston: Allyn and Bacon.

Sidak, Z. (1967). Rectangular confidence regions for the means of multivariate normal distributions. *Journal of the American Statistical Association, 62*, 626–633.

Smithson, M. (2001). Correct confidence intervals for various regression effect sizes and parameters: The importance of noncentral distributions in computing intervals. *Educational and Psychological Measurement, 61*, 605–632.

Steiger, J. H. & Fouladi, R. T. (1992). R2: A computer program in interval estimation, power calculation, and hypothesis testing for the squared multiple correlation. *Behavior Research Methods, Instruments, and Computers, 4*, 581–582.

Stevens, J. P. (2002). *Applied multivariate statistics for the social sciences* (4th ed.). Mahwah NJ: Lawrence Erlbaum Associates.

Stigler, S. M. (1986). *The history of statistics: The measurement of uncertainty before 1900*. Cambridge MA: Harvard.

Storer, B. E. & Kim, C. (1990). Exact properties of some exact test statistics for comparing two binomial proportions. *Journal of the American Statistical Association, 85*, 146–155.

Sudman, S. (1976). *Applied sampling*. New York: Academic.

Tabachnick, B. G. & Fidell, L. S. (2001). *Using multivariate statistics*. Boston: Allyn and Bacon.

Tabatabai, M. & Tan, W. (1985). Some comparative studies on testing parallelism of several straight lines under heteroscedastic variances. *Communications in Statistics—Simulation and Computation, 14*, 837–844.

Thompson, M. L. (1978). Selection of variables in multiple regression. Part I: A review and evaluation. Part II: Chosen procedures, computations and examples. *International Statistical Review, 46*, 1–19 and 129–146.

Tiku, M. L. & Singh, M. (1981). Robust test for means when population variances are unequal. *Communications in Statistics—Theory and Methods, A10*, 2057–2071.

Tijms, H. (2004). *Understanding probability: Chance rules in everyday life*. New York: Cambridge University Press.

Timm, N. H. (2002). *Applied multivariate analysis*. New York: Springer-Verlag.

Timm, N. H. & Carlson, J. E. (1975). Analysis of variance through full rank models. *Multivariate Behavioral Research Monographs*, No. 75-1.

Tomarken, A. & Serlin, R. (1986). Comparison of ANOVA alternatives under variance heterogeneity and specific noncentrality structures. *Psychological Bulletin, 99*, 90–99.

Tufte, E. R. (1992). *The visual display of quantitative information*. Cheshire CT: Graphics Press.

Tukey, J. W. (1949). One degree of freedom for nonadditivity. *Biometrics, 5*, 232–242.

Tukey, J. W. (1953). *The problem of multiple comparisons*. Ditto, Princeton University, 396 pp.

Tukey, J. W. (1977). *Exploratory data analysis*. Reading MA: Addison-Wesley.

Wainer, H. (1984). How to display data badly. *The American Statistician, 38*, 137–147.

Wainer, H. (1992). Understanding graphs and tables. *Educational Researcher, 21*, 14–23.

Wainer, H. (2000). *Visual revelations*. Mahwah, NJ: Lawrence Erlbaum Associates.

Wallgren, A., Wallgren, B., Persson, R., Jorner, U., & Haaland, J.-A. (1996). *Graphing statistics & data*. Thousand Oaks: Sage.

Weinberg, S. L. & Abramowitz, S. K. (2002). *Data analysis for the behavioral sciences using SPSS*. Cambridge United Kingdom: Cambridge University Press.

Weisberg, H. I. (1979). Statistical adjustments and uncontrolled studies. *Psychological Bulletin, 86*, 1149–1164.

Weisberg, S. (1985). *Applied linear regression* (2nd ed.). New York: Wiley.

Welch, B. L. (1951). On the comparison of several mean values: An alternative approach. *Biometrika, 38*, 330–336.

Wetherill, G. B. (1986). *Regression analysis with applications*. London: Chapman and Hall.

Wilcox, R. R. (1986). Controlling power in a heteroscedastic ANOVA procedure. *British Journal of Mathematical and Statistical Psychology, 39*, 65–68.

Wilcox, R. R. (1987). *New statistical procedures for the social sciences: Modern solutions to basic problems*. Hillsdale, NJ: Lawrence Erlbaum Associates.

Wilcox, R. R. (1988). A new alternative to the ANOVA F and new results on James'second- order method. *British Journal of Mathematical and Statistical Psychology, 41*, 109–117

Wilcox, R. R. (1989). Adjusting for unequal variances when comparing means in one-way and two-way fixed effects ANOVA models. *Journal of Educational Statistics, 14*, 269–278.

Wilcox, R. R. (1993). Comparing one-step M-estimators of location when there are more than two groups. *Psychometrika, 58*, 71–78.

Wilcox, R. R. (1996). *Statistics for the social sciences*. San Diego: Academic.

Wilcox, R. R. (1997). *Introduction to robust estimation and hypothesis testing*. San Diego: Academic.

Wilcox, R. R. (2002). Comparing the variances of two independent groups. *British Journal of Mathematical and Statistical Psychology, 55*, 169–175.

Wilcox, R. R. (2003). *Applying contemporary statistical procedures*. San Diego: Academic.

Wilkinson, L. (2005). *The grammar of statistics* (2nd ed.). New York: Springer.

Wonnacott, T. H. & Wonnacott, R. J. (1981). *Regression: A second course in statistics*. New York: Wiley.

Wright, R. E. (1995). Logistic regression. In L. G. Grimm & P. R. Arnold (Eds.). (1995). *Reading and understanding multivariate statistics* (pp. 217–244). Washington DC: American Psychological Association.

Wu, L. L. (1985). Robust M-estimation of location and regression. In N. B. Tuma (Ed.), *Sociological methodology, 1985*. San Francisco: Jossey-Bass.

Yu, M. C. & Dunn, O. J. (1982). Robust tests for the equality of two correlation coefficients: A monte carlo study. *Educational and Psychological Measurement, 42*, 987–1004.

Yuan, K.-H. & Maxwell, S. (2005). On the post hoc power in testing mean differences. *Journal of Educational and Behavioral Statistics, 30*, 141–167.

Zimmerman, D. W. (1997). A note of interpretation of the paired-samples t-test. *Journal of Educational and Behavioral Statistics, 22*, 349–360.

Zimmerman, D. W. (2003). A warning about the large-sample Wilcoxon-Mann-Whitney test. *Understanding Statistics, 2*, 267–280.

Appendix Tables

z	$P(z)$	z	$P(z)$	z	$P(z)$	z	$P(z)$
.00	.5000000	.50	.6914625	1.00	.8413447	1.50	.9331928
.01	.5039894	.51	.6949743	1.01	.8437524	1.51	.9344783
.02	.5079783	.52	.6984682	1.02	.8461358	1.52	.9357445
.03	.5119665	.53	.7019440	1.03	.8484950	1.53	.9369916
.04	.5159534	.54	.7054015	1.04	.8508300	1.54	.9382198
.05	.5199388	.55	.7088403	1.05	.8531409	1.55	.9394292
.06	.5239222	.56	.7122603	1.06	.8554277	1.56	.9406201
.07	.5279032	.57	.7156612	1.07	.8576903	1.57	.9417924
.08	.5318814	.58	.7190427	1.08	.8599289	1.58	.9429466
.09	.5358564	.59	.7224047	1.09	.8621434	1.59	.9440826
.10	.5398278	.60	.7257469	1.10	.8643339	1.60	.9452007
.11	.5437953	.61	.7290691	1.11	.8665005	1.61	.9463011
.12	.5477584	.62	.7323711	1.12	.8686431	1.62	.9473839
.13	.5517168	.63	.7356527	1.13	.8707619	1.63	.9484493
.14	.5556700	.64	.7389137	1.14	.8728568	1.64	.9494974
.15	.5596177	.65	.7421539	1.15	.8749281	1.65	.9505285
.16	.5635595	.66	.7453731	1.16	.8769756	1.66	.9515428
.17	.5674949	.67	.7485711	1.17	.8789995	1.67	.9525403
.18	.5714237	.68	.7517478	1.18	.8809999	1.68	.9535213
.19	.5753454	.69	.7549029	1.19	.8829768	1.69	.9544860
.20	.5792597	.70	.7580363	1.20	.8849303	1.70	.9554345
.21	.5831662	.71	.7611479	1.21	.8868606	1.71	.9563671
.22	.5870644	.72	.7642375	1.22	.8887676	1.72	.9572838
.23	.5909541	.73	.7673049	1.23	.8906514	1.73	.9581849
.24	.5948349	.74	.7703500	1.24	.8925123	1.74	.9590705
.25	.5987063	.75	.7733726	1.25	.8943502	1.75	.9599408
.26	.6025681	.76	.7763727	1.26	.8961653	1.76	.9607961
.27	.6064199	.77	.7793501	1.27	.8979577	1.77	.9616364
.28	.6102612	.78	.7823046	1.28	.8997274	1.78	.9624620
.29	.6140919	.79	.7852361	1.29	.9014747	1.79	.9632730
.30	.6179114	.80	.7881446	1.30	.9031995	1.80	.9640697
.31	.6217195	.81	.7910299	1.31	.9049021	1.81	.9648521
.32	.6255158	.82	.7938919	1.32	.9065825	1.82	.9656205
.33	.6293000	.83	.7967306	1.33	.9082409	1.83	.9663750
.34	.6330717	.84	.7995458	1.34	.9098773	1.84	.9671159
.35	.6368307	.85	.8023375	1.35	.9114920	1.85	.9678432
.36	.6405764	.86	.8051055	1.36	.9130850	1.86	.9685572
.37	.6443088	.87	.8078498	1.37	.9146565	1.87	.9692581
.38	.6480273	.88	.8105703	1.38	.9162067	1.88	.9699460
.39	.6517317	.89	.8132671	1.39	.9177356	1.89	.9706210
.40	.6554217	.90	.8159399	1.40	.9192433	1.90	.9712834
.41	.6590970	.91	.8185887	1.41	.9207302	1.91	.9719334
.42	.6627573	.92	.8212136	1.42	.9221962	1.92	.0725711
.43	.6664022	.93	.8238145	1.43	.9236415	1.93	.9731966
.44	.6700314	.94	.8263912	1.44	.9250663	1.94	.9738102
.45	.6736448	.95	.8289439	1.45	.9264707	1.95	.9744119
.46	.6772419	.96	.8314724	1.46	.9278550	1.96	.9750021
.47	.6808225	.97	.8339768	1.47	.9292191	1.97	.9755808
.48	.6843863	.98	.8364569	1.48	.9305634	1.98	.9761482
.49	.6879331	.99	.8389129	1.49	.9318879	1.99	.9767045
.50	.6914625	1.00	.8413447	1.50	.9331928	2.00	.9772499

$P(z)$ represents the area below that value of z.

(*continued*)

z	P(z)	z	P(z)	z	P(z)	z	P(z)
2.00	.9772499	2.50	.9937903	3.00	.9986501	3.50	.9997674
2.01	.9777844	2.51	.9939634	3.01	.9986938	3.51	.9997759
2.02	.9783083	2.52	.9941323	3.02	.9987361	3.52	.9997842
2.03	.9788217	2.53	.9942969	3.03	.9987772	3.53	.9997922
2.04	.9793248	2.54	.9944574	3.04	.9988171	3.54	.9997999
2.05	.9798178	2.55	.9946139	3.05	.9988558	3.55	.9998074
2.06	.9803007	2.56	.9947664	3.06	.9988933	3.56	.9998146
2.07	.9807738	2.57	.9949151	3.07	.9989297	3.57	.9998215
2.08	.9812372	2.58	.9950600	3.08	.9989650	3.58	.9998282
2.09	.9816911	2.59	.9952012	3.09	.9989992	3.59	.9998347
2.10	.9821356	2.60	.9953388	3.10	.9990324	3.60	.9998409
2.11	.9825708	2.61	.9954729	3.11	.9990646	3.61	.9998469
2.12	.9829970	2.62	.9956035	3.12	.9990957	3.62	.9998527
2.13	.9834142	2.63	.9957308	3.13	.9991260	3.63	.9998583
2.14	.9838226	2.64	.9958547	3.14	.9991553	3.64	.9998637
2.15	.9842224	2.65	.9959754	3.15	.9991836	3.65	.9998689
2.16	.9846137	2.66	.9960930	3.16	.9992112	3.66	.9998739
2.17	.9849966	2.67	.9962074	3.17	.9992378	3.67	.9998787
2.18	.9853713	2.68	.9963189	3.18	.9992636	3.68	.9998834
2.19	.9857379	2.69	.9964274	3.19	.9992886	3.69	.9998879
2.20	.9860966	2.70	.9965330	3.20	.9993129	3.70	.9998922
2.21	.9864474	2.71	.9966358	3.21	.9993363	3.71	.9998964
2.22	.9867906	2.72	.9967359	3.22	.9993590	3.72	.9999004
2.23	.9871263	2.73	.9968333	3.23	.9993810	3.73	.9999043
2.24	.9874545	2.74	.9969280	3.24	.9994024	3.74	.9999080
2.25	.9877755	2.75	.9970202	3.25	.9994230	3.75	.9999116
2.26	.9880894	2.76	.9971099	3.26	.9994429	3.76	.9999150
2.27	.9883962	2.77	.9971972	3.27	.9994623	3.77	.9999184
2.28	.9886962	2.78	.9972821	3.28	.9994810	3.78	.9999216
2.29	.9889893	2.79	.9973646	3.29	.9994991	3.79	.9999247
2.30	.9892759	2.80	.9974449	3.30	.9995166	3.80	.9999277
2.31	.9895559	2.81	.9975229	3.31	.9995335	3.81	.9999305
2.32	.9898296	2.82	.9975988	3.32	.9995499	3.82	.9999333
2.33	.9900969	2.83	.9976726	3.33	.9995658	3.83	.9999359
2.34	.9903581	2.84	.9977443	3.34	.9995811	3.84	.9999385
2.35	.9906133	2.85	.9978140	3.35	.9995959	3.85	.9999409
2.36	.9908625	2.86	.9978818	3.36	.9996103	3.86	.9999433
2.37	.9911060	2.87	.9979476	3.37	.9996242	3.87	.9999456
2.38	.9913437	2.88	.9980116	3.38	.9996376	3.88	.9999478
2.39	.9915758	2.89	.9980738	3.39	.9996505	3.89	.9999499
2.40	.9918025	2.90	.9981342	3.40	.9996631	3.90	.9999519
2.41	.9920237	2.91	.9981929	3.41	.9996752	3.91	.9999539
2.42	.9922397	2.92	.9982498	3.42	.9996869	3.92	.9999557
2.43	.9924506	2.93	.9983052	3.43	.9996982	3.93	.9999575
2.44	.9926564	2.94	.9983589	3.44	.9997091	3.94	.9999593
2.45	.9928572	2.95	.9984111	3.45	.9997197	3.95	.9999609
2.46	.9930531	2.96	.9984618	3.46	.9997299	3.96	.9999625
2.47	.9932443	2.97	.9985110	3.47	.9997398	3.97	.9999641
2.48	.9934309	2.98	.9985588	3.48	.9997493	3.98	.9999655
2.49	.9936128	2.99	.9986051	3.49	.9997585	3.99	.9999670
2.50	.9937903	3.00	.9986501	3.50	.9997674	4.00	.9999683

Percentage Points of the *t* Distribution

ν	$\alpha_1 = .10$ $\alpha_2 = .20$	.05 .10	.025 .050	.01 .02	.005 .010	.0025 .0050	.001 .002	.0005 .0010
1	3·078	6·314	12·706	31·821	63·657	127·32	318·31	636·62
2	1·886	2·920	4·303	6·965	9·925	14·089	22·327	31·598
3	1·638	2·353	3·182	4·541	5·841	7·453	10·214	12·924
4	1·533	2·132	2·776	3·747	4·604	5·598	7·173	8·610
5	1·476	2·015	2·571	3·365	4·032	4·773	5·893	6·869
6	1·440	1·943	2·447	3·143	3·707	4·317	5·208	5·959
7	1·415	1·895	2·365	2·998	3·499	4·029	4·785	5·408
8	1·397	1·860	2·306	2·896	3·355	3·833	4·501	5·041
9	1·383	1·833	2·262	2·821	3·250	3·690	4·297	4·781
10	1·372	1·812	2·228	2·764	3·169	3·581	4·144	4·587
11	1·363	1·796	2·201	2·718	3·106	3·497	4·025	4·437
12	1·356	1·782	2·179	2·681	3·055	3·428	3·930	4·318
13	1·350	1·771	2·160	2·650	3·012	3·372	3·852	4·221
14	1·345	1·761	2·145	2·624	2·977	3·326	3·787	4·140
15	1·341	1·753	2·131	2·602	2·947	3·286	3·733	4·073
16	1·337	1·746	2·120	2·583	2·921	3·252	3·686	4·015
17	1·333	1·740	2·110	2·567	2·898	3·222	3·646	3·965
18	1·330	1·734	2·101	2·552	2·878	3·197	3·610	3·922
19	1·328	1·729	2·093	2·539	2·861	3·174	3·579	3·883
20	1·325	1·725	2·086	2·528	2·845	3·153	3·552	3·850
21	1·323	1·721	2·080	2·518	2·831	3·135	3·527	3·819
22	1·321	1·717	2·074	2·508	2·819	3·119	3·505	3·792
23	1·319	1·714	2·069	2·500	2·807	3·104	3·485	3·767
24	1·318	1·711	2·064	2·492	2·797	3·091	3·467	3·745
25	1·316	1·708	2·060	2·485	2·787	3·078	3·450	3·725
26	1·315	1·706	2·056	2·479	2·779	3·067	3·435	3·707
27	1·314	1·703	2·052	2·473	2·771	3·057	3·421	3·690
28	1·313	1·701	2·048	2·467	2·763	3·047	3·408	3·674
29	1·311	1·699	2·045	2·462	2·756	3·038	3·396	3·659
30	1·310	1·697	2·042	2·457	2·750	3·030	3·385	3·646
40	1·303	1·684	2·021	2·423	2·704	2·971	3·307	3·551
60	1·296	1·671	2·000	2·390	2·660	2·915	3·232	3·460
120	1·289	1·658	1·980	2·358	2·617	2·860	3·160	3·373
∞	1·282	1·645	1·960	2·326	2·576	2·807	3·090	3·291

α_1 is the upper-tail value of the distribution with ν degrees of freedom, appropriate for use in a one-tailed test; use α_2 for a two-tailed test.

APPENDIX TABLE 3

Percentage Points of the χ^2 Distribution

α ν	0·990	0·975	0·950	0·900	0·100	0·050	0·025	0·010
1	157088.10^{-9}	982069.10^{-9}	393214.10^{-8}	0·0157908	2·70554	3·84146	5·02389	6·63490
2	0·0201007	0·0506356	0·102587	0·210721	4·60517	5·99146	7·37776	9·21034
3	0·114832	0·215795	0·351846	0·584374	6·25139	7·81473	9·34840	11·3449
4	0·297109	0·484419	0·710723	1·063623	7·77944	9·48773	11·1433	13·2767
5	0·554298	0·831212	1·145476	1·61031	9·23636	11·0705	12·8325	15·0863
6	0·872090	1·23734	1·63538	2·20413	10·6446	12·5916	14·4494	16·8119
7	1·239043	1·68987	2·16735	2·83311	12·0170	14·0671	16·0128	18·4753
8	1·64650	2·17973	2·73264	3·48954	13·3616	15·5073	17·5345	20·0902
9	2·08790	2·70039	3·32511	4·16816	14·6837	16·9190	19·0228	21·6660
10	2·55821	3·24697	3·94030	4·86518	15·9872	18·3070	20·4832	23·2093
11	3·05348	3·81575	4·57481	5·57778	17·2750	19·6751	21·9200	24·7250
12	3·57057	4·40379	5·22603	6·30380	18·5493	21·0261	23·3367	26·2170
13	4·10692	5·00875	5·89186	7·04150	19·8119	22·3620	24·7356	27·6882
14	4·66043	5·62873	6·57063	7·78953	21·0641	23·6848	26·1189	29·1412
15	5·22935	6·26214	7·26094	8·54676	22·3071	24·9958	27·4884	30·5779
16	5·81221	6·90766	7·96165	9·31224	23·5418	26·2962	28·8454	31·9999
17	6·40776	7·56419	8·67176	10·0852	24·7690	27·5871	30·1910	33·4087
18	7·01491	8·23075	9·39046	10·8649	25·9894	28·8693	31·5264	34·8053
19	7·63273	8·90652	10·1170	11·6509	27·2036	30·1435	32·8523	36·1909
20	8·26040	9·59078	10·8508	12·4426	28·4120	31·4104	34·1696	37·5662
21	8·89720	10·28293	11·5913	13·2396	29·6151	32·6706	35·4789	38·9322
22	9·54249	10·9823	12·3380	14·0415	30·8133	33·9244	36·7807	40·2894
23	10·19567	11·6886	13·0905	14·8480	32·0069	35·1725	38·0756	41·6384
24	10·8564	12·4012	13·8484	15·6587	33·1962	36·4150	39·3641	42·9798
25	11·5240	13·1197	14·6114	16·4734	34·3816	37·6525	40·6465	44·3141
26	12·1981	13·8439	15·3792	17·2919	35·5632	38·8851	41·9232	45·6417
27	12·8785	14·5734	16·1514	18·1139	36·7412	40·1133	43·1945	46·9629
28	13·5647	15·3079	16·9279	18·9392	37·9159	41·3371	44·4608	48·2782
29	14·2565	16·0471	17·7084	19·7677	39·0875	42·5570	45·7223	49·5879
30	14·9535	16·7908	18·4927	20·5992	40·2560	43·7730	46·9792	50·8922
40	22·1643	24·4330	26·5093	29·0505	51·8051	55·7585	59·3417	63·6907
50	29·7067	32·3574	34·7643	37·6886	63·1671	67·5048	71·4202	76·1539
60	37·4849	40·4817	43·1880	46·4589	74·3970	79·0819	83·2977	88·3794
70	45·4417	48·7576	51·7393	55·3289	85·5270	90·5312	95·0232	100·425
80	53·5401	57·1532	60·3915	64·2778	96·5782	101·879	106·629	112·329
90	61·7541	65·6466	69·1260	73·2911	107·565	113·145	118·136	124·116
100	70·0649	74·2219	77·9295	82·3581	118·498	124·342	129·561	135·807

APPENDIX TABLE 4

Percentage Points of the F Distribution, $\alpha = .10$

ν_2 \ ν_1	1	2	3	4	5	6	7	8	9	10	12	15	20	24	30	40	60	120	∞
1	39·86	49·50	53·59	55·83	57·24	58·20	58·91	59·44	59·86	60·19	60·71	61·22	61·74	62·00	62·26	62·53	62·79	63·06	63·33
2	8·53	9·00	9·16	9·24	9·29	9·33	9·35	9·37	9·38	9·39	9·41	9·42	9·44	9·45	9·46	9·47	9·47	9·48	9·40
3	5·54	5·46	5·39	5·34	5·31	5·28	5·27	5·25	5·24	5·23	5·22	5·20	5·18	5·18	5·17	5·16	5·15	5·14	5·13
4	4·54	4·32	4·19	4·11	4·05	4·01	3·98	3·95	3·94	3·92	3·90	3·87	3·84	3·83	3·82	3·80	3·79	3·78	3·76
5	4·06	3·78	3·62	3·52	3·45	3·40	3·37	3·34	3·32	3·30	3·27	3·24	3·21	3·19	3·17	3·16	3·14	3·12	3·10
6	3·78	3·46	3·29	3·18	3·11	3·05	3·01	2·98	2·96	2·94	2·90	2·87	2·84	2·82	2·80	2·78	2·76	2·74	2·72
7	3·59	3·26	3·07	2·96	2·88	2·83	2·78	2·75	2·72	2·70	2·67	2·63	2·59	2·58	2·56	2·54	2·51	2·49	2·47
8	3·46	3·11	2·92	2·81	2·73	2·67	2·62	2·59	2·56	2·54	2·50	2·46	2·42	2·40	2·38	2·36	2·34	2·32	2·29
9	3·36	3·01	2·81	2·69	2·61	2·55	2·51	2·47	2·44	2·42	2·38	2·34	2·30	2·28	2·25	2·23	2·21	2·18	2·16
10	3·29	2·92	2·73	2·61	2·52	2·46	2·41	2·38	2·35	2·32	2·28	2·24	2·20	2·18	2·16	2·13	2·11	2·08	2·06
11	3·23	2·86	2·66	2·54	2·45	2·39	2·34	2·30	2·27	2·25	2·21	2·17	2·12	2·10	2·08	2·05	2·03	2·00	1·97
12	3·18	2·81	2·61	2·48	2·39	2·33	2·28	2·24	2·21	2·19	2·15	2·10	2·06	2·04	2·01	1·99	1·96	1·93	1·90
13	3·14	2·76	2·56	2·43	2·35	2·28	2·23	2·20	2·16	2·14	2·10	2·05	2·01	1·98	1·96	1·93	1·90	1·88	1·85
14	3·10	2·73	2·52	2·39	2·31	2·24	2·19	2·15	2·12	2·10	2·05	2·01	1·96	1·94	1·91	1·89	1·86	1·83	1·80
15	3·07	2·70	2·49	2·36	2·27	2·21	2·16	2·12	2·09	2·06	2·02	1·97	1·92	1·90	1·87	1·85	1·82	1·79	1·76
16	3·05	2·67	2·46	2·33	2·24	2·18	2·13	2·09	2·06	2·03	1·99	1·94	1·89	1·87	1·84	1·81	1·78	1·75	1·72
17	3·03	2·64	2·44	2·31	2·22	2·15	2·10	2·06	2·03	2·00	1·96	1·91	1·86	1·84	1·81	1·78	1·75	1·72	1·69
18	3·01	2·62	2·42	2·29	2·20	2·13	2·08	2·04	2·00	1·98	1·93	1·89	1·84	1·81	1·78	1·75	1·72	1·69	1·66
19	2·99	2·61	2·40	2·27	2·18	2·11	2·06	2·02	1·98	1·96	1·91	1·86	1·81	1·79	1·76	1·73	1·70	1·67	1·63
20	2·97	2·59	2·38	2·25	2·16	2·09	2·04	2·00	1·96	1·94	1·89	1·84	1·79	1·77	1·74	1·71	1·68	1·64	1·61
21	2·96	2·57	2·36	2·23	2·14	2·08	2·02	1·98	1·95	1·92	1·87	1·83	1·78	1·75	1·72	1·69	1·66	1·62	1·59
22	2·95	2·56	2·35	2·22	2·13	2·06	2·01	1·97	1·93	1·90	1·86	1·81	1·76	1·73	1·70	1·67	1·64	1·60	1·57
23	2·94	2·55	2·34	2·21	2·11	2·05	1·99	1·95	1·92	1·89	1·84	1·80	1·74	1·72	1·69	1·66	1·62	1·59	1·55
24	2·93	2·54	2·33	2·19	2·10	2·04	1·98	1·94	1·91	1·88	1·83	1·78	1·73	1·70	1·67	1·64	1·61	1·57	1·53
25	2·92	2·53	2·32	2·18	2·09	2·02	1·97	1·93	1·89	1·87	1·82	1·77	1·72	1·69	1·66	1·63	1·59	1·56	1·52
26	2·91	2·52	2·31	2·17	2·08	2·01	1·96	1·92	1·88	1·86	1·81	1·76	1·71	1·68	1·65	1·61	1·58	1·54	1·50
27	2·90	2·51	2·30	2·17	2·07	2·00	1·95	1·91	1·87	1·85	1·80	1·75	1·70	1·67	1·64	1·60	1·57	1·53	1·49
28	2·89	2·50	2·29	2·16	2·06	2·00	1·94	1·90	1·87	1·84	1·79	1·74	1·69	1·66	1·63	1·59	1·56	1·52	1·48
29	2·89	2·50	2·28	2·15	2·06	1·99	1·93	1·89	1·86	1·83	1·78	1·73	1·68	1·65	1·62	1·58	1·55	1·51	1·47
30	2·88	2·49	2·28	2·14	2·05	1·98	1·93	1·88	1·85	1·82	1·77	1·72	1·67	1·64	1·61	1·57	1·54	1·50	1·46
40	2·84	2·44	2·23	2·09	2·00	1·93	1·87	1·83	1·79	1·76	1·71	1·66	1·61	1·57	1·54	1·51	1·47	1·42	1·38
60	2·79	2·39	2·18	2·04	1·95	1·87	1·82	1·77	1·74	1·71	1·66	1·60	1·54	1·51	1·48	1·44	1·40	1·35	1·29
120	2·75	2·35	2·13	1·99	1·90	1·82	1·77	1·72	1·68	1·65	1·60	1·55	1·48	1·45	1·41	1·37	1·32	1·26	1·19
∞	2·71	2·30	2·08	1·94	1·85	1·77	1·72	1·67	1·63	1·60	1·55	1·49	1·42	1·38	1·34	1·30	1·24	1·17	1·00

(continued)

ν_1 is the numerator degrees of freedom and ν_2 is the denominator degrees of freedom.

APPENDIX TABLE 4 *(continued)*

Percentage Points of the *F* Distribution, α = .05

v_1 \ v_2	1	2	3	4	5	6	7	8	9	10	12	15	20	24	30	40	60	120	∞
1	161.4	199.5	215.7	224.6	230.2	234.0	236.8	238.9	240.5	241.9	243.9	245.9	248.0	249.1	250.1	251.1	252.2	253.3	254.3
2	18.51	19.00	19.16	19.25	19.30	19.33	19.35	19.37	19.38	19.40	19.41	19.43	19.45	19.45	19.46	19.47	19.48	19.49	19.50
3	10.13	9.55	9.28	9.12	9.01	8.94	8.89	8.85	8.81	8.79	8.74	8.70	8.66	8.64	8.62	8.59	8.57	8.55	8.53
4	7.71	6.94	6.59	6.39	6.26	6.16	6.09	6.04	6.00	5.96	5.91	5.86	5.80	5.77	5.75	5.72	5.69	5.66	5.63
5	6.61	5.79	5.41	5.19	5.05	4.95	4.88	4.82	4.77	4.74	4.68	4.62	4.56	4.53	4.50	4.46	4.43	4.40	4.36
6	5.99	5.14	4.76	4.53	4.39	4.28	4.21	4.15	4.10	4.06	4.00	3.94	3.87	3.84	3.81	3.77	3.74	3.70	3.67
7	5.59	4.74	4.35	4.12	3.97	3.87	3.79	3.73	3.68	3.64	3.57	3.51	3.44	3.41	3.38	3.34	3.30	3.27	3.23
8	5.32	4.46	4.07	3.84	3.69	3.58	3.50	3.44	3.39	3.35	3.28	3.22	3.15	3.12	3.08	3.04	3.01	2.97	2.93
9	5.12	4.26	3.86	3.63	3.48	3.37	3.29	3.23	3.18	3.14	3.07	3.01	2.94	2.90	2.86	2.83	2.79	2.75	2.71
10	4.96	4.10	3.71	3.48	3.33	3.22	3.14	3.07	3.02	2.98	2.91	2.85	2.77	2.74	2.70	2.66	2.62	2.58	2.54
11	4.84	3.98	3.59	3.36	3.20	3.09	3.01	2.95	2.90	2.85	2.79	2.72	2.65	2.61	2.57	2.53	2.49	2.45	2.40
12	4.75	3.89	3.49	3.26	3.11	3.00	2.91	2.85	2.80	2.75	2.69	2.62	2.54	2.51	2.47	2.43	2.38	2.34	2.30
13	4.67	3.81	3.41	3.18	3.03	2.92	2.83	2.77	2.71	2.67	2.60	2.53	2.46	2.42	2.38	2.34	2.30	2.25	2.21
14	4.60	3.74	3.34	3.11	2.96	2.85	2.76	2.70	2.65	2.60	2.53	2.46	2.39	2.35	2.31	2.27	2.22	2.18	2.13
15	4.54	3.68	3.29	3.06	2.90	2.79	2.71	2.64	2.59	2.54	2.48	2.40	2.33	2.29	2.25	2.20	2.16	2.11	2.07
16	4.49	3.63	3.24	3.01	2.85	2.74	2.66	2.59	2.54	2.49	2.42	2.35	2.28	2.24	2.19	2.15	2.11	2.06	2.01
17	4.45	3.59	3.20	2.96	2.81	2.70	2.61	2.55	2.49	2.45	2.38	2.31	2.23	2.19	2.15	2.10	2.06	2.01	1.96
18	4.41	3.55	3.16	2.93	2.77	2.66	2.58	2.51	2.46	2.41	2.34	2.27	2.19	2.15	2.11	2.06	2.02	1.97	1.92
19	4.38	3.52	3.13	2.90	2.74	2.63	2.54	2.48	2.42	2.38	2.31	2.23	2.16	2.11	2.07	2.03	1.98	1.93	1.88
20	4.35	3.49	3.10	2.87	2.71	2.60	2.51	2.45	2.39	2.35	2.28	2.20	2.12	2.08	2.04	1.99	1.95	1.90	1.84
21	4.32	3.47	3.07	2.84	2.68	2.57	2.49	2.42	2.37	2.32	2.25	2.18	2.10	2.05	2.01	1.96	1.92	1.87	1.81
22	4.30	3.44	3.05	2.82	2.66	2.55	2.46	2.40	2.34	2.30	2.23	2.15	2.07	2.03	1.98	1.94	1.89	1.84	1.78
23	4.28	3.42	3.03	2.80	2.64	2.53	2.44	2.37	2.32	2.27	2.20	2.13	2.05	2.01	1.96	1.91	1.86	1.81	1.76
24	4.26	3.40	3.01	2.78	2.62	2.51	2.42	2.36	2.30	2.25	2.18	2.11	2.03	1.98	1.94	1.89	1.84	1.79	1.73
25	4.24	3.39	2.99	2.76	2.60	2.49	2.40	2.34	2.28	2.24	2.16	2.09	2.01	1.96	1.92	1.87	1.82	1.77	1.71
26	4.23	3.37	2.98	2.74	2.59	2.47	2.39	2.32	2.27	2.22	2.15	2.07	1.99	1.95	1.90	1.85	1.80	1.75	1.69
27	4.21	3.35	2.96	2.73	2.57	2.46	2.37	2.31	2.25	2.20	2.13	2.06	1.97	1.93	1.88	1.84	1.79	1.73	1.67
28	4.20	3.34	2.95	2.71	2.56	2.45	2.36	2.29	2.24	2.19	2.12	2.04	1.96	1.91	1.87	1.82	1.77	1.71	1.65
29	4.18	3.33	2.93	2.70	2.55	2.43	2.35	2.28	2.22	2.18	2.10	2.03	1.94	1.90	1.85	1.81	1.75	1.70	1.64
30	4.17	3.32	2.92	2.69	2.53	2.42	2.33	2.27	2.21	2.16	2.09	2.01	1.93	1.89	1.84	1.79	1.74	1.68	1.62
40	4.08	3.23	2.84	2.61	2.45	2.34	2.25	2.18	2.12	2.08	2.00	1.92	1.84	1.79	1.74	1.69	1.64	1.58	1.51
60	4.00	3.15	2.76	2.53	2.37	2.25	2.17	2.10	2.04	1.99	1.92	1.84	1.75	1.70	1.65	1.59	1.53	1.47	1.39
120	3.92	3.07	2.68	2.45	2.29	2.17	2.09	2.02	1.96	1.91	1.83	1.75	1.66	1.61	1.55	1.50	1.43	1.35	1.25
∞	3.84	3.00	2.60	2.37	2.21	2.10	2.01	1.94	1.88	1.83	1.75	1.67	1.57	1.52	1.46	1.39	1.32	1.22	1.00

(continued)

APPENDIX TABLE 4 (continued)
Percentage Points of the F Distribution, $\alpha = .01$

$\nu_2\backslash\nu_1$	1	2	3	4	5	6	7	8	9	10	12	15	20	24	30	40	60	120	∞
1	4052	4999·5	5403	5625	5764	5859	5928	5981	6022	6056	6106	6157	6209	6235	6261	6287	6313	6339	6366
2	98·50	99·00	99·17	99·25	99·30	99·33	99·36	99·37	99·39	99·40	99·42	99·43	99·45	99·46	99·47	99·47	99·48	99·49	99·50
3	34·12	30·82	29·46	28·71	28·24	27·91	27·67	27·49	27·35	27·23	27·05	26·87	26·69	26·60	26·50	26·41	26·32	26·22	26·13
4	21·20	18·00	16·69	15·98	15·52	15·21	14·98	14·80	14·66	14·55	14·37	14·20	14·02	13·93	13·84	13·75	13·65	13·56	13·46
5	16·26	13·27	12·06	11·39	10·97	10·67	10·46	10·29	10·16	10·05	9·89	9·72	9·55	9·47	9·38	9·29	9·20	9·11	9·02
6	13·75	10·92	9·78	9·15	8·75	8·47	8·26	8·10	7·98	7·87	7·72	7·56	7·40	7·31	7·23	7·14	7·06	6·97	6·88
7	12·25	9·55	8·45	7·85	7·46	7·19	6·99	6·84	6·72	6·62	6·47	6·31	6·16	6·07	5·99	5·91	5·82	5·74	5·65
8	11·26	8·65	7·59	7·01	6·63	6·37	6·18	6·03	5·91	5·81	5·67	5·52	5·36	5·28	5·20	5·12	5·03	4·95	4·86
9	10·56	8·02	6·99	6·42	6·06	5·80	5·61	5·47	5·35	5·26	5·11	4·96	4·81	4·73	4·65	4·57	4·48	4·40	4·31
10	10·04	7·56	6·55	5·99	5·64	5·39	5·20	5·06	4·94	4·85	4·71	4·56	4·41	4·33	4·25	4·17	4·08	4·00	3·91
11	9·65	7·21	6·22	5·67	5·32	5·07	4·89	4·74	4·63	4·54	4·40	4·25	4·10	4·02	3·94	3·86	3·78	3·69	3·60
12	9·33	6·93	5·95	5·41	5·06	4·82	4·64	4·50	4·39	4·30	4·16	4·01	3·86	3·78	3·70	3·62	3·54	3·45	3·36
13	9·07	6·70	5·74	5·21	4·86	4·62	4·44	4·30	4·19	4·10	3·96	3·82	3·66	3·59	3·51	3·43	3·34	3·25	3·17
14	8·86	6·51	5·56	5·04	4·69	4·46	4·28	4·14	4·03	3·94	3·80	3·66	3·51	3·43	3·35	3·27	3·18	3·09	3·00
15	8·68	6·36	5·42	4·89	4·56	4·32	4·14	4·00	3·89	3·80	3·67	3·52	3·37	3·29	3·21	3·13	3·05	2·96	2·87
16	8·53	6·23	5·29	4·77	4·44	4·20	4·03	3·89	3·78	3·69	3·55	3·41	3·26	3·18	3·10	3·02	2·93	2·84	2·75
17	8·40	6·11	5·18	4·67	4·34	4·10	3·93	3·79	3·68	3·59	3·46	3·31	3·16	3·08	3·00	2·92	2·83	2·75	2·65
18	8·29	6·01	5·09	4·58	4·25	4·01	3·84	3·71	3·60	3·51	3·37	3·23	3·08	3·00	2·92	2·84	2·75	2·66	2·57
19	8·18	5·93	5·01	4·50	4·17	3·94	3·77	3·63	3·52	3·43	3·30	3·15	3·00	2·92	2·84	2·76	2·67	2·58	2·49
20	8·10	5·85	4·94	4·43	4·10	3·87	3·70	3·56	3·46	3·37	3·23	3·09	2·94	2·86	2·78	2·69	2·61	2·52	2·42
21	8·02	5·78	4·87	4·37	4·04	3·81	3·64	3·51	3·40	3·31	3·17	3·03	2·88	2·80	2·72	2·64	2·55	2·46	2·36
22	7·95	5·72	4·82	4·31	3·99	3·76	3·59	3·45	3·35	3·26	3·12	2·98	2·83	2·75	2·67	2·58	2·50	2·40	2·31
23	7·88	5·66	4·76	4·26	3·94	3·71	3·54	3·41	3·30	3·21	3·07	2·93	2·78	2·70	2·62	2·54	2·45	2·35	2·26
24	7·82	5·61	4·72	4·22	3·90	3·67	3·50	3·36	3·26	3·17	3·03	2·89	2·74	2·66	2·58	2·49	2·40	2·31	2·21
25	7·77	5·57	4·68	4·18	3·85	3·63	3·46	3·32	3·22	3·13	2·99	2·85	2·70	2·62	2·54	2·45	2·36	2·27	2·17
26	7·72	5·53	4·64	4·14	3·82	3·59	3·42	3·29	3·18	3·09	2·96	2·81	2·66	2·58	2·50	2·42	2·33	2·23	2·13
27	7·68	5·49	4·60	4·11	3·78	3·56	3·39	3·26	3·15	3·06	2·93	2·78	2·63	2·55	2·47	2·38	2·29	2·20	2·10
28	7·64	5·45	4·57	4·07	3·75	3·53	3·36	3·23	3·12	3·03	2·90	2·75	2·60	2·52	2·44	2·35	2·26	2·17	2·06
29	7·60	5·42	4·54	4·04	3·73	3·50	3·33	3·20	3·09	3·00	2·87	2·73	2·57	2·49	2·41	2·33	2·23	2·14	2·03
30	7·56	5·39	4·51	4·02	3·70	3·47	3·30	3·17	3·07	2·98	2·84	2·70	2·55	2·47	2·39	2·30	2·21	2·11	2·01
40	7·31	5·18	4·31	3·83	3·51	3·29	3·12	2·99	2·89	2·80	2·66	2·52	2·37	2·29	2·20	2·11	2·02	1·92	1·80
60	7·08	4·98	4·13	3·65	3·34	3·12	2·95	2·82	2·72	2·63	2·50	2·35	2·20	2·12	2·03	1·94	1·84	1·73	1·60
120	6·85	4·79	3·95	3·48	3·17	2·96	2·79	2·66	2·56	2·47	2·34	2·19	2·03	1·95	1·86	1·76	1·66	1·53	1·38
∞	6·63	4·61	3·78	3·32	3·02	2·80	2·64	2·51	2·41	2·32	2·18	2·04	1·88	1·79	1·70	1·59	1·47	1·32	1·00

Fisher's *Z* Transformed Values

r	Z	r	Z
·00	·0000	·50	·5493
1	·0100	1	·5627
2	·0200	2	·5763
3	·0300	3	·5901
4	·0400	4	·6042
·05	·0500	·55	·6184
6	·0601	6	·6328
7	·0701	7	·6475
8	·0802	8	·6625
9	·0902	9	·6777
·10	·1003	·60	·6931
1	·1104	1	·7089
2	·1206	2	·7250
3	·1307	3	·7414
4	·1409	4	·7582
·15	·1511	·65	·7753
6	·1614	6	·7928
7	·1717	7	·8107
8	·1820	8	·8291
9	·1923	9	·8480
·20	·2027	·70	·8673
1	·2132	1	·8872
2	·2237	2	·9076
3	·2342	3	·9287
4	·2448	4	·9505
·25	·2554	·75	0·973
6	·2661	6	0·996
7	·2769	7	1·020
8	·2877	8	1·045
9	·2986	9	1·071
·30	·3095	·80	1·099
1	·3205	1	1·127
2	·3316	2	1·157
3	·3428	3	1·188
4	·3541	4	1·221
·35	·3654	·85	1·256
6	·3769	6	1·293
7	·3884	7	1 333
8	·4001	8	1·376
9	·4118	9	1·422
·40	·4236	·90	1·472
1	·4356	1	1·528
2	·4477	2	1·589
3	·4599	3	1·658
4	·4722	4	1·738
·45	·4847	·95	1·832
6	·4973	6	1·946
7	·5101	7	2·092
8	·5230	8	2·298
9	·5361	9	2·647

Orthogonal Polynomials

J	Trend	$j=1$	2	3	4	5	6	7	8	9	10	Σc_j^2
$J=3$	linear	−1	0	1								2
	quadratic	1	−2	1								6
$J=4$	linear	−3	−1	1	3							20
	quadratic	1	−1	−1	1							4
	cubic	−1	3	−3	1							20
$J=5$	linear	−2	−1	0	1	2						10
	quadratic	2	−1	−2	−1	2						14
	cubic	−1	2	0	−2	1						10
	quartic	1	−4	6	−4	1						70
$J=6$	linear	−5	−3	−1	1	3	5					70
	quadratic	5	−1	−4	−4	−1	5					84
	cubic	−5	7	4	−4	−7	5					180
	quartic	1	−3	2	2	−3	1					28
	quintic	−1	5	−10	10	−5	1					252
$J=7$	linear	−3	−2	−1	0	1	2	3				28
	quadratic	5	0	−3	−4	−3	0	5				84
	cubic	−1	1	1	0	−1	−1	1				6
	quartic	3	−7	1	6	1	−7	3				154
	quintic	−1	4	−5	0	5	−4	1				84
$J=8$	linear	−7	−5	−3	−1	1	3	5	7			168
	quadratic	7	1	−3	−5	−5	−3	1	7			168
	cubic	−7	5	7	3	−3	−7	−5	7			264
	quartic	7	−13	−3	9	9	−3	−13	7			616
	quintic	−7	23	−17	−15	15	17	−23	7			2184
$J=9$	linear	−4	−3	−2	−1	0	1	2	3	4		60
	quadratic	28	7	−8	−17	−20	−17	−8	7	28		2772
	cubic	−14	7	13	9	0	−9	−13	−7	14		990
	quartic	14	−21	−11	9	18	9	−11	−21	14		2002
	quintic	−4	11	−4	−9	0	9	4	−11	4		468
$J=10$	linear	−9	−7	−5	−3	−1	1	3	5	7	9	330
	quadratic	6	2	−1	−3	−4	−4	−3	−1	2	6	132
	cubic	−42	14	35	31	12	−12	−31	−35	−14	42	8580
	quartic	18	−22	−17	3	18	18	3	−17	−22	18	2860
	quintic	−6	14	−1	−11	−6	6	11	1	−14	6	780

Critical Values for Dunnett's Procedure

One-tailed, $\alpha = .05$

(The columns represent J = number of treatment means [excluding the control])

d.f.	1	2	3	4	5	6	7	8	9
5	2.02	2.44	2.68	2.85	2.98	3.08	3.16	3.24	3.30
6	1.94	2.34	2.56	2.71	2.83	2.92	3.00	3.07	3.12
7	1.89	2.27	2.48	2.62	2.73	2.82	2.89	2.95	3.01
8	1.86	2.22	2.42	2.55	2.66	2.74	2.81	2.87	2.92
9	1.83	2.18	2.37	2.50	2.60	2.68	2.75	2.81	2.86
10	1.81	2.15	2.34	2.47	2.56	2.64	2.70	2.76	2.81
11	1.80	2.13	2.31	2.44	2.53	2.60	2.67	2.72	2.77
12	1.78	2.11	2.29	2.41	2.50	2.58	2.64	2.69	2.74
13	1.77	2.09	2.27	2.39	2.48	2.55	2.61	2.66	2.71
14	1.76	2.08	2.25	2.37	2.46	2.53	2.59	2.64	2.69
15	1.75	2.07	2.24	2.36	2.44	2.51	2.57	2.62	2.67
16	1.75	2.06	2.23	2.34	2.43	2.50	2.56	2.61	2.65
17	1.74	2.05	2.22	2.33	2.42	2.49	2.54	2.59	2.64
18	1.73	2.04	2.21	2.32	2.41	2.48	2.53	2.58	2.62
19	1.73	2.03	2.20	2.31	2.40	2.47	2.52	2.57	2.61
20	1.72	2.03	2.19	2.30	2.39	2.46	2.51	2.56	2.60
24	1.71	2.01	2.17	2.28	2.36	2.43	2.48	2.53	2.57
30	1.70	1.99	2.15	2.25	2.33	2.40	2.45	2.50	2.54
40	1.68	1.97	2.13	2.23	2.31	2.37	2.42	2.47	2.51
60	1.67	1.95	2.10	2.21	2.28	2.35	2.39	2.44	2.48
120	1.66	1.93	2.08	2.18	2.26	2.32	2.37	2.41	2.45
∞	1.64	1.92	2.06	2.16	2.23	2.29	2.34	2.38	2.42

(continued)

Critical Values for Dunnett's Procedure

One-tailed, $\alpha = .01$

(The columns represent J = number of treatment means [excluding the control])

d.f.	1	2	3	4	5	6	7	8	9
5	3.37	3.90	4.21	4.43	4.60	4.73	4.85	4.94	5.03
6	3.14	3.61	3.88	4.07	4.21	4.33	4.43	4.51	4.59
7	3.00	3.42	3.66	3.83	3.96	4.07	4.15	4.23	4.30
8	2.90	3.29	3.51	3.67	3.79	3.88	3.96	4.03	4.09
9	2.82	3.19	3.40	3.55	3.66	3.75	3.82	3.89	3.94
10	2.76	3.11	3.31	3.45	3.56	3.64	3.71	3.78	3.83
11	2.72	3.06	3.25	3.38	3.48	3.56	3.63	3.69	3.74
12	2.68	3.01	3.19	3.32	3.42	3.50	3.56	3.62	3.67
13	2.65	2.97	3.15	3.27	3.37	3.44	3.51	3.56	3.61
14	2.62	2.94	3.11	3.23	3.32	3.40	3.46	3.51	3.56
15	2.60	2.91	3.08	3.20	3.29	3.36	3.42	3.47	3.52
16	2.58	2.88	3.05	3.17	3.26	3.33	3.39	3.44	3.48
17	2.57	2.86	3.03	3.14	3.23	3.30	3.36	3.41	3.45
18	2.55	2.84	3.01	3.12	3.21	3.27	3.33	3.38	3.42
19	2.54	2.83	2.99	3.10	3.18	3.25	3.31	3.36	3.40
20	2.53	2.81	2.97	3.08	3.17	3.23	3.29	3.34	3.38
24	2.49	2.77	2.92	3.03	3.11	3.17	3.22	3.27	3.31
30	2.46	2.72	2.87	2.97	3.05	3.11	3.16	3.21	3.24
40	2.42	2.68	2.82	2.92	2.99	3.05	3.10	3.14	3.18
60	2.39	2.64	2.78	2.87	2.94	3.00	3.04	3.08	3.12
120	2.36	2.60	2.73	2.82	2.89	2.94	2.99	3.03	3.06
∞	2.33	2.56	2.68	2.77	2.84	2.89	2.93	2.97	3.00

(*continued*)

Critical Values for Dunnett's Procedure

Two-tailed, $\alpha = .05$

(The columns represent $J =$ number of treatment means [excluding the control])

d.f.	1	2	3	4	5	6	7	8	9
5	2.57	3.03	3.29	3.48	3.62	3.73	3.82	3.90	3.97
6	2.45	2.86	3.10	3.26	3.39	3.49	3.57	3.64	3.71
7	2.36	2.75	2.97	3.12	3.24	3.33	3.41	3.47	3.53
8	2.31	2.67	2.88	3.02	3.13	3.22	3.29	3.35	3.41
9	2.26	2.61	2.81	2.95	3.05	3.14	3.20	3.26	3.32
10	2.23	2.57	2.76	2.89	2.99	3.07	3.14	3.19	3.24
11	2.20	2.53	2.72	2.84	2.94	3.02	3.08	3.14	3.19
12	2.18	2.50	2.68	2.81	2.90	2.98	3.04	3.09	3.14
13	2.16	2.48	2.65	2.78	2.87	2.94	3.00	3.06	3.10
14	2.14	2.46	2.63	2.75	2.84	2.91	2.97	3.02	3.07
15	2.13	2.44	2.61	2.73	2.82	2.89	2.95	3.00	3.04
16	2.12	2.42	2.59	2.71	2.80	2.87	2.92	2.97	3.02
17	2.11	2.41	2.58	2.69	2.78	2.85	2.90	2.95	3.00
18	2.10	2.40	2.56	2.68	2.76	2.83	2.89	2.94	2.98
19	2.09	2.39	2.55	2.66	2.75	2.81	2.87	2.92	2.96
20	2.09	2.38	2.54	2.65	2.73	2.80	2.86	2.90	2.95
24	2.06	2.35	2.51	2.61	2.70	2.76	2.81	2.86	2.90
30	2.04	2.32	2.47	2.58	2.66	2.72	2.77	2.82	2.86
40	2.02	2.29	2.44	2.54	2.62	2.68	2.73	2.77	2.81
60	2.00	2.27	2.41	2.51	2.58	2.64	2.69	2.73	2.77
120	1.98	2.24	2.38	2.47	2.55	2.60	2.65	2.69	2.73
∞	1.96	2.21	2.35	2.44	2.51	2.57	2.61	2.65	2.69

(*continued*)

Critical Values for Dunnett's Procedure

Two-tailed, $\alpha = .01$

(The columns represent J = number of treatment means [excluding the control])

d.f.	1	2	3	4	5	6	7	8	9
5	4.03	4.63	4.98	5.22	5.41	5.56	5.69	5.80	5.89
6	3.71	4.21	4.51	4.71	4.87	5.00	5.10	5.20	5.28
7	3.50	3.95	4.21	4.39	4.53	4.64	4.74	4.82	4.89
8	3.36	3.77	4.00	4.17	4.29	4.40	4.48	4.56	4.62
9	3.25	3.63	3.85	4.01	4.12	4.22	4.30	4.37	4.43
10	3.17	3.53	3.74	3.88	3.99	4.08	4.16	4.22	4.28
11	3.11	3.45	3.65	3.79	3.89	3.98	4.05	4.11	4.16
12	3.05	3.39	3.58	3.71	3.81	3.89	3.96	4.02	4.07
13	3.01	3.33	3.52	3.65	3.74	3.82	3.89	3.94	3.99
14	2.98	3.29	3.47	3.59	3.69	3.76	3.83	3.88	3.93
15	2.95	3.25	3.43	3.55	3.64	3.71	3.78	3.83	3.88
16	2.92	3.22	3.39	3.51	3.60	3.67	3.73	3.78	3.83
17	2.90	3.19	3.36	3.47	3.56	3.63	3.69	3.74	3.79
18	2.88	3.17	3.33	3.44	3.53	3.60	3.66	3.71	3.75
19	2.86	3.15	3.31	3.42	3.50	3.57	3.63	3.68	3.72
20	2.85	3.13	3.29	3.40	3.48	3.55	3.60	3.65	3.69
24	2.80	3.07	3.22	3.32	3.40	3.47	3.52	3.57	3.61
30	2.75	3.01	3.15	3.25	3.33	3.39	3.44	3.49	3.52
40	2.70	2.95	3.09	3.19	3.26	3.32	3.37	3.41	3.44
60	2.66	2.90	3.03	3.12	3.19	3.25	3.29	3.33	3.37
120	2.62	2.85	2.97	3.06	3.12	3.18	3.22	3.26	3.29
∞	2.58	2.79	2.92	3.00	3.06	3.11	3.15	3.19	3.22

242

APPENDIX TABLE 8
Critical Values for Dunn's (Bonferroni's) Procedure

ν	α	Number of contrasts										
		2	3	4	5	6	7	8	9	10	15	20
2	0.01	14.071	17.248	19.925	22.282	24.413	26.372	28.196	29.908	31.528	38.620	44.598
	0.05	6.164	7.582	8.774	9.823	10.769	11.639	12.449	13.208	13.927	17.072	19.721
	0.10	4.243	5.243	6.081	6.816	7.480	8.090	8.656	9.188	9.691	11.890	13.741
	0.20	2.828	3.531	4.116	4.628	5.089	5.512	5.904	6.272	6.620	8.138	9.414
3	0.01	7.447	8.565	9.453	10.201	10.853	11.436	11.966	12.453	12.904	14.796	16.300
	0.05	4.156	4.826	5.355	5.799	6.185	6.529	6.842	7.128	7.394	8.505	9.387
	0.10	3.149	3.690	4.115	4.471	4.780	5.055	5.304	5.532	5.744	6.627	7.326
	0.20	2.294	2.734	3.077	3.363	3.610	3.829	4.028	4.209	4.377	5.076	5.628
4	0.01	5.594	6.248	6.751	7.166	7.520	7.832	8.112	8.367	8.600	9.556	10.294
	0.05	3.481	3.941	4.290	4.577	4.822	5.036	5.228	5.402	5.562	6.214	6.714
	0.10	2.751	3.150	3.452	3.699	3.909	4.093	4.257	4.406	4.542	5.097	5.521
	0.20	2.084	2.434	2.697	2.911	3.092	3.250	3.391	3.518	3.635	4.107	4.468
5	0.01	4.771	5.243	5.599	5.888	6.133	6.346	6.535	6.706	6.862	7.491	7.968
	0.05	3.152	3.518	3.791	4.012	4.197	4.358	4.501	4.630	4.747	5.219	5.573
	0.10	2.549	2.882	3.129	3.327	3.493	3.638	3.765	3.880	3.985	4.403	4.718
	0.20	1.973	2.278	2.503	2.683	2.834	2.964	3.079	3.182	3.275	3.649	3.928
6	0.01	4.315	4.695	4.977	5.203	5.394	5.559	5.704	5.835	5.954	6.428	6.782
	0.05	2.959	3.274	3.505	3.690	3.845	3.978	4.095	4.200	4.296	4.675	4.956
	0.10	2.428	2.723	2.939	3.110	3.253	3.376	3.484	3.580	3.668	4.015	4.272
	0.20	1.904	2.184	2.387	2.547	2.681	2.795	2.895	2.985	3.066	3.385	3.620
7	0.01	4.027	4.353	4.591	4.782	4.941	5.078	5.198	5.306	5.404	5.791	6.077
	0.05	2.832	3.115	3.321	3.484	3.620	3.736	3.838	3.929	4.011	4.336	4.574
	0.10	2.347	2.618	2.814	2.969	3.097	3.206	3.302	3.388	3.465	3.768	3.990
	0.20	1.858	2.120	2.309	2.457	2.579	2.684	2.775	2.856	2.929	3.214	3.423
8	0.01	3.831	4.120	4.331	4.498	4.637	4.756	4.860	4.953	5.038	5.370	5.613
	0.05	2.743	3.005	3.193	3.342	3.464	3.569	3.661	3.743	3.816	4.105	4.316
	0.10	2.289	2.544	2.726	2.869	2.987	3.088	3.176	3.254	3.324	3.598	3.798
	0.20	1.824	2.075	2.254	2.393	2.508	2.605	2.690	2.765	2.832	3.095	3.286
9	0.01	3.688	3.952	4.143	4.294	4.419	4.526	4.619	4.703	4.778	5.072	5.287
	0.05	2.677	2.923	3.099	3.237	3.351	3.448	3.532	3.607	3.675	3.938	4.129
	0.10	2.246	2.488	2.661	2.796	2.907	3.001	3.083	3.155	3.221	3.474	3.658
	0.20	1.799	2.041	2.212	2.345	2.454	2.546	2.627	2.698	2.761	3.008	3.185
10	0.01	3.580	3.825	4.002	4.141	4.256	4.354	4.439	4.515	4.584	4.852	5.046
	0.05	2.626	2.860	3.027	3.157	3.264	3.355	3.434	3.505	3.568	3.813	3.989
	0.10	2.213	2.446	2.611	2.739	2.845	2.934	3.012	3.080	3.142	3.380	3.552
	0.20	1.779	2.014	2.180	2.308	2.413	2.501	2.578	2.646	2.706	2.941	3.108
11	0.01	3.495	3.726	3.892	4.022	4.129	4.221	4.300	4.371	4.434	4.682	4.860
	0.05	2.586	2.811	2.970	3.094	3.196	3.283	3.358	3.424	3.484	3.715	3.880
	0.10	2.186	2.412	2.571	2.695	2.796	2.881	2.955	3.021	3.079	3.306	3.468
	0.20	1.763	1.993	2.154	2.279	2.380	2.465	2.539	2.605	2.663	2.888	3.048
12	0.01	3.427	3.647	3.804	3.927	4.029	4.114	4.189	4.256	4.315	4.547	4.714
	0.05	2.553	2.770	2.924	3.044	3.141	3.224	3.296	3.359	3.416	3.636	3.793
	0.10	2.164	2.384	2.539	2.658	2.756	2.838	2.910	2.973	3.029	3.247	3.402
	0.20	1.750	1.975	2.133	2.254	2.353	2.436	2.508	2.571	2.628	2.845	2.999
13	0.01	3.371	3.582	3.733	3.850	3.946	4.028	4.099	4.162	4.218	4.438	4.595
	0.05	2.526	2.737	2.886	3.002	3.096	3.176	3.245	3.306	3.361	3.571	3.722
	0.10	2.146	2.361	2.512	2.628	2.723	2.803	2.872	2.933	2.988	3.198	3.347
	0.20	1.739	1.961	2.116	2.234	2.331	2.412	2.482	2.544	2.599	2.809	2.958
14	0.01	3.324	3.528	3.673	3.785	3.878	3.956	4.024	4.084	4.138	4.347	4.497
	0.05	2.503	2.709	2.854	2.967	3.058	3.135	3.202	3.261	3.314	3.518	3.662
	0.10	2.131	2.342	2.489	2.603	2.696	2.774	2.841	2.900	2.953	3.157	3.301
	0.20	1.730	1.949	2.101	2.217	2.312	2.392	2.460	2.520	2.574	2.779	2.924
15	0.01	3.285	3.482	3.622	3.731	3.820	3.895	3.961	4.019	4.071	4.271	4.414
	0.05	2.483	2.685	2.827	2.937	3.026	3.101	3.166	3.224	3.275	3.472	3.612
	0.10	2.118	2.325	2.470	2.582	2.672	2.748	2.814	2.872	2.924	3.122	3.262
	0.20	1.722	1.938	2.088	2.203	2.296	2.374	2.441	2.500	2.553	2.754	2.896

(*continued*)

Critical Values for Dunn's (Bonferroni's) Procedure

		Number of contrasts										
ν	α	2	3	4	5	6	7	8	9	10	15	20
16	0.01	3.251	3.443	3.579	3.684	3.771	3.844	3.907	3.963	4.013	4.206	4.344
	0.05	2.467	2.665	2.804	2.911	2.998	3.072	3.135	3.191	3.241	3.433	3.569
	0.10	2.106	2.311	2.453	2.563	2.652	2.726	2.791	2.848	2.898	3.092	3.228
	0.20	1.715	1.929	2.077	2.190	2.282	2.359	2.425	2.483	2.535	2.732	2.871
17	0.01	3.221	3.409	3.541	3.644	3.728	3.799	3.860	3.914	3.963	4.150	4.284
	0.05	2.452	2.647	2.783	2.889	2.974	3.046	3.108	3.163	3.212	3.399	3.532
	0.10	2.096	2.298	2.439	2.547	2.634	2.708	2.771	2.826	2.876	3.066	3.199
	0.20	1.709	1.921	2.068	2.179	2.270	2.346	2.411	2.468	2.519	2.713	2.849
18	0.01	3.195	3.379	3.508	3.609	3.691	3.760	3.820	3.872	3.920	4.102	4.231
	0.05	2.439	2.631	2.766	2.869	2.953	3.024	3.085	3.138	3.186	3.370	3.499
	0.10	2.088	2.287	2.426	2.532	2.619	2.691	2.753	2.806	2.857	3.043	3.174
	0.20	1.704	1.914	2.059	2.170	2.259	2.334	2.399	2.455	2.505	2.696	2.830
19	0.01	3.173	3.353	3.479	3.578	3.658	3.725	3.784	3.835	3.881	4.059	4.185
	0.05	2.427	2.617	2.750	2.852	2.934	3.004	3.064	3.116	3.163	3.343	3.470
	0.10	2.080	2.277	2.415	2.520	2.605	2.676	2.738	2.791	2.839	3.023	3.152
	0.20	1.699	1.908	2.052	2.161	2.250	2.324	2.388	2.443	2.493	2.682	2.813
20	0.01	3.152	3.329	3.454	3.550	3.629	3.695	3.752	3.802	3.848	4.021	4.144
	0.05	2.417	2.605	2.736	2.836	2.918	2.986	3.045	3.097	3.143	3.320	3.445
	0.10	2.073	2.269	2.405	2.508	2.593	2.663	2.724	2.777	2.824	3.005	3.132
	0.20	1.695	1.902	2.045	2.154	2.241	2.315	2.378	2.433	2.482	2.668	2.798
21	0.01	3.134	3.306	3.431	3.525	3.602	3.667	3.724	3.773	3.817	3.987	4.108
	0.05	2.408	2.594	2.723	2.822	2.903	2.970	3.028	3.080	3.125	3.300	3.422
	0.10	2.067	2.261	2.396	2.498	2.581	2.651	2.711	2.764	2.810	2.989	3.114
	0.20	1.691	1.897	2.039	2.147	2.234	2.306	2.369	2.424	2.472	2.656	2.785
22	0.01	3.118	3.289	3.410	3.503	3.579	3.643	3.698	3.747	3.790	3.957	4.075
	0.05	2.400	2.584	2.712	2.810	2.889	2.956	3.014	3.064	3.109	3.281	3.402
	0.10	2.061	2.254	2.387	2.489	2.572	2.641	2.700	2.752	2.798	2.974	3.098
	0.20	1.688	1.892	2.033	2.141	2.227	2.299	2.361	2.415	2.463	2.646	2.773
23	0.01	3.103	3.272	3.392	3.483	3.558	3.621	3.675	3.723	3.766	3.930	4.046
	0.05	2.392	2.574	2.701	2.798	2.877	2.943	3.000	3.050	3.094	3.264	3.383
	0.10	2.056	2.247	2.380	2.481	2.563	2.631	2.690	2.741	2.787	2.961	3.083
	0.20	1.685	1.888	2.028	2.135	2.221	2.292	2.354	2.407	2.455	2.636	2.762
24	0.01	3.089	3.257	3.375	3.465	3.539	3.601	3.654	3.702	3.744	3.905	4.019
	0.05	2.385	2.566	2.692	2.788	2.866	2.931	2.988	3.037	3.081	3.249	3.366
	0.10	2.051	2.241	2.373	2.473	2.554	2.622	2.680	2.731	2.777	2.949	3.070
	0.20	1.682	1.884	2.024	2.130	2.215	2.286	2.347	2.400	2.448	2.627	2.752
25	0.01	3.077	3.243	3.359	3.449	3.521	3.583	3.635	3.682	3.723	3.882	3.995
	0.05	2.379	2.558	2.683	2.779	2.856	2.921	2.976	3.025	3.069	3.235	3.351
	0.10	2.047	2.236	2.367	2.466	2.547	2.614	2.672	2.722	2.767	2.938	3.058
	0.20	1.679	1.881	2.020	2.125	2.210	2.280	2.341	2.394	2.441	2.619	2.743
26	0.01	3.066	3.230	3.345	3.433	3.505	3.566	3.618	3.664	3.705	3.862	3.972
	0.05	2.373	2.551	2.675	2.770	2.847	2.911	2.966	3.014	3.058	3.222	3.337
	0.10	2.043	2.231	2.361	2.460	2.540	2.607	2.664	2.714	2.759	2.928	3.047
	0.20	1.677	1.878	2.016	2.121	2.205	2.275	2.335	2.388	2.435	2.612	2.735
27	0.01	3.056	3.218	3.332	3.419	3.491	3.550	3.602	3.647	3.688	3.843	3.952
	0.05	2.368	2.545	2.668	2.762	2.838	2.902	2.956	3.004	3.047	3.210	3.324
	0.10	2.039	2.227	2.356	2.454	2.534	2.600	2.657	2.707	2.751	2.919	3.036
	0.20	1.675	1.875	2.012	2.117	2.201	2.270	2.330	2.383	2.429	2.605	2.727
28	0.01	3.046	3.207	3.320	3.407	3.477	3.536	3.587	3.632	3.672	3.825	3.933
	0.05	2.363	2.539	2.661	2.755	2.830	2.893	2.948	2.995	3.038	3.199	3.312
	0.10	2.036	2.222	2.351	2.449	2.528	2.594	2.650	2.700	2.744	2.911	3.027
	0.20	1.672	1.872	2.009	2.113	2.196	2.266	2.326	2.378	2.424	2.599	2.720
29	0.01	3.037	3.197	3.309	3.395	3.464	3.523	3.574	3.618	3.658	3.809	3.916
	0.05	2.358	2.534	2.655	2.748	2.823	2.886	2.940	2.987	3.029	3.189	3.301
	0.10	2.033	2.218	2.346	2.444	2.522	2.588	2.644	2.693	2.737	2.903	3.018
	0.20	1.671	1.869	2.006	2.110	2.193	2.262	2.321	2.373	2.419	2.593	2.713

(*continued*)

Critical Values for Dunn's (Bonferroni's) Procedure

ν	α	Number of contrasts										
		2	3	4	5	6	7	8	9	10	15	20
30	0.01	3.029	3.168	3.298	3.384	3.453	3.511	3.561	3.605	3.644	3.794	3.900
	0.05	2.354	2.528	2.649	2.742	2.816	2.878	2.932	2.979	3.021	3.180	3.291
	0.10	2.030	2.215	2.342	2.439	2.517	2.582	2.638	2.687	2.731	2.895	3.010
	0.20	1.669	1.867	2.003	2.106	2.189	2.258	2.317	2.369	2.414	2.587	2.707
40	0.01	2.970	3.121	3.225	3.305	3.370	3.425	3.472	3.513	3.549	3.689	3.787
	0.05	2.323	2.492	2.608	2.696	2.766	2.827	2.878	2.923	2.963	3.113	3.218
	0.10	2.009	2.189	2.312	2.406	2.481	2.544	2.597	2.644	2.686	2.843	2.952
	0.20	1.656	1.850	1.983	2.083	2.164	2.231	2.288	2.338	2.382	2.548	2.663
60	0.01	2.914	3.056	3.155	3.230	3.291	3.342	3.386	3.425	3.459	3.589	3.679
	0.05	2.294	2.456	2.568	2.653	2.721	2.777	2.826	2.869	2.906	3.049	3.148
	0.10	1.989	2.163	2.283	2.373	2.446	2.506	2.556	2.603	2.643	2.793	2.897
	0.20	1.643	1.834	1.963	2.061	2.139	2.204	2.259	2.308	2.350	2.511	2.621
120	0.01	2.859	2.994	3.087	3.158	3.215	3.263	3.304	3.340	3.372	3.493	3.577
	0.05	2.265	2.422	2.529	2.610	2.675	2.729	2.776	2.816	2.852	2.987	3.081
	0.10	1.966	2.136	2.254	2.342	2.411	2.469	2.519	2.562	2.600	2.744	2.843
	0.20	1.631	1.817	1.944	2.039	2.115	2.178	2.231	2.278	2.319	2.474	2.580
∞	0.01	2.806	2.934	3.022	3.089	3.143	3.188	3.226	3.260	3.289	3.402	3.480
	0.05	2.237	2.388	2.491	2.569	2.631	2.683	2.727	2.766	2.800	2.928	3.016
	0.10	1.949	2.114	2.226	2.311	2.378	2.434	2.482	2.523	2.560	2.697	2.791
	0.20	1.618	1.801	1.925	2.018	2.091	2.152	2.204	2.249	2.289	2.436	2.540

Critical Values for the Studentized Range Statistic, $\alpha = .10$

v \ J or r	2	3	4	5	6	7	8	9	10
1	8.929	13.44	16.36	18.49	20.15	21.51	22.64	23.62	24.48
2	4.130	5.733	6.773	7.538	8.139	8.633	9.049	9.409	9.725
3	3.328	4.467	5.199	5.738	6.162	6.511	6.806	7.062	7.287
4	3.015	3.976	4.586	5.035	5.388	5.679	5.926	6.139	6.327
5	2.850	3.717	4.264	4.664	4.979	5.238	5.458	5.648	5.816
6	2.748	3.559	4.065	4.435	4.726	4.966	5.168	5.344	5.499
7	2.680	3.451	3.931	4.280	4.555	4.780	4.972	5.137	5.283
8	2.630	3.374	3.834	4.169	4.431	4.646	4.829	4.987	5.126
9	2.592	3.316	3.761	4.084	4.337	4.545	4.721	4.873	5.007
10	2.563	3.270	3.704	4.018	4.264	4.465	4.636	4.783	4.913
11	2.540	3.234	3.658	3.965	4.205	4.401	4.568	4.711	4.838
12	2.521	3.204	3.621	3.922	4.156	4.349	4.511	4.652	4.776
13	2.505	3.179	3.589	3.885	4.116	4.305	4.464	4.602	4.724
14	2.491	3.158	3.563	3.854	4.081	4.267	4.424	4.560	4.680
15	2.479	3.140	3.540	3.828	4.052	4.235	4.390	4.524	4.641
16	2.469	3.124	3.520	3.804	4.026	4.207	4.360	4.492	4.608
17	2.460	3.110	3.503	3.784	4.004	4.183	4.334	4.464	4.579
18	2.452	3.098	3.488	3.767	3.984	4.161	4.311	4.440	4.554
19	2.445	3.087	3.474	3.751	3.966	4.142	4.290	4.418	4.531
20	2.439	3.078	3.462	3.736	3.950	4.124	4.271	4.398	4.510
24	2.420	3.047	3.423	3.692	3.900	4.070	4.213	4.336	4.445
30	2.400	3.017	3.386	3.648	3.851	4.016	4.155	4.275	4.381
40	2.381	2.988	3.349	3.605	3.803	3.963	4.099	4.215	4.317
60	2.363	2.959	3.312	3.562	3.755	3.911	4.042	4.155	4.254
120	2.344	2.930	3.276	3.520	3.707	3.859	3.987	4.096	4.191
∞	2.326	2.902	3.240	3.478	3.661	3.808	3.931	4.037	4.129

v \ J or r	11	12	13	14	15	16	17	18	19
1	25.24	25.92	26.54	27.10	27.62	28.10	28.54	28.96	29.35
2	10.01	10.26	10.49	10.70	10.89	11.07	11.24	11.39	11.54
3	7.487	7.667	7.832	7.982	8.120	8.249	8.368	8.479	8.584
4	6.495	6.645	6.783	6.909	7.025	7.133	7.233	7.327	7.414
5	5.966	6.101	6.223	6.336	6.440	6.536	6.626	6.710	6.789
6	5.637	5.762	5.875	5.979	6.075	6.164	6.247	6.325	6.398
7	5.413	5.530	5.637	5.735	5.826	5.910	5.988	6.061	6.130
8	5.250	5.362	5.464	5.558	5.644	5.724	5.799	5.869	5.935
9	5.127	5.234	5.333	5.423	5.506	5.583	5.655	5.723	5.786
10	5.029	5.134	5.229	5.317	5.397	5.472	5.542	5.607	5.668
11	4.951	5.053	5.146	5.231	5.309	5.382	5.450	5.514	5.573
12	4.886	4.986	5.077	5.160	5.236	5.308	5.374	5.436	5.495
13	4.832	4.930	5.019	5.100	5.176	5.245	5.311	5.372	5.429
14	4.786	4.882	4.970	5.050	5.124	5.192	5.256	5.316	5.373
15	4.746	4.841	4.927	5.006	5.079	5.147	5.209	5.269	5.324
16	4.712	4.805	4.890	4.968	5.040	5.107	5.169	5.227	5.282
17	4.682	4.774	4.858	4.935	5.005	5.071	5.133	5.190	5.244
18	4.655	4.746	4.829	4.905	4.975	5.040	5.101	5.158	5.211
19	4.631	4.721	4.803	4.879	4.948	5.012	5.073	5.129	5.182
20	4.609	4.699	4.780	4.855	4.924	4.987	5.047	5.103	5.155
24	4.541	4.628	4.708	4.780	4.847	4.909	4.966	5.021	5.071
30	4.474	4.559	4.635	4.706	4.770	4.830	4.886	4.939	4.988
40	4.408	4.490	4.564	4.632	4.695	4.752	4.807	4.857	4.905
60	4.342	4.421	4.493	4.558	4.619	4.675	4.727	4.775	4.821
120	4.276	4.353	4.422	4.485	4.543	4.597	4.647	4.694	4.738
∞	4.211	4.285	4.351	4.412	4.468	4.519	4.568	4.612	4.654

J for Tukey, r for Newman-Keuls

(continued)

Critical Values for the Studentized Range Statistic, $\alpha = .05$

v \ J or r	2	3	4	5	6	7	8	9	10
1	17.97	26.98	32.82	37.08	40.41	43.12	45.40	47.36	49.07
2	6.085	8.331	9.798	10.88	11.74	12.44	13.03	13.54	13.99
3	4.501	5.910	6.825	7.502	8.037	8.478	8.853	9.177	9.462
4	3.927	5.040	5.757	6.287	6.707	7.053	7.347	7.602	7.826
5	3.635	4.602	5.218	5.673	6.033	6.330	6.582	6.802	6.995
6	3.461	4.339	4.896	5.305	5.628	5.895	6.122	6.319	6.493
7	3.344	4.165	4.681	5.060	5.359	5.606	5.815	5.998	6.158
8	3.261	4.041	4.529	4.886	5.167	5.399	5.597	5.767	5.918
9	3.199	3.949	4.415	4.756	5.024	5.244	5.432	5.595	5.739
10	3.151	3.877	4.327	4.654	4.912	5.124	5.305	5.461	5.599
11	3.113	3.820	4.256	4.574	4.823	5.028	5.202	5.353	5.487
12	3.082	3.773	4.199	4.508	4.751	4.950	5.119	5.265	5.395
13	3.055	3.735	4.151	4.453	4.690	4.885	5.049	5.192	5.318
14	3.033	3.702	4.111	4.407	4.639	4.829	4.990	5.131	5.254
15	3.014	3.674	4.076	4.367	4.595	4.782	4.940	5.077	5.198
16	2.998	3.649	4.046	4.333	4.557	4.741	4.897	5.031	5.150
17	2.984	3.628	4.020	4.303	4.524	4.705	4.858	4.991	5.108
18	2.971	3.609	3.997	4.277	4.495	4.673	4.824	4.956	5.071
19	2.960	3.593	3.977	4.253	4.469	4.645	4.794	4.924	5.038
20	2.950	3.578	3.958	4.232	4.445	4.620	4.768	4.896	5.008
24	2.919	3.532	3.901	4.166	4.373	4.541	4.684	4.807	4.915
30	2.888	3.486	3.845	4.102	4.302	4.464	4.602	4.720	4.824
40	2.858	3.442	3.791	4.039	4.232	4.389	4.521	4.635	4.735
60	2.829	3.399	3.737	3.977	4.163	4.314	4.441	4.550	4.646
120	2.800	3.356	3.685	3.917	4.096	4.241	4.363	4.468	4.560
∞	2.772	3.314	3.633	3.858	4.030	4.170	4.286	4.387	4.474

v \ J or r	11	12	13	14	15	16	17	18	19
1	50.59	51.96	53.20	54.33	55.36	56.32	57.22	58.04	58.83
2	14.39	14.75	15.08	15.38	15.65	15.91	16.14	16.37	16.57
3	9.717	9.946	10.15	10.35	10.53	10.69	10.84	10.98	11.11
4	8.027	8.208	8.373	8.525	8.664	8.794	8.914	9.028	9.134
5	7.168	7.324	7.466	7.596	7.717	7.828	7.932	8.030	8.122
6	6.649	6.789	6.917	7.034	7.143	7.244	7.338	7.426	7.508
7	6.302	6.431	6.550	6.658	6.759	6.852	6.939	7.020	7.097
8	6.054	6.175	6.287	6.389	6.483	6.571	6.653	6.729	6.802
9	5.867	5.983	6.089	6.186	6.276	6.359	6.437	6.510	6.579
10	5.722	5.833	5.935	6.028	6.114	6.194	6.269	6.339	6.405
11	5.605	5.713	5.811	5.901	5.984	6.062	6.134	6.202	6.265
12	5.511	5.615	5.710	5.798	5.878	5.953	6.023	6.089	6.151
13	5.431	5.533	5.625	5.711	5.789	5.862	5.931	5.995	6.055
14	5.364	5.463	5.554	5.637	5.714	5.786	5.852	5.915	5.974
15	5.306	5.404	5.493	5.574	5.649	5.720	5.785	5.846	5.904
16	5.256	5.352	5.439	5.520	5.593	5.662	5.727	5.786	5.843
17	5.212	5.307	5.392	5.471	5.544	5.612	5.675	5.734	5.790
18	5.174	5.267	5.352	5.429	5.501	5.568	5.630	5.688	5.743
19	5.140	5.231	5.315	5.391	5.462	5.528	5.589	5.647	5.701
20	5.108	5.199	5.282	5.357	5.427	5.493	5.553	5.610	5.663
24	5.012	5.099	5.179	5.251	5.319	5.381	5.439	5.494	5.545
30	4.917	5.001	5.077	5.147	5.211	5.271	5.327	5.379	5.429
40	4.824	4.904	4.977	5.044	5.106	5.163	5.216	5.266	5.313
60	4.732	4.808	4.878	4.942	5.001	5.056	5.107	5.154	5.199
120	4.641	4.714	4.781	4.842	4.898	4.950	4.998	5.044	5.086
∞	4.552	4.622	4.685	4.743	4.796	4.845	4.891	4.934	4.974

(*continued*)

Critical Values for the Studentized Range Statistic, $\alpha = .01$

v \ J or r	2	3	4	5	6	7	8	9	10
1	90.03	135.0	164.3	185.6	202.2	215.8	227.2	237.0	245.6
2	14.04	19.02	22.29	24.72	26.63	28.20	29.53	30.68	31.69
3	8.261	10.62	12.17	13.33	14.24	15.00	15.64	16.20	16.69
4	6.512	8.120	9.173	9.958	10.58	11.10	11.55	11.93	12.27
5	5.702	6.976	7.804	8.421	8.913	9.321	9.669	9.972	10.24
6	5.243	6.331	7.033	7.556	7.973	8.318	8.613	8.869	9.097
7	4.949	5.919	6.543	7.005	7.373	7.679	7.939	8.166	8.368
8	4.746	5.635	6.204	6.625	6.960	7.237	7.474	7.681	7.863
9	4.596	5.428	5.957	6.348	6.658	6.915	7.134	7.325	7.495
10	4.482	5.270	5.769	6.136	6.428	6.669	6.875	7.055	7.213
11	4.392	5.146	5.621	5.970	6.247	6.476	6.672	6.842	6.992
12	4.320	5.046	5.502	5.836	6.101	6.321	6.507	6.670	6.814
13	4.260	4.964	5.404	5.727	5.981	6.192	6.372	6.528	6.667
14	4.210	4.895	5.322	5.634	5.881	6.085	6.258	6.409	6.543
15	4.168	4.836	5.252	5.556	5.796	5.994	6.162	6.309	6.439
16	4.131	4.786	5.192	5.489	5.722	5.915	6.079	6.222	6.349
17	4.099	4.742	5.140	5.430	5.659	5.847	6.007	6.147	6.270
18	4.071	4.703	5.094	5.379	5.603	5.788	5.944	6.081	6.201
19	4.046	4.670	5.054	5.334	5.554	5.735	5.889	6.022	6.141
20	4.024	4.639	5.018	5.294	5.510	5.688	5.839	5.970	6.087
24	3.956	4.546	4.907	5.168	5.374	5.542	5.685	5.809	5.919
30	3.889	4.455	4.799	5.048	5.242	5.401	5.536	5.653	5.756
40	3.825	4.367	4.696	4.931	5.114	5.265	5.392	5.502	5.599
60	3.762	4.282	4.595	4.818	4.991	5.133	5.253	5.356	5.447
120	3.702	4.200	4.497	4.709	4.872	5.005	5.118	5.214	5.299
∞	3.643	4.120	4.403	4.603	4.757	4.882	4.987	5.078	5.157

v \ J or r	11	12	13	14	15	16	17	18	19
1	253.2	260.0	266.2	271.8	277.0	281.8	286.3	290.4	294.3
2	32.59	33.40	34.13	34.81	35.43	36.00	36.53	37.03	37.50
3	17.13	17.53	17.89	18.22	18.52	18.81	19.07	19.32	19.55
4	12.57	12.84	13.09	13.32	13.53	13.73	13.91	14.08	14.24
5	10.48	10.70	10.89	11.08	11.24	11.40	11.55	11.68	11.81
6	9.301	9.485	9.653	9.808	9.951	10.08	10.21	10.32	10.43
7	8.548	8.711	8.860	8.997	9.124	9.242	9.353	9.456	9.554
8	8.027	8.176	8.312	8.436	8.552	8.659	8.760	8.854	8.943
9	7.647	7.784	7.910	8.025	8.132	8.232	8.325	8.412	8.495
10	7.356	7.485	7.603	7.712	7.812	7.906	7.993	8.076	8.153
11	7.128	7.250	7.362	7.465	7.560	7.649	7.732	7.809	7.883
12	6.943	7.060	7.167	7.265	7.356	7.441	7.520	7.594	7.665
13	6.791	6.903	7.006	7.101	7.188	7.269	7.345	7.417	7.485
14	6.664	6.772	6.871	6.962	7.047	7.126	7.199	7.268	7.333
15	6.555	6.660	6.757	6.845	6.927	7.003	7.074	7.142	7.204
16	6.462	6.564	6.658	6.744	6.823	6.898	6.967	7.032	7.093
17	6.381	6.480	6.572	6.656	6.734	6.806	6.873	6.937	6.997
18	6.310	6.407	6.497	6.579	6.655	6.725	6.792	6.854	6.912
19	6.247	6.342	6.430	6.510	6.585	6.654	6.719	6.780	6.837
20	6.191	6.285	6.371	6.450	6.523	6.591	6.654	6.714	6.771
24	6.017	6.106	6.186	6.261	6.330	6.394	6.453	6.510	6.563
30	5.849	5.932	6.008	6.078	6.143	6.203	6.259	6.311	6.361
40	5.686	5.764	5.835	5.900	5.961	6.017	6.069	6.119	6.165
60	5.528	5.601	5.667	5.728	5.785	5.837	5.886	5.931	5.974
120	5.375	5.443	5.505	5.562	5.614	5.662	5.708	5.750	5.790
∞	5.227	5.290	5.348	5.400	5.448	5.493	5.535	5.574	5.611

Critical Values for the Bryant-Paulson Procedure, $\alpha = .05$

v	$J = 2$	$J = 3$	$J = 4$	$J = 5$	$J = 6$	$J = 7$	$J = 8$	$J = 10$	$J = 12$	$J = 16$	$J = 20$
					$X = 1$						
2	7·96	11·00	12·99	14·46	15·61	16·56	17·36	18·65	19·68	21·23	22·40
3	5·42	7·18	8·32	9·17	9·84	10·39	10·86	11·62	12·22	13·14	13·83
4	4·51	5·84	6·69	7·32	7·82	8·23	8·58	9·15	9·61	10·30	10·82
5	4·06	5·17	5·88	6·40	6·82	7·16	7·45	7·93	8·30	8·88	9·32
6	3·79	4·78	5·40	5·86	6·23	6·53	6·78	7·20	7·53	8·04	8·43
7	3·62	4·52	5·09	5·51	5·84	6·11	6·34	6·72	7·03	7·49	7·84
8	3·49	4·34	4·87	5·26	5·57	5·82	6·03	6·39	6·67	7·10	7·43
10	3·32	4·10	4·58	4·93	5·21	5·43	5·63	5·94	6·19	6·58	6·87
12	3·22	3·95	4·40	4·73	4·98	5·19	5·37	5·67	5·90	6·26	6·53
14	3·15	3·85	4·28	4·59	4·83	5·03	5·20	5·48	5·70	6·03	6·29
16	3·10	3·77	4·19	4·49	4·72	4·91	5·07	5·34	5·55	5·87	6·12
18	3·06	3·72	4·12	4·41	4·63	4·82	4·98	5·23	5·44	5·75	5·98
20	3·03	3·67	4·07	4·35	4·57	4·75	4·90	5·15	5·35	5·65	5·88
24	2·98	3·61	3·99	4·26	4·47	4·65	4·79	5·03	5·22	5·51	5·73
30	2·94	3·55	3·91	4·18	4·38	4·54	4·69	4·91	5·09	5·37	5·58
40	2·89	3·49	3·84	4·09	4·29	4·45	4·58	4·80	4·97	5·23	5·43
60	2·85	3·43	3·77	4·01	4·20	4·35	4·48	4·69	4·85	5·10	5·29
120	2·81	3·37	3·70	3·93	4·11	4·26	4·38	4·58	4·73	4·97	5·15
					$X = 2$						
2	9·50	13·18	15·59	17·36	18·75	19·89	20·86	22·42	23·66	25·54	26·94
3	6·21	8·27	9·60	10·59	11·37	12·01	12·56	13·44	14·15	15·22	16·02
4	5·04	6·54	7·51	8·23	8·80	9·26	9·66	10·31	10·83	11·61	12·21
5	4·45	5·68	6·48	7·06	7·52	7·90	8·23	8·76	9·18	9·83	10·31
6	4·10	5·18	5·87	6·37	6·77	7·10	7·38	7·84	8·21	8·77	9·20
7	3·87	4·85	5·47	5·92	6·28	6·58	6·83	7·24	7·57	8·08	8·46
8	3·70	4·61	5·19	5·61	5·94	6·21	6·44	6·82	7·12	7·59	7·94
10	3·49	4·31	4·82	5·19	5·49	5·73	5·93	6·27	6·54	6·95	7·26
12	3·35	4·12	4·59	4·93	5·20	5·43	5·62	5·92	6·17	6·55	6·83
14	3·26	3·99	4·44	4·76	5·01	5·22	5·40	5·69	5·92	6·27	6·54
16	3·19	3·90	4·32	4·63	4·88	5·07	5·24	5·52	5·74	6·07	6·33
18	3·14	3·82	4·24	4·54	4·77	4·96	5·13	5·39	5·60	5·92	6·17
20	3·10	3·77	4·17	4·46	4·69	4·88	5·03	5·29	5·49	5·81	6·04
24	3·04	3·69	4·08	4·35	4·57	4·75	4·90	5·14	5·34	5·63	5·86
30	2·99	3·61	3·98	4·25	4·46	4·62	4·77	5·00	5·18	5·46	5·68
40	2·93	3·53	3·89	4·15	4·34	4·50	4·64	4·86	5·04	5·30	5·50
60	2·88	3·46	3·80	4·05	4·24	4·39	4·52	4·73	4·89	5·14	5·33
120	2·82	3·38	3·72	3·95	4·13	4·28	4·40	4·60	4·75	4·99	5·17

X is the number of covariates

(*continued*)

Critical Values for the Bryant-Paulson Procedure, $\alpha = .05$

v	$J = 2$	$J = 3$	$J = 4$	$J = 5$	$J = 6$	$J = 7$	$J = 8$	$J = 10$	$J = 12$	$J = 16$	$J = 20$
						$X = 3$					
2	10·83	15·06	17·82	19·85	21·45	22·76	23·86	25·66	27·08	29·23	30·83
3	6·92	9·23	10·73	11·84	12·72	13·44	14·06	15·05	15·84	17·05	17·95
4	5·51	7·18	8·25	9·05	9·67	10·19	10·63	11·35	11·92	12·79	13·45
5	4·81	6·16	7·02	7·66	8·17	8·58	8·94	9·52	9·98	10·69	11·22
6	4·38	5·55	6·30	6·84	7·28	7·64	7·94	8·44	8·83	9·44	9·90
7	4·11	5·16	5·82	6·31	6·70	7·01	7·29	7·73	8·08	8·63	9·03
8	3·91	4·88	5·49	5·93	6·29	6·58	6·83	7·23	7·55	8·05	8·42
10	3·65	4·51	5·05	5·44	5·75	6·01	6·22	6·58	6·86	7·29	7·62
12	3·48	4·28	4·78	5·14	5·42	5·65	5·85	6·17	6·43	6·82	7·12
14	3·37	4·13	4·59	4·93	5·19	5·41	5·59	5·89	6·13	6·50	6·78
16	3·29	4·01	4·46	4·78	5·03	5·23	5·41	5·69	5·92	6·27	6·53
18	3·23	3·93	4·35	4·66	4·90	5·10	5·27	5·54	5·76	6·09	6·34
20	3·18	3·86	4·28	4·57	4·81	5·00	5·16	5·42	5·63	5·96	6·20
24	3·11	3·76	4·16	4·44	4·67	4·85	5·00	5·25	5·45	5·75	5·98
30	3·04	3·67	4·05	4·32	4·53	4·70	4·85	5·08	5·27	5·56	5·78
40	2·97	3·57	3·94	4·20	4·40	4·56	4·70	4·92	5·10	5·37	5·57
60	2·90	3·49	3·83	4·08	4·27	4·43	4·56	4·77	4·93	5·19	5·38
120	2·84	3·40	3·73	3·97	4·15	4·30	4·42	4·62	4·77	5·01	5·19

$\alpha = .01$

v	$J = 2$	$J = 3$	$J = 4$	$J = 5$	$J = 6$	$J = 7$	$J = 8$	$J = 10$	$J = 12$	$J = 16$	$J = 20$
						$X = 1$					
2	19·09	26·02	30·57	33·93	36·58	38·76	40·60	43·59	45·95	49·55	52·24
3	10·28	13·32	15·32	16·80	17·98	18·95	19·77	21·12	22·19	23·82	25·05
4	7·68	9·64	10·93	11·89	12·65	13·28	13·82	14·70	15·40	16·48	17·29
5	6·49	7·99	8·97	9·70	10·28	10·76	11·17	11·84	12·38	13·20	13·83
6	5·83	7·08	7·88	8·48	8·96	9·36	9·70	10·25	10·70	11·38	11·90
7	5·41	6·50	7·20	7·72	8·14	8·48	8·77	9·26	9·64	10·24	10·69
8	5·12	6·11	6·74	7·20	7·58	7·88	8·15	8·58	8·92	9·46	9·87
10	4·76	5·61	6·15	6·55	6·86	7·13	7·35	7·72	8·01	8·47	8·82
12	4·54	5·31	5·79	6·15	6·43	6·67	6·87	7·20	7·46	7·87	8·18
14	4·39	5·11	5·56	5·89	6·15	6·36	6·55	6·85	7·09	7·47	7·75
16	4·28	4·96	5·39	5·70	5·95	6·15	6·32	6·60	6·83	7·18	7·45
18	4·20	4·86	5·26	5·56	5·79	5·99	6·15	6·42	6·63	6·96	7·22
20	4·14	4·77	5·17	5·45	5·68	5·86	6·02	6·27	6·48	6·80	7·04
24	4·05	4·65	5·02	5·29	5·50	5·68	5·83	6·07	6·26	6·56	6·78
30	3·96	4·54	4·89	5·14	5·34	5·50	5·64	5·87	6·05	6·32	6·53
40	3·88	4·43	4·76	5·00	5·19	5·34	5·47	5·68	5·85	6·10	6·30
60	3·79	4·32	4·64	4·86	5·04	5·18	5·30	5·50	5·65	5·89	6·07
120	3·72	4·22	4·52	4·73	4·89	5·03	5·14	5·32	5·47	5·69	5·85

(*continued*)

Critical Values for the Bryant-Paulson Procedure, $\alpha = .01$

ν	$J = 2$	$J = 3$	$J = 4$	$J = 5$	$J = 6$	$J = 7$	$J = 8$	$J = 10$	$J = 12$	$J = 16$	$J = 20$
					$X = 2$						
2	23·11	31·55	37·09	41·19	44·41	47·06	49·31	52·94	55·82	60·20	63·47
3	11·97	15·56	17·91	19·66	21·05	22·19	23·16	24·75	26·01	27·93	29·38
4	8·69	10·95	12·43	13·54	14·41	15·14	15·76	16·77	17·58	18·81	19·74
5	7·20	8·89	9·99	10·81	11·47	12·01	12·47	13·23	13·84	14·77	15·47
6	6·36	7·75	8·64	9·31	9·85	10·29	10·66	11·28	11·77	12·54	13·11
7	5·84	7·03	7·80	8·37	8·83	9·21	9·53	10·06	10·49	11·14	11·64
8	5·48	6·54	7·23	7·74	8·14	8·48	8·76	9·23	9·61	10·19	10·63
10	5·02	5·93	6·51	6·93	7·27	7·55	7·79	8·19	8·50	8·99	9·36
12	4·74	5·56	6·07	6·45	6·75	7·00	7·21	7·56	7·84	8·27	8·60
14	4·56	5·31	5·78	6·13	6·40	6·63	6·82	7·14	7·40	7·79	8·09
16	4·42	5·14	5·58	5·90	6·16	6·37	6·55	6·85	7·08	7·45	7·73
18	4·32	5·00	5·43	5·73	5·98	6·18	6·35	6·63	6·85	7·19	7·46
20	4·25	4·90	5·31	5·60	5·84	6·03	6·19	6·46	6·67	7·00	7·25
24	4·14	4·76	5·14	5·42	5·63	5·81	5·96	6·21	6·41	6·71	6·95
30	4·03	4·62	4·98	5·24	5·44	5·61	5·75	5·98	6·16	6·44	6·66
40	3·93	4·48	4·82	5·07	5·26	5·41	5·54	5·76	5·93	6·19	6·38
60	3·83	4·36	4·68	4·90	5·08	5·22	5·35	5·54	5·70	5·94	6·12
120	3·73	4·24	4·54	4·75	4·91	5·05	5·16	5·35	5·49	5·71	5·88
					$X = 3$						
2	26·54	36·26	42·64	47·36	51·07	54·13	56·71	60·90	64·21	69·25	73·01
3	13·45	17·51	20·17	22·15	23·72	25·01	26·11	27·90	29·32	31·50	33·13
4	9·59	12·11	13·77	15·00	15·98	16·79	17·47	18·60	19·50	20·87	21·91
5	7·83	9·70	10·92	11·82	12·54	13·14	13·65	14·48	15·15	16·17	16·95
6	6·85	8·36	9·34	10·07	10·65	11·13	11·54	12·22	12·75	13·59	14·21
7	6·23	7·52	8·36	8·98	9·47	9·88	10·23	10·80	11·26	11·97	12·51
8	5·81	6·95	7·69	8·23	8·67	9·03	9·33	9·84	10·24	10·87	11·34
10	5·27	6·23	6·84	7·30	7·66	7·96	8·21	8·63	8·96	9·48	9·88
12	4·94	5·80	6·34	6·74	7·05	7·31	7·54	7·90	8·20	8·65	9·00
14	4·72	5·51	6·00	6·36	6·65	6·89	7·09	7·42	7·69	8·10	8·41
16	4·56	5·30	5·76	6·10	6·37	6·59	6·77	7·08	7·33	7·71	8·00
18	4·44	5·15	5·59	5·90	6·16	6·36	6·54	6·83	7·06	7·42	7·69
20	4·35	5·03	5·45	5·75	5·99	6·19	6·36	6·63	6·85	7·19	7·45
24	4·22	4·86	5·25	5·54	5·76	5·94	6·10	6·35	6·55	6·87	7·11
30	4·10	4·70	5·06	5·33	5·54	5·71	5·85	6·08	6·27	6·56	6·78
40	3·98	4·54	4·88	5·13	5·32	5·48	5·61	5·83	6·00	6·27	6·47
60	3·86	4·39	4·72	4·95	5·12	5·27	5·39	5·59	5·75	6·00	6·18
120	3·75	4·25	4·55	4·77	4·94	5·07	5·18	5·37	5·51	5·74	5·90

ANSWERS
TO SELECTED CHAPTER PROBLEMS

Chapter 1

Odd-Numbered Answers to Conceptual Problems

1. a (if the sample means are all equal, then MS_{betw} is 0)
3. c (lose 1 df from each group; $63 - 3 = 60$)
5. a (for between source $= 3 - 1 = 2$ and for within source $= 30 - 3 = 27$)
7. c (an F ratio of 1.0 implies between- and within-groups variation are the same)
9. true (mean square is a variance estimate)
11. true (F ratio must be greater than or equal to 0)
13. no (rejecting in ANOVA only indicates that there is some difference among the means, not that all of the means are different)
15. c (the more t tests conducted, the more likely a Type I error for the set of tests)
17. true (basically the definition of independence)
19. no (find a new statistician as a negative F value is not possible in this context).

Odd-Numbered Answers to Computational Problems

1. $df_{betw} = 3$, $df_{with} = 60$, $df_{total} = 63$, $SS_{with} = 9.00$, $MS_{betw} = 3.25$, $MS_{with} = 0.15$, $F = 21.6666$, critical value $= 2.76$ (reject H_0).
3. $SS_{betw} = 150$, $SS_{total} = 1,110$, $df_{betw} = 3$, $df_{with} = 96$, $df_{total} = 99$, $MS_{betw} = 50$, $MS_{with} = 10$, critical value approximately 2.7 (reject H_0).

Chapter 2

Odd-Numbered Answers to Conceptual Problems

1. false (requires equal n's and equal variances; we hope the means are different)
3. d (with two groups, no need to follow up the ANOVA)
5. d (see definition of a priori comparisons)
7. b (POC are planned, not post hoc)
9. c (when null is rejected and there are more than two groups, then want to know which means are different)
11. true (see table of critical values for studentized range; easier to reject with more observations)
13. false (n's need not be equal for Dunnett; see characteristics)
15. yes (each contrast is orthogonal to the others as they rely on independent information)
17. d (see Fig. 2.2)
19. no (with equal sample means, the numerator of any t will be zero, thus nothing can possibly be significant).

Selected Answers to Odd-Numbered Computational Problems

1. contrast $= -5$; standard error $= 1$; $t = -5$; critical value $= 5.10$; fail to reject.
3. a) $\mu_{.1} - \mu_{.2}, \mu_{.3} - \mu_{.4}, (\mu_{.1} + \mu_{.2})/2 - (\mu_{.3} + \mu_{.4})/2$; b) no as Σc_j not equal to 0; c) H_0: $\mu_{.1} - [(\mu_{.2} + \mu_{.3} + \mu_{.4})/3]$

Chapter 3

Odd-Numbered Answers to Conceptual Problems

1. c (a plot of the cell means reveals an interaction)
3. a (a nonsignificant interaction results in the greatest generalizability of the main effects)
5. c (c is one definition of an interaction)
7. e (3 levels of A, 2 levels of B, thus 6 cells)
9. b ($170 \times 2 = 340$)
11. b (interaction df = product of main effects df)
13. d (the effect of one factor depends on the second factor; see definition of interaction as well as example profile plots in Fig. 3.1)
15. false (when the interaction is significant, this imples nothing about the main effects)
17. no (the numerator degrees of freedom for factor B can be anything).

Odd-Numbered Answers to Computational Problems

1. $SS_{with} = 225$, $df_A = 1$, $df_B = 2$, $df_{AB} = 2$, $df_{with} = 150$, $df_{total} = 155$, $MS_A = 6.15$, $MS_B = 5.30$, $MS_{AB} = 4.55$, $MS_{with} = 1.50$, $F_A = 4.10$, $F_B = 3.5333$, $F_{AB} = 3.0333$, critical value for A approximately 3.91, reject H_0 for A, critical value for B and AB approximately 3.06, reject H_0 for B and fail to reject H_0 for AB.

3. $F_A = 14.555$, $F_B = 9.093$, $F_{AB} = .6863$, critical value for A approximately 7.31, reject H_0 for A, critical value for B and AB approximately 5.18, reject H_0 for B, but not for AB.

    means: factor A − level 1 = 62, level 2 = 97

    factor B − level 1 = 54.688, level 2 = 81.313, level 3 = 102.5

    with Tukey HSD for factor B, only levels 1 and 3 are different

5. $F_A = 21.350$, $F_B = 0.133$, $F_{AB} = 21.184$, critical value for A and AB = 3.01, reject H_0 for A and for AB, critical value for B = 4.26, fail to reject H_0 for B.

Chapter 4

Odd-Numbered Answers to Conceptual Problems

1. b (see discussion on homogeneity of regression slopes)
3. b (14 df per group, 3 groups, 42 df − 2 df for covariates = 40)
5. c (want covariate having a high correlation with dependent variable)
7. c (the covariate and dependent variable need not be the same measure; could be pretest and posttest, but does not have to be)
9. b (an interaction indicates that the regression lines are not parallel across the groups)
11. c (a posthoc covariate typically results in an underestimate of the treatment effect, due to confounding or interference of the covariate)
13. no (if the correlation is substantial, then error variance will be reduced in ANCOVA regardless of its sign)
15. b (11 df per group, 6 groups, 66 df − 1 df for covariate = 65)
17. no (there will be no adjustment due to the covariate and one df will be lost from the error term)

Odd-Numbered Answers to Computational Problems

1. the adjusted groups means are all equal to 150; this resulted because the adjustment moved the mean for Group 1 up to 150 and the mean for Group 3 down to 150.

3. $df_{betw} = 4$, $MS_{betw} = 24$, $F = 3$, critical value 2.78 (reject H_0), $df_{with} = 24$, $MS_{with} = 8$, $SS_{cov} = 40$, $df_{cov} = 1$, $MS_{cov} = 40$, $F_{cov} = 5$, critical value 4.26 (reject H_0).

Chapter 5

Odd-Numbered Answers to Conceptual Problems

1. b (when there are both random and fixed factors, then the design is mixed)
3. c (gender is fixed, order is random, thus a mixed-effects model)
5. false (a repeated measures model can involve fixed and/or random factors)
7. no (MS_{with} is not used as the denominator for all models)
9. b (strategy is a repeated factor)
11. a (interactions require the two factors to be crossed; the other aspects are not relevant)
13. b (review the summary table for that model)

Odd-Numbered Answers to Computational Problems

1. $SS_{with} = 1.9$, $df_A = 2$, $df_B = 1$, $df_{AB} = 2$, $df_{with} = 18$, $df_{total} = 23$, $MS_A = 1.82$, $MS_B = .57$, $MS_{AB} = 1.035$, $MS_{with} = .1056$, $F_A = 1.7585$, $F_B = 5.3977$, $F_{AB} = 9.8011$, critical value for AB $= 6.01$ (reject H_0 for AB), critical value for B $= 8.29$ (fail to reject H_0 for B), critical value for A $= 99$ (fail to reject H_0 for A).
3. $SS_{time} = 126.094$, $SS_{time \times program} = 2.594$, $SS_{program} = 3.781$, $MS_{time} = 42.031$, $MS_{time \times program} = 0.865$, $MS_{program} = 3.781$, $F_{time} = 43.078$ ($p < .001$), $F_{time \times program} = 0.886$ ($p > .05$), $F_{program} = 0.978$ ($p > .05$).

Chapter 6

Odd-Numbered Answers to Conceptual Problems

1. d (subjects are randomly sampled within a range of IQ scores)
3. d (interactions only occur among factors that are crossed)
5. a (this is the notation for teachers nested within methods; see also problem 2)
7. false (cannot be a nested design; must be a crossed design)
9. yes (see the discussion on the types of blocking)
11. c (physician is nested within method)
13. b (there will be two main effects tests and no interaction test)
15. false (IQ cannot be randomly assigned to individuals; IQ must be a blocking factor or a covariate)

Odd-Numbered Answers to Computational Problems

1. a) yes; b) at age 4 type 1 is most effective, at age 6 type 2 is most effective, and at age 8 type 2 is most effective.

3. $F_{section} = 44.385$, $p = .002$; $F_{GRE-Q} = 61.000$, $p = .001$; thus reject H_0 for both effects; Bonferroni results: all but sections 1 and 2 are different, and all but blocks 1 and 2 are different.

Chapter 7

Odd-Numbered Answers to Conceptual Problems

1. c (see definition of intercept — a and b refer to the slope and d to the correlation)
3. a (the predicted value is a constant value of 14 regardless of X, thus the variance of the predicted values is 0)
5. d (linear relationships are best represented by a straight line, although all of the points need not fall on the line)
7. a (as the slope $= 0$, then the correlation $= 0$)
9. b (with the same predictor score, they will have the same predicted score; whether the residuals are the same will only depend on the observed Y)
11. d (see definition of homogeneity)
13. true (value of Y is irrelevant when correlation $= 0$, so mean of Y is best prediction)
15. false (if the variables are positively correlated, then the slope would be positive and a low score on the pretest would predict a low score on the posttest)
17. no (the regression equation may generate any number of points on the regression line).

Selected Answers to Odd-Numbered Computational Problems

1. a, $b = .8571$, $a = 1.9716$, b, $Y' = 7.1142$.
3. a, $b = .7447$, $a = 1.8136$, b, $F = 14.9431$ $(p < .05)$, $t = 3.8646$ $(p < .05)$.

Chapter 8

Odd-Numbered Answers to Conceptual Problems

1. a (as variable 3 has the largest correlation with variable 1 and the smallest with variable 2)
3. false (the intercept can be any value)
5. false (best prediction is when there is a high correlation of the predictors with the dependent variable, and low correlations among the predictors)
7. no (the partial correlation may be larger than, the same as, or smaller than .6)
9. no (the purpose of the adjustment is to take the number of predictors into account; thus R^2_{adj} may actually be smaller for the most predictors)

Odd-Numbered Answers to Computational Problems

1. intercept $= 28.0952$, $b_1 = .0381$, $b_2 = .8333$, $SS_{res} = 21.4294$, $SS_{reg} = 1,128.5706$, $F = 105.3292$ (reject at .01), $s^2_{res} = 5.3574$, $s(b_1) = .0058$, $s(b_2) = .1545$, $t_1 = 6.5343$ (reject at .01), $t_2 = 5.3923$ (reject at .01).

3. $r_{12.3} = .0934$.

5. $df_{reg} = 4$, $df_{res} = 40$, $df_{total} = 44$, $SS_{reg} = 80$, $SS_{total} = 480$, $MS_{res} = 10$, $F = 2$, critical value $= 2.61$, fail to reject H_0.

7. $r_{13.2} = .5305$, $r_{1(3.2)} = .5187$.

INDEX

The following typographical conventions are used in the index: *f* and *t* identify figures and tables, respectively